Hi Mom
JD Connet

Oct 4 1957 - SPUTNIK

The
Literature
of
Learning

The Literature of Learning

A Teacher's Anthology

Edited

With Notes and Commentary

by

Bernard Johnston

HOLT, RINEHART AND WINSTON, INC.

New York   Chicago   San Francisco
Atlanta   Dallas   Montreal   Toronto

COPYRIGHT ACKNOWLEDGMENTS

The Atlantic Monthly
   for James Ballard, "Man Overboard," *The Atlantic Monthly*, November 1964, copyright by James Ballard. Reprinted by permission of the author and *The Atlantic Monthly*.

Brandt & Brandt
   for Mark Schorer, "What We Don't Know Hurts Us" from *The State of Mind*. Reprinted by permission of Brandt & Brandt. Copyright © 1946 by Mark Schorer.

Chatto and Windus Ltd
   for Aldous Huxley, pp. 1–38 from *Brave New World*. Reprinted with permission from Mrs. Laura Huxley. Published in Canada by Chatto and Windus Ltd.

The Dial Press, Inc.
   for Herbert Gold, "A Dog in Brooklyn, A Girl in Detroit: A Life Among

For Georgia and George Dini

Preface

Teachers in America have customarily been trained in a literature that is understandably eclectic, restrictively abstract, and young. Though the arts of teaching predate Greek antiquity, the tenure of pedagogy as a field distinct from the traditional arts and sciences consumes scarcely five decades. Such a brief history requires that proper clichés be mulled. One such platitude murmurs that eclecticism should not merely enlarge the professional bibliography—it must enrich it. A second platitude insists that an abstract literature and its empirical data must clarify, not occlude, the complex realities of teaching. And a third cliché dictates that concurrently we shun mere fashions as we urge bright reforms. Overtly true, unglamorously true, these propositions are mocked by educators who ostensibly convene to assess their methods and materials but who are actually content to wallow in apologetics, then to carp, then to adjourn in the calm of a shy consensus.

Promiscuous experiment and inertia, versatility and cant—these are the extremes pervading teacher education in America. Predictably, the best and worst of books compose the bibliography. Formulas for reform abound. Statistical abstracts abound. Spiteful tracts compete against bloodless surveys. And amid this welter are gifted educators who struggle for a hearing against rivals who merely strike a pose, or announce an attitude, or offer a placebo, or bully the conventions of their time.

Though copious and diffuse, the literature of American pedagogy has long been criticized for its ingrown perspectives, for it has ingested countless sources and suppositions from the social sciences while its acquisitions from the humanities have been minimal. Until an enriching balance between the sciences and humanities is struck, with each tradition lending its proper strength, men of the liberal arts will continue to disparage—at times cantankerously but with cause—the provincialism of the curricula purporting to train our teachers.

The reform I advocate is not new. Nor is it self-styled. Nor does it overlook the conventional place of the humanities in higher education: it would be fatuous to urge, for example, that the School of Education undertake the humanistic schooling of its candidates because the College of Arts and Sciences had, in its own attempt, failed. Rather, the enrichment I propose involves sources of art, world literature, social criticism, and cultural history that are pedagogically germane and which interpret radiantly the modes of education in our time—the very sources that educators have devotedly ignored. Though an integration of philosophy (and intellectual history) with the special aims of teacher training has indeed been practiced, this union is timid and lacks too much, among other nourishments the novels, stories, poems, and personal narratives that evoke the *atmospheres* of teaching and learning. In short, the bibliographers of teacher education have ignored the entire amplitude and vision of imaginative literature. In light of this disregard, *The Literature of Learning* is simply an introduction to a pervasive wealth that lies beyond the claims of an anthology.

So broadly disposed toward the abstract, so youthful, the bibliography of education needs the accuracy of experience that only fiction and personal narrative provide. Credential candidates are besieged with theoretics, with statistics, with disembodied ideas. Except for intern programs of varying worth, no way exists for candidates to explore emotionally and imaginatively the *daily* obligations of their calling. I do not plead for a Rousseauistic romanticism, if by the term one means a woolly disregard for scientific method. But however pious in its science, a training bearing little relation to the dailyness of classroom life is as derelict as one ignoring evidential data in its pursuit of chimeras. Educators must ruthlessly distinguish between Laputian theory-spinning and the integral use of ideas. The former is derelict, having small regard for the exigencies it pretends to serve. Always must our curricula, our methods, and our in-service training be moored to the demands our ideals inflict on us.

In recent years some improvements in teacher education have been gingerly broached. In more than a few schools, elementary and secondary credential programs have been revised. The better liberal arts colleges are requiring that prospective teachers meet respectable undergraduate standards in the traditional academic areas. Fewer methods courses are now mandatory. In-service training, always problematical, tends to be more rigorous now. Stiffer prerequisites for advanced degrees in education have been smuggled into some graduate schools. But assuming the most tenuous of circumstances, that widespread agreement was reached on the wisdom of these measures, decisive reform would still depend on the best minds being known through the better books being read. No shifting of standards and curricula will raise the quality of teacher education if its literature remains dilute, or totally abstract, or ingrown, or desultory, or minimally inspired.

The Literature of Learning: A Teacher's Anthology invites a marriage of fiction with the preceding reforms. Such use of imaginative literature harbors no pinched didacticism, no betrayal of fiction as an art. Rather, an inspired didacticism, generous and unparochial, can result. Superior fiction not only enlivens the utility of our ideas, but annotates them, brings life to them, renders them humane. Just as a good story evokes the moods of the classroom with a precision impossible to match in the idioms of the social sciences, so does a graphic autobiography invoke that most severe of trials, the testing of one's ideas by life.

Conceived basically for introductory courses in education and as a reader for students involved in student teaching and other forms of in-service training, The Literature of Learning may also be used in graduate courses devoted to thematic investigations of topical and perennial controversies. Emphatically, this book is meant to be savored as well as studied, and to be read unrequiredly even when assigned.

The anthology is arranged in eight parts. Time Past in Time Present, the opening section, explores a continuity of past and present. Historical arguments are exposed and their application to current problems sketched. Implicit in these readings is the freshness of good instincts expended on worthy themes, each entry a proof that true modernity is seldom a trait of fashion.

Part Two, The Arts of Teaching, provides views of inspired pedagogy. Stressing the brilliance of five teachers, these stories strike paths between the hackneyed routes of mindless experimentalism and stony custom.

Part Three, Present Discontents, is a diagnosis of educational failure and hardship. Sham educationism, the myopia of pedagogical bureaucrats, the doughty incompetence of some tenured teachers, the corruption of ideals in the public schools, the unpublicized tyrannies that plague young and veteran teachers alike—these are among the discontents portrayed. Beyond naïve cheer and feckless pessimism, Present Discontents will seem not sad enough for the dour, and for the bovine too caustic.

Environments: the City, the Suburb, the Slum, the fourth section, explores the public ways whereby the lives of students are enriched or depleted. Like entries in other sections, these narratives render conditions rarely noted in commencement orations and the minutes of the PTA.

Part Five, The Rites of Prejudice, offers three portrayals of racial conflict that avoid simplistic resolutions. The characters are not caricatures; they affect beyond the headlines of their anguish.

Scenes from Childhood and The Rites of Adolescence, the sixth and seventh sections, hold diverse views of problems mutually besetting parents, teachers, and students. The word *rites* is central to the editorial bias in Part Seven, wherein the perilous, sometimes funny, often absurd, but *recurring* patterns of adolescence are dramatized. Though the vogue term "unique personality" is still parroted among schoolmen, the gifted writer persuades us of more than facile solemnities; he persuades us of our deep similitudes, of our separateness mocked by compassion.

As in Part One, the concluding section *Time Future in Time Present* stresses a historical continuity for educational progress and failure. Part One and Part Eight frame the anthology, alerting readers to recurring themes, to the recurring sentiments of students and teachers, and to those profound controversies that lie within but also beyond our topical arguments.

The narratives were placed for sequential reading, but the literary roof will not collapse if readers sample the stories according to whim or their own necessities. For the most part, the responsibility (and enjoyment) of interpreting these stories belongs to the reader, for I have chosen to relate each narrative to an educational theme but not to explain away its other and often richer implications. Any good story deserves to enrich or fester the reader's consciousness, unfettered by editorial asides. Though the temptation to give this book an emphasis constrictingly toward issues was slight, such issues are nonetheless apparent throughout. Ultimately, however, the stories must live in their own air, touched by the private weather of each reader. Literary quality was always the dominant criterion for a story's inclusion, and a narrative that offered nothing beyond its topicality was never acceptable.

The absence of poetry is conspicuous and is due to limitations of space and, consequently, to my own dislike for stranding lone poems within octavos of fiction. Perhaps a future book will bring together the poetry of education, with work by Shakespeare, Rilke, Yeats, Theodore Roethke, and Stephen Spender, among others. For readers who desire germane essays by men decidedly within the humanities, there is Robert Ulich's superb *Three Thousand Years of Educational Wisdom* (Harvard University Press, 1954) and my own *Issues in Education: An Anthology of Controversy* (Houghton Mifflin Company, 1964).

Suggestions for Further Reading, a bibliography, is found on page 445 and lists novels, stories, and personal narratives not provided or otherwise suggested in *The Literature of Learning*. On page xvii the regular *Contents* arranges selections according to a broadly thematic plan. The *Chronological Contents*, an alternate design, is found on page xxi and arranges entries by categories appropriate to the elementary, secondary, collegial progression. Original publication facts for all sources are cited in the *Acknowledgments*.

The palpable but unprovable influences that led to this book came from teachers, all of whom displayed forebearance and afforded me their generosity and those special charities that only talent can bestow: Margaret Abbott and Paul Barrett of Oakland High School; Eleanor Bushnell, Vladimir Brenner, and Matthew Evans of San Francisco State; Donald Dike, Thornton Parsons, Abraham Veinus, and William Wasserstrom of Syracuse University; and Theodore Roethke.

Yet any faults of this book are loyally my own.

B. J.

Piedmont, California
July 20, 1969

Contents

Chronological Contents

Part One

Time Past in Time Present

History, the most abused of human measurements, is distrusted by rebels and ignored by politicians. It is exploited by liberals to promote fashions and by conservatives to discredit reforms. Men of doctrine distort it; some mystics would abolish it. Whether defined as the gospel of causation, or as the tragic attempt of humanity to remember, or simply as a fable agreed upon, history remains a handmaiden to the present. Incessantly it is redefined to flatter the academic specialist or to comfort the generalist. But however defined, and for whatever motives, history survives as a spur to hope, as a means of despair, as an apology for action, as needed myth, as a litany of fact—a thrust of meanings willed into prominence. In the clamorous present these meanings are fragile, but they are tenacious too. They survive their admirers.

As Americans we equivocate about our own history. With more than annual grandiloquence we celebrate the treaties drawn, the elections won, the machines invented, and the wars survived. But, contradictorily, we accuse our past of coercion, of being *Old World*, of threatening the unself-conscious audacity that encouraged the fresh start of Puritan America. With one bent we insist that a society desiring its freedom must annihilate its past: the present must never be slowed by the weight of antiquity. But with another impulse we crave a preserved heritage that tells us what we are and have been.

Similarly, depending on partisan convictions, the history of American education can be viewed as a dormant tradition or as an evolution palsied with experiment. One educator, somber before his microphone, complains that the time for change in education is rotten before it is ripe, while another lambasts overdue reforms as frills. If history *is* the memory of mankind, then such partisanship may rely as much upon our cultural amnesia as upon our willful bias.

This amnesia—our collective inability to *remember* vast influences in our history—implies as much our contempt for history as our ignorance of it. Such contempt is partly derived, no doubt, from the way history has typically been taught in the public schools. Who cannot recall his adolescent gaze drearily cast on double-column texts replete with moronic lithographs? Recalling their own educations, how many young teachers wince at their recollection of history drowned in a porridge which, lacking all integrity and form, was factitiously named *social studies*?

In higher education the teaching of history, by whatever curricular name, remains compartmentalized. Students uneasily elaborate their study of American culture by amassing chunks of data from disparate courses in political history, economic history, intellectual history, and art history. Upon graduation from college, if not from high school, they discover in themselves an antihistorical attitude: *if the past can be known only in weak fragments, then what is the quality of this knowledge?* This distrust of history is further whetted by the cult of novelty, the narcissism of the present, found everywhere in America. Given these disadvantages, how may the past excite in us a comprehension of the present world and the fateful choices which have dictated that world?

The history of American education, like other histories, has been taught conventionally, in segments usually unrelated by sentiment, style, or hypothesis. With few exceptions, courses in the history of education examine discrete philosophical systems or, as in the case of intellectual history, the evolution of ideas within arbitrary periods. Still other courses inspect not evolutions or systems but institutional history, the literal data of American educational practices. The complaint is not that these patches of alienated history are *invalid*—they are simply incomplete by a margin too wide to tolerate. Teachers charged with bringing the stranded past into the ken of the present must not, through their methods, incite an even greater estrangement. Doubtless one history of American education must be known through the ideas we have about it. To know the origins of our public schools, we study, among other sources, *The Old Deluder Law* of 1647, Thomas Jefferson's plea for "a more general diffusion of knowledge," the *Annual Reports* of Horace Mann, and the Morrill (Land-Grant College) Act of 1862. However, to encourage more than a bland familiarity with our past, to seek a sharper involvement, a history of sentiment can also be reached—a history of feeling, predicament, and desire that complements our histories of system, idea, document, and event.

And so the writings in Part One form a kind of sensorium for educational history, a depot for experience, in which ideas are surrounded by life and not abstracted from it. The reader may find a rhythm of recurring educational questions wherein past attitudes are found to be ingenuously more current than today's journalism.

Certainly the timeliness of the past is not questioned by one who believes even faintly in historical causation, who suspects that time past does dwell through its effects in time present. Correspondingly, if one's memory of that past is vivid, then his recall is bound to influence imminent choices, and therefore the future. But beyond these routine perceptions is an awareness of similitude, of an intelligibility that past experience bestows on the present, an arousal of pattern in the affairs of men that strikes the senses as well as the intellect.

It is not quite amusing to hear symposia speakers bewail an educational problem as if it were starkly an invention of the twentieth century, beyond the advantage of old answers. Such problems and the controversies they engender will appear unique to disputants who are trapped in a nonhistorical present, in their busy voids. The truly modern mind distrusts not history but obsolete ideas; it rejects the dithering notions that are at least as prevalent in today's pamphlet as in yesterday's document. If he aspires to true modernity, the educator must first appreciate the didactic methods, the courses of study, and the forms of tradition and rebellion that are vital not because opinion makers have endorsed them but because they have endured, with remarkably small revisions, through the changes of civilization. As a professional enterprise, American education has yet to distinguish comprehensively, *for the uses of our time*, the writers who possess historical stamina from those who do not.

The authors in Part One display this stamina. Though outlines of educational arguments are in constant shift, it is rare that motives behind these disputes are innocently new. Plato's journey to the underworld of ignorance and his exploration of the Cave portray a trek of mankind still underway. In the tone of his homage to his teachers, Marcus Aurelius bestows a gratitude that is relentless, consummate, and unsentimental. Set within the larger drama of Faust's education, the counseling session between a naïve student and Mephistopheles is a spoof, with grave undertones, of scholastic attitudes rampant today. Charles Dickens satirizes a surviving pedantry in elementary schools, and, as always, the follies exposed are denied most by those who live them. Through the characters of Uncle Wadsworth and Nephew Alvin, Randall Jarrell scorns the results of flaccid education, of a training imperviously smug and still pursued in many American high schools. The melancholia of Henry Adams mirrors a reality unblurred by jargon and cliché, a reminiscence of personal fate vivid within the national destiny.

Situations change, but feelings recur. The narratives in Part One display a cohesion of sentiment as reliable as the bonds of jurisprudence, economics, politics, and war. Though difficult to define, the palpable data of life—the experience of men—is impossible to mistake.

Whether or not they are read sequentially, these writings provide an introduction to issues that recur in subsequent pages devoted to contemporary narratives. Even so, a personal education cannot be known wholly through the issues aroused by it, nor can it be stripped down to categories of argument. Through circumstances and his own making, a man's education is a flow of sentience, sloth, pride, mastery, contrition, mediocrity, and hope; it is a subtlety not to be wrecked by formulas or insulted by bromides. The writers assembled here respect this complexity. Time past in time present, as personal and collective history, is shown to dwell in one's consciousness not as invader, not as oppressor, but as interpreter. History, thus allowed, not only conserves and remembers the collective education of mankind, but also fulfills that education in the living present. The purpose of history need not be a secret we vainly try to find, but a kind of inner life our reason and passion enable us to live.

Plato

(*c.* 428–347 B.C.)

The dialogues of Plato fare poorly in classrooms where analysis is encouraged at the expense of imagination. "The Allegory of the Cave," a scene from *The Republic*, must be invented rather than dissected. Though the dialogue should be read scrupulously, its details fit a dramatic fantasy rather than a discursive argument. Readers who dwell only on the facts of Plato's message will miss his grander intentions, for he usually writes *toward* a realization rather than about it. For Plato, and for his teacher Socrates (469–399 B.C.), the act of philosophizing was favored over the subject of philosophy: hence their use of dialogues instead of lectures. Certainly this allegory *is* philosophical, its ideas are formidable, its aspirations are epistemologically impressive. But its truth is that of poetry.

So the allegory moves in the ways of a poem, teasing the reader toward speculations not exhausted by the parable's literal message. Interpreted strictly, the scene teaches of two worlds, the lower one a dark retreat from knowledge, the higher a radiant utopia illumined by the Ideal Forms lighting Plato's incorporeal cosmos. Within this contrast is a third vision of the endless search for an earthbound education, a search not damned by its terrible infinity but made free through its abundant possibilities. Nietzsche preached that a man knowing everything goes mad. For Plato this threat could not be a human worry.

In a symbolic way at least, the exchange between Socrates and Glaucon, led by Socrates in the first person, opens a discussion on the nature of ignorance, a debate that still flourishes. The Socrates who speaks here is a fictional character, but he undoubtedly mirrors the spirit of the actual man, a teacher who was by turns gregarious and ascetic, voluble and taciturn, eloquent, testy, and certainly untenured. For a reasonably accurate narrative of Socrates' final days, of the teacher's spiritual summation and physical death, one may read the *Apology, Crito,* and *Phaedo,* a dramatic trilogy written by his most distinguished pupil.

Implicit in the poetry of this allegory is a nonideological tone: there is

7

one cave vivid in shadows, imprisoning. But within its scarred walls are varieties of ignorance, men and women of all persuasions, each locked in an inner cave of his own consciousness. These masses who believe in their shadows may be likened to combatants in American education—administrators and teachers, students and taxpayers, board members and parents—who play out contemporary dramas of deception, popular politics, and humane quest.

First-year Latin students learn that the word *education* is derived from the Roman verb *educere*, which means *to lead out*. In Plato's terms the education of a man, his being led from the cave of ignorance, depends not on tidy lessons learned from a tutor but on the learner's own personal excellence, his *areté*, and on the sublimity of the ideals he strives to know.

The notes which follow are by the translator, F. M. Cornford.

THE ALLEGORY OF THE CAVE

The progress of the mind from the lowest state of unenlightenment to knowledge of the Good is now illustrated by the famous parable comparing the world of appearance to an underground Cave. In Empedocles' religious poem the powers which conduct the soul to its incarnation say, "We have come under this cavern's roof." The image was probably taken from mysteries held in caves or dark chambers representing the underworld, through which the candidates for initiation were led to the revelation of sacred objects in a blaze of light. The idea that the body is a prison-house, to which the soul is condemned for past misdeeds, is attributed by Plato to the Orphics.

One moral of the allegory is drawn from the distress caused by a too sudden passage from darkness to light. The earlier warning against plunging untrained minds into the discussion of moral problems . . . , as the Sophists and Socrates himself had done, is reinforced by the picture of the dazed prisoner dragged out into the sunlight. Plato's ten years' course of pure mathematics is to habituate the intellect to abstract reasoning before moral ideas are called in question. . . .

Next, said I, here is a parable to illustrate the degrees in which our nature may be enlightened or unenlightened. Imagine the condition of men living in a sort of cavernous chamber underground, with an entrance open to the light and a long passage all down the cave.[1] Here they have been from childhood, chained by the leg and also by the neck, so that

---

[1] The *length* of the "way in" (*eisodos*) to the chamber where the prisoners sit is an essential feature, explaining why no daylight reaches them.

they cannot move and can see only what is in front of them, because the chains will not let them turn their heads. At some distance higher up is the light of a fire burning behind them; and between the prisoners and the fire is a track[2] with a parapet built along it, like the screen at a puppet-show, which hides the performers while they show their puppets over the top.

I see, said he.

Now behind this parapet imagine persons carrying along various artificial objects, including figures of men and animals in wood or stone or other materials, which project above the parapet. Naturally, some of these persons will be talking, others silent.[3]

It is a strange picture, he said, and a strange sort of prisoners.

Like ourselves, I replied; for in the first place prisoners so confined would have seen nothing of themselves or of one another, except the shadows thrown by the fire-light on the wall of the Cave facing them, would they?

Not if all their lives they had been prevented from moving their heads.

And they would have seen as little of the objects carried past.

Of course.

Now, if they could talk to one another, would they not suppose that their words referred only to those passing shadows which they saw?[4]

Necessarily.

And suppose their prison had an echo from the wall facing them? When one of the people crossing behind them spoke, they could only suppose that the sound came from the shadow passing before their eyes.

No doubt.

In every way, then, such prisoners would recognize as reality nothing but the shadows of those artificial objects.[5]

Inevitably.

Now consider what would happen if their release from the chains and the healing of their unwisdom should come about in this way. Sup-

[2] The track crosses the passage into the cave at right angles, and is *above* the parapet built along it.

[3] A modern Plato would compare his Cave to an underground cinema, where the audience watch the play of shadows thrown by the film passing before a light at their backs. The film itself is only an image of "real" things and events in the world outside the cinema. For the film Plato has to substitute the clumsier apparatus of a procession of artificial objects carried on their heads by persons who are merely part of the machinery, providing for the movement of the objects and the sounds whose echo the prisoners hear. The parapet prevents these persons' shadows from being cast on the wall of the Cave.

[4] Adam's text and interpretation. The prisoners, having seen nothing but shadows, cannot think their words refer to the objects carried past behind their backs. For them shadows (images) are the only realities.

[5] The state of mind called *eikasia* in the previous chapter.

pose one of them set free and forced suddenly to stand up, turn his head, and walk with eyes lifted to the light; all these movements would be painful, and he would be too dazzled to make out the objects whose shadows he had been used to see. What do you think he would say, if someone told him that what he had formerly seen was meaningless illusion, but now, being somewhat nearer to reality and turned towards more real objects, he was getting a truer view? Suppose further that he were shown the various objects being carried by and were made to say, in reply to questions, what each of them was. Would he not be perplexed and believe the objects now shown him to be not so real as what he formerly saw?[6]

Yes, not nearly so real.

And if he were forced to look at the fire-light itself, would not his eyes ache, so that he would try to escape and turn back to the things which he could see distinctly, convinced that they really were clearer than these other objects now being shown to him?

Yes.

And suppose someone were to drag him away forcibly up the steep and rugged ascent and not let him go until he had hauled him out into the sunlight, would he not suffer pain and vexation at such treatment, and, when he had come out into the light, find his eyes so full of its radiance that he could not see a single one of the things that he was now told were real?

Certainly he would not see them all at once.

He would need, then, to grow accustomed before he could see things in that upper world.[7] At first it would be easiest to make out shadows, and then the images of men and things reflected in water, and later on the things themselves. After that, it would be easier to watch the heavenly bodies and the sky itself by night, looking at the light of the moon and stars rather than the Sun and the Sun's light in the day-time.

Yes, surely.

Last of all, he would be able to look at the Sun and contemplate its nature, not as it appears when reflected in water or any alien medium, but as it is in itself in its own domain.

No doubt.

And now he would begin to draw the conclusion that it is the Sun that produces the seasons and the course of the year and controls everything in the visible world, and moreover is in a way the cause of all that he and his companions used to see.

Clearly he would come at last to that conclusion.

---

[6] The first effect of Socratic questioning is perplexity. . . .

[7] Here is the moral—the need of habituation by mathematical study before discussing moral ideas and ascending through them to the Form of the Good.

Then if he called to mind his fellow prisoners and what passed for wisdom in his former dwelling-place, he would surely think himself happy in the change and be sorry for them. They may have had a practice of honouring and commending one another, with prizes for the man who had the keenest eye for the passing shadows and the best memory for the order in which they followed or accompanied one another, so that he could make a good guess as to which was going to come next.[8] Would our released prisoner be likely to covet those prizes or to envy the men exalted to honour and power in the Cave? Would he not feel like Homer's Achilles, that he would far sooner "be on earth as a hired servant in the house of a landless man"[9] or endure anything rather than go back to his old beliefs and live in the old way?

Yes, he would prefer any fate to such a life.

Now imagine what would happen if he went down again to take his former seat in the Cave. Coming suddenly out of the sunlight, his eyes would be filled with darkness. He might be required once more to deliver his opinion on those shadows, in competition with the prisoners who had never been released, while his eyesight was still dim and unsteady; and it might take some time to become used to the darkness. They would laugh at him and say that he had gone up only to come back with his sight ruined; it was worth no one's while even to attempt the ascent. If they could lay hands on the man who was trying to set them free and lead them up, they would kill him.[10]

Yes, they would.

Every feature in this parable, my dear Glaucon, is meant to fit our earlier analysis. The prison dwelling corresponds to the region revealed to us through the sense of sight, and the fire-light within it to the power of the Sun. The ascent to see the things in the upper world you may take as standing for the upward journey of the soul into the region of the intelligible; then you will be in possession of what I surmise, since that is what you wish to be told. Heaven knows whether it is true; but this, at any rate, is how it appears to me. In the world of knowledge, the last thing to be perceived and only with great difficulty is the essential Form of Goodness. Once it is perceived, the conclusion must follow that, for all things, this is the cause of whatever is right and good; in the visible world it gives birth to light and to the lord of light, while it is itself

[8] The empirical politician, with no philosophic insight, but only a "knack of remembering what usually happens" (*Gorgias*). He has *eikasia* = conjecture as to what is likely (*eikos*).

[9] This verse (already quoted . . .), being spoken by the ghost of Achilles, suggests that the Cave is comparable with Hades.

[10] An allusion to the fate of Socrates.

sovereign in the intelligible world and the parent of intelligence and truth. Without having had a vision of this Form no one can act with wisdom, either in his own life or in matters of state.

So far as I can understand, I share your belief.

Then you may also agree that it is no wonder if those who have reached this height are reluctant to manage the affairs of men. Their souls long to spend all their time in that upper world—naturally enough, if here once more our parable holds true. Nor, again, is it at all strange that one who comes from the contemplation of divine things to the miseries of human life should appear awkward and ridiculous when, with eyes still dazed and not yet accustomed to the darkness, he is compelled, in a law-court or elsewhere, to dispute about the shadows of justice or the images that cast those shadows, and to wrangle over the notions of what is right in the minds of men who have never beheld Justice itself.[11]

It is not at all strange.

No; a sensible man will remember that the eyes may be confused in two ways—by a change from light to darkness or from darkness to light; and he will recognize that the same thing happens to the soul. When he sees it troubled and unable to discern anything clearly, instead of laughing thoughtlessly, he will ask whether, coming from a brighter existence, its unaccustomed vision is obscured by the darkness, in which case he will think its condition enviable and its life a happy one; or whether, emerging from the depths of ignorance, it is dazzled by excess of light. If so, he will rather feel sorry for it; or, if he were inclined to laugh, that would be less ridiculous than to laugh at the soul which has come down from the light.

That is a fair statement.

If this is true, then, we must conclude that education is not what it is said to be by some, who profess to put knowledge into a soul which does not possess it, as if they could put sight into blind eyes. On the contrary, our own account signifies that the soul of every man does possess the power of learning the truth and the organ to see it with; and that, just as one might have to turn the whole body round in order that the eye should see light instead of darkness, so the entire soul must be turned away from this changing world, until its eye can bear to contemplate reality and that supreme splendour which we have called the Good. Hence there may well be an art whose aim would be to effect this very thing, the conversion of the soul, in the readiest way; not to put the power of sight into the soul's eye, which already has it, but to ensure

---

[11] In the *Gorgias* . . . , Callicles, forecasting the trial of Socrates, taunts him with the philosopher's inability to defend himself in a court.

that, instead of looking in the wrong direction, it is turned the way it ought to be.

Yes, it may well be so.

It looks, then, as though wisdom were different from those ordinary virtues, as they are called, which are not far removed from bodily qualities, in that they can be produced by habituation and exercise in a soul which has not possessed them from the first. Wisdom, it seems, is certainly the virtue of some diviner faculty, which never loses its power, though its use for good or harm depends on the direction towards which it is turned. You must have noticed in dishonest men with a reputation for sagacity the shrewd glance of a narrow intelligence piercing the objects to which it is directed. There is nothing wrong with their power of vision, but it has been forced into the service of evil, so that the keener its sight, the more harm it works.

Quite true.

And yet if the growth of a nature like this had been pruned from earliest childhood, cleared of those clinging overgrowths which come of gluttony and all luxurious pleasure and, like leaden weights charged with affinity to this mortal world, hang upon the soul, bending its vision downwards; if, freed from these, the soul were turned round towards true reality, then this same power in these very men would see the truth as keenly as the objects it is turned to now.

Yes, very likely.

Is it not also likely, or indeed certain after what has been said, that a state can never be properly governed either by the uneducated who know nothing of truth or by men who are allowed to spend all their days in the pursuit of culture? The ignorant have no single mark before their eyes at which they must aim in all the conduct of their own lives and of affairs of state; and the others will not engage in action if they can help it, dreaming that, while still alive, they have been translated to the Islands of the Blest.

Quite true.

It is for us, then, as founders of a commonwealth, to bring compulsion to bear on the noblest natures. They must be made to climb the ascent to the vision of Goodness, which we called the highest object of knowledge; and, when they have looked upon it long enough, they must not be allowed, as they now are, to remain on the heights, refusing to come down again to the prisoners or to take any part in their labours and rewards, however much or little these may be worth.

Shall we not be doing them an injustice, if we force on them a worse life than they might have?

You have forgotten again, my friend, that the law is not concerned to make any one class specially happy, but to ensure the welfare of the commonwealth as a whole. By persuasion or constraint it will unite the citizens in harmony, making them share whatever benefits each class can contribute to the common good; and its purpose in forming men of that spirit was not that each should be left to go his own way, but that they should be instrumental in binding the community into one.

True, I had forgotten.

You will see, then, Glaucon, that there will be no real injustice in compelling our philosophers to watch over and care for the other citizens. We can fairly tell them that their compeers in other states may quite reasonably refuse to collaborate: there they have sprung up, like a self-sown plant, in despite of their country's institutions; no one has fostered their growth, and they cannot be expected to show gratitude for a care they have never received. "But," we shall say, "it is not so with you. We have brought you into existence for your country's sake as well as for your own, to be like leaders and king-bees in a hive; you have been better and more thoroughly educated than those others and hence you are more capable of playing your part both as men of thought and as men of action. You must go down, then, each in his turn, to live with the rest and let your eyes grow accustomed to the darkness. You will then see a thousand times better than those who live there always; you will recognize every image for what it is and know what it represents, because you have seen justice, beauty, and goodness in their reality; and so you and we shall find life in our commonwealth no mere dream, as it is in most existing states, where men live fighting one another about shadows and quarrelling for power, as if that were a great prize; whereas in truth government can be at its best and free from dissension only where the destined rulers are least desirous of holding office."

Quite true.

Then will our pupils refuse to listen and to take their turns at sharing in the work of the community, though they may live together for most of their time in a purer air?

No; it is a fair demand, and they are fair-minded men. No doubt, unlike any ruler of the present day, they will think of holding power as an unavoidable necessity.

Yes, my friend; for the truth is that you can have a well-governed society only if you can discover for your future rulers a better way of life than being in office; then only will power be in the hands of men who are rich, not in gold, but in the wealth that brings happiness, a good and wise life. All goes wrong when, starved for lack of anything good in their own lives, men turn to public affairs hoping to snatch from thence the happiness they hunger for. They set about fighting for power, and this internecine conflict ruins them and their country. The life of true philosophy is the only one that looks down upon offices of state; and access to power must be confined to men who are not in love with it;

otherwise rivals will start fighting. So whom else can you compel to undertake the guardianship of the commonwealth, if not those who, besides understanding best the principle of government, enjoy a nobler life than the politician's and look for rewards of a different kind?

There is indeed no other choice.

Marcus Aurelius

(A.D. 121–180)

Marcus Aurelius fulfilled perhaps better than any other Roman emperor the Platonic virtues of the philosopher king. Aurelius, however, took his personal philosophy from the Roman Stoics and, by derivation, from Zeno, the father of Greek Stoicism. Referring to Aurelius and his immediate predecessor, Antoninus Pius, Edward Gibbon wrote, "Their united reigns are possibly the only period of history in which the happiness of a great people was the sole object of government." Even so, the reforms of Aurelius were hindered by famine and pestilence and by Rome's constant wars with such forces as the Parthians in the east and the Marcomanni in the territory that is now Germany. But despite these torments Aurelius preserved a nature both judicious and ironic: "Even in a palace," he wrote, "it is possible to live well."

The Stoicism of Aurelius was due in part to the influence of one of his teachers, the slave Epictetus, who urged the value of a rigorous but unpedantic education in harmony with the Stoic moral code, which stressed forebearance, tranquillity within an active life, emotional discipline, and generosity. In his discourse "To Those Who Would Undertake the Profession of Teacher with a Light Heart" Epictetus contrasts the presumption of the fledgling teacher with the real demands of his chosen art:

> Those who have learnt precepts and nothing more are anxious to give them out at once, just as men with weak stomachs vomit food. First digest your precepts, and then you will not vomit them. Show us that you have digested them to some purpose . . . as athletes can show their shoulders, as a result of training and eating, and as those who have acquired the arts can show the result of their learning. The carpenter does not come and say, "Hear me discourse on carpentry," but he undertakes a contract and builds a house and so shows that he has acquired the art.

Just this integration of precept and art is exhibited throughout the twelve books of *The Meditations*: each passage carries the beat of a knowing modesty, of passion reined by an ideal.

The import of such an integration of learning with behavior is obvious. How many current slogans like "educating for citizenship," "teaching the whole child," and "teaching not subjects but how to think" find their real applications in the following meditation? If these sayings beg for satire, if they pretend to an integrity they do not have, it is because they exist not as tactical resources but as undigested clichés. For example, if educators define *citizenship* as mere playacting with the jargon of democracy, then any curriculum purporting to educate for this brand of citizenship will inevitably be trivial.

In truth, this meditation defends the foregoing slogans, but not as if they were ritualized trappings. The precepts of Aurelius are stripped of pretense and are tempered by his suffering, by his affection for the lessons of experience, and by his scholarship. As the endorsement of a carpenter's skill is found in the house he builds, so the proof of a versatile education is discovered in the man it makes.

MEDITATION

(BOOK I)

From my grandfather Verus I learned good morals and the government of my temper.

2. From the reputation and remembrance of my father,[1] modesty and a manly character.

3. From my mother,[2] piety and beneficence, and abstinence, not only from evil deeds, but even from evil thoughts; and further, simplicity in my way of living, far removed from the habits of the rich.

4. From my great-grandfather,[3] not to have frequented public schools, and to have had good teachers at home, and to know that on such things a man should spend liberally.

5. From my governor, to be neither of the green nor of the blue party at the games in the Circus, nor a partizan either of the Parmularius or the Scutarius at the gladiators' fights; from him too I learned endurance of labour, and to want little, and to work with my own hands, and

---

[1] His real father's name was Annius Verus.
[2] Domita Calvilla, also called Lucilla.
[3] Perhaps his mother's grandfather, Catilius Severus.

not to meddle with other people's affairs, and not to be ready to listen to slander.

6. From Diognetus, not to busy myself about trifling things, and not to give credit to what was said by miracle-workers and jugglers about incantations and the driving away of daemons and such things; and not to breed quails for fighting, nor to give myself up passionately to such things; and to endure freedom of speech; and to have become intimate with philosophy; and to have been a hearer, first of Bacchius, then of Tandasis and Marcianus; and to have written dialogues in my youth; and to have desired a plank bed and skin, and whatever else of the kind belongs to the Grecian discipline.

7. From Rusticus I received the impression that my character required improvement and discipline; and from him I learned not to be led astray to sophistic emulation, nor to writing on speculative matters, nor to delivering little hortatory orations, nor to showing myself off as a man who practises much discipline, or does benevolent acts in order to make a display; and to abstain from rhetoric, and poetry, and fine writing; and not to walk about in the house in my outdoor dress, nor to do other things of the kind; and to write my letters with simplicity, like the letter which Rusticus wrote from Sinuessa to my mother; and with respect to those who have offended me by words, or done me wrong, to be easily disposed to be pacified and reconciled, as soon as they have shown a readiness to be reconciled; and to read carefully, and not to be satisfied with a superficial understanding of a book; nor hastily to give my assent to those who talk overmuch; and I am indebted to him for being acquainted with the discourses of Epictetus, which he communicated to me out of his own collection.

8. From Apollonius I learned freedom of will and undeviating steadiness of purpose; and to look to nothing else, not even for a moment, except to reason; and to be always the same, in sharp pains, on the occasion of the loss of a child, and in long illness; and to see clearly in a living example that the same man can be both most resolute and yielding, and not peevish in giving his instruction; and to have had before my eyes a man who clearly considered his experience and his skill in expounding philosophical principles as the smallest of his merits; and from him I learned how to receive from friends what are esteemed favours, without being either humbled by them or letting them pass unnoticed.

9. From Sextus, a benevolent disposition, and the example of a family governed in a fatherly manner, and the idea of living conformably to nature; and gravity without affectation, and to look carefully after the interests of friends, and to tolerate ignorant persons, and those who form opinions without consideration: he had the power of readily accommodating himself to all, so that intercourse with him was more agreeable than any flattery; and at the same time he was most highly venerated

by those who associated with him: and he had the faculty both of discovering and ordering, in an intelligent and methodical way, the principles necessary for life; and he never showed anger or any other passion, but was entirely free from passion, and also most affectionate; and he could express approbation without noisy display, and he possessed much knowledge without ostentation.

10. From Alexander the grammarian, to refrain from fault-finding, and not in a reproachful way to chide those who uttered any barbarous or solecistic or strange-sounding expression; but dexterously to introduce the very expression which ought to have been used, and in the way of answer or giving confirmation, or joining in an inquiry about the thing itself, not about the word, or by some other fit suggestion.

11. From Fronto I learned to observe what envy, and duplicity, and hypocrisy are in a tyrant, and that generally those among us who are called Patricians are rather deficient in paternal affection.

12. From Alexander the Platonic, not frequently nor without necessity to say to any one, or to write in a letter, that I have no leisure; nor continually to excuse the neglect of duties required by our relation to those with whom we live, by alleging urgent occupations.

13. From Catulus, not to be indifferent when a friend finds fault, even if he should find fault without reason, but to try to restore him to his usual disposition; and to be ready to speak well of teachers, as it is reported of Domitius and Athenodotus; and to love my children truly.

14. From my brother Severus, to love my kin, and to love truth, and to love justice; and through him I learned to know Thrasea, Helvidius, Cato, Dion, Brutus; and from him I received the idea of a polity in which there is the same law for all, a polity administered with regard to equal rights and equal freedom of speech, and the idea of a kingly government which respects most of all the freedom of the governed; I learned from him also consistency and undeviating steadiness in my regard for philosophy; and a disposition to do good, and to give to others readily, and to cherish good hopes, and to believe that I am loved by my friends; and in him I observed no concealment of his opinions with respect to those whom he condemned, and that his friends had no need to conjecture what he wished or did not wish, but it was quite plain.

15. From Maximus I learned self-government, and not to be led aside by anything; and cheerfulness in all circumstances, as well as in illness; and a just admixture in the moral character of sweetness and dignity, and to do what was set before me without complaining. I observed that everybody believed that he thought as he spoke, and that in all that he did he never had any bad intention; and he never showed amazement and surprise, and was never in a hurry, and never put off doing a thing, nor was perplexed nor dejected, nor did he ever laugh to disguise his vexation, nor, on the other hand, was he ever passionate or

suspicious. He was accustomed to do acts of beneficence, and was ready to forgive, and was free from all falsehood; and he presented the appearance of a man who could not be diverted from right rather than of a man who had been improved. I observed, too, that no man could ever think that he was despised by Maximus, or ever venture to think himself a better man. He had also the art of being humorous in an agreeable way.

16. In my father[4] I observed mildness of temper, and unchangeable resolution in the things which he had determined after due deliberation; and no vainglory in those things which men call honours; and a love of labour and perseverance; and a readiness to listen to those who had anything to propose for the common weal; and undeviating firmness in giving to every man according to his deserts; and a knowledge derived from experience of the occasions for vigorous action and for remission. And I observed that he had overcome all passion for boys; and he considered himself no more than any other citizen; and he released his friends from all obligation to sup with him or to attend him of necessity when he went abroad, and those who had failed to accompany him, by reason of any urgent circumstances, always found him the same. I observed too his habit of careful inquiry in all matters of deliberation, and his persistency, and that he never stopped his investigation through being satisfied with appearances which first present themselves; and that his disposition was to keep his friends, and not to be soon tired of them, nor yet to be extravagant in his affection; and to be satisfied on all occasions, and cheerful; and to foresee things a long way off, and to provide for the smallest without display; and to check immediately popular applause and all flattery; and to be ever watchful over the things which were necessary for the administration of the empire, and to be a good manager of the expenditure, and patiently to endure the blame which he got for such conduct; and he was neither superstitious with respect to the gods, nor did he court men by gifts or by trying to please them, or by flattering the populace; but he showed sobriety in all things and firmness, and never any mean thoughts or action, nor love of novelty. And the things which conduce in any way to the commodity of life, and of which fortune gives an abundant supply, he used without arrogance and without excusing himself; so that when he had them, he enjoyed them without affectation, and when he had them not, he did not want them. No one could ever say of him that he was either a sophist or a home-bred flippant slave or a pedant; but every one acknowledged him to be a man ripe, perfect, above flattery, able to manage his own and other men's affairs. Besides this, he honoured those who were true philosophers, and he did not reproach those who pretended to be philoso-

---

[4] His adoptive father, the Emperor Antoninus Pius.

phers, nor yet was he easily led by them. He was also easy in conversation, and he made himself agreeable without any offensive affectation. He took a reasonable care of his body's health, not as one who was greatly attached to life, nor out of regard to personal appearance, nor yet in a careless way, but so that, through his own attention, he very seldom stood in need of the physician's art or of medicine or external applications. He was most ready to give way without envy to those who possessed any particular faculty, such as that of eloquence or knowledge of the law or of morals, or of anything else; and he gave them his help, that each might enjoy reputation according to his deserts; and he always acted conformably to the institutions of his country, without showing any affectation of doing so. Further, he was not fond of change nor unsteady, but he loved to stay in the same places, and to employ himself about the same things; and after his paroxysms of headache he came immediately fresh and vigorous to his usual occupations. His secrets were not many, but very few and very rare, and these only about public matters; and he showed prudence and economy in the exhibition of the public spectacles and the construction of public buildings, his donations to the people, and in such things, for he was a man who looked to what ought to be done, not to the reputation which is got by a man's acts. He did not take the bath at unseasonable hours; he was not fond of building houses, nor curious about what he ate, nor about the texture and colour of his clothes, nor about the beauty of his slaves. His dress came from Lorium, his villa on the coast, and from Lanuvium generally. We know how he behaved to the toll-collector at Tusculum who asked his pardon; and such was all his behaviour. There was in him nothing harsh, nor implacable, nor violent, nor, as one may say, anything carried to the sweating point; but he examined all things severally, as if he had abundance of time, and without confusion, in an orderly way, vigorously and consistently. And that might be applied to him which is recorded of Socrates,[5] that he was able both to abstain from, and to enjoy, those things which many are too weak to abstain from, and cannot enjoy without excess. But to be strong enough both to bear the one and to be sober in the other is the mark of a man who has a perfect and invincible soul, such as he showed in the illness of Maximus.

17. To the gods I am indebted for having good grandfathers, good parents, a good sister, good teachers, good associates, good kinsmen and friends, nearly everything good. Further, I owe it to the gods that I was not hurried into any offence against any of them, though I had a disposition which, if opportunity had offered, might have led me to do something of this kind; but, through their favour, there never was such

[5] See Xenophon, *Memorabilia*, I.3. 15.

a concurrence of circumstances as put me to the trial. Further, I am
thankful to the gods that I was not longer brought up with my grandfather's concubine, and that I preserved the flower of my youth, and
that I did not make proof of my virility before the proper season, but
even deferred the time; that I was subjected to a ruler and a father who
was able to take away all pride from me, and to bring me to the knowledge that it is possible for a man to live in a palace without wanting
either guards or embroidered dresses, or torches and statues, and such-
like show; but that it is in such a man's power to bring himself very near
to the fashion of a private person, without being for this reason either
meaner in thought, or more remiss in action, with respect to the things
which must be done for the public interest in a manner that befits a
ruler. I thank the gods for giving me such a brother,[6] who was able by
his moral character to rouse me to vigilance over myself, and who, at the
same time, pleased me by his respect and affection; that my children
have not been stupid nor deformed in body; that I did not make more
proficiency in rhetoric, poetry, and the other studies, in which I should
perhaps have been completely engaged, if I had seen that I was making
progress in them; that I made haste to place those who brought me up
in the station of honour, which they seemed to desire, without putting
them off with hope of my doing it some time after, because they were
then still young; that I knew Apollonius, Rusticus, Maximus; that I
received clear and frequent impressions about living according to nature,
and what kind of a life that is, so that, so far as depended on the gods,
and their gifts, and help, and inspirations, nothing hindered me from
forthwith living according to nature, though I still fall short of it through
my own fault, and through not observing the admonitions of the gods,
and, I may almost say, their direct instructions; that my body has held
out so long in such a kind of life; that I never touched either Benedicta
or Theodotus, and that, after having fallen into amatory passions, I was
cured; and, though I was often out of humour with Rusticus, I never did
anything of which I had occasion to repent; that, though it was my
mother's fate to die young, she spent the last years of her life with me;
that, whenever I wished to help any man in his need, or on any other
occasion, I was never told that I had not the means of doing it; and that
to myself the same necessity never happened, to receive anything from
another; that I have such a wife, so obedient, and so affectionate, and
so simple; that I had abundance of good masters for my children; and
that remedies have been shown to me by dreams, both others, and against
bloodspitting and giddiness[7] . . . ; and that, when I had an inclina-

---

[6] Presumably his brother by adoption, L. Verus.
[7] The text is uncertain here.

tion to philosophy, I did not fall into the hands of any sophist, and that I did not waste my time on writers of histories, or in the resolution of syllogisms, or occupy myself about the investigation of appearances in the heavens; for all these things require the help of the gods and fortune.

Among the Quadi at the Granua.[8]

[8] The Quadi, against whom Aurelius campaigned successfully in A.D. 174, lived in the southeast of Germany.

Johann Wolfgang von Goethe
(1749–1832)

During Goethe's lifetime the intellectual climate of Europe was suffused with warring doctrines that are described in *Faust* as "the garbage cans, the attics, the high-flown political dramas . . . raked for the proper didactic maxims for the marionettes to mouth." As a child Goethe lived through The Seven Years' War, which deeply divided Germany. As a man he witnessed the tragedy of the French Revolution. As a scholar at work amid social crises he became prodigiously versed in literature, jurisprudence, philosophy, the natural sciences, alchemy, and religious mysticism. His education was as versatile as the talents it refined.

A party to no popular ideology, Goethe felt disinherited from any coherent past and estranged from hope. The poem *Faust* was composed in two parts, over a span of sixty years, and reflects the spiritual wanderings, the satirical versatility, and the instinctive isolation of its creator. *Faust* should not mistakenly be read as a tragic epic, for Goethe's milieu lacked the cultural homogeneity that epic verse seems to require, that poets living in Hellenic, medieval, and Elizabethan times enjoyed. But as a vast lyrical comedy *Faust* is convincingly dramatic, even distinctly modern; its meanings are shaded, its moods are diverse.

Like Goethe, the hero Faust strives to know deeply, insatiably, the mysteries of art and science. He wills a breadth of experience too ambitious for one man, an eternal education that drives him to conflicting moods of disillusionment, ecstasy, and cynicism. Knowing that Faust is an idealized embodiment for the strivings of mankind, Mephistopheles and God wage a contest for his soul. Faust enters the wager when he tells the demon that he, Faust, will strive to embrace all nuances of human wisdom and experience. If the demon can induce in Faust one thrill of contentment, one moment of satisfaction to which Faust pleads, "Linger, you are wonderful," then Mephistopheles can claim his soul forever and mankind inherits the symbolic defeat wherein satiety, not accomplishment, prevails.

"The Counseling Session" occurs in *Faust, Part One* shortly before the hero and Mephistopheles depart on their cosmic odyssey in search of the satisfying moment. Using the naïve student as a foil, the demon exploits educational questions of Goethe's day that are embarrassingly unresolved in ours. As in the larger poem, the truth of "The Counseling Session" is not found exclusively in the characters' rhetoric but, also, in the weaving of dialogue that evokes an interplay, a dynamism at the heart of the scene.

The translation is by the scholar and poet C. F. MacIntyre.

THE COUNSELING SESSION

Faust

> When do we start?

Mephistopheles

> As soon as we can.
> This place is a torment.
> What sort of life is it where a man
> bores both himself and his students?
> Leave that to your neighbor, Doctor Paunch!
> Why should you slave to thresh out that old straw?
> The best you know you can't show to the boys.
> Right now I hear one at the door.

Faust

> It's quite impossible for me to see him.

Mephistopheles

> The poor boy's waited so long already,
> he mustn't go away uncomforted.
> Come, give me your doctor's gown and hood.
> This mask will suit me wonderfully.

> *(He changes his clothes.)*

> Go now and leave it to my wits!
> A quarter-hour is all I'll need,
> in which time go get ready for our trip!

(*Faust goes out.*)

Mephistopheles

   (*in the doctor's gown*)

   Scoff at all knowledge and despise
   reason and science, those flowers of mankind.
   Let the father of all lies
   with dazzling necromancy make you blind,
   then I'll have you unconditionally—
   fate gave him a spirit that's ever pressing forward,
   uncurbed; his rash impulses overleap
   the joys of earth. I'll drag him through the wild life,
   through the flat wasteland. I'll let him flounder,
   stiffen, stick fast, and food and drink
   shall bait his insatiate sense,
   hovering before his greedy lips.
   Vainly he'll beg me for refreshment,
   and even if he hadn't given himself to the Devil,
   he'd still be ruined in the end.

   (*A Student enters.*)

Student

   I've been here just a little while
   and come, full of devotion,
   to meet and know a man of whom
   the world speaks with such reverence.

Mephistopheles

   I'm flattered by your courtesy.
   You see a man like any other.
   Have you already been around elsewhere?

Student

   Please, sir, assist me. I have come
   with the best intentions, good health, and a little money.
   My mother didn't like to have me leave her;
   I want to learn something here that's practical.

Mephistopheles

   That's fine. You've come to the right place.

Student

But honestly I don't like it here at all
and would love to get away from these walls and halls
and these narrow gloomy lecture-rooms.
I feel so cramped: no grass, no trees—
and on a bench in the auditorium
I cannot think and I am deaf and dumb.

Mephistopheles

That comes with practice; as a child at first
unwillingly receives the mother's breast,
but soon takes to the feeding eagerly;
so you, nursed on the breasts of wisdom
will satisfy your thirst more gladly every day.

Student

I'll hang with joy about her neck!
But only tell me the best means to use.

Mephistopheles

Before proceeding, you must tell me:
what subject will you choose?

Student

I want to be very learned and understand
the secrets of the earth and of the firmament—
the natural sciences, that is to say!

Mephistopheles

You're starting out on the right paths,
but you mustn't let any distraction lead you astray.

Student

I'm set upon it, body and soul;
but I'd like some time to play
in freedom and not have to study
during the summer holidays!

Mephistopheles

Use your time well. It glides away so swiftly,
but system will teach you how to conserve it.

My friend, take logic. There your spirit's deftly
laced in the tight Spanish boot.[1]
Thereafter you'll proceed more circumspectly,
crawling down the road of reason, but never veer,
like a will o' the wisp, and criss-cross here and there.
Each day you'll learn that what required no thought
for its performance, as when you eat and drink,
must now be done in order—one, two, three!
And really in these thinking-mills
it's like a masterpiece worked on a weaver's loom:
one treadle moves like a thousand threads on spools;
the humming shuttles dart from side to side;
threads flow invisibly; one stroke
will tie a thousand knots—then the philosopher steps in
and shows you that it must be so:
the first was thus and the second so;
therefore the third and fourth are likewise so;
but if it weren't for the first and second,
the third and fourth just never could have been.
Everywhere the scholars praise
this sort of thing, but never become weavers.
The man who wants to know
organic truth and describe it well
seeks first to drive the living spirit out;
he's got the parts in hand there,
it's merely the breath of life that's lacking.
The chemists call it *encheiresin naturae*
and mock themselves and don't know how or why.

Student

I don't quite understand you.

Mephistopheles

You'll get the hang of it by and by.
Everything will be simplified
after it's properly classified.

Student

I'm all confused from what you've said,
as if a mill-wheel were turning in my brain.

---

[1] An instrument of torture.

Mephistopheles

> Then, before studying any further,
> you must try metaphysics; but take care
> to grasp the deepest meanings and explore
> what isn't suitable for human brains.
> There's always a pompous word to serve
> for what we may or may not understand.
> See that throughout the first semester
> you follow the routine most carefully.
> When the chimes ring in the tower,
> be at class punctually—don't miss a day.
> Be well prepared for five long lectures;
> study each paragraph so well
> that you can check up on the teacher;
> don't let him put in a syllable
> that isn't in the book.
> And busily write down his every word
> as though the Holy Ghost were dictating to you!

Student

> That you won't have to tell me more than once!
> I think that's very good advice.
> What one gets down in black and white in notes
> he can carry home to comfort him at night.

Mephistopheles

> Now you must choose your major subject.

Student

> The study of law does not seem too attractive.

Mephistopheles

> I can't hold that against you, I admit,
> for I know well just how that matter stands.
> The statutes and the laws are handed on
> like some disease that never ends,
> stealthily creeping from race to race.
> Reason turns nonsense; beneficence becomes a plague.
> It's too bad that you're a grandchild, my lad.
> But of natural rights, unfortunately,
> there's never any question.

Student

> You have increased my own aversion for the law.
> The students you teach are lucky indeed.
> Maybe I'd like to study theology.

Mephistopheles

> I wouldn't want to be leading you astray,
> but in the subject matter of this field
> it's difficult to keep on the right track;
> there's so much poison hidden here
> it's hard to tell it from the medicine.
> You'll find it's best to have just one professor
> and swear by the master's words. In general,
> stick fast to words, and through that trusty gateway
> you'll get into the temple of assurance.

Student

> But there ought to be some idea behind a word.

Mephistopheles

> Of course! But don't torment yourself too much.
> Just where the idea's lacking a word pops up.
> Words are splendid weapons for fighting;
> with words you can prepare a system;
> words are grand to put your faith in—
> and you can't take anything from one.

Student

> Excuse me if I ask too many questions;
> but won't you please make some suggestions for the study
> of medicine? Three years go by so quickly
> and, God, the field's so wide!
> If only I could get a pointer
> then I could grope my way ahead.

Mephistopheles

> *(aside)*

> I'm bored with this dry tone
> and now I'll really play the Devil again.

> *(aloud)*

> The spirit of medicine is easily comprehended;
> you study through the macrocosm and microcosm,

but in the end let it all go, as pleases God.
In vain you rummage learnedly far and wide;
each one learns only what he can;
but he who seizes the instant boldly,
he is the clever one!
Now you, you're pretty well built
and will not be lacking in daring.
As long as you thoroughly trust yourself,
all the simple souls will have confidence in you.
Above all, learn how to manage the women:
all their eternal Ah's and Oh's
of a thousand sorts
can be cured at a single point.
And if you act discreetly,
you'll keep them all under your thumb.
First, your M. D. will give them confidence
that your skill and learning are immense.
Right at the start you can fumble them here and there,
when another man would have to coax for years.
Learn how to press the pulse in the little wrist
and with fiery furtive glances slip
your arm around her slender hips
to see how tightly she is laced.

Student

Already it seems better!
Now I begin to see the where and how.

Mephistopheles

My friend, all theory is gray,
and the golden tree of life is green.

Student

I swear to you it's like a dream.
May I return another time and trouble you
to expound your system to the bottom?

Mephistopheles

I'll do all that I can for you and more.

Student

I cannot possibly leave
until I get your autograph.
I wonder if you'd be so kind.

Mephistopheles

> With pleasure.

> (*He writes in the book and returns it.*)

Student

> (*reading*)

> *Eritis sicut Deus, scientes bonum et malum.*[2]

> (*He closes the book reverently and goes out.*)

Mephistopheles

> Just follow the old proverb and my cousin the snake;
> and in spite of your likeness to God,
> your soul will soon be quaking!

> (*Faust comes in.*)

Faust

> Where do we go from here?

Mephistopheles

> Wherever you please. First we can see
> the world of little people, then the great.
> With pleasure and profit
> you can crib through the course.

Faust

> But admit that it's pretty hard to be
> a man of the world, with a beard as long as mine.
> I lack the *savoir vivre.* I won't succeed.
> I never did know how to get around;
> indeed, I feel so small before most other men,
> that often I could sink into the dirt.

Mephistopheles

> Time will take care of that, my friend.
> Gain some self-confidence and you'll know how to live.

Faust

> But how shall we get away from here?
> Where have you a coach, driver and horses?

---

[2] You shall be as God, knowing good and evil.

Mephistopheles

We only need to spread this cloak
and it will carry us through the sky.
Of course, upon this daring journey
your baggage must be very light.
A puff of hydrogen which I'll prepare
will hoist us quickly to the upper regions.
Congratulations on your new career!

Charles Dickens

(1812–1870)

The most popular English novelist of the last century, Charles Dickens created a memorable pedant in the character of Mr. Gradgrind, whose fetish for fact anticipated the complaint of Alfred North Whitehead that the merely well-informed man is the most useless bore on God's earth.

Though the ensuing excerpt from *Hard Times*, a novel published in 1854, ridicules the atmosphere of nineteenth-century British schools, the author's attack extends to contemporary American classrooms as well. When Dickens describes M'Choakumchild as one of many teachers "lately turned at the same time, in the same factory, on the same principles, like so many pianoforte legs," he indicts a kind of intellectual pettiness capable of many guises. Though the doctrines of M'Choakumchild's training no longer lure most educators, a question remains: Which of *today's* educational tenets are correspondingly unquestioned, slavishly purveyed, and meekly adopted?

Dickens feared not the substance of oppressive doctrines so much as their effect, the paralyzing of the believer's imagination. For Dickens, the task of the good teacher is neither to worship nor to disparage factual knowledge, but to excite in students its relation to human affairs.

M'Choakumchild's Schoolroom

I

"Now, what I want is, Facts. Teach these boys and girls nothing but Facts. Facts alone are wanted in life. Plant nothing else, and root out everything else. You can only form the minds of reasoning animals upon Facts: nothing else will ever be of any service to them. This is the principle on which I bring up my own children, and this is the principle on which I bring up these children. Stick to Facts, sir!"

The scene was a plain, bare, monotonous vault of a schoolroom, and the speaker's square forefinger emphasised his observations by underscoring every sentence with a line on the schoolmaster's sleeve. The emphasis was helped by the speaker's square wall of a forehead, which had his eyebrows for its base, while his eyes found commodious cellarage in two dark caves, overshadowed by the wall. The emphasis was helped by the speaker's mouth, which was wide, thin, and hard set. The emphasis was helped by the speaker's voice, which was inflexible, dry, and dictatorial. The emphasis was helped by the speaker's hair, which bristled on the skirts of his bald head, a plantation of firs to keep the wind from its shining surface, all covered with knobs, like the crust of a plum pie, as if the head had scarcely warehouseroom for the hard facts stored inside. The speaker's obstinate carriage, square coat, square legs, square shoulders,—nay, his very neckcloth, trained to take him by the throat with an unaccommodating grasp, like a stubborn fact, as it was,—all helped the emphasis.

"In this life, we want nothing but Facts, sir; nothing but Facts!"

The speaker, and the schoolmaster, and the third grown person present, all backed a little, and swept with their eyes the inclined plane of little vessels then and there arranged in order, ready to have imperial gallons of facts poured into them until they were full to the brim.

II

Thomas Gradgrind, sir. A man of realities. A man of facts and calculations. A man who proceeds upon the principle that two and two are four, and nothing over, and who is not to be talked into allowing for anything over. Thomas Gradgrind, sir—peremptorily Thomas—Thomas Gradgrind. With a rule and a pair of scales, and the multiplication table always in his pocket, sir, ready to weigh and measure any parcel of human nature, and tell you exactly what it comes to. It is a mere question of figures, a case of simple arithmetic. You might hope to get some other nonsensical belief into the head of George Gradgrind, or Augustus Gradgrind, or John Gradgrind, or Joseph Gradgrind (all suppositious, nonexistent persons), but into the head of Thomas Gradgrind—no, sir!

In such terms Mr. Gradgrind always mentally introduced himself, whether to his private circle of acquaintance, or to the public in general. In such terms, no doubt, substituting the words "boys and girls," for "sir," Thomas Gradgrind now presented Thomas Gradgrind to the little pitchers before him, who were to be filled so full of facts.

Indeed, as he eagerly sparkled at them from the cellarage before mentioned, he seemed a kind of cannon loaded to the muzzle with facts, and prepared to blow them clean out of the regions of childhood at one discharge. He seemed a galvanizing apparatus, too, charged with a grim mechanical substitute for the tender young imaginations that were to be stormed away

"Girl number twenty," said Gradgrind, squarely pointing with his square forefinger, "I don't know that girl. Who is that girl?"

"Sissy Jupe, sir," explained number twenty, blushing, standing up, and curtseying.

"Sissy is not a name," said Mr. Gradgrind. "Don't call yourself Sissy. Call yourself Cecilia."

"It's father as calls me Sissy, sir," returned the young girl in a trembling voice, and with another curtsey.

"Then he has no business to do it," said Mr. Gradgrind. "Tell him he mustn't. Cecilia Jupe. Let me see. What is your father?"

"He belongs to the horse-riding, if you please, sir."

Mr. Gradgrind frowned, and waved off the objectionable calling with his hand.

"We don't want to know anything about that, here. You mustn't tell us about that, here. Your father breaks horses, don't he?"

"If you please, sir, when they can get any to break, they do break horses in the ring, sir."

"You mustn't tell us about the ring, here. Very well, then. Describe your father as a horsebreaker. He doctors sick horses, I dare say?"

"Oh yes, sir."

"Very well, then. He is a veterinary surgeon, a farrier, and horsebreaker. Give me your definition of a horse."

(Sissy Jupe thrown into the greatest alarm by this demand.)

"Girl number twenty unable to define a horse!" said Mr. Gradgrind, for the general behoof of all the little pitchers. "Girl number twenty possessed of no facts, in reference to one of the commonest of animals! Some boy's definition of a horse. Bitzer, yours."

The square finger, moving here and there, lighted suddenly on Bitzer, perhaps because he chanced to sit in the same ray of sunlight which, darting in at one of the bare windows of the intensely whitewashed room, irradiated Sissy. For, the boys and girls sat on the face of the inclined plane in two compact bodies, divided up the centre by a narrow interval; and Sissy, being at the corner of a row on the sunny side, came in for the beginning of a sunbeam, of which Bitzer, being at the corner of a row on the other side, a few rows in advance, caught the end. But, whereas the girl was so dark-eyed and dark-haired, that she seemed to receive a deeper and more lustrous colour from the sun, when it shone upon her, the boy was so light-eyed and light-haired that the self-same rays appeared to draw out of him what little colour he ever possessed. His cold eyes would hardly have been eyes, but for the short ends of lashes which, by bringing them into immediate contrast with something paler than themselves, expressed their form. His short-cropped hair might have been a mere continuation of the sandy freckles on his forehead and face. His skin was so unwholesomely deficient in the natural tinge, that he looked as though, if he were cut, he would bleed white.

"Bitzer," said Thomas Gradgrind. "Your definition of a horse."

"Quadruped. Graminivorous. Forty teeth, namely twenty-four grinders, four eye-teeth, and twelve incisive. Sheds coat in the spring; in marshy countries, sheds hoofs, too. Hoofs hard, but requiring to be shod with iron. Age known by marks in mouth." Thus (and much more) Bitzer.

"Now girl number twenty," said Mr. Gradgrind. "You know what a horse is."

She curtseyed again, and would have blushed deeper, if she could have blushed deeper than she had blushed all this time. Bitzer, after rapidly blinking at Thomas Gradgrind with both eyes at once, and so catching the light upon his quivering ends of lashes that they looked like the antennae of busy insects, put his knuckles to his freckled forehead, and sat down again.

The third gentleman now stepped forth. A mighty man at cutting and drying, he was; a government officer; in his way (and in most other people's too), a professed pugilist; always in training, always with a system to force down the general throat like a bolus, always to be heard of at the bar of his little Public-office, ready to fight all England. To continue in fistic phraseology, he had a genius for coming up to the scratch, wherever and whatever it was, and proving himself an ugly customer. He would go in and damage any subject whatever with his right, follow up with his left, stop, exchange, counter, bore his opponent (he always fought All England) to the ropes, and fall upon him neatly. He was certain to knock the wind out of common sense, and render that unlucky adversary deaf to the call of time. And he had it in charge from high authority to bring about the great public-office Millennium, when Commissioners should reign upon earth.

"Very well," said this gentleman, briskly smiling, and folding his arms. "That's a horse. Now, let me ask you girls and boys, Would you paper a room with representations of horses?"

After a pause, one half of the children cried in chorus, "Yes, sir!" Upon which the other half, seeing in the gentleman's face that Yes was wrong, cried out in chorus, "No, sir!"—as the custom is, in these examinations.

"Of course, No. Why wouldn't you?"

A pause. One corpulent slow boy, with a wheezy manner of breathing, ventured the answer, Because he wouldn't paper a room at all, but would paint it.

"You *must* paper it," said the gentleman, rather warmly.

"You must paper it," said Thomas Gradgrind, "whether you like it or not. Don't tell *us* you wouldn't paper it. What do you mean, boy?"

"I'll explain to you, then," said the gentleman, after another and a dismal pause, "why you wouldn't paper a room with representations of horses. Do you ever see horses walking up and down the sides of rooms in reality—in fact? Do you?"

"Yes, sir!" from one half. "No, sir!" from the other.

"Of course, No," said the gentleman, with an indignant look at the wrong half. "Why, then, you are not to see anywhere, what you don't see in fact; you are not to have anywhere, what you don't have in fact. What is called Taste, is only another name for Fact."

Thomas Gradgrind nodded his approbation.

"This is a new principle, a discovery, a great discovery," said the gentleman. "Now, I'll try you again. Suppose you were going to carpet a room. Would you use a carpet having a representation of flowers upon it?"

There being a general conviction by this time that "No, sir!" was always the right answer to this gentleman, the chorus of No was very strong. Only a few feeble stragglers said Yes: among them Sissy Jupe.

"Girl number twenty," said the gentleman, smiling in the calm strength of knowledge.

Sissy blushed, and stood up.

"So you would carpet your room—or your husband's room, if you were a grown woman, and had a husband—with representations of flowers, would you?" said the gentleman. "Why would you?"

"If you please, sir, I am very fond of flowers," returned the girl.

"And is that why you would put tables and chairs upon them, and have people walking over them with heavy boots?"

"It wouldn't hurt them, sir. They wouldn't crush and wither, if you please, sir. They would be the pictures of what was very pretty and pleasant, and I would fancy——"

"Ay, ay, ay! But you mustn't fancy," cried the gentleman, quite elated by coming so happily to his point. "That's it! You are never to fancy."

"You are not, Cecilia Jupe," Thomas Gradgrind solemnly repeated, "to do anything of that kind."

"Fact, fact, fact!" said the gentleman. And "Fact, fact, fact!" repeated Thomas Gradgrind.

"You are to be in all things regulated and governed," said the gentleman, "by fact. We hope to have, before long, a board of fact, composed of commissioners of fact, who will force the people to be a people of fact, and of nothing but fact. You must discard the word Fancy altogether. You have nothing to do with it. You are not to have, in any object of use or ornament, what would be a contradiction in fact. You don't walk upon flowers in fact; you cannot be allowed to walk upon flowers in carpets. You don't find that foreign birds and butterflies come and perch upon your crockery; you cannot be permitted to paint foreign birds and butterflies upon your crockery. You never meet with quadrupeds going up and down walls; you must not have quadrupeds represented upon walls. You must use," said the gentleman, "for all these purposes, combinations and modifications (in primary colours) of mathematical figures which are susceptible of proof and demonstration. This is the new discovery. This is fact. This is taste."

The girl curtseyed, and sat down. She was very young, and she looked as if she were frightened by the matter of fact prospect the world afforded.

"Now, if Mr. M'Choakumchild," said the gentleman, "will proceed to give his first lesson here, Mr. Gradgrind, I shall be happy, at your request, to observe his mode of procedure."

Mr. Gradgrind was much obliged. "Mr. M'Choakumchild, we only wait for you."

So, Mr. M'Choakumchild began in his best manner. He and some one hundred and forty other schoolmasters had been lately turned at the same time, in the same factory, on the same principles, like so many pianoforte legs. He had been put through an immense variety of paces, and had answered volumes of head-breaking questions. Orthography, etymology, syntax, and prosody, biography, astronomy, geography, and general cosmography, the sciences of compound proportion, algebra, land-surveying and levelling, vocal music, and drawing from models, were all at the ends of his ten chilled fingers. He had worked his stony way into Her Majesty's most Honourable Privy Council's Schedule B, and had taken the bloom off the higher branches of mathematics and physical science, French, German, Latin, and Greek. He knew all about all the Water Sheds of all the world (whatever they are), and all the histories of all the peoples, and all the names of all the rivers and mountains, and all the productions, manners, and customs of all the countries, and all their boundaries and bearings on the two and thirty points of the compass. Ah, rather overdone, M'Choakumchild. If he had only learnt a little less, how infinitely better he might have taught much more!

He went to work in this preparatory lesson, not unlike Morgiana in the Forty Thieves: looking into all the vessels ranged before him, one after another, to see what they contained. Say, good M'Choakumchild. When from thy boiling store, thou shalt fill each jar brim full by-and-by, dost thou think that thou wilt always kill outright the robber Fancy lurking within—or sometimes only maim him and distort him!

Henry Adams
(1838–1918)

Henry Adams, a descendant of two Presidents, believed that education is ceaseless, in many ways accidental, costly to one's comfort, and damned to incompletion by the brevity of life. Published in 1907 in a small private edition meant only for friends, *The Education of Henry Adams* has since been issued in numerous public editions. Written in the third person, a point of view that grants a tone of objectivity to the recounting, *The Education* is the most distinguished autobiography yet written by an American. It is as dense as a New England virgin forest; thickets of experience detain the good reader. It is a book that yields most when read slowly. Henry Adams' mind, which he sometimes doubted, and his heart, which he usually distrusted, unite in *The Education* as they seemed rarely to do in his life.

Henry Adams would agree with Plato to the extent that an education, to be worth anything at all, must be worth everything: it is plainly the most ambitious task that a man can undertake. Consequently, the following passages, though taken from Adams' years as a student and teacher, reflect but a small part of his real education. Nevertheless, the questions about formal education raised by Adams are perennial ones, not because they are without solution, but because each era must ask them anew.

The autobiography spans a period of American life which saw the decline of New England idealism, the rise of national disillusionment during the Civil War, a recrudescence of hope in the years of the Industrial Revolution, and an ensuing realism which replaced the Victorian view of man and nature. This realism created a milieu in which Henry James could declare through one of his feminine characters: "It was not in the least of American barbarism that she was afraid. Her dread was all of American civilization."

Like Henry James, Adams was both an artist of manners and a prophet. By his own admission he owned an eighteenth-century mind fated to live in the nineteenth, yet it was a mind able to discern the fledgling energies of the twentieth, among them the awful contingency that "the human race may commit suicide by blowing up the world."

Other works by Adams include a monumental nine-volume *History of the United States During the Administrations of Jefferson and Madison* (1891), a theory of history defined in Chapter XXXIII of *The Education*, and a masterful study of thirteenth-century unity in *Mont-Saint-Michel and Chartres* (1904).

THREE EDUCATIONS

I. Quincy (1838–1848)

Under the shadow of Boston State House, turning its back on the house of John Hancock, the little passage called Hancock Avenue runs, or ran, from Beacon Street, skirting the State House grounds, to Mount Vernon Street, on the summit of Beacon Hill; and there, in the third house below Mount Vernon Place, February 16, 1838, a child was born, and christened later by his uncle, the minister of the First Church after the tenets of Boston Unitarianism, as Henry Brooks Adams.

Had he been born in Jerusalem under the shadow of the Temple and circumcised in the Synagogue by his uncle the high priest, under the name of Israel Cohen, he would scarcely have been more distinctly branded, and not much more heavily handicapped in the races of the coming century, in running for such stakes as the century was to offer; but, on the other hand, the ordinary traveller, who does not enter the field of racing, finds advantage in being, so to speak, ticketed through life, with the safeguards of an old, established traffic. Safeguards are often irksome, but sometimes convenient, and if one needs them at all, one is apt to need them badly. A hundred years earlier, such safeguards as his would have secured any young man's success; and although in 1838 their value was not very great compared with what they would have had in 1738, yet the mere accident of starting a twentieth-century career from a nest of associations so colonial—so troglodytic—as the First Church, the Boston State House, Beacon Hill, John Hancock and John Adams, Mount Vernon Street and Quincy, all crowding on ten pounds of unconscious babyhood, was so queer as to offer a subject of curious speculation to the baby long after he had witnessed the solution. What could become of such a child of the seventeenth and eighteenth centuries, when he should wake up to find himself required to play the game of the twentieth? Had he been consulted, would he have cared to play the game at all, holding such cards as he held, and suspecting that the game was to be one of which neither he nor any one else back to the beginning of time knew the rules or the risks or the stakes? He was not consulted and was not responsible, but had he been taken into the confidence of his parents, he would certainly have told them to change nothing as far as concerned him. He would have been astounded by his own luck. Probably no child, born in the year, held better cards than he. Whether life was an honest game of chance, or whether the cards were marked and forced, he could not refuse to play his excellent hand. He could never make the usual plea of irresponsibility. He accepted the situation as though he had been a party to it, and under the same circumstances would do it again, the more readily for knowing the exact values. To his life as a whole he was a consenting, contracting party and partner from the moment he was born to the moment he died. Only with that understanding—as a consciously assenting member in full partnership with the society of his age—had his education an interest to himself or to others.

As it happened, he never got to the point of playing the game at all; he lost himself in the study of it, watching the errors of the players; but this is the only interest in the story, which otherwise has no moral and little incident. A story of education—seventy years of it—the practical value remains to the end in doubt, like other values about which men have disputed since the birth of Cain and Abel; but the practical value of the universe has never been stated in dollars. Although every one cannot be a Gargantua-Napoleon-Bismarck and walk off with the great bells of Notre Dame, every one must bear his own universe, and most persons are moderately interested in learning how their neighbors have managed to carry theirs.

This problem of education, started in 1838, went on for three years, while the baby grew, like other babies, unconsciously, as a vegetable, the outside world working as it never had worked before, to get his new universe ready for him. Often in old age he puzzled over the question whether, on the doctrine of chances, he was at liberty to accept himself or his world as an accident. No such accident had ever happened before in human experience. For him, alone, the old universe was thrown into the ash-heap and a new one created. He and his eighteenth-century, troglodytic Boston were suddenly cut apart—separated forever—in act if not in sentiment, by the opening of the Boston and Albany Railroad; the appearance of the first Cunard steamers in the bay; and the telegraphic messages which carried from Baltimore to Washington the news that Henry Clay and James K. Polk were nominated for the Presidency. This was in May, 1844; he was six years old; his new world was ready for use, and only fragments of the old met his eyes.

Of all this that was being done to complicate his education, he knew only the color of yellow. He first found himself sitting on a yellow kitchen floor in strong sunlight. He was three years old when he took this earliest step in education; a lesson of color. The second followed soon; a lesson of taste. On December 3, 1841, he developed scarlet fever. For several days he was as good as dead, reviving only under the careful nursing of his family. When he began to recover strength, about January 1, 1842, his hunger must have been stronger than any other pleasure or pain, for while in after life he retained not the faintest recollection of his illness, he remembered quite clearly his aunt entering the sick-room bearing in her hand a saucer with a baked apple.

The order of impressions retained by memory might naturally be that of color and taste, although one would rather suppose that the sense of pain would be first to educate. In fact, the third recollection of the child was that of discomfort. The moment he could be removed, he was bundled up in blankets and carried from the little house in Hancock Avenue to a larger one which his parents were to occupy for the rest of their lives in the neighboring Mount Vernon Street. The season was midwinter, January 10, 1842, and he never forgot his acute distress for want of air under his blankets, or the noises of moving furniture.

As a means of variation from a normal type, sickness in childhood ought to have a certain value not to be classed under any fitness or unfitness of natural selection; and especially scarlet fever affected boys seriously, both physically and in character, though they might through life puzzle themselves to decide whether it had fitted or unfitted them for success; but this fever of Henry Adams took greater and greater importance in his eyes, from the point of view of education, the longer he lived. At first, the effect was physical. He fell behind his brothers two or three inches in height, and proportionally in bone and weight. His character and processes of mind seemed to share in this fining-down process of scale. He was not good in a fight, and his nerves were more delicate than boys' nerves ought to be. He exaggerated these weaknesses as he grew older. The habit of doubt; of distrusting his own judgment and of totally rejecting the judgment of the world; the tendency to regard every question as open; the hesitation to act except as a choice of evils; the shirking of responsibility; the love of line, form, quality; the horror of ennui; the passion for companionship and the antipathy to society—all these are well-known qualities of New England character in no way peculiar to individuals but in this instance they seemed to be stimulated by the fever, and Henry Adams could never make up his mind whether, on the whole, the change of character was morbid or healthy, good or bad for his purpose. His brothers were the type; he was the variation.

As far as the boy knew, the sickness did not affect him at all, and he grew up in excellent health, bodily and mental, taking life as it was given; accepting its local standards without a difficulty, and enjoying much of it as keenly as any other boy of his age. He seemed to himself quite normal, and his companions seemed always to think him so. Whatever was peculiar about him was education, not character, and came to him, directly and indirectly, as the result of that eighteenth-century inheritance which he took with his name.

The atmosphere of education in which he lived was colonial, revolutionary, almost Cromwellian, as though he were steeped, from his greatest grandmother's birth, in the odor of political crime. Resistance to something was the law of New England nature; the boy looked out of the world with the instinct of resistance; for numberless generations his predecessors had viewed the world chiefly as a thing to be reformed, filled with evil forces to be abolished, and they saw no reason to suppose that they had wholly succeeded in the abolition; the duty was unchanged. That duty implied not only resistance to evil, but hatred of it. Boys naturally look on all force as an enemy, and generally find it so, but the New Englander, whether boy or man, in his long struggle with a stingy or hostile universe, had learned also to love the pleasure of hating; his joys were few.

Politics, as a practice, whatever its professions, had always been the systematic organization of hatreds, and Massachusetts politics had been as harsh as the climate. The chief charm of New England was harshness of contrasts and extremes of sensibility—a cold that froze the blood, and a heat that boiled it—so that the pleasure of hating—one's self is no better victim offered—was not its rarest amusement; but the charm was a true and natural child of the soil, not a cultivated weed of the ancients. The violence of the contrast was real and made the strongest motive of education. The double exterior nature gave life its relative values. Winter and summer, cold and heat, town and country, force and freedom, marked two modes of life and thought, balanced like lobes of the brain. Town was winter confinement, school, rule, discipline; straight, gloomy streets, piled with six feet of snow in the middle; frosts that made the snow sing under wheels or runners; thaws when the streets became dangerous to cross; society of uncles, aunts, and cousins who expected children to behave themselves, and who were not always gratified; above all else, winter represented the desire to escape and go free. Town was restraint, law, unity. Country, only seven miles away, was liberty, diversity, outlawry, the endless delight of mere sense impressions given by nature for nothing, and breathed by boys without knowing it.

Boys are wild animals, rich in the treasures of sense, but the New England boy had a wider range of emotions than boys of more equable climates. He felt his nature crudely, as it was meant. To the boy Henry Adams, summer was drunken. Among senses, smell was the strongest—smell of hot pine-woods and sweet-fern in the scorching summer noon; of new-mown hay; of ploughed earth; of box hedges; of peaches, lilacs, syringas; of stables, barns, cow-yards; of salt water and low tide on the marshes; nothing came amiss. Next to smell came taste, and the children knew the taste of everything they saw or touched, from pennyroyal and flagroot to the shell of a pignut and the letters of a spelling-book—the taste of A-B, AB, suddenly revived on the boy's tongue sixty years afterwards. Light, line, and color as sensual pleasures, came later and were as crude as the rest. The New England light is glare, and the atmosphere harshens color. The boy was a full man before he ever knew what was meant by atmosphere; his idea of pleasure in light was the blaze of a New England sun. His idea of color was a peony, with the dew of early morning on its petals. The intense blue of the sea, as he saw it a mile or two away, from the Quincy hills; the cumuli in a June afternoon sky; the strong reds and greens and purples of colored prints and children's picture-books, as the American colors then ran; these were ideals. The opposites or antipathies, were the cold grays of November evenings, and the thick, muddy thaws of Boston winter. With such standards, the Bostonian could not but develop a double nature. Life was a double thing. After a January blizzard, the boy who could look with pleasure into the violent snow-glare of the cold white sunshine, with its intense light and shade, scarcely knew what was meant by tone. He could reach it only by education.

Winter and summer, then, were two hostile lives, and bred two separate natures. Winter was always the effort to live; summer was tropical license. Whether the children rolled in the grass, or waded in the brook, or swam in the salt ocean, or sailed in the bay, or fished for smelts in the creeks, or netted minnows in the salt-marshes, or took to the pine-woods and the granite quarries, or chased muskrats and hunted snapping-turtles in the swamps, or mushrooms or nuts on the autumn hills, summer and country were always sensual living, while winter was always compulsory learning. Summer was the multiplicity of nature; winter was school.

The bearing of the two seasons on the education of Henry Adams was no fancy; it was the most decisive force he ever knew; it ran through life, and made the division between its perplexing, warring, irreconcilable problems, irreducible opposites, with growing emphasis to the last year of study. From earliest childhood the boy was accustomed to feel that, for him, life was double. Winter and summer, town and country, law and liberty, were hostile, and the man who pretended they were not, was in his eyes a schoolmaster—that is, a man employed to tell lies to little boys.

II. Boston (1848-1854)

In 1848, a few months after the death of John Quincy Adams, a convention of antislavery delegates met at Buffalo, New York, to organize a new political party. Nominated at this convention were Martin Van Buren for President and Charles Francis Adams for Vice President. Henry's family subsequently moved to Boston, the center of New England politics, and settled in a house on Mount Vernon Street.

Of all the conditions of his youth which afterwards puzzled the grown-up man, this disappearance of religion puzzled him most. The boy went to church twice every Sunday; he was taught to read his Bible, and he learned religious poetry by heart; he believed in a mild deism; he prayed; he went through all the forms; but neither to him nor to his brothers or sisters was religion real. Even the mild discipline of the Unitarian Church was so irksome that they all threw it off at the first possible moment, and never afterwards entered a church. The religious instinct had vanished, and could not be revived, although one made in later life many efforts to recover it. That the most powerful emotion of man, next to the sexual, should disappear, might be a personal defect of his own; but that the most intelligent society, led by the most intelligent clergy, in the most moral conditions he ever knew, should have solved all the problems of the universe so thoroughly as to have quite ceased making itself anxious about past or future, and should have persuaded itself that all the problems which had convulsed human thought from earliest recorded time, were not worth discussing, seemed to him the most curious social phenomenon he had to account for in a long life. The faculty of turning away one's eyes as one approaches a chasm is not unusual, and Boston showed, under the lead of Mr. Webster, how successfully it could be done in politics; but in politics a certain number of men did at least protest. In religion and philosophy no one protested. Such protest as was made took forms more simple than the silence, like the deism of Theodore Parker, and of the boy's own cousin Octavius Frothingham, who distressed his father and scandalized Beacon Street by avowing scepticism that seemed to solve no old problems, and to raise many new ones. The less aggressive protest of Ralph Waldo Emerson, was, from an old-world point of view, less serious. It was *naïf*.

The children reached manhood without knowing religion, and with the certainty that dogma, metaphysics, and abstract philosophy were not worth knowing. So one-sided an education could have been possible in no other country or time, but it became, almost of necessity, the more literary and political. As the children grew up, they exaggerated the literary and the political interests. They joined in the dinner-table discussions and from childhood the boys were accustomed to hear, almost every day, table-talk as good as they were ever likely to hear again. The eldest child, Louisa, was one of the most sparkling creatures her brother met in a long and varied experience of bright women. The oldest son, John, was afterwards regarded as one of the best talkers in Boston society, and perhaps the most popular man in the State, though apt to be on the unpopular side. Palfrey and Dana could be entertaining when they pleased, and though Charles Sumner could hardly be called light in hand, he was willing to be amused, and smiled grandly from time to time;

while Mr. Adams, who talked relatively little, was always a good listener, and laughed over a witticism till he choked.

By way of educating and amusing the children, Mr. Adams read much aloud, and was sure to read political literature, especially when it was satirical, like the speeches of Horace Mann and the "Epistles" of "Hosea Biglow," with great delight to the youth. So he read Longfellow and Tennyson as their poems appeared, but the children took possession of Dickens and Thackeray for themselves. Both were too modern for tastes founded on Pope and Dr. Johnson. The boy Henry soon became a desultory reader of every book he found readable, but these were commonly eighteenth-century historians because his father's library was full of them. In the want of positive instincts, he drifted into the mental indolence of history. So, too, he read shelves of eighteenth-century poetry, but when his father offered his own set of Wordsworth as a gift on condition of reading it through, he declined. Pope and Gray called for no mental effort; they were easy reading; but the boy was thirty years old before his education reached Wordsworth.

This is the story of an education, and the person or persons who figure in it are supposed to have values only as educators or educated. The surroundings concern it only so far as they affect education. Sumner, Dana, Palfrey, had values of their own, like Hume, Pope, and Wordsworth, which any one may study in their works; here all appear only as influences on the mind of a boy very nearly the average of most boys in physical and mental stature. The influence was wholly political and literary. His father made no effort to force his mind, but left him free play, and this was perhaps best. Only in one way his father rendered him a great service by trying to teach him French and giving him some idea of a French accent. Otherwise the family was rather an atmosphere than an influence. The boy had a large and overpowering set of brothers and sisters, who were modes or replicas of the same type, getting the same education, struggling with the same problems, and solving the question, or leaving it unsolved much in the same way. They knew no more than he what they wanted or what to do for it, but all were conscious that they would like to control power in some form; and the same thing could be said of an ant or an elephant. Their form was tied to politics or literature. They amounted to one individual with half-a-dozen sides or facets; their temperaments reacted on each other and made each child more like the other. This was also education, but in the type, and the Boston or New England type was well enough known. What no one knew was whether the individual who thought himself a representative of this type, was fit to deal with life.

As far as outward bearing went, such a family of turbulent children, given free rein by their parents, or indifferent to check, should have come to more or less grief. Certainly no one was strong enough to control them, least of all their mother, the queen-bee of the hive, on whom nine-tenths of the burden fell, on whose strength they all depended, but whose children were much too self-willed and self-confident to take guidance from her, or from any one else, unless in the direction they fancied. Father and mother were about equally helpless. Almost every large family in those days produced at least one black sheep, and if this generation of Adamses escaped, it was as much a matter of surprise to them as to their neighbors. By some happy chance they grew up to be decent citizens, but Henry Adams, as a brand escaped from the burning, always looked back with astonishment at their luck. The fact seemed to prove that they were born, like birds, with a certain innate balance. Home influences alone never saved the New England boy from ruin, though sometimes they may have helped to ruin him; and the influences outside of home were negative. If school helped, it was only by reaction. The dislike of school was so strong as to be a positive gain. The passionate hatred of school methods was almost a method in itself. Yet the dayschool of that time was respectable, and the boy had nothing to complain of. In fact, he never complained. He hated it because he was here with a crowd of other boys and compelled to learn by memory a quantity of things that did not amuse him. His memory was slow, and the effort painful. For him to conceive that his memory could compete for school prizes with machines of two or three times its power, was to prove himself wanting not only in memory, but flagrantly in mind. He thought his mind a good enough machine, if it were given time to act, but it acted wrong if hurried. Schoolmasters never gave time.

In any and all its forms, the boy detested school, and the prejudice became deeper with years. He always reckoned his school days, from ten to sixteen years old, as time thrown away. Perhaps his needs turned out to be exceptional, but his existence was exceptional. For success in the life imposed on him he needed, as afterwards appeared, the facile use of only four tools: Mathematics, French, German, and Spanish. With these, he could master in very short time any special branch of inquiry, and feel at home in any society. Latin and Greek, he could, with the help of the modern languages, learn more completely by the intelligent work of six weeks than in the six years he spent on them at school. These four tools were necessary to his success in life, but he never controlled any one of them.

Thus, at the outset, he was condemned to failure more or less complete in the life awaiting him, but not more so than his companions. Indeed, had his father kept the boy at home, and given him half an hour's direction every day, he would have done more for him than school ever could do for them. Of course, school-taught men and boys looked down on home-bred boys, and rather prided themselves on their own ignorance, but the man of sixty can generally see what he needed in life, and in Henry Adams's opinion it was not school.

Most school experience was bad. Boy associations at fifteen were worse than none. Boston at that time offered few healthy resources for boys or men. The bar-room and billiard-room were more familiar than parents knew. As a rule boys could skate and swim and were sent to dancing-school; they played a rudimentary game of baseball, football, and hockey; a few could sail a boat; still fewer had been out with a gun to shoot yellow-legs or a stray wild duck; one or two may have learned something of natural history if they came from the neighborhood of Concord; none could ride across country, or knew what shooting with dogs meant. Sport as a pursuit was unknown. Boat-racing came after 1850. For horse-racing, only the trotting-course existed. Of all pleasures, winter sleighing was still the gayest and most popular. From none of these amusements could the boy learn anything likely to be of use to him in the world. Books remained as in the eighteenth century, the source of life, and as they came out—Thackeray, Dickens, Bulwer, Tennyson, Macaulay, Carlyle, and the rest—they were devoured; but as far as happiness went, the happiest hours of the boy's education were passed in summer lying on a musty heap of Congressional Documents in the old farmhouse at Quincy, reading "Quentin Durward," "Ivanhoe," and "The Talisman," and raiding the garden at intervals for peaches and pears. On the whole he learned most then.

III. Failure (1871)

In the fall of 1854, at the age of sixteen, Adams entered Harvard University. After his graduation in 1858, he traveled extensively in Europe. In 1861, President Lincoln's appointment of Charles Francis Adams as Minister to England determined that Henry was to view the Civil War from the strange vantage of a foreign country. Following the Union victory, Adams dabbled in art criticism and began to write articles for the *North American Review*, a magazine he was later to edit. During these years he read Marx and Darwin closely, wrote for the *Nation* and the *Review*, and investigated the vagaries of Washington politics. During a tour of Europe in 1870, Adams received an offer from President Norton of Harvard to teach history. He assumed this professorship in the autumn of 1871.

Far back in childhood, among its earliest memories, Henry Adams could recall his first visit to Harvard College. He must have been nine years old when on one of the singularly gloomy winter afternoons which beguiled Cambridgeport, his mother drove him out to visit his aunt, Mrs. Everett. Edward Everett was then President of the college and lived in the old President's House on Harvard Square. The boy remembered the drawing-room, on the left of the hall door, in which Mrs. Everett received them. He remembered a marble greyhound in the corner. The house had an air of colonial self-respect that impressed even a nine-year-old child.

When Adams closed his interview with President Eliot, he asked the Bursar about his aunt's old drawing-room, for the house had been turned to base uses. The room and the deserted kitchen adjacent to it were to let. He took them. Above him, his brother Brooks, then a law student, had rooms, with a private staircase. Opposite was J. R. Dennett, a young instructor almost as literary as Adams himself, and more rebellious to conventions. Inquiry revealed a boarding-table, somewhere in the neighborhood, also supposed to be superior in its class. Chauncey Wright, Francis Wharton, Dennett, John Fiske, or their equivalents in learning and lecture, were seen there, among three or four law students like Brooks Adams. With these primitive arrangements, all of them had to be satisfied. The standard was below that of Washington, but it was, for the moment, the best.

For the next nine months the Assistant Professor had no time to waste on comforts or amusements. He exhausted all his strength in trying to keep one day ahead of his duties. Often the stint ran on, till night and sleep ran short. He could not stop to think whether he were doing the work rightly. He could not get it done to please him, rightly or wrongly, for he never could satisfy himself what to do.

The fault he had found with Harvard College as an undergraduate must have been more or less just, for the college was making a great effort to meet these self-criticisms, and had elected President Eliot in 1869 to carry out its reforms. Professor Gurney was one of the leading performers, and had tried his hand on his own department of History. The two full Professors of History—Torrey and Gurney, charming men both—could not cover the ground. Between Gurney's classical courses and Torrey's modern ones, lay a gap of a thousand years, which Adams was expected to fill. The students had already elected courses numbered 1, 2, and 3, without knowing what was to be taught or who was to teach. If their new professor had asked what idea was in their minds, they must have replied that nothing at all was in their minds, since their professor had nothing in his, and down to the moment he took his chair and looked his scholars in the face, he had given, as far as he could remember, an hour, more or less, to the Middle Ages.

Not that his ignorance troubled him! He knew enough to be ignorant. His course had led him through oceans of ignorance; he had tumbled from one ocean into another till he had learned to swim; but even to him education was a serious thing. A parent gives life, but as parent, gives no more. A murderer takes life, but his deed stops there. A teacher affects eternity; he can never tell where his influence stops. A teacher is expected to teach truth, and may perhaps flatter himself that he does so, if he stops with the alphabet or the multiplication table, as a mother teaches truth by making her child eat with a spoon; but morals are quite another truth and philosophy is more complex still. A teacher must either treat history as a catalogue, a record, a romance, or as an evolution; and whether he affirms or denies evolution, he falls into all the burning faggots of the pit. He makes of his scholars either priests or atheists, plutocrats or socialists, judges or anarchists, almost in spite of himself. In essence incoherent and immoral, history had either to be taught as such—or falsified.

Adams wanted to do neither. He had no theory of evolution to teach, and could not make the facts fit one. He had no fancy for telling agreeable tales to amuse sluggish-minded boys, in order to publish them afterwards as lectures. He could still less compel his students to learn the Anglo-Saxon Chronicle and the Venerable Bede by heart. He saw no relation whatever between his students and the Middle Ages unless it were the Church, and there the ground was particularly dangerous. He knew better than though he were a professional historian that the man who should solve the riddle of the Middle Ages and bring them into the line of evolution from past to present, would be a greater man than Lamarck or Linnæus; but history had nowhere broken down so pitiably, or avowed itself so hopelessly bankrupt, as there. Since Gibbon, the spectacle was almost a scandal. History had lost even the sense of shame. It was a hundred years behind the experimental sciences. For all serious purpose, it was less instructive than Walter Scott and Alexandre Dumas.

All this was without offence to Sir Henry Maine, Tyler, McLennan, Buckle, Auguste Comte, and the various philosophers who, from time to time, stirred the scandal, and made it more scandalous. No doubt, a teacher might make some use of these writers on their theories; but Adams could fit them into no theory of his own. The college expected him to pass at least half his time in teaching the boys a few elementary dates and relations, that they might not be a disgrace to the university. This was formal; and he could frankly tell the boys that, provided they passed their examinations, they might get their facts where they liked, and use the teacher only for questions. The only privilege a student had that was worth his claiming, was that of talking to the professor, and the professor was bound to encourage it. His only difficulty on that side was to get them to talk at all. He had to devise schemes to find what they were thinking about, and induce them to risk criticism from their fellows. Any large body of students stifles the student. No man can instruct more than half-a-dozen students at once. The whole problem of education is one of its cost in money.

The lecture system to classes of hundreds, which was very much that of the twelfth century, suited Adams not at all. Barred from philosophy and bored by facts, he wanted to teach his students something not wholly useless. The number of students whose minds were of an order above the average was, in his experience, barely one in ten; the rest could not be much stimulated by any inducements a teacher could suggest. All were respectable, and in seven years of contact, Adams never had cause to complain of one; but nine minds in ten take polish passively, like a hard surface; only the tenth sensibly reacts.

Adams thought that, as no one seemed to care what he did, he would try to cultivate this tenth mind, though necessarily at the expense of the other nine. He frankly acted on the rule that a teacher, who knew nothing of his subject, should not pretend to teach his scholars what he did not know, but should join them in trying to find the best way of learning it. The rather pretentious name of historical method was sometimes given to this process of instruction, but the name smacked of German pedagogy, and a young professor who respected neither history nor method, and whose sole object of interest was his students' minds, fell into trouble enough without adding to it a German parentage.

The task was doomed to failure for a reason which he could not control. Nothing is easier than to teach historical method, but, when learned, it has little use. History is a tangled skein that one may take up at any point, and break when one has unravelled enough; but complexity precedes evolution. The *Pteraspis* grins horribly from the closed entrance. One may not begin at the beginning, and one has but the loosest relative truths to follow up. Adams found himself obliged to force his material into some shape to which a method could be applied. He could think only of law as subject; the Law School as end; and he took, as victims of his experiment, half-a-dozen highly intelligent young men who seemed willing to work. The course began with the beginning, as far as the books showed a beginning in primitive man, and came down through the Salic Franks to the Norman English. Since no textbooks existed, the professor refused to profess, knowing no more than his students, and the students read what they pleased and compared their results. As pedagogy, nothing could be more triumphant. The boys worked like rabbits, and dug holes all over the field of archaic society; no difficulty stopped them; unknown languages yielded before their attack, and customary law became familiar as the police court; undoubtedly they learned, after a fashion, to chase an idea, like a hare, through as dense a thicket of obscure facts as they were likely to meet at the bar; but their teacher knew from his own experience that his wonderful method led nowhere, and they would have to exert themselves to get rid of it in the Law School even more than they exerted themselves to acquire it in the college. Their science had no system, and could have none, since its subject was merely antiquarian. Try as hard as he might, the professor could not make it actual.

What was the use of training an active mind to waste its energy? The experiments might in time train Adams as professor, but this result was still less to his taste. He wanted to help the boys to a career, but not one of his many devices to stimulate the intellectual reaction of the student's mind satisfied either him or the students. For himself he was clear that the fault lay in the system, which could lead only to inertia. Such little knowledge of himself as he possessed warranted him in affirming that his mind required conflict, competition, contradiction even more than that of the student. He too wanted a rank-list to set his name upon. His reform of the system would have begun in the lecture-room at his own desk. He would have seated a rival assistant professor opposite him, whose business should be strictly limited to expressing opposite views. Nothing short of this would ever interest either the professor or the student; but of all university freaks, no irregularity shocked the intellectual atmosphere so much as contradiction or competition between teachers. In that respect the thirteenth-century university system was worth the whole teaching of the modern school.

All his pretty efforts to create conflicts of thought among his students failed for want of system. None met the needs of instruction. In spite of President Eliot's reforms and his steady, generous, liberal support, the system remained costly, clumsy and futile. The university—as far as it was represented by Henry Adams—produced at great waste of time and money results not worth reaching.

He made use of his lost two years of German schooling to inflict their results on his students, and by a happy chance he was in the full tide of fashion. The Germans were crowning their new emperor at Versailles, and surrounding his head with a halo of Pepins and Merwigs, Othos and Barbarossas. James Bryce had even discovered the Holy Roman Empire. Germany was never so powerful, and the Assistant Professor of History had nothing else as his stock in trade. He imposed Germany on his scholars with a heavy hand. He was rejoiced; but he sometimes doubted whether they should be grateful. On the whole, he was content neither with what he had taught nor with the way he had taught it. The seven years he passed in teaching seemed to him lost.

The uses of adversity are beyond measure strange. As a professor, he regarded himself as a failure. Without false modesty he thought he knew what he meant. He had tried a great many experiments, and wholly succeeded in none. He had succumbed to the weight of the system. He had accomplished nothing that he tried to do. He regarded the system as wrong; more mischievous to the teachers than to the students; fallacious from the beginning to end. He quitted the university at last, in

1877, with a feeling, that, if it had not been for the invariable courtesy and kindness shown by every one in it, from the President to the injured students, he should be sore at his failure.

These were his own feelings, but they seemed not to be felt in the college. With the same perplexing impartiality that had so much disconcerted him in his undergraduate days, the college insisted on expressing an opposite view. John Fiske went so far in his notice of the family in "Appleton's Cyclopedia," as to say that Henry had left a great reputation at Harvard College; which was a proof of John Fiske's personal regard that Adams heartily returned; and set the kind of expression down to *camaraderie*. The case was different when President Eliot himself hinted that Adams's service merited recognition. Adams could have wept on his shoulder in hysterics, so grateful was he for the rare good-will that inspired the compliment; but he could not allow the college to think that he esteemed himself entitled to distinction. He knew better, and his was among the failures which were respectable enough to deserve self-respect. Yet nothing in the vanity of life struck him as more humiliating than that Harvard College, which he had persistently criticised, abused, abandoned, and neglected, should alone have offered him a dollar, an office, an encouragement, or a kindness. Harvard College might have its faults, but at least it redeemed America, since it was true to its own.

The only part of education that the professor thought a success was the students. He found them excellent company. Cast more or less in the same mould, without violent emotions or sentiment, and, except for the veneer of American habits, ignorant of all that man had ever thought or hoped, their minds burst open like flowers at the sunlight of a suggestion. They were quick to respond; plastic to a mould; and incapable of fatigue. Their faith in education was so full of pathos that one dared not ask them what they thought they could do with education when they got it. Adams did put the question to one of them, and was surprised at the answer: "The degree of Harvard College is worth money to me in Chicago." This reply upset his experience; for the degree of Harvard College had been rather a drawback to a young man in Boston and Washington. So far as it went, the answer was good, and settled one's doubts. Adams knew no better, although he had given twenty years to pursuing the same education, and was no nearer a result than they. He still had to take for granted many things that they need not—among the rest, that his teaching did them more good than harm. In his own opinion the greatest good he could do them was to hold his tongue. They needed much faith then; they were likely to need more if they lived long.

He never knew whether his colleagues shared his doubts about their own utility. Unlike himself, they knew more or less their business. He could not tell his scholars that history glowed with social virtue; the Professor of Chemistry cared not a chemical atom whether society was virtuous or not. Adams could not pretend that mediæval society proved evolution; the Professor of Physics smiled at evolution. Adams was glad to dwell on the virtues of the Church and the triumphs of its art: the Professor of Political Economy had to treat them as waste of force. They knew what they had to teach; he did not. They might perhaps be frauds without knowing it; but he knew certainly nothing else of himself. He could teach his students nothing; he was only educating himself at their cost.

Education, like politics, is a rough affair, and every instructor has to shut his eyes and hold his tongue as though he were a priest. The students alone satisfied. They thought they gained something. Perhaps they did, for even in America and in the twentieth century, life could not be wholly industrial. Adams fervently hoped that they might remain content; but supposing twenty years more to pass, and they should turn on his as fiercely as he had turned on his old instructors—what answer could he make? The college had pleaded guilty, and tried to reform. He had pleaded guilty from the start, and his reforms had failed before those of the college.

The lecture-room was futile enough, but the faculty-room was worse. American society feared total wreck in the maelstrom of political and corporate administration, but it could not look for help to college dons. Adams knew, in that capacity, both Congressmen and professors, and he preferred Congressmen. The same failure marked the society of a college. Several score of the best-educated, most agreeable, and personally the most sociable people in America united in Cambridge to make a social desert that would have starved a polar bear. The liveliest and most agreeable of men—James Russell Lowell, Francis J. Child, Louis Agassiz, his son Alexander, Gurney, John Fiske, William James and a dozen others, who would have made the joy of London or Paris—tried their best to break out and be like other men in Cambridge and Boston, but society called them professors, and professors they had to be. While all these brilliant men were greedy for companionship, all were famished for want of it. Society was a faculty-meeting without business. The elements were there; but society cannot be made up of elements—people who are expected to be silent unless they have observations to make—and all the elements are bound to remain apart if required to make observations.

Thus it turned out that of all his many educations, Adams thought that of school-teacher the thinnest. Yet he was forced to admit that the education of an editor, in some ways, was thinner still. The editor had barely time to edit; he had none to write. If copy fell short, he was obliged to scribble a book-review on the virtues of the Anglo-Saxons or the vices of the Popes; for he knew more about Edward the Confessor or Boniface VIII than he did about President Grant. For seven years he wrote nothing; the *Review* lived on his brother Charles's railway articles. The editor could help others, but could do nothing for himself. As a writer, he was totally forgotten by the time he had been an editor for twelve months. As editor he could find no writer to take his place for politics and affairs of current concern. The *Review* became chiefly historical. Russell Lowell and Frank Palgrave helped him to keep it literary. The editor was a helpless drudge whose successes, if he made any, belonged to his writers; but whose failures might easily bankrupt himself. Such a Review may be made a sink of money with captivating ease. The secrets of success as an editor were easily learned; the highest was that of getting advertisements. Ten pages of advertising made an editor a success; five marked him as a failure. The merits or demerits of his literature had little to do with his results except when they led to adversity.

A year or two of education as editor satiated most of his appetite for that career as a profession. After a very slight experience, he said no more on the subject. He felt willing to let any one edit, if he himself might write. Vulgarly speaking, it was a dog's life when it did not succeed, and little better when it did. A professor had at least the pleasure of associating with his students; an editor lived the life of an owl. A professor commonly became a pedagogue or a pedant; an editor became an authority on advertising. On the whole, Adams preferred his attic in Washington. He was educated enough. Ignorance paid better, for at least it earned fifty dollars a month.

Randall Jarrell

(1914–1967)

There is a superstition that enchants only the open-minded. It is the notion that all things are incessantly open to question. Accordingly, such liberated idolators swear to an oath and thereafter deem all opinions to be intrinsically equal. Captive to this new emancipation, debates become centerless. Controversies become insincere. Under the guise of prudence, decisions are indefinitely forestalled. Intellectual caution becomes cowardice. Wrongheaded ideas are gracefully shortlived, but so are all worthy ones.

This suspension of judgment cannot be mistaken for fair-minded objectivity, for it is too arrogantly pursued and too evangelical in its deployment. Actually a form of bigotry, this superstition confuses many debates in education, perhaps its most notorious victim being the controversy over elementary reading materials and methods. In the following dialogue, admittedly one-sided, the late poet Randall Jarrell supports the teaching of children's classics rather than Dick-and-Jane journalism. A liberal in politics, a traditionalist in his literary preferences for children, Jarrell risks censure because he does not victimize his theme with shuffling qualifications. Timorous readers who can indefinitely mull any thesis so long as it lacks iron definition will probably be more in sympathy with young Alvin than with Uncle Wadsworth, whose opposition to the confections of Dick and Jane is untentative.

Uncle Wadsworth, a curricular *amateur* in the Renaissance sense of a lover, has received recent professional support from such educators as Harvard's Jeanne Chall. In her detailed study *Learning to Read: The Great Debate*, Professor Chall concludes that children in elementary grades need classics rather than Dick-and-Jane materials, expanded rather than controlled vocabularies in their readers, and exposure to "code-emphasis" techniques (methods of reading instruction which stress the alphabetic code and its sounds), of which intensive phonics is the most proven.

Within the contemporary tone of Jarrell's dialogue, and throughout the issues it explores, is a deep regard for historical currents, for the continuity of human experience. In pleading for the child's right to read "the best that has

57

been thought and said in the world," Uncle Wadsworth does not defend a return to the schools of yesteryear. He does implore the indecisive among us to awake to the rough fact that time past does indeed imbue time present, in the subtle forms of wisdom, sloth, and tyranny, whether or not we invite its presence. A democracy that belittles high literacy ignores the means by which its citizens may govern themselves rationally. However well-intentioned, ideas and emotions that are loosely expressed have as their result a chaos that enslaves.[1]

The Schools of Yesteryear:
A One-Sided Dialogue

Uncle Wadsworth

>(a deep, slightly grained or corrugated, comfortable-sounding voice, accompanied by an accordion)

>School days, school days, dear old golden rule—

Alvin

>(Alvin's voice is young)

>Stop, Uncle Wadsworth!

Uncle Wadsworth

>Why should I stop, Alvin boy?

Alvin

>Because it isn't so, Uncle Wadsworth.

>(With scorn.)

>Dear old golden rule days! That's just nostalgia, just sentimentality. The man that wrote that song was just too old to remember what it was really like. Why, kids hated school in those days—they used to play hookey all the time. It's different now. Children like to go to school now.

---

[1] With the ostensible purpose of securing *minimum* literacy standards, California's State Board of Education recently decreed that high school seniors need possess only an eighth-grade level of literacy to satisfy the English prerequisite for graduation. Such precautions are ominous.

Uncle Wadsworth

Finished, Alvin boy?

Alvin

Finished, Uncle Wadsworth.

Uncle Wadsworth

School days, school days, dear old golden rule days, Readin' and 'ritin' and 'rithmetic, Taught to—

Alvin

Stop, Uncle Wadsworth!

Uncle Wadsworth

Why should I stop this time, Alvin boy?

Alvin

Reading and writing and arithmetic! What a curriculum! Why, it sounds like it was invented by an illiterate. How could a curriculum like that prepare you for life? No civics, no social studies, no hygiene; no home economics, no manual training, no physical education! And extra-curricular activities—where were they?

Uncle Wadsworth

Where indeed? Where are the extra-curricular activities of yester-year? Shall I go on, Alvin boy?

Alvin

Go ahead, Uncle Wadsworth.

Uncle Wadsworth

School days, school days, dear old golden rule days, Readin' and 'ritin' and 'rithmetic, Taught to the tune of a hick'ry stick—

Alvin

Stop! Stop! Stop, Uncle Wadsworth!

(He pants with emotion.)

Honestly, Uncle, I don't see how you can bear to say it. *Taught to the tune of a hickory stick!* . . . Imagine having to *beat* poor little children with a *stick!* Thank God those dark old days of ignorance and fear and compulsion are over, and we just appeal to the child's better nature, and get him to adjust, and try to make him see that what he likes to do is what we want him to do.

Uncle Wadsworth

Finished, Alvin boy?

Alvin

Finished, Uncle Wadsworth.

Uncle Wadsworth

Well, so am I. I can't seem to get going in this song—every fifty yards I get a puncture and have to stop for air. You go on for a while and let me interrupt you. Go ahead, Alvin.

Alvin

Go ahead where?

Uncle Wadsworth

Go ahead about those dark old days of ignorance and fear and compulsion. It makes my flesh creep—and I'm just like the fat boy, I *like* to have my flesh creep.

Alvin

What fat boy?

Uncle Wadsworth

The one in *Pickwick Papers.*

(Silence from Alvin.)

You know, *Pickwick Papers.*

(Silence from Alvin.)

It's a book, son—a book by Charles Dickens. Ever read any Dickens?

Alvin

Oh, sure, sure. I read *The Tale of Two Cities* in high school. And *Oliver Twist*—well, really I didn't read it exactly, I read it in *Illustrated Classics.* And I saw *Great Expectations* in the movies.

Uncle Wadsworth

Why, you and Dickens are old friends. But go on about the—the schools of yesteryear.

Alvin

Well, I will, Uncle Wadsworth. After all, it's only because I was lucky enough to be born now that I didn't have to go to one of those schools myself. I can just see myself trudging to school barefooted in my overalls—because they didn't even have school buses then, you know—

Uncle Wadsworth

Not a one! If a school bus had come for me I'd have thought it was a patrol wagon someone had painted orange for Hallowe'en.

Alvin

Well, there I am trudging along, and I'm not only trudging, I'm *limping*.

Uncle Wadsworth

Stub your toe?

Alvin

(*with bitter irony*)

Stub my toe! I'm limping because I'm *sore*—sore all over, where the teacher beat me.

Uncle Wadsworth

All over isn't where the teacher beat you, Alvin boy—I know.

Alvin

All right, all right! And when I get to the school is it the Consolidated School? Is there a lunch-room and a 'chute-the-'chute and a jungle-gym? Is it—is it like schools ought to be? Uh-*uh!* That school has one room, and it's *red*.

Uncle Wadsworth

You mean that even in those days the Communists—

Alvin

No, no, not Red, *red!* Red like a barn. And when I get inside, the teacher is an old maid that looks like a broomstick, or else a man that looks like a—that looks like Ichabod Crane. And then this Crane-type teacher says to me, real stern: "Alvin McKinley, stand up! Are you aware, Alvin, that it is *three minutes past seven?*"

Uncle Wadsworth

Three minutes past seven! What on earth are you and Ichabod Crane doing in school at that ungodly hour?

Alvin

That's when school starts then! Or six, maybe. . . . Then he says, pointing his finger at me in a terrible voice: "Three minutes tardy! And what, Alvin, what did I warn you would happen to you if you ever again were so much as one minute tardy? What did I tell you that I would do to you?" And I say in a little meek voice, because I'm scared, I say: "Whip me." And he says: "YES, WHIP YOU!" And I say—

Uncle Wadsworth

You say, "Oh, *don't* whip pore Uncle Tom, massa! If only you won't whip him he won't never—"

Alvin

Oh, stop it, Uncle Wadsworth! That's not what I say at all, and you know it. How can I tell about the schools of yesteryear if you won't be serious? Well, anyway, he says to me: "Have you anything to say for yourself?" And I say, "Please, Mr. Crane, it was four miles, and I had the cows to milk, and Ma was sick and I had to help Sister cook the hoe-cakes—"

Uncle Wadsworth

Hoe-cakes!

(With slow relish.)

Hoe-cakes. . . . Why, I haven't had any hoe-cakes since. . . . How'd you hear about hoe-cakes, Alvin boy?

Alvin

Uncle Wadsworth, if you keep interrupting me about irrevu—irrelevancies, how can I get anywhere?

Uncle Wadsworth

I apologize, Alvin; I am silent, Alvin.

Alvin

Then he looks at me and he smiles like—like somebody in *Dick Tracy*, and he says: "Alvin, *spare your breath*." And then he walks over to the corner next to the stove, and do you know what's in the corner?

Uncle Wadsworth

What's in the corner?

Alvin

Sticks. Sticks of every size. Hundreds of sticks. And then he reaches down and takes the biggest one and—and—

Uncle Wadsworth

And—and—

Alvin

And he *beats* me.

Uncle Wadsworth

(with a big sigh)

The Lord be praised! For a minute I was afraid he was going to burn you at the stake. But go ahead, Alvin.

Alvin

Go ahead?

Uncle Wadsworth

It's still just ten minutes after seven. Tell me about your day—your school-day—your dear old golden rule day.

Alvin

Well, then he says: "Take your Readers!" And I look around and everybody in the room, from little kids just six years old with their front teeth out to great big ones, grown men practically that look like they ought to be on the Chicago Bears—everybody in the room picks up the same book and they all start reading aloud out of the— *McGuffey Reader!* Ha-ha-ha! The McGuffey Reader!

Uncle Wadsworth

And why, Alvin, do you laugh?

Alvin

Because it's funny, that's why! The McGuffey Reader!

Uncle Wadsworth

Have you ever seen a McGuffey Reader, Alvin?

Alvin

How could I of, Uncle Wadsworth? I didn't go to school back in those days.

Uncle Wadsworth

Your account was so vivid that for a moment I forgot. . . . You've never seen such a Reader. Well, I have.

Alvin

Oh, sure—you used one in school yourself, didn't you?

Uncle Wadsworth

No, Alvin—strange as it seems, I did not; nor did I ever shake the hand of Robert E. Lee, nor did I fight in the War of 1812, nor did I get to see Adam and Eve and the Serpent. My father used a McGuffey Reader; I did not.

Alvin

I'm sorry, Uncle Wadsworth.

Uncle Wadsworth

No need, no need. . . . Alvin, if you will go over to the bookcase and reach into the right hand corner of the top shelf, you will find a book—a faded, dusty, red-brown book.

Alvin

Here it is. It's all worn, and there're gold letters on the back, and it says *Appletons' Fifth Reader*.

Uncle Wadsworth

Exactly. *Appletons' Fifth Reader*. Week before last, at an antique-dealer's over near Hillsboro, side by side with a glass brandy-flask bearing the features of the Father of our Country, George Washington, I found this Reader.

Alvin

Look how yellow the paper is! And brown spots all over it. . . . Gee, they must have used it all over the country; it says New York, Boston, and Chicago, 1880, and it was printed in 1878 and 1879 too, and—look at the picture across from it, it's one of those old engravings. I guess they didn't have photographs in those days.

Uncle Wadsworth

Guess again, Alvin boy. And what is the subject of this old engraving?

Alvin

A girl with a bucket, and back behind her somebody's plowing, and it's dawn. And there's some poetry underneath.

Uncle Wadsworth

> *While the plowman near at hand*
> *Whistles o'er the furrowed land*
> *And the milkmaid singeth blithe. . . .*

Alvin

That's right! You mean to say you *memorized* it?

Uncle Wadsworth

Fifty years ago, Alvin. Doesn't any of it have a—a familiar ring?

Alvin

Well, to tell the truth, Uncle Wadsworth. . . .

Uncle Wadsworth

What does it say in small letters down at the right-hand corner of the page?

Alvin

It says—"*L'Allegro*, page 420." *L'Allegro!* Sure! sure! Why, I read it in sophomore English. We spent two whole days on that poem and on—you know, that other one that goes with it. They're by John Milton.

Uncle Wadsworth

Yes, Milton. And in that same—

Alvin

But Uncle Wadsworth, you don't mean to say they had Milton in a Fifth Reader! Why, we were sophomores in college, and there were two football players that were juniors, and believe me, it was all Dr. Taylor could do to get us through that poem. How could little kids in the fifth grade read Milton?

Uncle Wadsworth

Sit down, Alvin. Do you remember reading, at about the same time you read "L'Allegro," a poem called "Elegy Written in a Country Churchyard"?

Alvin

Well—

Uncle Wadsworth

Gray's "Elegy"?

Alvin

Say me some, Uncle Wadsworth.

Uncle Wadsworth

> *Full many a gem of purest ray serene*
> *The dark unfathom'd caves of ocean bear;*
> *Full many a flower is born to blush unseen*
> *And waste its sweetness on the desert air.*

Alvin

Sure, I remember that one. I liked that one.

Uncle Wadsworth

Well, Alvin, that very poem—

Alvin

Oh *no*, Uncle Wadsworth! You're not going to tell me that that poem was in a Fifth Reader!

Uncle Wadsworth

No, Alvin, I am not. I want you to . . . to steel yourself. That poem was not in Appletons' Fifth Reader, that poem was in Appletons' Fourth Reader.

(Alvin groans in awe.)

And Wordsworth—you studied Wordsworth in your sophomore English?

Alvin

(lifelessly)

Uh-huh.

Uncle Wadsworth

There are four of Wordsworth's poems in Appletons' Fourth Reader.

Alvin

I guess in the Sixth Reader they were reading Einstein.

Uncle Wadsworth

No, but in the Fifth Reader—run your eye down the table of contents, Alvin—there are selections by Addison, Bishop Berkeley, Bunyan, Byron, Coleridge, Carlyle, Cervantes, Coleridge—the whole *Ancient Mariner*, Alvin—Defoe, De Quincy, Dickens, Emerson, Fielding, Hawthorne, George Herbert, Hazlitt, Jefferson, Dr. Johnson, Shakespeare, Shelley, Sterne, Swift, Tennyson, Thoreau, Mark Twain—

Alvin

It's hard to believe.

Uncle Wadsworth

And there are also selections from simpler writers—

Alvin

Yeah, simple ones—

Uncle Wadsworth

Simpler writers such as Scott, Burns, Longfellow, Cooper, Audubon, Poe, Oliver Wendell Holmes, Benjamin Franklin, Washington Irving. Alvin, have you ever—at college perhaps—ever read anything by Goethe?

Alvin

I don't *believe* so.

Uncle Wadsworth

Well, Alvin boy, if after milking the cow and baking the hoe-cakes, you had limped four miles barefoot to that one-room red schoolhouse of yours, and had been beaten by that Ichabod Crane of a teacher, you would still have got to read, in your Appletons' Fifth Reader, one poem and five pages of prose from Goethe's immortal *Wilheim Meister*. . . . As it is you don't limp, nobody beats you, and you read—whom *do* you read, Alvin? Tell me some of the writers you read in the fifth grade.

Alvin

I don't exactly remember their *names*.

Uncle Wadsworth

There in the bookcase—that red and yellow and black book there—is the Fifth Reader of today. *Days and Deeds*, it is called; it is, I believe, the most popular Fifth Reader in the country. That's right, hand it over. Here on page 3 is its table of contents; come, Alvin, read out to me the names of the writers from whom the children of today get their knowledge of life and literature.

Alvin

Well, the first one's Fletcher D. Slater, and then Nora Burglon, and Sterling North and Ruth G. Plowhead—

Uncle Wadsworth

Plowhead?

Alvin

That's what it says. Then Ruth E. Kennell, Gertrude Robinson, Philip A. Rollins, J. Walker McSpadden, Merlin M.—

Uncle Wadsworth

You're sure you're not making up some of these names?

Alvin

How could I? Merlin M. Taylor, Sanford Tousey, Gladys M. Wick, Marie Barton, Margaret Leighton, Edward C. James—no, Janes, Leonard K. Smith, P. L. Travers, Esther Shepherd, James C. Bowman, Dr. Seuss—

Uncle Wadsworth

Land! Land!

Alvin

No, Seuss. Seuss.

Uncle Wadsworth

I speak figuratively. I mean that here, at last, is a name I recognize, the name of a well-known humorist and cartoonist.

Alvin

Oh. Then there's Armstrong Sperry, Myra M. Dodds, Alden G. Stevens, Lavinia R. Davis, Lucy M. Crockett, Raymond Jannson, Hubert Evans, Ruth E. Tanner, Three Boy Scouts—

Uncle Wadsworth

Three Boy Scouts. An Indian, no doubt. . . . Never heard of him.

Alvin

Heard of *them*. There're three of them.

Uncle Wadsworth

Three? Thirty! Three hundred! They're *all* Boy Scouts! Alvin, these are names only a mother could love—names only a mother would know. That they are honest names, respected names, the names of worthy citizens, I have not the slightest doubt; but when I reflect that it is *these* names that have replaced those of Goethe, of Shakespeare, of Cervantes, of Dr. Johnson—of all the other great and good writers of the Appleton Fifth Reader—when I think of this, Alvin, I am confused, I am dismayed, I am *astounded.*

Alvin

Uncle Wadsworth, you've got all red in the face.

Uncle Wadsworth

There are also in the Appleton Fifth Reader, Alvin, elaborate analyses of the style, rhetoric, and organization of the literary works included; penetrating discussions of their logic; highly technical instructions for reading them aloud in the most effective way; discussions of etymology, spelling, pronunciation, the general development of the English language. And, Alvin, these are *not* written in the insipid baby-talk thought appropriate for children today. Here, in a paragraph about *Don Quixote*, is one of the Fifth Reader's typical discussions of logic: "The question here involved is the old sophism of Eubulides. . . . Is a man a liar who says that he tells lies? If he is, then he does not tell lies; and if he does not tell lies, is he a liar? If not, then is not his assertion a lie? . . . It will be noticed that the perplexity comes from the fact of self-relation: the one assertion relates to another assertion of the same person; and the one assertion being conditioned upon the other, the difficulty arises. It is the question of self-contradiction—of two mutually contradictory statements, one must be false. It is a sophism, but one that continually occurs among unsophisticated reasoners. It is also a practical sophism, for it is continually being acted in the world around us (e.g., a person seeks pleasure by such means that, while he enjoys himself, he undermines his health, or sins against his conscience, and thus draws inevitably on him physical suffering and an uneasy soul). It is therefore well worthy of study in its purely logical form. . . . All universal negative assertions (and a lie is a negation) are liable to involve the assertion itself in self-contradiction."

Alvin

Ohhhhh. . . . *Ohhhhh.* . . . If I'd gone to school then, I'd have known what that means in the *fifth grade?*

Uncle Wadsworth

You'd have known it or you never would have got into the sixth grade.

Alvin

Then I'd be the oldest settler in the fifth grade, because I'm a junior in college and I still can't understand it.

Uncle Wadsworth

Yes, it's surprising what those fifth-graders were expected to know. The Reader contains a little essay called "Hidden Beauties of Classic Authors," by a writer named N. P. Willis.

Alvin

N. P. Willis. . . . I guess he was Ruth G. Plowhead's grandpa.

Uncle Wadsworth

Yes, he isn't exactly a classic author himself. He tells you how he fell in love with Beaumont and Fletcher, and the *Faerie Queene*, and *Comus*, and *The Rape of the Lock*; he says that he knows "no more exquisite sensation than this warming of the heart to an old author; and it seems to me that the most delicious portion of intellectual existence is the brief period in which, one by one, the great minds of old are admitted with all their time-mellowed worth to the affections." Well, at the end of the essay there're some questions; what do you think is the first thing they ask those fifth-graders?

Alvin

What?

Uncle Wadsworth

"Have you read Milton's *Comus?*—Pope's *Rape of the Lock?*"

Alvin

Now Uncle Wadsworth, you've got to admit that that's a terrible thing to ask a little boy in the fifth grade.

Uncle Wadsworth

I think it's a terrible thing. But they didn't. As a matter of fact, *I* think it's a terrible thing to ask a big boy in his junior year in college. How about it, Alvin? Have *you* read Milton's *Comus?* Pope's *Rape of the Lock?*

Alvin

Well, to tell you the truth, Uncle Wadsworth—

Uncle Wadsworth

Tell ahead.

Alvin

Well, to—well—well, it just isn't the *sort* of question you can answer yes or no. I *may* have read Milton's *Comus;* it's the kind of thing we read hundreds of things like in our sophomore survey course; I guess the chances are ten to one I read it, and a year ago I could have told you for certain whether or not I read it, but right now all I can say is if I didn't read it, it would surprise me a lot.

Uncle Wadsworth

And *The Rape of the Lock?*

Alvin

No.

Uncle Wadsworth

No? You mean you *know* you didn't read it?

Alvin

Uh-huh.

Uncle Wadsworth

How do you know?

Alvin

I—

Uncle Wadsworth

Go on, go on.

Alvin

Well Uncle Wadsworth, it seems to me that a book with a title like that, if I'd read it I'd remember it.

Uncle Wadsworth

Alvin, if you weren't my own nephew I'd—I'd be proud to have invented you. . . . Here's another of those poems, the kind that *you* read in your sophomore year in college and that your great-grandfather read in the Fifth Reader. It's by George Herbert, the great religious poet George Herbert. Read it to me, Alvin; and when you've read it, tell me what it means.

Alvin

(in careful singsong)

Sunday. By George Herbert.

> *O Day most calm, most bright!*
> *The fruit of this, the next world's bud;*
> *The endorsement of supreme delight,*
> *Writ by a Friend, and with his blood;*
> *The couch of Time: Care's calm and bay:*
> *The week were dark but for thy light;*
> *Thy torch doth show the way.*
>
> *The other days and thou*
> *Make up one man, whose face thou art,*
> *Knocking at heaven with thy brow:*
> *The working-days are the back part;*
> *The burden of the week lies there;*
> *Making the whole to stoop and bow,*
> *Till thy release appear.*
>
> *Man had—man had—*

Uncle Wadsworth, I'm all mixed up. I've *been* all mixed up. And if you ask me that fifth grade was mixed up too.

Uncle Wadsworth

Where did you first begin to feel confused?

Alvin

I never did not feel confused.

Uncle Wadsworth

Surely the first line—

Alvin

Yeah. Yeah. The first one was all right. *O Day most calm, most bright!* That means it's Sunday, and it's all calm and bright, the weather's all calm and bright. Then it says, *the fruit of this. . . . The fruit of this.* What's the fruit of this?

Uncle Wadsworth

The fruit of this, the next world's bud. World is understood.

Alvin

Understood?

Uncle Wadsworth

Yes. The fruit of this world and the bud of the next world.

Alvin

Oh. . . . *The endorsement of supreme delight. (Pauses.) The endorsement of supreme delight.* . . . Uncle Wadsworth, a line like that— you've got to admit a line like that's *obscure.*

Uncle Wadsworth

It means that—it *says* that Sunday is like the endorsement of a check or note; because of the endorsement this supreme delight, our salvation, is negotiable, we can cash it.

Alvin

Oh. . . . Like endorsing a check. *Writ by a Friend—Friend's* got a capital *F.* . . . Oh! That means it was written by a Quaker. (*Uncle Wadsworth laughs.*) But that's what it does mean. We live on a road named the Friendly Road because it goes to a Quaker church. If *Friend* doesn't mean *Quaker* why's it got a capital *F?*

Uncle Wadsworth

Writ by a Friend, and with his blood. If you're talking about church and Sunday and the next world, and mention a Friend who has written something with his blood, who is that Friend, Alvin?

Alvin

Oh. . . . *The couch of Time; Care's calm and bay.* . . . (*Pauses.*) Uncle Wadsworth, do we *have* to read poetry?

Uncle Wadsworth

Of course not, Alvin. Nobody else does, why should we? Let's get back to prose. Here's the way the Fifth Reader talks about climbing a mountain: "Some part of the beholder, even some vital part, seems to escape through the loose grating of his ribs as he ascends. . . . He is more lone than you can imagine. There is less of substantial thought and fair understanding in him than in the plains where men inhabit. His reason is dispersed and shadowy, more thin and subtle, like the air. Vast, Titanic, inhuman Nature has got him at disadvantage, caught him alone, and pilfers him of some of his divine faculty. She does not smile on him as in the plains. She seems to say sternly, 'Why come ye here before your time? . . . Why seek me where I have not called you, and then complain because you find me but a stepmother? Shouldst thou freeze, or starve, or shudder thy life away, here is no shrine, nor altar, nor any access to my ear. "Chaos and ancient Night, I come no spy/ With purpose to explore or to disturb/ The secrets of your realm—"'"

Alvin

Uncle Wadsworth, if the prose is like that, I'd just as soon have stayed with the poetry. Didn't they have any plain American writers in that Fifth Reader?

Uncle Wadsworth

Plain American writers? That was Thoreau I was reading you. Well, if he's too hard, here's what the Fifth Reader has to say about him. It's talking about his account of the battle between the black ants and the red: "The style of this piece is an imitation of the heroic style of Homer's 'Iliad,' and is properly a 'mock-heroic.' The intention of the author is two-fold: half-seriously endowing the incidents of everyday life with epic dignity, in the belief that there is nothing mean and trivial to the poet and philosopher, and that it is the man that adds dignity to the occasion, and not the occasion that dignifies the man; half-satirically treating the human events alluded to as though they were non-heroic, and only fit to be applied to the events of animal life."

Alvin

(wonderingly)

Why, it's just like old Taylor!

Uncle Wadsworth

Professor Taylor would lecture to you in that style?

Alvin

He'd get going that way, but pretty soon he'd see we didn't know what he meant, and then he'd talk so we could understand him. . . .

Well, if the Fifth Reader sounds like that about ants, I sure don't want to hear it about scansion and etymology!

Uncle Wadsworth

But Alvin, wouldn't you *like* to be able to understand it? Don't you wish you'd had it in the fifth grade and known what it was talking about?

Alvin

Sure, sure! Would I have made old Taylor's eyes pop out! All we ever had in the fifth grade was Boy Scouts going on hikes, and kids going to see their grandmother for Thanksgiving; it was easy.

Uncle Wadsworth

And interesting?

Alvin

Nah, it was corny—the same old stuff; how can you make stuff like that interesting?

Uncle Wadsworth

How indeed?

Alvin

But how did things like Shakespeare and Milton and Dickens ever get in a Fifth Reader?

Uncle Wadsworth

Alvin, they've always *been* there. Yesterday, here in the United States, those things were in the Fifth Reader; today, everywhere else in the world, those things or their equivalent are in the Fifth Reader; it is only here in the United States, today, that the Fifth Reader consists of *Josie's Home Run*, by Ruth G. Plowhead, and *A Midnight Lion Hunt*, by Three Boy Scouts. I read, in a recent best-seller, this sentence: "For the first time in history Americans see their children getting less education than they got themselves." That may be; and for the first time in history Americans see a book on why their children can't read becoming a best-seller, being serialized in newspapers across the nation. Alvin, about school-buildings, health, lunches, civic responsibility, kindness, good humor, spontaneity, we have nothing to learn from the schools of the past; but about reading, with pleasure and understanding, the best that has been thought and said in the world—about *that* we have much to learn. The child who reads and understands the Appleton Fifth Reader is well on the way to becoming an educated, cultivated human being—and if he has to do it sitting in a one-room schoolhouse, if he has to do it sitting on a hollow log, he's better off than a boy sitting in the Pentagon reading *Days and Deeds*. There's a jug of cider in the icebox, Alvin; you get it, I'll get the glasses; and let's drink a toast to—

Alvin

To the Appleton Fifth Reader! long may she read!

(They drink.)

Uncle Wadsworth

And now, Alvin, let us conclude the meeting with a song.

Alvin

What song?

Uncle Wadsworth

What song? Alvin, can you ask? Start us off, Alvin!

Alvin

School days, school days. . . .

Both

Dear old golden rule days. . . .

Alvin

Louder, Uncle Wadsworth, louder!

Both

Readin' and 'ritin' and 'rithmetic
Taught to the tune of a hick'ry stick. . . .

(Alvin and Uncle Wadsworth and the accordion disappear into the distance.)

Part Two

The Arts
of Teaching

---

*Nothing in education needs explaining more than this,
that a teacher may be neither a professor nor an educator,
that a professor may mature to the age of retirement without teaching or educating, and that an educator, without
loss of reputation, may profess nothing and never face a
class.*

John Erskine

The arts of teaching, like all other arts, are summoned more vividly by examples than by axioms. Any formal analysis of a teacher's actions involves harrowing questions of method, subject matter, and didactic intent. But to witness the craft of a gifted teacher is to absorb these questions by facing their answers. Too often our attempts to describe the ideal teacher are really veiled pleas for various philosophies of learning. The result of such advocacy is that the goal of artful teaching—a student precisely inspired, made heedlessly curious about the nature of things— is often relegated to a forsaken place in some organon of methodology, whereas this aim ought to have been celebrated alone, conspicuously. It is really all that matters.

But to celebrate a goal is not to shun its means. Between Plato's extreme view that nothing truly worth learning is teachable, and a pedant's delusion that nothing unteachable is worth learning, lies a wealth of philosophy and experiment that describes (but cannot invoke) the pedagogic arts. Because the powers that permit men to learn are more wondrous than behaviorists can know (and less occult than Rousseauians insist), the prospective teacher can study to good effect the diverse philosophies of learning. In America alone the influences of Neo-Thomism, Progressivism, Essentialism, and lately of Existentialism are impressively documented and lucidly compared.[1] Moreover, the student of education should weigh severely the questions of didactic form: Should the teacher be a paradigm, an ideal model, for his students to follow? Or should he eschew the extremes of the ideal and cultivate a humbler realism about the nature of this world and the place of students

[1] Descriptions of these and other axiologies may be found in *Philosophy and the American School* by Van Cleve Morris (Boston: Houghton Mifflin Company, 1961).

within it? And how does the case now stand for the mental disciplinarian who is not afraid to encourage rational powers in his pupils at the possible expense of social amenities? Or should the teacher be a partner to the learner, a comrade in experiment? Or, to take the existentialist tack, should he be a provocateur of selfhood, urging upon his pupils a moral autonomy usually associated with the completely mature? These questions and their resolutions are never inappropriate to an understanding of what *may* constitute good and great teaching. But an attentive suspicion toward such analysis is still in order. Analysis is, after all, limited by its prowess; it falls short because it does two things so well, dividing the inseparable, wrecking the organic whole so that its parts may be known.

And consider the codes of evaluation open to survey: How do we know when a teacher is teaching well, or superbly, or not at all? Test scores achieved by his students may reflect his excellence or merely his slavishness. The motivations of one teacher's students may be fierce, but misdirected or plainly benighted, while another's develop good habits of study simply because their parents have coerced them well. And who among us—parent, teacher, board member, administrator—can wait smugly for the exonerations of history, for the children under our tutelage to show in adulthood the informed passion and integrity of mind that, assuming our own dubious wisdom, we will unto them?

If inspired teaching, however defined, enables students to come upon the knowledge that matters, then it seems to do so through paradoxes that dwell deeply in the learner's consciousness: in the intellectual curiosity that was never teased until it was somehow satisfied; in ideas never glimpsed until they were mastered; and in the great needs of us all, the emotional hungers, which seem never so starved, so utterly imperiled, as after they have first known fulfillment.

So examples, not axioms. Of the necessary arts, probably the teacher's love for his subject matter should be mentioned prior to his broader passion for knowledge in general. The other virtues? Surely good teachers, most of them, have a disciplined flexibility toward methods and the classroom moods encouraged by them. Some patience, yes; and persistence, and a dignity that is guilty of wit. Also, the superior teacher aspires to a mien that reaches, without betraying accuracy, as many aptitudes within the class as possible.

To these imposing traits should be added the shaping of *style* in a teacher's manner; that is, the power of right means used precisely to achieve right ends. A teacher who cavalierly dismisses pedagogic methods because he fears pedantry (whether these methods be external techniques or possessions of his temperament) may turn out to be like a singing cab driver on amateur night—inflated with purpose but helpless to please.

Still to be mentioned is the very *character* of a teacher's manner that can endow his students with a wisdom that is beyond specialty, elusive of summary, and unhemmed by circumstance. *Kharakter* in ancient Greek referred to an engraving instrument, a tool for etching, and is suggestive of the kind of influence a modern teacher can have—not that he may literally mark his students with an ideology or moral outlook but rather that he invokes a version of reality, his own, that they can preserve as a reference, as an alternative among others, by which to weigh in their futures the antics of life.

Part Two may disappoint some readers. These stories lack formal discourse about techniques. Nor do the teachers portrayed here share equally the virtues hitherto praised. Nowhere will be found a testimonial for lesson plans, or a tribute to tutorial methods, or a sermon on the merits or defects of team teaching. The jargon of symposia and the bromides of summer seminars are absent. No revolutionary schema is advertised. But imitations of inspired teaching are nonetheless discovered in Richard Lockridge's Miss Fox, in Sherwood Anderson's Kate Swift, and in Irwin Edman's first lesson of the term. As in life, the experience of a story like Hortense Calisher's "A Wreath for Miss Totten" reflects the viewpoint of an observer involved in, yet separate from, the central action of the narrative. The narrator herself is not only an observer in the world's classroom, but also a participant. Hortense Calisher, like the stuttering Mooley, like the reader, and Miss Totten, is *in medias res*. Her story bestows a form, an order, on the mercurial experiences that at once endow and forfeit our lives.

Irwin Edman

(1896–1954)

Maudlin paeans about the joys of teaching are too handy, too ceremoniously quoted, to be endured; they cheapen the origins of their tribute. In "Former Students" and "First Lesson" Irwin Edman risks saying too little so that he will not say too much. His restraint is more than a virtue: it works rhetorically, moving us closer to the renewing feelings of affection, of mastery, of salvageable error, and of humor that good teachers acknowledge as their casual recompense.

Edman muses about former students, then about a semester's first day. Each narrative hoards a career's experience and engages the larger truths that outlive the quick history of this class, that pupil; of these years, that term.

Though attuned to the environment of Columbia University, Edman's point of view bears on other levels of teaching, indeed on any classroom wherein the vibrant seance of an hour takes hold: ". . . once in a way, in the midst of the routine of the classroom, it was something not himself that spoke, something not themselves that listened."

A popular teacher, Edman's reputation also rests on his writings, among them *Arts and the Man* (1928), *Philosopher's Holiday* (1938), *Fountainheads of Freedom* (1942), and *Philosopher's Quest* (1947).

FORMER STUDENTS

Once at a gathering in New York various people were mentioned who in diverse ways had begun to make their young presence felt in the world. One had written a play; another had become a psycho-analyst; still another a distinguished literary critic; one a radical editor; still another a foreign correspondent; and one even "the Iron Man" of big-league baseball. Every once in a while I found myself murmuring with not greatly concealed pride: "He is a former student of mine." Finally, a rather bored young lady looked at me pointedly. "Tell me," she asked, "was Chaliapin a former student of yours?"

I have since tried, not very successfully, to refrain from muttering proudly when the brighter young minds among contemporaries are mentioned: "Former student of mine!" For I cannot pretend to have taught any of them their present accomplishments. They did not learn playwriting, psychiatry, literary criticism, foreign correspondence, or baseball from me. And if I were honest, I should have to claim as former students of mine the hundreds of boring and unpleasant people, the failures and the complacent, successful non-entities, the rakes and the time-servers, whom I had the opportunity once to lecture to and whose quiz papers I once read. There are ten thousand former students of mine, I have calculated, roaming about the world. That does not include half a dozen, including some of the best, I have outlived. It does include hundreds I have forgotten and doubtless hundreds who have forgotten me. I met one of the latter once. It was at a club in New York. He was a little drunk, and he looked at me vaguely. He seemed to recall that he had seen me somewhere. A light dawned.

"I greatly enjoyed that course of yours in—in history."

"Mathematics," I corrected him gently.

"That's it," he said, "mathematics. You made calculus interesting, I must say."

"No," I said, "it was the theory of functions." I thought I might as well be credited with something even more majestic that I knew nothing about.

I must admit former students generally do better than that, and they greet a former teacher with a touching sense that once long ago they did get something from him. Sometimes it is nothing more than a joke, used to illustrate something they have completely forgotten. But the joke remains, and probably the theory it was meant to illustrate is dated by now, anyway. Sometimes they surprise you by remembering a quite incidental remark. Occasionally it is good enough for you to wish you could be sure you *had* said it and they had not heard it from some other professor—a professor of calculus, for instance. Or they remember some trick of gesture you had, or the way you suddenly, for emphasis, write a single word on the blackboard, or the mordant things you try to say to listeners, cruelties invariably regarded as merely gently whimsical. Or they even remember ideas that, being the first time they had heard them, made a great impression. They are ideas, often, about which by this time you have changed your mind, or lost faith in. One former student told me he had still the notebook he kept in the first year I taught anybody. He promises not to use it for blackmail against me. He insists that I misspelt Malebranche on the blackboard and, as a result, he has misspelt it almost automatically ever since.

Among the students one does remember, there is a tendency to remember them as they were, as, with notebooks before them, they sat as young men of nineteen or twenty in your classroom, or talked with you in your office. I find it hard to realize that time passes, or to realize that though freshmen and sophomores always look the same each year, they don't look the same (though they often are) ten years or fifteen years later. Meeting some of them after a lapse of years, one wonders what has happened to them, or whether one could ever have taught them anything, or where they can have learned all they seem to have found out about books and life, or how they could, who had once been so eager and bright, be so stodgy now.

I have had them look at me, too, in obvious wonder that they could ever have believed I could teach them anything and, once or twice, frankly express resentment at what they had learned.

I often wonder what students remember of a "former teacher," and can judge of their memories only by my own. But I wonder, too, what it is that one teaches them; how much difference a teacher can make. The psycho-analysts assure us these days that the great damage we call education is done largely in the first six years of a child's life, and that a teacher can do less and less fundamentally to the mind and character of a pupil after that as he passes from grade school to college. I hope that is so. It appears to relieve many of us of great responsibilities. The freshman comes with a kind of fatal predestination; he is what he is, and a course or a seminar cannot make any very great difference. I realize how momentary a tangent any teaching is upon a student's psyche, or his mental equipment.

Yet it is something, and something for which students, doubtless with justice, are not grateful.

"Teaching," Santayana writes in *Character and Opinion in the United States*, "is a delightful paternal art, and especially teaching intelligent and warm-hearted youngsters, as most American collegians are; but it is an art like acting, where the performance, often rehearsed, must be adapted to an audience hearing it only once. The speaker must make concessions to their impatience, their taste, their capacity, their prejudices, their ultimate good; he must neither bore nor perplex nor demoralize them. His thoughts must be such as can flow daily, and be set down in notes; they must come when the bell rings and stop appropriately when the bell rings a second time. The best that is in him, as Mephistopheles says in *Faust*, he dare not tell them; and as the substance of this possession is spiritual, to withhold is often to lose it."

What boredom, perplexity, and demoralization do one's students remember! I once caught a glimpse of what it was. I ran into a former student at a week-end in the country. I had known him fairly well and, even before I knew him, had noticed, as had some colleagues, the sharp, critical eye which he fixed upon one during a lecture. There are always half a dozen students in a class in whose presence one would not willingly be boring or stupid or inaccurate. When one is so unwillingly, one sees the immediate register of disappointment (or is it fulfilled expectation?) in their eyes. S——— had been one of those.

The conversation had been general and desultory. At the end of the evening he came into my room. He sat down on a chair and looked at me sharply. He seemed older than he had been, but he had always seemed grown up. He had, I had heard, had various reasons for discouragement, both personal and professional, since he had left college. At one point some years ago he had suddenly turned up and asked if I couldn't think of a good reason for his not committing suicide, since he was about to do so. My reasons were not too good, but they seemed good enough. He was here still, not much happier apparently.

"Look here," he said, "I have been wanting to tell you for some years that your former students have a lot to hold against you, especially the good ones, those who got what you gave them."

"What harm did I do?" I asked, weakly. "I am in a worse case than Socrates. At least he could boast at his trial that none of his former students—those whom he was supposed to have corrupted—had appeared to testify against him. But here you come yourself, saying I have done you irreparable damage. Really, a course in the Philosophy of Art can't do that much harm to anyone, not even to those who get an A."

"Yes it can, and did," he insisted, "and I'm not the only one who was damaged, and you're not the only one who did the damage, though you did a good deal. You taught me and a good many others to think that contemplation, detachment, eternal things, that Truth, Goodness, and Beauty, were the proper preoccupations for a young man in this world. Well, that isn't the kind of world we are living in, and you gave us a profound sense of unreality. It's taken me years to get over it and I'm not quite over it yet. But Freud and Marx have helped me, and I wish I had found out about them sooner. I must admit I first heard about them from you, but you didn't sound as if you thought them as important as Plato or Santayana. You made me live beyond my intellectual income; you made me set store by a lot of things that had no more relation to the moving things in the world and to the lives of men than backgammon or Venetian brocades. I admit you woke me up to a few beautiful things and moving ideas, but it was a fool's Paradise. I've reversed the usual order and gone through Purgatory since."

"Well, you've found a new Paradise of your own—the revolution—haven't you?"

"Call it that, but it's one of the forces going on in the world; it isn't the lost causes of sweetness and light."

I tried to say something about the lost causes being the only enduring ones; but S——— suddenly softened a little. "It was a pleasant enough trance while it lasted," he said.

"I'm sorry the coming to was so bad," I said.

Former students are not often so bitter, I must admit. They are frequently almost embarrassing in their assertion that you awakened them to think, or to think clearly, or to feel qualities in things and ideas and people they had never perceived before. They can be incredibly kind, even or especially when they think they are being objective and just. For it is difficult to distinguish the persons from the things they communicate, and many a teacher gets a certain glamour in a student's memory because the teacher is associated with that student's first encounter with Plato or Shakespeare, Bach or Phidias. A teacher dealing with great things cannot help sometimes seeming—if only to the undistinguishing young—to be their voice or their oracle; and to a very young mind, if only for a short time, the teacher is confused with the things taught. This may, indeed, be very bad for the teacher, who, in the mirror of his student's generosity, makes something like the same identification, too. His colleagues will correct him, and many of his unbemused students would, too, given the opportunity. For even the luckiest teacher dealing with students avid for ideas will have a good many who look at him as if they dared him to teach them anything. I met one of that category once. He looked at me curiously. "I never could understand," he said, "why you thought philosophy interesting. And yet you seemed to do so. I was quite struck with that fact. That's the only thing I remember from the course."

It should really be a most discouraging fact (I am convinced it is a fact, in any case) that there is nothing much one does for the good student, and nothing very much that one can do for the poor one. In the case of the brilliant successes among former students of mine, I am convinced they were in essence as sophomores what they are now. If they are now learned men, they were already on the road to learning in their sophomore year. One of my former pupils can lay claim now to an erudition that I shall never have. But he was an erudite sophomore, and a little disturbing to an instructor in his first year of teaching. Another, though he is wiser about the world now, was wiser then than I shall ever be about it, and wrote almost as clearly and well then as he does now. The campus politicians are now real politicians, some of them, and not only in the field of politics. Sometimes there are apparent changes: the æsthetes become hardboiled or disillusioned; the sentimentalists, cynics. But even in those cases the change is not always a real one.

Now that I have been teaching more than twenty years and have thus seen five generations—a college generation being four years—of college students, former students seem to return. I do not mean that they come back in the flesh as one did recently with his ten-year-old child to the campus; I mean one recognizes in the sophomore or junior there in the first row a replica of some predecessor not so very different of classes long ago. If I had known fewer students I should have been readier to predict what will become of them. It is easy enough with the run of the mill, though even with them, so rapidly is our world changing, it is not so easy as it used to be. There are not so many fathers' businesses to go into; the typical pre-lawyer may not find an office to be a lawyer in; the young snob and richling may find the world in which he can be both of those things vanishing under his feet. It is not easy even with the "originals," who also, for a teacher long in harness, fall into types. How was I to guess—how would anyone have guessed—that the editor of the best college humorous magazine in ten years, neatly ironic, merrily sceptical, and amusedly disillusioned, would turn into an uncompromising revolutionary, the Washington correspondent of the *Daily Worker*? How was one to suspect that the playboy whose life was bounded by fraternities and dances and drinking would be sobered by something or other into becoming a diligent professional classical scholar—a pedantic one at that? How could I have dreamed (though I might have done so) that the withering cynic of his class, whose god was Swift, should have become a mystical and fanatical rabbi?

I suspect that in each of these cases, had I been wiser or known my student better, I should not have had much occasion for surprise. There is much one does not find out about students, since it is natural that a teacher does rather more of the talking. And there is a lot one would never find out from the way in which students talk to a teacher.

There is only one thing by which I continue, with a foolish and persistent naïveté, to be surprised. I expect, somehow, that a student ten years after college will still have the brightness and enthusiasm, the disinterested love of ideas, and the impersonal passion for them that some develop during their undergraduate days. Time and again I have run into them, and wondered what the world has done to them that that passionate detachment should have gone. I know some of the things, brutal or familiar enough to the point almost of banality: a family, the struggle for a living, a disillusion with the status of contemplation in the nightmare of a violent world. But it is not revolution or disillusion that surprises me; both are intelligible. It is the death-in-life that assails the spirits of young men who had been alive when I knew them at college. A fierce hate, a transcendent revolutionary contempt for ideas, especially traditional ones, a revolt against the academy; all these things are not dismaying. They are symptoms that life is not dead and that spirit lives in some form, however tortured or fantastic or unprecedented. It is when spirit is utterly dead, when the one-time eager youth becomes precociously middle-aged, that one feels above all that education is a failure. One awakened something for a short time. But did one? Perhaps I have, like a good many teachers, flattered myself. It was not we who awakened them;

it was the season of their lives, and the things and ideas which, despite us, for a moment—if only for a moment—stirred them. There are times when, if one thought about former students too much, one could not go on teaching. For the teacher meeting his former students is reminded of the fact that Plato long ago pointed out in the *Republic*. It is not what the teacher but what the world teaches them that will in the long run count, and what they can learn from the latter comes from habits fixed soon after birth and temperaments fixed long before it. There are just a few things a teacher can do, and that only for the sensitive and the spirited. He can initiate enthusiasms, clear paths, and inculcate discipline. He can communicate a passion and a method; no more. His most serious triumph as a teacher is the paradoxical one of having his students, while he is teaching them and perhaps afterwards, forget him in the absorption of the tradition or the inquiry of which he is the transient voice. Lucky for him if later his students feel his voice was just. As in the playing of music, it is the music, not the musician, that is ultimate. And in the art of teaching, it is what is taught that counts, not the teacher. It is a great tribute to an artist to say that he plays Beethoven or Bach, and puts nothing between them and his audience. But in so doing he becomes one with both the composer and the listener. In the listener's memory he anonymously shares the composer's immortality. The teacher, too, is best remembered who is thus forgotten. He lives in what has happened to the minds of his students, and in what they remember of things infinitely greater than themselves or than himself. They will remember, perhaps, that once in a way, in the midst of the routine of the classroom, it was something not himself that spoke, something not themselves that listened. The teacher may well be content to be otherwise forgotten, or to live in something grown to ripeness in his students that he, however minutely, helped bring to birth. There are many students thus come to fruition whom I should be proud to have say: "He was my teacher." There is no other immortality a teacher can have.

FIRST LESSON

Every autumn in normal times I walk, with rather deliberate briskness, into a classroom in which are gathered about forty young men who have voluntarily enrolled themselves in a course entitled "Introduction to Philosophy." They have come to this class not as they come to similar enterprises in physics, chemistry, or history. They come to those subjects expecting to find out more about what they already know something about. They come to this class hoping to find out by the end of the year what it is that they are studying. And, as I am a disciple of Socrates, I do not propose to tell them. I propose, by asking the proper questions, to have them tell me, and to assist them in the discovery that they have in essence always known what philosophy is.

I look around and light on the most likely looking candidate. I find a young man whom I know by sight, Alfred Jeremy, hitherto undebauched by philosophy.

"Mr. Jeremy," I say without preamble, "I suppose you believe you exist?"

Young Jeremy looks at me quizzically. I feel he is wondering if this is what professors of philosophy are paid to do.

"Of course I exist," he says, and I detect the slightest tone of impatience in his courteous and somewhat surprised tone.

"What makes you so sure?" I ask.

The large football player in the second row shifts his bulk impatiently in the seat too small for him, as if suddenly wondering what is going on here.

"Well," says Jeremy, "it's me. I mean I. I brought myself in here." The class smiles a little at that.

"How do you know it's you?" I say.

"I can pinch myself," he says. The football player does that very thing. Then he pinches his neighbor. I tap warningly on the table with a piece of chalk.

"I can feel my hands if I press them hard, and I have a pain in the crick of my neck."

"You mean you have sensations," I say. "But how do you know they're yours?"

"Well, whose else would they be?" asks Jeremy in great surprise.

"But who are you?" I insist. "Simply this cluster of sensations at the present moment?"

"Oh, no," says Jeremy. "I'm the guy, excuse me, the fellow, who went through the Horace Mann School, and who entered Columbia College last year as a freshman. I left the dormitory this morning and had breakfast at the Sandwich Shop, no, it was the Lion's Den, and I had a class in advanced French, and I talked to a couple of guys, I mean fellows, and now I'm here."

"But all that was up to the present moment; it was all in the past, wasn't it?"

"Yes, sir," says Jeremy.

"It was pure memory," I say. "Might it not be false memory, pure fiction? You know how difficult it is to get a reliable witness of what has happened in the past. You can't be sure, can you, that it *was* you, can you now?"

"Who else could it be?" asks Jeremy.

"It might be a dream that you in the present are having of what you call the immediate past, mightn't it?"

During this colloquy some members of the class are sitting in absorbed attention. There is a bright-looking, very young man who can scarcely wait until I ask him a question. His hand is already up. The football player is not exactly absorbed, but he looks a little as if he would like really very much now to know what is going on here. The nice-looking boy in the third row seems vaguely troubled. Several look as if they think I am trying to play some trick on them.

The very young-looking boy can wait no longer.

"Well?" I say. (I recognize him, too. He had come to interview me yesterday for the college paper.) "Mr. Gottesman, what do *you* think?"

"Well, I not only remember, but I expect," he says. "I know for pretty certain that I'm going to be around tomorrow, having breakfast and lunch and coming to classes."

"But that," I say, "is mere expectation, is it not? It's an act of faith. You can't really believe you exist on the ground that somebody to whom unhappened things have not yet happened is going to be there to have them happen to him. And is that the ground for your believing that you now exist—because somebody not in existence is going to exist? That future 'you' does not yet exist, does he?"

"No," says young Gottesman ruefully, "I suppose he doesn't."

There is a hand raised in the back row. I look at the pleasant blue-eyed Irish face behind it.

"Your name, please."

"Farrell, John."

"Well, Mr. Farrell, what do you think? Why do *you* think you exist?"

"Because I can't think of myself not existing while I'm sitting here talking—or thinking," he adds after a moment's thought. "Who else is doing it?"

"Have you ever read Descartes?" I ask.

"Never heard of him," he says, almost in a tone of disclaiming unsavory acquaintance.

"Well, he is a famous French philosopher of three centuries ago. He would be inclined to agree with you."

"He would?" asks Farrell.

"Well, let's see where we are," I say. "The past is an illusion, the future a gamble. We have only ourselves of the moment—feeling, thinking, sensing—to be sure of. But surely, Mr. Farrell, you wouldn't call that enough to call 'Mr. Farrell,' would you? The John Farrell your parents know has a past and a future, hasn't he?"

"I sure hope so," says Mr. Farrell. "So do my parents, especially about the future."

"Well," I say, "let's take a vote for a moment. How many are willing to assume they exist?"

The class is unanimous in favor of their own existence.

"But it's only an assumption, mind," I say. "We haven't proved it yet. Now how about other people?"

John Farrell looks appraisingly at his neighbor to the left and then to the right. Many members of the class do the same. The football player looks appraisingly at me.

"How do we know other people exist?"

"How do we know other people exist?" Farrell repeats.

Jeremy raises his hand. I nod.

"Well, I hear them, I see them. Seeing is believing, as they say."

"Yes, but gentlemen, we are obviously often deceived. There are mirages in the desert; we think we see things that turn out to be not there, or to be something else. The man you see is not the one you thought you saw, but his brother. The stick looks broken in water, but it is the shadow, not the stick, that you see. Perhaps it is a devil who has masked as your friend and classmate. Perhaps it is a dream, or a nightmare."

The bright youngster in the front row looks at me as if he wondered if I were more than half joking.

"And how about *things*, this blackboard, this desk?" I ask, turning to Farrell, whose blue eyes seem to be speculating curiously on this panorama of illusion I have opened before him.

"Me?" he says, his attention recalled. "Well, the same thing as other people. I see it, I can touch it. The blackboard has a sort of odor, too."

I take the class on a little imaginary tour through the history of thought. I remind them how uneasy Plato was about the senses; how Berkeley whisked the world away into a semblance constituted by our ideas; how Schopenhauer emphasizes the dreamlike quality of existence, despite the regularity and order of the dream.

"But things," persists the bright young boy, "are there in space, and that blackboard will be there tomorrow when we come back. Or," he added, "if we don't."

I had been rather waiting for this opening.

"What," I say, turning to Smith, having found his name next to his seat number, "what, Mr. Smith, is *space*?"

Mr. Smith considers a moment. He waves his hand comprehensively in the air. "Space is what everything else is in," he says.

The football player leans forward. "Yeah, like a box," he bursts out.

"But what," I say, "is space in?" Some of the boys look faintly disgusted, some perplexed.

"Yes, sir," says the football player slowly and ruefully, "what *is* it in?"

For the next fifteen minutes or so, without knowing the words, the young men, aided and abetted by myself, explore, in elementary form, some of the mysteries and paradoxes that Immanuel Kant turned up. We come out at about the same place he did. Perhaps space is just a way our mind has of arranging our sensations. Experience, we determine tentatively, is impossible without space, and yet it is impossible to find space in experience.

"Is it the same about time?" says a rather blasé youth in the third row who has not up to that point taken any part in the discussion.

"Well, surely the present is here," says Mr. Gottesman.

"And the past *has* been here," says the football player.

"And the future is surely going to be here," says Mr. Jeremy.

"You are going too fast for me, gentlemen," I interrupt. "Why are you so sure, Mr. Jeremy, that the past *was* here? Is it not, like yourself of yesterday, a memory? You cannot see the past clearly, can you? Or hear it? It's gone forever.

"And as for the future, you can bet, if you care to, that it is going to take place, but surely at the present moment it does not exist. If it did, it would be the present, wouldn't it? There's just this moment, isn't there? All the rest is memory or imagination."

"It doesn't leave us very much," says Mr. Smith.

There are several students who have not entered into the discussion at all. But I suspect I know what is going on in their heads. Some of them look bored, and I am not sure they will not change their registration after all. Some of them are pleasantly bewildered, some embarrassed by their bewilderment. The football player finally says, "But that's all very well, maybe, for philosophers. But for plain ordinary people, time and space and other people and themselves do exist, don't they now, professor? Right here now, aren't we in this actual room, talking to each other, today, Monday?"

For the next ten minutes we have quite a heated controversy. There are those who side with the football player, who take the side of common-sense men in all ages, who will have no traffic with such nonsense. In a class every sort of temperament in the history of mankind is likely to reveal itself. Young Gottesman is a kind of poet, and I can see already that he is impressed by the poetry and suasion of the idea that all that we see and hear is a dream.

I intend myself before the term is over to try to show these young men that it would be silly to pretend that they need seriously doubt their own existence, that of the world, of time and space and other people and things. My purpose this morning has been to get them to look at these things with a difference. If only one can get them to be critical of their most usual preconceptions, one is on the road. A little later we'll see what we can do about good and evil, right and wrong, justice and injustice. These students are very young, but they are already full of age-old prejudices. At least an Introduction to Philosophy may start them on the quest for more rational standards of life, of knowledge, of action, of society.

The bell is ringing, announcing the end of the hour. Young Farrell leans forward. "But *do* we exist?" he says.

"Here endeth the first lesson," I say.

Hortense Calisher

It is a truism that a teacher cannot accurately measure the extent of his influence nor even the breadth of his ineptitude. The best of teachers suffer long doubts about their efficacy; so may the worst of teachers. All teachers, in private moments, probably fret about their reputations, the caricatures of themselves that their pupils carry forth in memory.

In this era of methodology, when a theory of pedagogy is often more honored than its practitioners, Hortense Calisher's Miss Totten is a poignant affront. Miss Totten is not kind in the cozy sense nor masterful in the ways that stun. She survives as an exemplar who is not Olympian but who is decent in the ways that civilize. She allows for a learning of disparate virtues.

A distinguished novelist and short story writer, Hortense Calisher has recently published *Journal from Ellipsia* (1965), *The Railway Police* and *The Last Trolley Ride* (1966), and *The New Yorkers* (1969).

A WREATH FOR MISS TOTTEN

Children growing up in the country take their images of integrity from the land. The land, with its changes, is always about them, a pervasive truth, and their midget foregrounds are crisscrossed with minute dramas which arc the animalcules of a larger vision. But children who grow in a city where there is nothing greater than the people brimming up out of subways, riveleting in the streets—these children must take their archetypes where and if they find them.

In P.S. 146, between periods, when the upper grades were shunted through the halls in that important procedure known as "departmental," although most of the teachers stood about chatting relievedly in couples, Miss Totten always stood at the door of her "home room," watching us straightforwardly, alone. As, straggling and muffled, we lined past the other teachers, we often caught snatches of upstairs gossip which we later perverted and enlarged; passing before Miss Totten we deflected only that austere look, bent solely on us.

Perhaps, with the teachers, as with us, she was neither admired nor loathed but simply ignored. Certainly none of us ever fawned on her as we did on the harshly blond and blue-eyed Miss Steele, who never wooed us with a smile but slanged us delightfully in the gym, giving out the exercises in a voice like scuffed gravel. Neither did she obsess us in the way of the Misses Comstock, two liverish, stunted women who could have had nothing so vivid about them as our hatred for them, and though all of us had a raffish hunger for metaphor, we never dubbed Miss Totten with a nickname.

Miss Totten's figure, as she sat tall at her desk or strode angularly in front of us rolling down the long maps over the blackboard, had that instantaneous clarity, one metallic step removed from the real, of the daguerreotype. Her clothes partook of this period too—long, saturnine waists and skirts of a stuff identical with that in a good family umbrella. There was one like it in the umbrella-stand at home—a high black one with a seamed ivory head. The waists enclosed a vestee of dim, but steadfast lace; the skirts grazed narrow boots of that etiolated black leather, venerable with creases, which I knew to be a sign both of respectability and foot trouble. But except for the vestee, all of Miss Totten, too, folded neatly to the dark point of her shoes, and separated from these by her truly extraordinary length, her face presided above, a lined, ocher ellipse. Sometimes, as I watched it on drowsy afternoons, her face floated away altogether and came to rest on the stand at home. Perhaps it was because of this guilty image that I was the only one who noticed Miss Totten's strange preoccupation with "Mooley" Davis.

Most of us in Miss Totten's room had been together as a group since first grade, but we had not seen Mooley since down in second grade, under the elder and more frightening of the two Comstocks. I had forgotten Mooley completely, but when she reappeared I remembered clearly the incident which had given her her name.

That morning, very early in the new term, back in Miss Comstock's, we had lined up on two sides of the classroom for a spelling bee. These were usually a relief to good and bad spellers alike, since it was the only part of our work which resembled a game, and even when one had to miss and sit down, there was a kind of dreamy catharsis in watching the tenseness of those still standing. Miss Comstock always rose for these occasions and came forward between the two lines, standing there in an oppressive close-up in which we could watch the terrifying action of the cords in her spindling gray neck and her slight smile as a boy or a girl was spelled down. As the number of those standing was reduced, the smile grew, exposing the oversize slabs of her teeth, through which the words issued in a voice increasingly unctuous and soft.

On this day the forty of us still shone with the first fall neatness of new clothes, still basked in that delightful anonymity in which neither our names nor our capacities were already part of the dreary foreknowledge of the teacher. The smart and quick had yet to assert themselves with their flying, staccato hands; the uneasy dull, not yet forced into recitations which would make their status clear, still preserved in the small, sinking corners of their hearts a lorn, factitious hope. Both teams were still intact when the word "mule" fell to the lot of a thin colored girl across the room from me, in clothes perky only with starch, her rusty fuzz of hair drawn back in braids so tightly sectioned that her eyes seemed permanently widened.

"Mule," said Miss Comstock, giving out the word. The ranks were still full. She had not yet begun to smile.

The girl looked back at Miss Comstock, soundlessly. All her face seemed drawn backward from the silent, working mouth, as if a strong, pulling hand had taken hold of the braids.

My turn, I calculated, was next. The procedure was to say the word, spell it out, and say it again. I repeated it in my mind: "Mule. M-u-l-e. Mule."

Miss Comstock waited quite a long time. Then she looked around the class, as if asking them to mark well and early this first malfeasance, and her handling of it.

"What's your name?" she said.

"Ull—ee." The word came out in a glottal, molasses voice, hardly articulate, the *l*'s scarcely pronounced.

"Lilly?"

The girl nodded.

"Lilly what?"

"Duh-avis."

"Oh. Lilly Davis. Mmmm. Well, spell 'mule,' Lilly." Miss Comstock trilled out the name beautifully.

The tense brown bladder of the girl's face swelled desperately, then broke at the mouth. "Mool," she said, and stopped. "Mmm—oo—"

The room tittered. Miss Comstock stepped closer.

"*Mule!*"

The girl struggled again. "Mool."

This time we were too near Miss Comstock to dare laughter.

Miss Comstock turned to our side. "Who's next?"

I half raised my hand.

"Go on." She wheeled around on Lilly, who was sinking into her seat. "No. Don't sit down."

I lowered my eyelids, hiding Lilly from my sight. "Mule," I said. "M-u-l-e. Mule."

The game continued, words crossing the room uneventfully. Some children survived. Others settled, abashed, into their seats, craning around to watch us. Again the turn came around to Lilly.

Miss Comstock cleared her throat. She had begun to smile.

"Spell it now, Lilly," she said. "Mule."

The long-chinned brown face swung from side to side in an odd writhing movement. Lilly's eyeballs rolled. Then the thick sound from her mouth was lost in the hooting, uncontrollable laughter of the whole class. For there was no doubt about it: the long, coffee-colored face, the whitish glint of the eyeballs, the bucking motion of the head suggested it to us all—a small brown quadruped, horse of mule, crazily stubborn, or at bay.

"Quiet!" said Miss Comstock. And we hushed, although she had not spoken loudly. For the word had smirked out from a wide, flat smile and on the stringy neck beneath there was a creeping, pleasurable flush which made it pink as a young girl's.

That was how Mooley Davis got her name, although we had a chance to use it only for a few weeks, in a taunting singsong when she hung up her coat in the morning, or as she flicked past the little dust-bin of a store where we shed our pennies for nigger-babies and tasteless, mottoed hearts. For after a few weeks, when it became clear that her cringing, mucoused talk was getting worse, she was transferred to the "ungraded" class. This group, made up of the mute, the shambling, and the oddly tall, some of whom were delivered by bus, was housed in a basement part of the school, with a separate entrance which was forbidden us not only by rule but by a lurking distaste of our own.

The year Mooley reappeared in Miss Totten's room, a dispute in the school system had disbanded all the ungraded classes in the city. Here and there, now, in the back seat of a class, there would be some grown-size boy who read haltingly from a primer, fingering the stubble on his slack jaw. Down in 4-A there was a shiny, petted doll of a girl, all crackling hairbow and nimble wheelchair, over whom the teachers shook their heads feelingly, saying: "Bright as a dollar! Imagine!" as if there were something sinister in the fact that useless legs had not impaired the musculature of a mind. And in our class, in harshly clean, faded dresses which were always a little too infantile for her, her spraying ginger hair cut short now and held by a round comb which circled the back of her head like a snaggle-toothed tiara which had slipped, there was this bony, bug-eyed wraith of a girl who raised her hand instead of say-ing "Present!" when Miss Totten said "Lilly Davis?" at roll call, and never spoke at all.

It was Juliet Hoffman, the pace-setter among the girls in the class, who spoke Mooley's nickname first. A jeweller's daughter, Juliet had achieved an eminence even beyond that due her curly profile, embroi-dered dresses, and prancing, leading-lady ways when, the Christmas before, she had brought as her present to teacher a real diamond ring. It had been a modest diamond, to be sure, but undoubtedly real, and set in real gold. Juliet had heralded it for weeks before and we had all seen it—it and the peculiar look on the face of the teacher, a young substitute whom we hardly knew—when she had lifted it from the pile of hankies and fancy notepaper on her desk. The teacher, over the syrupy protests of Mrs. Hoffman, had returned the ring, but its sparkle lingered on, iridescent around Juliet's head.

On our way out at three o'clock that first day with Miss Totten, Juliet nudged at me to wait. Obediently, I waited behind her. Twiddling her bunny muff, she minced over to the clothes closet and confronted the new girl.

"I know you," she said. "Mooley Davis, that's who you are!" A couple of the other children hung back to watch.

"Aren't you? Aren't you Mooley Davis?"

I remember just how Mooley stood there because of the coat she wore. She just stood there holding her coat against her stomach with both hands. It was a coat of some pale, vague tweed, cut the same length as mine. But it wrapped the wrong way over for a girl and the revers, wide ones, came all the way down and ended way below the pressing hands.

"Where you been?" Juliet flipped us all a knowing grin. "You been in ungraded?"

One of Mooley's shoulders inched up so that it almost touched her ear, but beyond that, she did not seem able to move. Her eyes looked at us, wide and fixed. I had the feeling that all of her had retreated far, far back behind the eyes which—large and light, and purposefully empty—had been forced to stay.

My back was to the room, but on the suddenly wooden faces of the others I saw Miss Totten's shadow. Then she loomed thinly over Juliet, her arms, which were crossed at her chest, hiding the one V of white in her garments, so that she looked like an umbrella which had been tightly furled.

"What's *your* name?" she asked, addressing not so much Juliet as the white muff which, I noticed now, was slightly soiled.

"Jooly-ette."

"Hmm. Oh, yes. Juliet Hoffman."

"Jooly-ette, it is." She pouted creamily up at Miss Trotten, her glance narrow with the assurance of finger rings to come.

Something flickered in the nexus of yellow wrinkles around Miss Totten's lips. Poking out a bony forefinger, she held it against the muff. "You tell your mother," she said slowly, "that the way she spells it, it's *Juliet.*"

Then she dismissed the rest of us but put a delaying hand on Mooley. Turning back to look, I saw that she had knelt down painfully, her skirt-hem graying in the floor dust, and staring absently over Mooley's head she was buttoning up the queerly shaped coat.

After a short, avid flurry of speculation we soon lost interest in Mooley, and in the routine Miss Totten devised for her. At first, during any kind of oral work, Mooley took her place at the blackboard and wrote down her answers, but later, Miss Totten sat her in the front row and gave her a small slate. She grew very quick at answering, particularly in "mental arithmetic" and in the card drills, when Miss Totten held up large Manila cards with significant locations and dates inscribed in her Palmer script, and we went down the rows, snapping back the answers.

Also, Mooley had acquired a protector in Ruby Green, the other Negro girl in the class—a huge, black girl with an arm-flailing, hee-haw way of talking and a rich, contralto singing voice which we had often heard in solo at Assembly. Ruby, boasting of her singing in night clubs on Saturday nights, of a father who had done time, cowed us all with these pungent inklings of the world on the other side of the dividing line of Amsterdam Avenue—that deep, velvet murk of Harlem which she lit for us with the flash of razors, the honky-tonk beat of the "numbahs," and the plangent wails of the mugged. Once, hearing David Hecker, a doctor's son, declare "Mooley has a cleft palate, that's what," Ruby wheeled and put a large hand on his shoulder, holding it there in menacing caress.

"She ain' got no cleff palate, see? She talk sometime, 'roun' home." She glared at us each in turn with such a pug-scowl that we flinched, thinking she was going to spit. Ruby giggled.

"She got no cause to talk, 'roun' here. She just don' need to bother." She lifted her hand from David, spinning him backward, and joined arms with the silent Mooley. "Me neither!" she added, and walked Mooley away, flinging back at us her gaudy, syncopated laugh.

Then one day, lolloping home after three, I suddenly remembered my books and tam, and above all my homework assignment, left in the pocket of my desk at school. I raced back there. The janitor, grumbling, unlocked the side door at which he had been sweeping and let me in. In the mauve, settling light the long maw of the gym held a rank, uneasy stillness. I walked up the spiral metal stairs feeling that I thieved on some part of the school's existence not intended for me. Outside the ambushed quiet of Miss Totten's room I stopped, gathering breath.

Then I heard voices, one of them surely Miss Totten's dark, firm tones, the other no more than an arrested gurgle and pause.

I opened the door slowly. Miss Totten and Mooley raised their heads. It was odd, but although Miss Totten sat as usual at her desk, her hands clasped to one side of her hat, lunch-box, and the crinkly boa she wore all spring, and although Mooley was at her own desk in front of a spread copy of our thick reader, I felt the distinct, startled guilt of someone who interrupts an embrace.

"Yes?" said Miss Totten. Her eyes had the drugged look of eyes raised suddenly from close work. I fancied that she reddened slightly, like someone accused.

"I left my books."

Miss Totten nodded, and sat waiting. I walked down the row to my desk and bent over, fumbling for my things, my haunches awkward under the watchfulness behind me. At the door, with my arms full, I stopped, parroting the formula of dismissal.

"Good afternoon, Miss Totten."

"Good afternoon."

I walked home slowly. Miss Totten, when I spoke to her, had seemed to be watching my mouth, almost with enmity. And in front of Mooley there had been no slate.

In class the next morning, as I collected the homework in my capacity as monitor, I lingered a minute at Mooley's desk, expecting some change, perhaps in her notice of me, but there was none. Her paper was the same as usual, written in a neat script quite legible in itself, but in a spidery backhand which just faintly silvered the page, like a communiqué issued out of necessity, but begrudged.

Once more I had a glimpse of Miss Totten and Mooley together, on a day when I had joined the slangy, athletic Miss Steele who was striding capably along in her Ground Grippers on the route I usually took home. Almost at once I had known I was unwelcome, but I trotted desperately in her wake, not knowing how to relieve her of my company. At last a stitch in my side forced me to stop, in front of a corner fishmongers'.

"Folks who want to walk home with me have to step on it!" said Miss Steele. She allotted me one measuring, stone-blue glance, and moved on.

Disposed on the bald white window stall of the fish store there was a rigidly mounted eel which looked as if only its stuffing prevented it from growing onward, sinuously, from either impersonal end. Beside it were several tawny shells. A finger would have to avoid the spines on them before being able to touch their rosy, pursed throats. As the pain in my side lessened, I raised my head and saw my own face in the window, egg-shaped and sad. I turned away. Miss Totten and Mooley stood on the corner, their backs to me, waiting to cross. A trolley clanged by, then the street was clear, and Miss Totten, looking down, nodded gently into the black boa and took Mooley by the hand. As they passed down the hill to St. Nicholas Avenue and disappeared, Mooley's face, smoothed out and grave, seemed to me, enviably, like the serene, guided faces of the children I had seen walking securely under the restful duennaship of nuns.

Then came the first day of Visiting Week, during which, according to convention, the normal school day would be on display, but for which we had actually been fortified with rapid-fire recitations which were supposed to erupt from us in sequence, like the somersaults which climax acrobatic acts. On this morning, just before we were called to order, Dr. Piatt, the principal, walked in. He was a gentle man, keeping to his office like a snail, and we had never succeeded in making a bogey of him, although we tried. Today he shepherded a group of mothers and two men, officiously dignified, all of whom he seated on some chairs up front at Miss Totten's left. Then he sat down too, looking upon us benignly, his head cocked a little to one side in a way he had, as if he hearkened to some unseen arbiter who whispered constantly to him of how bad children could be, but he benevolently, insistently, continued to disagree.

Miss Totten, alone among the teachers, was usually immune to visitors, but today she strode restlessly in front of us and as she pulled down the maps one of them slipped from her hand and snapped back up with a loud, flapping roar. Fumbling for the roll-book, she sat down and began to call the roll from it, something she usually did without looking at the book and favouring each of us, instead, with a warming nod.

"Arnold Ames?"

"Pres-unt!"

"Mary Bates?"

"Pres-unt!"

"Wanda Becovic?"

"Pres-unt!"

"Sidney Cohen?"

"Pres-unt!"

"L—Lilly Davis?"

It took us a minute to realize that Mooley had not raised her hand. A light, impatient groan rippled over the class. But Mooley, her face uplifted in a blank stare, was looking at Miss Totten. Miss Totten's own lips moved. There seemed to be a cord between her lips and Mooley's. Mooley's lips moved, opened.

"Pres-unt!" said Mooley.

The class caught its breath, then righted itself under the sweet, absent smile of the visitors. With flushed, lowered lids, but in a rich full voice, Miss Totten finished calling the roll. Then she rose and came forward with the Manila cards. Each time, she held up the name of a state and we answered with its capital city.

Pennsylvania.

"Harrisburg!" said Arnold Ames.

Illinois.

"Springfield!" said Mary Bates.

Arkansas.

"Little Rock!" said Wanda Becovic.

North Dakota.

"Bismark!" said Sidney Cohen.

Idaho.

We were afraid to turn our heads.

"Buh . . . Boise!" said Mooley Davis.

After this, we could hardly wait for the turn to come around to Mooley. When Miss Totten, using a pointer against the map, indicated that Mooley was to "bound" the state of North Carolina, we focused on one spot with such attention that the visitors, grinning at each other, shook their heads at such zest. But Dr. Piatt was looking straight at Miss Totten, his lips parted, his head no longer to one side.

"N-north Cal . . . Callina." Just as the deaf gaze at the speaking, Mooley's eyes never left Miss Totten's. Her voice issued, burred here, choked there, but unmistakably a voice. "Bounded by Virginia on the north . . . Tennessee on the west . . . South Callina on the south . . . and on the east . . . and on the east . . ." She bent her head and gripped her desk with her hands. I gripped my own desk, until I saw that she suffered only from the common failing—she had only forgotten. She raised her head.

"And on the east," she said joyously, "and on the east by the Atlannic Ocean."

Later that term Miss Totten died. She had been forty years in the school system, we heard in the eulogy at Assembly. There was no immediate family, and any of us who cared to might pay our respects at the chapel. After this, Mr. Moloney, who usually chose *Whispering* for the dismissal march, played something slow and thrumming which forced us to drag our feet until we reached the door.

Of course none of us went to the chapel, nor did any of us bother to wonder whether Mooley went. Probably she did not. For now that the girl withdrawn for so long behind those rigidly empty eyes had stepped forward into them, they flicked about quite normally, as captious as anyone's.

Once or twice in the days that followed we mentioned Miss Totten, but it was really death that we honored, clicking our tongues like our elders. Passing the umbrella-stand at home, I sometimes thought of Miss Totten, furled forever in her coffin. Then I forgot her too, along with the rest of the class. After all this was only reasonable in a class which had achieved Miss Steele.

But memory, after a time, dispenses its own emphasis, making a *feuilleton* of what we once thought most ponderable, laying its wreath on what we never thought to recall. In the country, the children stumble upon the griffin mask of the mangled pheasant, and they learn; they come upon the murderous love-knot of the mantis, and they surmise. But in the city, although no man looms very large against the sky, he is silhouetted all the more sharply against his fellows. And sometimes the children there, who know so little about the natural world, stumble still upon that unsolicited good which is perhaps only a dislocation in the insensitive rhythm of the natural world. And if they are lucky, memory holds it in waiting. For what they have stumbled upon is their own humanity—their aberration, and their glory. That must be why I find myself wanting to say aloud to someone: "I remember . . . a Miss Elizabeth Totten."

William Melvin Kelley
(1937–   )

Frequently an artist discovers his themes and traps his meanings during the act of creation rather than before. Similarly, during the act of teaching, artful teachers often find what they need to know: their theories become intelligible after the fact of experience. The boy Mance in "The Life You Save" is taught a truth about his place in the world; indeed, he is taught that he may *have* a place. As important, however, is the implied lesson he gives his counselor, who works in a ghetto settlement house.

Mance lives in the Bronx and, in the words of the settlement house director, has seen it all. But in another sense Mance has seen nothing; the larger world is unknown to him. With an unencumbered, really instinctive act, his counselor, Peter Dunford, is able to reach the boy after allegedly prudent tactics have failed. The artful teacher, it would seem, must respect instinct and trust his urges even as he distrusts tumid emotions.

William Melvin Kelley shuns the easy appellation of "young black writer," the tag condescendingly used to excuse amateurish prose or to veil the independent cut of good writing. Kelley studied at Harvard under Archibald MacLeish and John Hawkes, and later received a Breadloaf Writing Fellowship. His first novel, *A Different Drummer* (1963), has been followed by a collection of short stories, *Dancers on the Shore* (1964), and a second novel, *A Drop of Patience* (1965).

The Life You Save

"You mean his brother really tried to burn him alive?" Peter leaned forward onto the table, and smiled involuntarily at the horror of it.

The director nodded; he too could not help smiling. "Right. Carlyle, the older brother, told the mother he was just initiating Mance into a club. But she didn't buy it. She told the father, but he wouldn't believe it, not about his oldest boy, his namesake. He doesn't even know what kind of place we got here. He thinks it's just a regular day camp. He'd probably pull the kid out if he found out—disgrace and all that stuff."

Peter sat back. "Wow!" He shook out a cigarette and lit it.

The director tore the cellophane from a cigar. "So anyway, that's what you got. At eleven, this Mance Bedlow's seen it all. I can only tell you one thing: don't hit him, don't even try to punish him, or any of them. They've been smacked enough to last them a lifetime. That's why they're here. If you hit them, you'll lose them, sure." He pulled himself forward, lit the cigar, and continued through dense smoke. "I'll give you all this stuff." He tapped Mance Bedlow's folder with a thick brown finger. "Okay?"

"Okay." Peter sighed, put out his cigarette and left the director's office. He went down the hall to the room, where, in an hour, he would greet his eight eleven-year-olds. They were all so-called emotionally disturbed children. Some of them had already flirted with minor crime. Peter would be their counselor for the next eight weeks.

The settlement house had recently moved from a small, old building to the ground floor of one of the buildings in a new low-rent housing project; the walls of the room were bleak, bare, pale-green cinder blocks. In the room, there were only two tables and ten folding chairs. Peter sat in one of the chairs, lit a cigarette, and waited for his boys to come, a bit nervous now with the thought that in a short while he would have the responsibility of helping to guide, or even the opportunity to change the lives of eight small human beings. When he realized what was running through his mind, he laughed at his earnestness. The feeling was honest, but to put it into words made it seem conceited and pompous. He would have to watch such attitudes. If his boys sensed them, they would never trust him.

The boys entered one by one, in shapeless, beltless dungarees, in torn and faded T-shirts. Each carried, in a brown paper bag, his lunch. Their mothers had pomaded and brushed their heads fervently, flattening the tiny beads of black hair. As they came in, Peter introduced himself, and each in turn, mumbled a name. Finally, eight had arrived. But there was no Mance Bedlow.

"I guess one of us isn't here." Peter, seated now at the head of one of the tables, scanned their dark faces. "Anybody here know Mance Bedlow?"

The boys glanced at one another. One of them, who had introduced himself as Randolph Wayne, said he did.

"Have you seen him, Randolph?"

"I seed him on the way over here, Mister Dunford. He say he ain't making it. He say this a wasted gig." There was an impish look on the boy's dark-brown face, as if he held the same view. His eyes were dark, and twinkled.

"Okay. You fellows wait here." Peter got up. "I'll go check on him." He left the room and headed for the director's office. Halfway down the hall he realized there was no Randolph Wayne on the list the director had given him.

"What's the problem, Peter?" The director was reading his mail.

Peter remained in the doorway. "I have the right number of kids, but no Mance Bedlow."

"Oh?" The director put down a letter he had just opened. "Who's the extra?"

"A kid named Randolph Wayne."

The director sighed. "They do that sometimes. They see their buddies on the way here and just tag along." He got up.

They walked back down the hall and stopped at the door. The director looked in at the boys. "Which is the Wayne boy?"

The boys turned to the door now, some smiling politely.

Peter indicated Randolph Wayne.

The director shook his head and chuckled. "That is Mance Bedlow."

The room filled with high squealing and cackling, the boys talking to each other: "Man, you see that cat go for that shit?"

"Yeah. Man, he dumb!"

Mance Bedlow sat at the table, basking in his triumph, staring at Peter, interested to see what he might do. Peter felt his embarrassed anger bubbling, and knowing he could not afford to let the boys see it, left the door, took two steps, and leaned against the wall, trying to control himself.

The director put a hand on Peter's shoulder. "Don't let it get you. That's the way they live."

Peter nodded.

The director went back to his office.

Peter fixed a smile on his face, and entered the room. "That's a point for you, Mance." He looked into hard brown eyes, understanding now what the director had told him before. Mance Bedlow's eyes were not at all those of an eleven-year-old. Peter realized suddenly that at eleven, he would not have survived in Mance Bedlow's world, even though he had always lived in Harlem. Peter's father was a doctor and earned a good living; Peter had been sent to private schools.

Mance returned his stare. Finally Peter looked at another boy. "Well, let's paint a little bit."

The boys were not enthusiastic. They waited quietly as Peter brought out huge sheets of paper, brushes, and jars of paint, and passed them around. Finally one of them, George, light-skinned and shaved bald, asked what Peter wanted them to paint.

"What do you guys want to paint?" Peter was sitting again, and looked around the table. The boys were surprised. The director had told Peter that most of the time boys like these were told exactly what to do. Their choice was to obey or rebel. Obedience brought little reward or admiration; rebellion brought harsh punishment. "You can paint anything you want. But if you can't think of anything, paint a picture of your family." He suggested that purposely, knowing the settlement house psychologist might learn something from the paintings.

Automatically, the boys painted their families. Peter walked around behind them. As he approached, they would usually tighten their bony shoulders. He encouraged them all and from time to time received smiles.

Mance Bedlow's picture was entirely in brown. There were three figures, the two biggest on one side of the page, the smallest on the other side. Peter asked Mance to name them. The two big ones were his father and brother. He was the small one.

"Where's your mother?"

"She in the kitchen cooking their dinner." He looked up at Peter. "Mister Dunford, what color should I paint the sun?"

"Any color you want; it's your picture." Peter smiled and went on to George, who smiled at him timidly.

Behind him, Peter heard scuffling. "Cut that shit out, boy."

Peter turned around to find Mance glaring at the boy on the other side of him. Then he picked up his own picture and began ripping it into tiny pieces. Peter decided not to stop him.

When he was through destroying his picture, Mance turned to Peter. "This place is shit!"

Peter smiled.

"And you're a cock-sucker!"

Still Peter smiled, although now it was an effort.

"I'm going home!" Standing up, he knocked over his chair, then raced around the table away from Peter, and scrambled out the door. Peter stood his ground. The boy would come back.

Five minutes later, Mance had not re-appeared. Peter, who had started the boys painting again, told them he would return in a few moments and went down to the front door and looked out.

The settlement house was in one of twenty buildings in the red-brick project. Black asphalt paths connected the buildings, which were separated by chained-off plots of grass. Wooden benches lined the paths. Mance sat watching the door of the settlement house. When he saw Peter at the door window, he stood up.

Peter opened the door. "Why don't you come back inside?"

"I'm going home!"

Peter stepped through the door. "What do you want to do that for?"

"I'm going home!" His fists were clenched; he was yelling.

Peter came part way down the front stairs, speaking softly. "Come on, Mance, don't . . ."

He had gotten too close and the boy was running. Peter trotted after him, closing the space between them. He did not want to catch and drag him back, knowing it would be better to convince the boy to return of his own free will. They ran past a brown woman wheeling a baby carriage, shouting at a toddler clinging to her skirts, past a seated old man leaning his white-whiskered chin on his cane, past a group of young girls chanting and skipping rope. Finally, Mance neared the curb, the outer boundary of the project, and without looking, darted out into the street, avoiding cars, the drivers startled behind their windshields, stopping only when he had reached the other side.

Peter waited until the cars passed, then started across. "Why don't you tell me what's wrong?"

Mance watched Peter drawing closer to him until they were only five steps apart, then began to run again, along the sidewalks now, in front of the brownstone houses' high stairs, occupied by Negro men and women sitting in undershirts and housecoats. They ran around groups of conversing brown people, through mobs of playing children. Peter could see Mance was tiring now, his thin legs growing heavy and wobbly.

Peter slowed to a walk. Mance looked over his shoulder, and began to walk himself. "Why don't you tell me what's wrong?" Peter was shouting; several people turned around. He felt foolish.

"I don't like painting pictures!" They were still walking, a distance now of two cars between them.

"We aren't going to paint pictures all day."

Mance stopped. "What was we going to do?"

They stood shouting at each other. "I don't know—we were going to the park and play some ball."

"Who wants to do that?"

Peter wondered if Mance would sit down if he did, and moved back to some empty steps behind him. "We're taking trips downtown and on the Staten Island ferry, and to the car show." He saw Mance Bedlow's face flicker with interest, but did not know exactly what had interested him. He guessed. "You like cars?"

"When you got a car nobody can mess with you." Mance inched closer. He was standing in the gutter directly in front of Peter. "One of these days I'll hit the number and buy me a Cadillac and won't nobody mess with me." He was staring at the middle of the sidewalk.

Peter wanted to keep this conversation going and grabbed at a question. "What color car will you get?"

"I'm getting me a black one, with air conditioning and a radio." He was in the middle of the sidewalk now. "Some niggers run out and get white Cadillacs; they get dirty and look jive. But I'm getting me a black one, and even when it dirty it'll still look good." He paused for an instant. "I'll get in that car and nobody'll mess with me and I'll go away."

Peter was tempted to ask why Mance wanted to go away, but he suspected the boy would balk. "Why did you want to go home?"

"I told you—I don't want to paint no pictures."

"Well, you don't have to. You can do something else when the other guys are painting."

"What?" His chin was lifted high.

"I don't know. You decide." Peter got up, planning something new. Mance backed up. "Look, I'd like you to come back. You don't have to, of course, but I do, because I'm taking the other guys to the park." Peter descended the steps. Mance had retreated to the gutter. "Why don't you come along? We'll have a good time." Peter knew he was overacting but he did not think Mance would see it. "Well, so long. I hope you come back." He started up the street.

He walked slowly, not turning around and came to a store, the window of which was slanted so he could see behind himself. At a distance of three cars, Mance was following him. Peter smiled to himself, a little proud. Perhaps, he had broken through.

Peter soon found it was not that easy. Mance ran out two times that afternoon, racing in a different direction each time. Contrary to the declaration—"I'm going home!"—he never seemed to be heading toward any particular place. He simply ran until he got tired, or until Peter could engage him in conversation. Between flights he talked to no one. He would seem as engrossed as the other boys, then suddenly, he would bolt.

At the end of the day, alone now, Peter had a chance to read Mance Bedlow's report. Two things particularly interested him. The first was that Mance had a recurring nightmare: He would be standing with his parents on a grassy mound. He would be quite happy. A wolf would appear then, and, snapping at his legs, would drive him off the mound, away from his parents. He would try to outsmart the wolf by running around to the other side of the mound to sneak to the top again. But the wolf would always get there before him and keep him away.

The second thing was that Mance lived in the Bronx. Yet, though the settlement house was in Manhattan, when he ran away, he never went anywhere near the subway.

Next day, Peter had the boys paint animals. Predictably, Mance painted a wolf standing on top of a mound of grass. Peter stood watching. "What's that?" He tried to give the question no weight.

"That's my wolf." Mance seemed indignant. "Didn't they tell you about my wolf? They all know about it—all the people here."

Peter was startled by the answer, but went on as he had planned. "They didn't tell me about him."

"Hell, they should-a. He's important. I got this wolf, see? I dream about him most every night and . . ." He stopped short. "You're jiving me. You know all about my wolf."

Peter shook his head. "No. No, I don't know a thing about it."

Mance tilted his head, studying Peter. "Then," he started slowly, "you are one stupid bastard and I ain't wasting my time telling you." He stood up, rather slowly this time. "I'm going home." He did not even bother to run; he ambled.

Peter stood fighting anger, waited until he had calmed himself before he followed, catching up to the boy in a small playground at the other end of the project. He was still a bit angry, but remembered all the director had told him, and all he had learned from the report. He told himself again that a counselor was supposed to be a good example for boys like Mance. He fixed a gentle look on his face, but before he could say anything, Mance was coming toward him. "You go to college?"

"Yes, I do." Peter sat down and was surprised when the boy sat beside him, quite close.

"What they teach you there?" The boy was genuinely interested. Peter wished he knew what turn his mind had taken.

"I guess the same things you learn, only harder." Mance Bedlow's interest in his personal affairs was a good sign.

"You ever get into any fights there?" Mance was inspecting Peter's hands.

"No, I don't." Peter had the unsettling feeling his answers were all wrong.

"What happens when somebody robs your stuff?"

"Nobody does." In front of them, two small boys were pretending to be airplanes.

Mance scowled. "Don't nobody hate you at college?"

"I hope not." Peter chuckled. "I don't think so."

"Must be a jive place." He stood up. "I guess you want me to go back, huh?"

"Yes, I do." Peter did not know what to make of all this.

"Okay. I'll save you a speech. Come on." Mance started toward the settlement house, Peter following obediently.

Mance did not run away again. But as the weeks went by, Peter realized this was not a sign of progress. Mance got along no better with the rest of the boys. He got into his share of fights. But despite these brief signs of involvement, Peter knew Mance was lonely and unhappy. It seemed that he knew he had to attend the day camp, and had decided to endure it, but no more. Even Peter's success with the other boys did not balance the disappointment of having failed with Mance Bedlow.

Peter did not know if it was this failure, or simply the demands the entire group made on him, but he began to get more tense, more tired, and more frustrated. When he arrived home at night, he would skip dinner with his parents, go to his room, and sleep. He could not rid himself of his tight feelings and could not show them to the boys, and so after six weeks of hiding them, each day was harder to get through. He was fighting anger all the time.

In the afternoons, if they had not gone on a trip, Peter would take his boys to the project's large playground, which was used not only by the settlement house, but by all of the children, boys, and young men in the neighborhood. One hot, humid day, the air conditioner had burned out and the room had steamed, forcing sweat down the dark faces of his boys, staining their shirts. Peter took them to the playground an hour early; Mance as usual tagged behind.

Peter organized seven of the boys into a game of basketball, leaving Mance to wander the playground alone. Then he sat down to watch, mopping himself with an already damp and wilted handkerchief.

The game would have been laughable if Peter had felt like laughing. The boys' shots either did not reach the backboard or went over it. Instead of dribbling, they ran, and when one had the ball, the others, no matter what team, descended on him like a mob. Even so, they seemed to be having a good time.

Peter did not see the older boys until it was too late. They were standing at the far end of the court, watching and laughing. They wore tight dark pants, button-down shirts in browns and wine-red, and thin brimmed hats.

George, his bald head glistening with sweat, threw the wild pass. It bounced down the court and was caught by one of the older boys, who began to dribble it, neatly, between his legs. George ran down the court after it, yelling: "Hey, man! Hey! Give me that ball!"

The older boy, thin and dark, ignored him, continued to bounce the ball, low and hard, behind his back.

"Hey, man, give me the ball!" George stood ten feet away, watching, and after asking for the ball once more, charged the boy, who laughing, passed the ball to one of his friends.

George did not change direction. He was swinging his fists wildly, his blows falling on the boy's thighs and stomach. Peter was up now, running down the court, telling George to stop. Just as Peter reached them, the older boy stopped laughing, stepped back, and punched George square in the face, knocking him to the ground, where he burst into fuming tears.

Peter, whose only aim until then had been to retrieve the ball and to stop George, found himself flying at the boy, a loud rushing, like heavy rain, filling his ears, his fists clenched. He caught the boy by surprise with a punch on the ear, and when the boy turned, shocked, followed through with two punches to the stomach and one to the eye. The boy stumbled, and backed up, holding his eye. "Hey, man, what you do that for?"

Peter was screaming. "What did you hit that kid for?"

"Awh, man, I was only playing." The boy was still backing up. His friends stood behind him, timidly, not looking at him.

"Well, you play some place else or I'll break your ass for you!" Peter marched forward and took the ball from the boy who was holding it. Then suddenly he realized what he had done. He spun around and found his boys in a group, staring at him, their mouths open. To one side of them, his hands in his pockets, a scowl on his face, stood Mance Bedlow.

Avoiding their gaze, Peter helped George up and hurried his boys back to the settlement house, where he let them go home immediately though it was a half hour early. He sat alone in the room, smoking, thinking how he would repair the damage he had done. All summer, he had tried to build an image they could see and perhaps copy; he had tried to show them there were people in the world who were completely different from their aggressive, brutal fathers and brothers. In ten seconds, he had destroyed six weeks' work, and now he could not discover a way to salvage himself in their eyes.

As he was just about to push open the front door, he saw Mance sitting on one of the benches in front of the settlement house. He was still scowling.

Peter did not want to speak to him; he pushed open the door quickly and waved: "Good night, Mance." He walked as fast as he could.

Behind him, he heard running footsteps. "You learn to fight like that in college?"

"No!" He stopped now, and spun on his heels, expecting to find the boy taunting him. The boy's face was blank. Peter changed his tone. "No, I didn't. Look, Mance, it's not good to settle things by—"

Mance cut him off. "Where'd you learn to fight?"

Peter sighed. "I don't know—I guess my father taught me." He started to walk again.

Mance tagged along at his elbow. "What do he do?"

"My father? He's a doctor."

"And he really taught you how to fight?" Mance did not seem to believe him.

"That's right." They were out of the project now, almost to the corner where Peter waited for his bus. He hoped one would come soon.

"You mean, doctor's really get in fights?"

He looked up the block for the bus. "Sometimes. I guess sometimes everybody gets into a fight."

"Just like me."

Something in the boy's tone forced Peter to look at him. Mance was staring at him. "When I was a kid I wanted to be a doctor."

Peter was about to speak, when behind him, he heard the gasping of a bus door. He turned around uncertain whether to get on. This was too good to let slip.

"He leaving without you. You better get on."

Peter did as the boy directed. After he had paid his fare and found a seat, and the bus had begun to move, he looked out of the window, back to the bus stop and saw Mance Bedlow, standing on tiptoes, his hand just at ear level, waving him a timid, tentative good-by.

Richard Lockridge

(1898–   )

An anachronism is described here—a Kansas City teacher of English grammar, one Miss Fox, who recently died in California, "where the laxity of the climate probably disagreed with her." The art of Miss Fox is obdurate, predictable, and rare—the malpractice of which has led some critics to indict our country as a nation of semiliterates. We read and write, so of course we are not *ill*iterate. But we read and write negligibly, narrowly, gracelessly, vaguely; so we are far short of literate.

Whatever her flaws to the educator schooled in the curriculum of mindless cheer, Miss Fox does not shrink from her professional obligation, that of teaching respect for "the hard, bare bones on which the language hangs." However, the shirking of just this duty is legend in American education. College English instructors, themselves not guiltless, scoff at the illiteracy of each freshman crop by thumbing their rhetorical noses at high school English teachers, who in turn grieve over the laxity of the junior high faculty, whose refuge lies in attacking the compulsory-pass system adopted by most elementary schools. Elementary teachers and their administrators can blame the parents, most of whom take little interest in curriculum and methods. Completing this cycle of recrimination, the parents oust school board members and replace them with candidates often no better qualified to find remedies. But the buck stopped with Miss Fox.

Of wider import is Lockridge's implicit argument that teachers must rigorously serve their subject matter and must not, for motives subtle and deceitful, bargain their students' futures for a temporary equanimity. Many of the arts of teaching are sublime. A few may even be reposeful. But some are hardnosed.

Richard Lockridge is a drama critic and mystery writer and has often contributed to *The New Yorker*.

THE GRAMMARIAN

I heard only recently that Miss Fox, after a few years of retirement, had died in California, where the laxity of the climate probably disagreed with her. It was a little startling to learn that her death had happened so recently, because I had somehow fallen to thinking of her, as I did rather often, and usually with a feeling of guilt, as a historical character. It was difficult to realize that she came so close to the contemporary. She was a little woman, and made, I suspect, of flint, and when I was in high school she taught me English.

She seemed to be rather old even then, and that was a fairly long time ago. She was a little stooped, and gave the impression of being done almost entirely in gray, in spite of her black dresses, which had high collars held up with stays, and the little flutter of her white W.C.T.U. ribbon. But you never thought of her as frail; after you had been in her class for a while, you got to thinking of yourself as frail, but never of her. She walked two miles to the school every day and two miles back again, carrying a great load of papers to correct, and her own inflexibility. So far as I know she never had a first name, and, if she had had, I do not think anyone would ever have thought of calling her by it.

It is odd to think that, for many years after I passed through the disinfection of her class, she kept on hitting boys and girls over the head with grammar and working herself and them to a frazzle in a dour, uncompromising search for perfection. It is also a little odd to think that she is no longer doing this, but possibly she is giving the angels a few lessons and fighting grimly against a certain grammatical looseness which she has probably found where she is now. I wouldn't put it past her to go above the angels, either; she would snip away at bad grammar wherever she found it.

She found a lot of it, of course, in second-year English, which was what she taught. We drifted up to her vaguely, I realize now, our English a boneless thing in spite of all the diagrams of sentences we had made on blackboards, and, if we thought of English letters at all, it was with a kind of yeasty sentiment. Miss Fox took all that out of us. She was not sentimental about English letters; she didn't, I suspect, even like them very well, and considered that a good bit of laxity had crept into them from time to time. She was beautifully free from that expansive desire, which one found in some of the other instructors, to help us see the beauty of literature, and she had no thought of making us love it.

It is this method, I gather from rumors which trickle from the educa-

115

tive fields, which is in vogue just now, and even then there were a few instructors who took the larger view. I had one or two of them; one particularly I remember. He was an odd, impassioned gentleman, and he used to act out the beauties of literature for us on occasion. One of the grimmest memories of my youth concerns an afternoon when we all came to his classroom and found the shades drawn, so that the room was an unhealthy, yellow murk—the shades were a rather tired yellow. He was sitting at his desk, with his gray hair pulled down, and was staring in a rather awful way at a bottle of ink. We crept in, silenced and a little frightened, and nobody said anything for several minutes. We just sat there, troubled. Then, with no warning, the instructor let out a little shriek. We all jumped and wished we could get out. In another minute, I think, we would have got out, but then the instructor spoke.

"Is this a dagger which I see before me?" he screamed, in tones of anguish. We all settled back then, of course, and quieted down, although he grew noisier and noisier. After a while it began to seem, in a rather unpleasant way, a little funny, and it still does.

Miss Fox never did anything like that, and never gave, I am sure, a rap whether we appreciated the beauties of the English speech or not, so long as we learned its grammar. There was a certain amount of literature to be got through, naturally, and we went through Milton, a little grimly. I don't think Miss Fox really cared much for Milton's, or anybody else's, poetry, and she lightened up the ordeal with curious little side trips to visit the horrors of alcohol and tobacco. In the middle of "Comus" there was one such bitter little excursion to the subject of General Grant, who had, it seemed, died because he insisted on smoking a lot. But, even if her heart was not entirely in it, she took us resolutely through Milton, with only a few mishaps. One of the more arresting of the mishaps was mine.

We had been told to pick a passage—a good, long passage—and memorize it. The only stipulation was about the length. Aside from that, we could pick any passage which, by its beauty, appealed to us. (Miss Fox always uttered the word "beauty" in a flat, disapproving tone.) In alphabetical order, the next day we recited what we had learned, and, as the turn came down toward me, I began to have serious misgivings. Everybody else, or almost everybody, had picked a pleasant, idyllic passage about, as I recall it, birds and clouds, and it came over me that I had made a mistake. But it was the only passage I had learned, so there was nothing to do but give it, and I did. I've forgotten most of it, but it concerned the amorous gambols of a couple of Miltonian immortals, and the lines which loomed up when I came to them were those which described how the male immortal had, on beds of something or other,

> Fill'd her with thee a daughter fair,
> So bucksom, blith, and debonair.

I think it was not until I saw the expression on Miss Fox's face that I realized the full enormity of this couplet. Miss Fox's face turned slightly grayer, and all the sharp bones stood out in it, and the white W.C.T.U. ribbon quivered on what would, under happier circumstances, have been her breast. Quite unintentionally I had put her in a spot; she was torn between the conviction that I had committed this offense by intention, and should have something dire befall me, and the realization that anything she did would only make matters worse. Finally she just said "Well!" in a tone which I hope never to hear again from human lips, and called the name of the next student.

Probably it was the lurking danger that things like that might come up in literature which made Miss Fox suspect it; and there was always, too, the likelihood that the classics had been written by loose persons who smoked and drank and, hence, were likely to abuse grammar. And English grammar was the god before which Miss Fox burned the sharp, acrid, but infinitely penetrating incense of her devotion. The prohibition of alcohol, tobacco, and the hanging participle—this was the goal toward which she strove with a valiance and disregard of self which, even now, a little frightens me. She made us work hard, but she herself worked many times as hard; she must, indeed, have put in almost as much labor on each member of her rather large class as each student she was trying to save did on himself.

Miss Fox kept us writing almost constantly about literature and allied subjects, such as the evils of alcohol. We found it a good idea to put in a few licks against liquor and cigarettes when the occasion arose, and to make it arise if possible, but even this did not soften Miss Fox's harsh integrity if your grammar slipped. She was ruthlessly fair; I got in rather bad by writing, in conscious perversity this time, an essay mildly questioning the toxic qualities of nicotine, but this merely made her dislike me and didn't affect my grades one way or the other.

Miss Fox took home all the papers from all the boys and girls and went over them with a blue pencil, marking in the margins the existence of grammatical errors. She did not correct the errors; she did not even specify them. She merely, with the cold distaste of a housewife in the presence of an untoward insect, noted the presence of sin. It was up to the student to find the sin out and correct it. It was up to him then to write the paper over, correcting all the errors and not making any new ones, and have the result "checked." A paper was checked when not even Miss Fox could find an infraction of the least of grammar's formalities. Usually a paper went back three or four times before it was checked, and you went back with it, during "seventh hour." There were six regular periods in a day, and overtime, almost all the overtime being devoted to Miss Fox.

Out of those sessions boys and girls used to go white with weariness and vexation, their hands shaking from copying essays and their minds reeling with grammar. As dusk crept on, and after the slowest of them had gone, little Miss Fox would trot out smartly, her round black hat bobbing, and walk rapidly the two miles home, clutching the bundle of that day's papers. She must have sat up most of the night with them, her blue pencil and her black eyes flashing coldly, and her mouth set hard against error. Now and then, perhaps, her expression would soften a little as some wily pupil took a slash at the cigarette evil, but it would harden again at the next paragraph as an infinitive split wide open.

You came out of all this with, surprisingly enough, a good deal of precisely what Miss Fox was determined to give you—respect for the hard, bare bones on which the language hangs. If you went on to one of the near-by state universities, you were astonished and gratified to learn that, if you had survived Miss Fox, you did not need to take Freshman Rhetoric. Perhaps they thought that exemption was as little as they could give you in recompense. If, years afterward—ten years, at any rate —you began to write letters to your closer friends in a style slightly more colloquial than Miss Fox would have approved, it was always with some sense of guilt and a fleeting, absurd thought that Miss Fox might find you out and make you come back to seventh hour and be checked.

She was a hard, uncompromising little woman, our Miss Fox of Kansas City, and I shudder to think what her blue pencil would do to what I have written about her. I would not please her, I know; I never did. But she was the best teacher I ever had.

Sherwood Anderson

(1876–1941)

"The Teacher" is a selection from Sherwood Anderson's *Winesburg, Ohio*, a collection of interwoven stories depicting the lives of midwesterners early in this century. One of the book's cyclic themes is of deprivation, the spiritual starvation suffered by the townspeople, a meagerness they fail to comprehend even as it withers lives. At odds with this circumstance, though victimized by it herself, is Kate Swift, a high school teacher who becomes involved with a gifted pupil, George Willard. The story is true to its facts: though the teacher is tragically unable to convey the import of her perceptions, partly because Willard's immaturity withholds the range of sentiment needed, the boy's confusion at the end of the story discloses that he may yet develop the gifts first discerned by his teacher. Kate Swift's art is stringent, borne by a suffering generosity, and selflessly applied to the conditions of Winesburg. Though she may be the victim of isolation, she is not its casualty.

Sherwood Anderson, the fourth of seven children, grew up in Clyde, Ohio, and later held various jobs on farms, in factories, and in advertising agencies. An influence on writers as disparate as Ernest Hemingway and William Faulkner, Anderson is probably best known for *Winesburg, Ohio* (1919), *A Story Teller's Story* (1924), *Dark Laughter* (1925), and his *Memoirs* (1942).

THE TEACHER

Snow lay deep in the streets of Winesburg. It had begun to snow about ten o'clock in the morning and a wind sprang up and blew the snow in clouds along Main Street. The frozen mud roads that led into town were fairly smooth and in places ice covered the mud. "There will be good sleighing," said Will Henderson, standing by the bar in Ed Griffith's saloon. Out of the saloon he went and met Sylvester West the druggist

119

stumbling along in the kind of heavy overshoes called arctics. "Snow will bring the people into town on Saturday," said the druggist. The two men stopped and discussed their affairs. Will Henderson, who had on a light overcoat and no overshoes, kicked the heel of his left foot with the toe of the right. "Snow will be good for the wheat," observed the druggist sagely.

Young George Willard, who had nothing to do, was glad because he did not feel like working that day. The weekly paper had been printed and taken to the post office Wednesday evening and the snow began to fall on Thursday. At eight o'clock, after the morning train had passed, he put a pair of skates in his pocket and went up to Waterworks Pond but did not go skating. Past the pond and along a path that followed Wine Creek he went until he came to a grove of beech trees. There he built a fire against the side of a log and sat down at the end of the log to think. When the snow began to fall and the wind to blow he hurried about getting fuel for the fire.

The young reporter was thinking of Kate Swift, who had once been his school teacher. On the evening before he had gone to her house to get a book she wanted him to read and had been alone with her for an hour. For the fourth or fifth time the woman had talked to him with great earnestness and he could not make out what she meant by her talk. He began to believe she might be in love with him and the thought was both pleasing and annoying.

Up from the log he sprang and began to pile sticks on the fire. Looking about to be sure he was alone he talked aloud pretending he was in the presence of the woman. "Oh, you're just letting on, you know you are," he declared. "I am going to find out about you. You wait and see."

The young man got up and went back along the path toward town leaving the fire blazing in the wood. As he went through the streets the skates clanked in his pocket. In his own room in the New Willard House he built a fire in the stove and lay down on top of the bed. He began to have lustful thoughts and pulling down the shade of the window closed his eyes and turned his face to the wall. He took a pillow into his arms and embraced it thinking first of the school teacher, who by her words had stirred something within him, and later of Helen White, the slim daughter of the town banker, with whom he had been for a long time half in love.

By nine o'clock of that evening snow lay deep in the streets and the weather had become bitter cold. It was difficult to walk about. The stores were dark and the people had crawled away to their houses. The evening train from Cleveland was very late but nobody was interested in its arrival. By ten o'clock all but four of the eighteen hundred citizens of the town were in bed.

Hop Higgins, the night watchman, was partially awake. He was lame and carried a heavy stick. On dark nights he carried a lantern. Between nine and ten o'clock he went his rounds. Up and down Main Street he stumbled through the drifts trying the doors of the stores. Then he went into alleyways and tried the back doors. Finding all tight he hurried around the corner to the New Willard House and beat on the door. Through the rest of the night he intended to stay by the stove. "You go to bed. I'll keep the stove going," he said to the boy who slept on a cot in the hotel office.

Hop Higgins sat down by the stove and took off his shoes. When the boy had gone to sleep he began to think of his own affairs. He intended to paint his house in the spring and sat by the stove calculating the cost of paint and labor. That led him into other calculations. The night watchman was sixty years old and wanted to retire. He had been a soldier in the Civil War and drew a small pension. He hoped to find some new method of making a living and aspired to become a professional breeder of ferrets. Already he had four of the strangely shaped savage little creatures, that are used by sportsmen in the pursuit of rabbits, in the cellar of his house. "Now I have one male and three females," he mused. "If I am lucky by spring I shall have twelve or fifteen. In another year I shall be able to begin advertising ferrets for sale in the sporting papers."

The night watchman settled into his chair and his mind became a blank. He did not sleep. By years of practice he had trained himself to sit for hours through the long nights neither asleep nor awake. In the morning he was almost as refreshed as though he had slept.

With Hop Higgins safely stowed away in the chair behind the stove only three people were awake in Winesburg. George Willard was in the office of the *Eagle* pretending to be at work on the writing of a story but in reality continuing the mood of the morning by the fire in the wood. In the bell tower of the Presbyterian Church the Reverend Curtis Hartman was sitting in the darkness preparing himself for a revelation from God, and Kate Swift, the school teacher, was leaving her house for a walk in the storm.

It was past ten o'clock when Kate Swift set out and the walk was unpremeditated. It was as though the man and the boy, by thinking of her, had driven her forth into the wintry streets. Aunt Elizabeth Swift had gone to the county seat concerning some business in connection with mortgages in which she had money invested and would not be back until the next day. By a huge stove, called a base burner, in the living room of the house sat the daughter reading a book. Suddenly she sprang to her feet and, snatching a cloak from a rack by the front door, ran out of the house.

At the age of thirty Kate Swift was not known in Winesburg as a pretty woman. Her complexion was not good and her face was covered with blotches that indicated ill health. Alone in the night in the winter streets she was lovely. Her back was straight, her shoulders square, and her features were as the features of a tiny goddess on a pedestal in a garden in the dim light of a summer evening.

During the afternoon the school teacher had been to see Doctor Welling concerning her health. The doctor had scolded her and had declared she was in danger of losing her hearing. It was foolish for Kate Swift to be abroad in the storm, foolish and perhaps dangerous.

The woman in the streets did not remember the words of the doctor and would not have turned back had she remembered. She was very cold but after walking for five minutes no longer minded the cold. First she went to the end of her own street and then across a pair of hay scales set in the ground before a feed barn and into Trunion Pike. Along Trunion Pike she went to Ned Winters' barn and turning east followed a street of low frame houses that led over Gospel Hill and into Sucker Road that ran down a shallow valley past Ike Smead's chicken farm to Water-works Pond. As she went along, the bold, excited mood that had driven her out of doors passed and then returned again.

There was something biting and forbidding in the character of Kate Swift. Everyone felt it. In the schoolroom she was silent, cold, and stern, and yet in an odd way very close to her pupils. Once in a long while something seemed to have come over her and she was happy. All of the children in the schoolroom felt the effect of her happiness. For a time they did not work but sat back in their chairs and looked at her.

With hands clasped behind her back the school teacher walked up and down in the schoolroom and talked very rapidly. It did not seem to matter what subject came into her mind. Once she talked to the children of Charles Lamb and made up strange, intimate little stories concerning the life of the dead writer. The stories were told with the air of one who had lived in a house with Charles Lamb and knew all the secrets of his private life. The children were somewhat confused, thinking Charles Lamb must be someone who had once lived in Winesburg.

On another occasion the teacher talked to the children of Benvenuto Cellini. That time they laughed. What a bragging, blustering, brave, lovable fellow she made of the old artist! Concerning him also she invented anecdotes. There was one of a German music teacher who had a room above Cellini's lodgings in the city of Milan that made the boys guffaw. Sugars McNutts, a fat boy with red cheeks, laughed so hard that he became dizzy and fell off his seat and Kate Swift laughed with him. Then suddenly she became again cold and stern.

On the winter night when she walked through the deserted snow-covered streets, a crisis had come into the life of the school teacher. Although no one in Winesburg would have suspected it, her life had been very adventurous. It was still adventurous. Day by day as she worked in the schoolroom or walked in the streets, grief, hope, and desire fought within her. Behind a cold exterior the most extraordinary events transpired in her mind. The people of the town thought of her as a confirmed old maid and because she spoke sharply and went her own way thought her lacking in all the human feeling that did so much to make and mar their own lives. In reality she was the most eagerly passionate soul among them, and more than once, in the five years since she had come back from her travels to settle in Winesburg and become a school teacher, had been compelled to go out of the house and walk half through the night fighting out some battle raging within. Once on a night when it rained she had stayed out six hours and when she came home had a quarrel with Aunt Elizabeth Swift. "I am glad you're not a man," said the mother sharply. "More than once I've waited for your father to come home, not knowing what new mess he had got into. I've had my share of uncertainty and you cannot blame me if I do not want to see the worst side of him reproduced in you."

Kate Swift's mind was ablaze with thoughts of George Willard. In something he had written as a school boy she thought she had recognized the spark of genius and wanted to blow on the spark. One day in the summer she had gone to the *Eagle* office and finding the boy unoccupied had taken him out Main Street to the Fair Ground, where the two sat on a grassy bank and talked. The school teacher tried to bring home to the mind of the boy some conception of the difficulties he would have to face as a writer. "You will have to know life," she declared, and her voice trembled with earnestness. She took hold of George Willard's shoulders and turned him about so that she could look into his eyes. A passer-by might have thought them about to embrace. "If you are to become a writer you'll have to stop fooling with words," she explained. "It would be better to give up the notion of writing until you are better prepared. Now it's time to be living. I don't want to frighten you, but I would like to make you understand the import of what you think of attempting. You must not become a mere peddler of words. The thing to learn is to know what people are thinking about, not what they say."

On the evening before that stormy Thursday night when the Reverend Curtis Hartman sat in the bell tower of the church waiting to look at her body, young Willard had gone to visit the teacher and to borrow a book.[1] It was then the thing happened that confused and puzzled the boy. He had the book under his arm and was preparing to depart. Again Kate Swift talked with great earnestness. Night was coming on and the

[1] In another story in *Winesburg, Ohio*, entitled "The Strength of God," Reverend Curtis Hartman is depicted as a frantic cleric who voyeuristically spies on Kate from his bell tower, as she reads nightly in her bedroom next door.—Ed.

light in the room grew dim. As he turned to go she spoke his name softly and with an impulsive movement took hold of his hand. Because the reporter was rapidly becoming a man something of his man's appeal, combined with the winsomeness of the boy, stirred the heart of the lonely woman. A passionate desire to have him understand the import of life, to learn to interpret it truly and honestly, swept over her. Leaning forward, her lips brushed his cheek. At the same moment he for the first time became aware of the marked beauty of her features. They were both embarrassed, and to relieve her feeling she became harsh and domineering. "What's the use? It will be ten years before you begin to understand what I mean when I talk to you," she cried passionately.

On the night of the storm and while the minister sat in the church waiting for her, Kate Swift went to the office of the *Winesburg Eagle,* intending to have another talk with the boy. After the long walk in the snow she was cold, lonely, and tired. As she came through Main Street she saw the light from the printshop window shining on the snow and on an impulse opened the door and went in. For an hour she sat by the stove in the office talking of life. She talked with passionate earnestness. The impulse that had driven her out into the snow poured itself out into talk. She became inspired as she sometimes did in the presence of the children in school. A great eagerness to open the door of life to the boy, who had been her pupil and who she thought might possess a talent for the understanding of life, had possession of her. So strong was her passion that it became something physical. Again her hands took hold of his shoulders and she turned him about. In the dim light her eyes blazed. She arose and laughed, not sharply as was customary with her, but in a queer, hesitating way. "I must be going," she said. "In a moment, if I stay, I'll be wanting to kiss you."

In the newspaper office a confusion arose. Kate Swift turned and walked to the door. She was a teacher but she was also a woman. As she looked at George Willard, the passionate desire to be loved by a man, that had a thousand times before swept like a storm over her body, took possession of her. In the lamplight George Willard looked no longer a boy, but the man ready to play the part of a man.

The school teacher let George Willard take her into his arms. In the warm little office the air became suddenly heavy and the strength went out of her body. Leaning against a low counter by the door she waited. When he came and put a hand on her shoulder she turned and let her body fall heavily against him. For George Willard the confusion was immediately increased. For a moment he held the body of the woman tightly against his body and then it stiffened. Two sharp little fists began to beat on his face. When the school teacher had run away and left him alone, he walked up and down in the office swearing furiously.

It was into this confusion that the Reverend Curtis Hartman protruded himself.[2] When he came in George Willard thought the town had gone mad. Shaking a bleeding fist in the air, the minister proclaimed the woman George had only a moment before held in his arms an instrument of God bearing a message of truth.

George blew out the lamp by the window and locking the door of the printshop went home. Through the hotel office, past Hop Higgins lost in his dream of the raising of ferrets, he went and up into his own room. The fire in the stove had gone out and he undressed in the cold. When he got into bed the sheets were like blankets of dry snow.

George Willard rolled about in the bed on which he had lain in the afternoon hugging the pillow and thinking thoughts of Kate Swift. The words of the minister, who he thought had gone suddenly insane, rang in his ears. His eyes stared about the room. The resentment, natural to the baffled male, passed and he tried to understand what had happened. He could not make it out. Over and over he turned the matter in his mind. Hours passed and he began to think it must be time for another day to come. At four o'clock he pulled the covers up about his neck and tried to sleep. When he became drowsy and closed his eyes, he raised a hand and with it groped about in the darkness. "I have missed something. I have missed something Kate Swift was trying to tell me," he muttered sleepily. Then he slept and in all Winesburg he was the last soul on that winter night to go to sleep.

---

[2] As described in "The Strength of God," Reverend Hartman, from his bell tower, sees Kate's reaction to Willard's embrace: She prays in her bedroom, and the minister takes this event as a sign of divine intervention. His pronouncement above therefore takes on ironic overtones.—Ed.

Part Three

Present Discontents

To think of progress as a certainty is superstitious—the most splendid and animated of all superstitions, if you like, yet a superstition still. It is a kind of fatalism— radiant, confident and infinitely hopeful, yet a fatalism still, and like fatalism in all its other forms, inevitably dangerous to the effective sense of individual responsibility.

John Morley

Readers of *Candide*, Voltaire's enduring satire, recall with delight the antics of Doctor Pangloss, the jargon-spouting pundit who revels in the creed that "All is for the best in this best of all possible worlds." With irritating frequency the pedant turns to his young student Candide and, with eyebrows arched and body stanced, declares his optimistic themes. Energetic and naïve, Candide listens reverently. The reader may curse impatiently for respite from the self-congratulatory sermons of the good Doctor, but there is no respite. Pangloss and his student stroll with a throng of companions through a series of adventures that should discourage even the most stalwart believer in the Good, the True, and the Beautiful. Finally, when Candide is about to graduate with honors for his obsequious allegiance to the optimism of Pangloss, Voltaire allows for his maturity. With his fellow sufferers, Candide avers that "We must cultivate our gardens," that men must forsake abstract theories of optimism and tend to the weeds and brambles of their lives. Confronted with this revolt, Doctor Pangloss admits that he, too, had felt the dishonesty of his philosophy but had lacked the courage to shun its comfort.

Until about a decade ago, Voltaire's hatred of the fatuous optimist might well have been resurrected and leveled at many of education's spokesmen. Cheery platitudes about the "joys of teaching" were rampant. Conference speakers, gorged with gratuitous dinners, warmed to their duties. We heard them extol the happy factories of education that were manned by rosy pedagogues, policed by sanguine administrators, guided by folksy school boards, and financed by a sympathetic public. Our speakers comfortably referred to desperate faults as *problem areas*. The euphemism was pleasantly challenging, unabrasive. Between conferences our educational gardens remained unkempt. The Panglossian deception thrived.

In the past decade, however, the atmosphere of optimism has been banished by a new tone of criticism principally aroused by the competitive advances of Communist technology, by the citizen's growing dissatisfaction with the intellectual standards of his public schools, and by a late-found awareness of the educational deprivations suffered by the poor. However salutary and overdue, the new criticism threatens to become as irrelevantly versatile as the optimism it replaced. Hasty pessimism is now the rage, and some of it is well-founded. Self-styled messiahs, some of them belligerently astute, measure the quality of our schools by criteria zealously protected from cross-examination. Ours is a time of omens and acronyms. Whether bent on reform or reaction, on right- or left-wing suppressions of learning, the messiahs venture forth, with few followers or many, to subdue reasoned debate and plausible reform.

But there are other voices. Between the extremes of pallid optimism and faithless pessimism exists a climate of criticism that observes the evil of this world as well as its correctives. The words of these special critics, these meliorists, are heard impatiently by the advocates of cheer and despair. Although tolerated, given room for their grief and aspiration, at times even comprehended, the meliorists are often characterized as uncooperative by the optimists and as naïve (or corrupted) by the pessimists. Though not always in agreement amongst themselves, either in regard to viewpoint or conclusions, the meliorists are nevertheless of special value. They are able to confirm the solid states of good and evil in American education and to separate the remediable failings in teaching from those problems that are intrinsic to the demands of the profession and not to be cured. Low salaries, community apathy or intimidation, insufficient instructional supplies, administrational myopia, poor professional training—such conditions as these are plausibly reformable, and any teacher who still owns his soul must demand and work for solutions to these blights.

But there are other discontents that are not to be consoled. How does a teacher ever know, beyond great guesses, what his real influence on students is, or what his real breakthroughs were, even which of his failures was clean? Can there ever be an *oeuvre* for a teacher, a record of accomplishment measurable in itself, and public? Who has yet calculated the draining obligations of a teacher's public life, the welter of expectation and rue that he must face daily in his classrooms? When he fails, there is usually an audience; when he succeeds in arousing a thought or in tempering and attitude or in ordering a chaos, his success is likely to be obliquely acknowledged by the recipient if indeed it is recognized at all. And how even the most spirited teachers stave off the fatigue of routine, the sanctified habits of institutional life that even the best schools seem unable to evade?

Also to contend with, every semester, is the incorrigible child who is made so through neurosis or his own inventive wickedness or any number of enigmatic causes. Incorrigibility is not merely to be borne: it must be confronted daily, contested, and dispatched. What teacher, to delve further, has not known the yearly contest with those bureaucratic imperatives that are common to his profession because it is endowed by public funds? How many ceremonies of separate peace does one perform?

The fledgling teacher cannot escape most of the conditions which have made these questions mandatory; but he can survive them; though they wear him down each spring and trouble his summers, he can return to them each fall with a composure that is not meek and not quite without scorn.

So, then, there are discontents remediable and discontents beyond hope in this life. Certainly the narratives in Part Three do not compose a happy literature; nor do they constitute a despairing attitude. The heralded joys of teaching are shadowed in the concern of the authors presented here: but to extol such pleasures is not to ensure their existence. And no teacher worthy of his task need be taught the benefits of his calling.

Bel Kaufman

For years a teacher in the New York City school system, Bel Kaufman, collected her experiences, gave them the form of fiction, and provided readers with a sustained view of the inner-city school.

What distinguishes *Up the Down Staircase* from autobiographical novels of similar intent is a resiliency of tone which evokes the shades of anguish, humor, exacerbation, boredom, and compassion that pervade schools like Calvin Coolidge High. The situations of the novel are representative but not stereotyped, and the major characters escape cliché because they own a reality not wholly dependent on their topicality.

How Sylvia Barrett, an untenured young teacher, survives her disillusionment (and why she should) is the real story of *Up the Down Staircase*, a novel which reached the audience that most needed it—the millions of lay readers who, for reasons understandable and sad, never read the formal expositions which have for so long denounced the conditions dramatized in the following excerpts.

LETTERS TO ELLEN

Sept. 7

Dear Ellen,

It's a far cry from our dorm in Lyons Hall (Was it only four years ago?); a far cry from the sheltered Graduate School Library stacks; a far cry from Chaucer; and a far and desperate cry from *Education 114* and Prof. Winters' lectures on "The Psychology of the Adolescent." I have met the Adolescent face to face; obviously, Prof. Winters had not.

You seem to have done better with your education than I: while you are strolling through your suburban supermarket with your baby in the cart, or taking a shower in the middle of the third period, I am automatically erasing "Fuck Teacher" from the blackboard.

What I really had in mind was to do a little teaching. "And gladly wolde he lerne, and gladly teche"—like Chaucer's Clerke of Oxenford, I had come eager to share all I know and feel; to imbue the young with a love for their language and literature; to instruct and to inspire. What happened in real life (when I had asked why they were taking English, a boy said: "To help us in real life") was something else again, and even if I could describe it, you would think I am exaggerating.

But I'm not.

In homeroom (that's the official class, where the kids report in the morning and in the afternoon for attendance and vital statistics) they went after me with all their ammunition: whistling, shouting, drumming on desks, clacking inkwell lids, playing catch with the board eraser, sprawling in their seats to trip each other in the aisles—all this with an air of vacant innocence, while I stood there, pleading for attention, wary as a lion-tamer, my eyes on all 46 at once.

By the time I got to my subject classes, I began to stagger under an inundation of papers—mimeos, directives, circulars, letters, notices, forms, blanks, records. The staggering was especially difficult because I am what's known as a "floater"—I float from room to room.

There's a whole glossary to be learned. My 3rd termers are "special-slows"; my 5th termers are "low-normal" and "average-normal." So far, it's hard to tell which is which, or who I am, for that matter.

I made one friend—Bea Schachter, and one enemy—Admiral Ass, who signs himself JJ McH. And I saw hate and contempt on the face of a boy—because I am a teacher.

The building itself is hostile: cracked plaster, broken windows, splintered doors and carved up desks, gloomy corridors, metal stairways, dingy cafeteria (they can eat sitting down only in 20 minute shifts) and an auditorium which has no windows. It does have murals, however, depicting mute, muscular harvesters, faded and immobilized under a mustard sun.

That's where we had assembly this morning.

Picture it: the air heavy with hundreds of bodies, the principal's blurred face poised like a pale balloon over the lectern, his microphone-voice crackling with sudden static:

". . . a new leaf, for here at Calvin Coolidge we are all free and equal, with the same golden opportunity . . ."

The students are silent in their seats. The silence has nothing to do with attention; it's a glazed silence, ready to be shattered at a moment. The girl next to me examines her teeth in her pocket mirror. I sit straight on the wooden seat, smoothed by the restless bottoms of how many children, grown now, or dead, or where? On the back of the seat directly in front of me, carefully chiseled with some sharp instrument, is the legend: *Balls*.

". . . knocks but once, and your attitude . . ." *Tude* booms, unexpectedly amplified by the erratic microphone, "towards your work and your teachers, who so selflessly . . ."

The teachers dot the aisles: a hen-like little woman with a worried profile; a tall young man with amused eyebrows; a round lady with a pepper-and-salt pompadour—my colleagues, as yet unknown.

". . . precious than rubies. Education means . . ."—he's obviously winding up for a finish—"not only preparation for citizenship and life *plus* a sound academic foundation. Don't forget to have your teachers sign your program cards, and if you have any problems, remember my door is always open." Eloquent pause. "And so, with this thought in mind, I hope you will show the proper school spirit, one and all."

Released at last, they burst, clang-banging the folding seats, as they spill out on a wave of forbidden voices, and I with them, into the hall.

"Wherezya pass?" says the elevator man gloomily. "Gotcher elevator pass?"

"I'm a teacher," I say sheepishly, as if caught in a lie.

For only teachers, and students with proof of a serious disability, may ride in the elevators. Looking young has certain disadvantages here; if I were a man, I'd grow a mustache.

This morning, the students swarming on the street in front of the entrance parted to let me pass—the girls, their faces either pale or masked with makeup; the boys eyeing me exaggeratedly: "Hey eeahhowzabidis! Gedaloadadis—whee-uh!" the two-note whistle of insolent admiration following me inside.

(Or better still—a beard.)

It seems to me kids were different when I was in high school. But the smell in the lobby was the same unmistakable school smell—chalk dust? paper filings? musty metal? rotting wood?

I joined the other teachers on line at the time clock, and gratefully found my card. I was expected: Someone had put my number on it—#91. I punched the time on my card and stuck it into the IN rack. I was *in*.

But when I had written my name on the blackboard in my room, for a moment I had the strange feeling that it wasn't spelled right. It looked unfamiliar—white and drowning in that hard black sea. . . .

I am writing this during my lunch period, because I need to reach towards the outside world of sanity, because I am overwhelmed by the sheer weight of the clerical work still to be done, and because at this hour of the morning normal ladies are still sleeping.

We have to punch—

Sept. 7

Dear Ellen,

I had begun a letter to you this morning but was interrupted, and now I can't find it in the flood of papers in which I am drowning.

Perhaps it's just as well; I couldn't possibly succeed in describing this place to you: the homeroom, the Assembly, the chaos of clerical work, the kids—whom I had come to guide and "gladly teche."

I've been here less than a day, and already I'm in hot water. A boy had "incurred a fall" in class, and I failed to report it on the proper form. Another left the room without a pass and is suspected of stealing a wallet from a locker which wasn't locked because I had neglected to inspect it. This was Joe Ferone, *the* problem-boy of Calvin Coolidge, who earlier, in homeroom, had been flagrantly rude to me, and insolent, and contemptuous.

While I was writing you the other letter (Where can it be? Among the Circulars? Directives? Faculty Mimeos? Department Notices? In the right-hand desk drawer? Left-hand? In my wastebasket, perhaps), during what was presumably my lunch period, Admiral Ass (a Mr. McHabe, who signs himself Adm. Asst.) appeared in my room with Joe Ferone.

"This boy is on probation," he said. "Did he show up in homeroom this morning"

"Yes," I said.

"Any trouble?" the Admiral asked.

There we stood, the three of us, taking each other's measure. Ferone was watching me through narrowed eyes.

"No. No trouble," I said.

I am writing this during my free . . . oops! unassigned period, at the end of my first day of teaching. So far, I have taught nothing—but I have learned a great deal. To wit:

We have to punch a time clock and abide by the Rules.

We must make sure our students likewise abide, and that they sign the time sheet whenever they leave or reenter a room.

We have keys but no locks (except in lavatories), blackboards but no chalk, students but no seats, teachers but no time to teach.

The library is closed to the students.

Yet I'm told that Calvin Coolidge is not unique; it's as average as a large metropolitan high school can be. There are many schools worse than this (the official phrase is "problem-area schools for the lower socio-economic groups") and a few better ones. Kids with an aptitude in a trade can go to vocational high schools; kids with outstanding talents in math, science, drama, dance, music, or art can attend special high schools which require entrance tests or auditions; kids with emotional problems or difficulties in learning are sent to the "600 schools." But the great majority, the ordinary kids, find themselves in Calvin Coolidge or its reasonable facsimile. And so do the teachers.

Do you remember Rhoda, who left Lyons Hall before graduation? She is now writing advertising copy for a cosmetics firm at three times my salary. I often think of her. And of Mattie, who was in graduate school with me, and who is teaching at Willowdale Academy, holding seminars on James Joyce under the philosophic maples. And I think of you, in a far away town, walking serene in daylight from Monday to Friday, and I think I must be crazy to stay on here. And yet—there is a certain phrase we have, a kind of in-joke: "Let it be a challenge."

There goes the bell. Or is it only the warning signal? The bells have gone berserk. I now go to check the PM attendance in my homeroom— Admiral Ass says it prevents escapes.

Love, *Syl*

P. S. Did you know that according to the Board of Education's estimate it would cost the city $8 million to reduce the size of classes "by a single child" throughout the city?

Sept. 25

Dear Ellen,

It's FTG (Friday Thank God), which means I need not set the alarm for 6:30 tomorrow morning; I can wash a blouse, think a thought, write a letter.

Congratulations on the baby's new tooth. Soon there is bound to be another tooth and another and another, and before you know it, little Suzie will start going to school, and her troubles will just begin. Though I hope that by the time she gets into the public high school system, things will be different. At least, they keep *promising* that things will be different. I'm told that since the recent strike threats, negotiations with the United Federation of Teachers, and greater public interest, we are enjoying "improved conditions." But in the two weeks that I've been here, conditions seem greatly unimproved.

You ask what I am teaching. Hard to say. Professor Winters advised teaching "not the subject but the whole child." The English Syllabus urges "individualization and enrichment"—which means giving individual attention to each student to bring out the best in him and enlarge his scope beyond the prescribed work. Bester says to "motivate and distribute" books—that is, to get students ready and eager to read. All this is easier said than done. In fact, all this is plain impossible.

Many of our kids—though physically mature—can't read beyond 4th or 5th grade level. Their background consists of the simplest comics and thrillers. They've been exposed to some ten years of schooling, yet they don't know what a sentence is.

The books we are required to teach frequently have nothing to do with anything except the fact that they have always been taught, or that there is an oversupply of them, or that some committee or other was asked to come up with some titles.

For example: I've distributed Shakespeare's *Julius Caesar* to my 5th term class of "slow non-readers." (Question: How would "fast non-readers" read?) This is in lieu of *The Mill on the Floss*. I am supposed to teach *Romeo and Juliet* OR *A Tale of Two Cities* (strange bedfellows!) to my "low-normal" class, and *Essays Old and New* to my "special-slows." So far, however, I've been unable to give out any books because of problems having to do with Purloined Book Receipts, Book Labels without Glue, Inaccurate Inventory of Book Room, and Traffic Conditions on the Stairs.

I have let it be a challenge to me: I've been trying to teach without books. There was one heady moment when I was able to excite the class by an idea: I had put on the blackboard Browning's "A man's reach should exceed his grasp, or what's a heaven for?" and we got involved in a spirited discussion of aspiration vs. reality. Is it wise, I asked, to aim higher than one's capacity? Does it not doom one to failure? No, no, some said, that's ambition and progress! No, no, others cried, that's frustration and defeat! What about hope? What about despair?—You've got to be practical!—You've got to have a dream! They said this in their own words, you understand, startled into discovery. To the young, clichés seem freshly minted. Hitch your wagon to a star! Shoemaker, stick to your last! And when the dismissal bell rang, they paid me the highest compliment: they groaned! They crowded in the doorway, chirping like agitated sparrows, pecking at the seeds I had strewn—when who should materialize but Admiral Ass.

"What is the meaning of this noise?"

"It's the sound of thinking, Mr. McHabe," I said.

In my letter-box that afternoon was a note from him, with copies to my principal and chairman (and—who knows?—perhaps a sealed indictment dispatched to the Board?) which read (sic):

"I have observed that in your class the class entering your room is held up because the pupils exiting from your room are exiting in a disorganized fashion, blocking the doorway unnecessarily and *talking*. An orderly flow of traffic is the responsibility of the teacher whose class is exiting from the room."

The cardinal sin, strange as it may seem in an institution of learning, is talking. There are others, of course—sins, I mean, and I seem to have committed a good number. Yesterday I was playing my record of Gielgud reading Shakespeare. I had brought my own phonograph to school (no one could find the Requisition Forms for "Audio-Visual Aids"—that's the name for the school record player) and I had succeeded, I thought, in establishing a mood. I mean, I got them to be quiet, when—enter Admiral Ass, in full regalia, epaulettes quivering with indignation. He snapped his fingers for me to stop the phonograph, waited for the turntable to stop turning, and pronounced:

"There will be a series of three bells rung three times indicating Emergency Shelter Drill. Playing records does not encourage the orderly evacuation of the class."

I mention McHabe because he has crystallized into The Enemy.

But there are other difficulties. There are floaters floating in during class (these are peripatetic, or unanchored teachers) to rummage through my desk drawers for a forgotten Delaney Book. (I have no idea why it's called that. Perhaps because it was invented by a Mr. Delaney. It's a seating-plan book, with cards with kids' names stuck into slots.)

There are questionnaires to be filled out in the middle of a lesson, such as: "Are there any defective electrical outlets in your home?"

There is money to be collected for publications, organizations, milk, G.O. (the General Organization), basketball tickets, and "Voluntary Contributions to the Custodial Staff." The latter is some kind of tacit appeasement of Mr. Grayson, who lives in the basement, if he exists at all; he is the mystery man of Calvin Coolidge.

There is the drilling on the street below that makes the windows vibrate; the Orchestra tuning up down the hall; the campaigners (this is the election season) bursting into the room to blazon on my sole blackboard in curlicued yellow chalk:

> HARRY KAGAN WINS RESPECT
> IF YOU WILL HIM FOR PRES. ELECT!

and

> GLORIA EHRLICH IS PRETTY AND NICE
> VOTE FOR GLORIA FOR VICE!

And the shelter area drills, which usually come at the most interesting point in the lesson. Bells clanging frantically, we all spill out into the gym, where we stand silent and safe between parallel bars, careful not to lean on horses, excused, for the moment, from destruction.

Sometimes the lesson is interrupted by life: the girl who, during grammar drill, rushed out of the room to look for her lost $8.70 for the gas and electric bill, crying: "My mother will kill me, for sure!" And for sure, she might. The boy who apologized for not doing his homework because he had to go to get married. "I got this girl into trouble all right, and we're Catholics, but the thing is, I don't *like* her."

Chaos, waste, cries for help—strident, yet unheard. Or am I romanticizing? That's what Paul says; he only shrugs and makes up funny verses about everyone. That's Paul Barringer—a writer who teaches English on one foot, as it were, just waiting to be published. He's very attractive: a tan crew cut; a white smile with lots of teeth; one eyebrow higher than the other. All the girls are in love with him.

There are a few good, hard-working, patient people like Bea—a childless widow—"Mother Schachter and her cherubs," as the kids say, who manage to teach against insuperable odds; a few brilliantly endowed teachers who——unknown and unsung—work their magic in the classroom; a few who truly love young people. The rest, it seems to me, have either given up, or are taking it out on the kids. "Those who can, do; those who can't, teach." Like most sayings, this is only half true. Those who can, teach; those who can't—the bitter, the misguided, the failures from other fields—find in the school system an excuse or a refuge.

There is Mary Lewis, bowed and cowed, who labors through the halls as overloaded as a pack mule, thriving on discomfort and overwork, compulsively following all directions from supervisors, a willing martyr to the system. She's an old-timer who parses sentences and gives out zeros to kids who chew gum.

There is Henrietta Pastorfield, a hearty spinster who is "married to the school," who woos the kids by entertaining them, convinced that lessons must be fun, knowledge sugar-coated, and that teacher should be pal.

There is Fred Loomis, a math teacher stuck with two out-of-license English classes, who hates kids with a pure and simple hatred. "At the age of 15," he said to me, "they should all be kicked out of school and the girls sterilized so they don't produce others like themselves." These were his words. And he comes in contact with some 200 children a day.

The school nurse, Frances Egan, wears white space shoes and is mad for nutrition; Mrs. Wolf, the librarian, cannot bear to see a book removed from its shelf; and Miss Ella Friedenberg, an ambitious typing teacher promoted to Guidance Counselor, swoops upon the kids and impales them with questions about masturbation. She has evolved a PPP (Pupil Personality Profile) into which she fits each youngster, branding him with pseudo-Freudian phrases. She has most of the teachers bamboozled, and some of the kids terrorized.

My other colleagues I know just by sight: Desk Despots, Blackboard Barons, Classroom Caesars and Lords of the Loose-Leaf, Paul calls them. He has the gift of words. Lyrics are his forte; he composed an amusing song about our principal: "Hark, hark, the Clarke/ At heaven's gate . . . something—something," I forget. He wrote a verse about me too: rhymed me with "14 carat." Very attractive man.

McHabe, of course, is the kind of petty tyrant who flourishes best in the school system, the army, or a totalitarian state. To me he personifies all that is picayune, mean and degrading to the human spirit. I've had a head-on clash with him over one of my boys, Joe Ferone, whom he had accused of theft—unjustifiably, as it turned out; and he has alluded darkly to the danger of my getting a U (Unsatisfactory) end-term rating.

I don't know why I am championing Ferone, who is the most difficult discipline problem in the school, except, perhaps, that I dimly sense in him a rebelliousness, like mine, against the same things. When he is in school, which isn't often, he is rude and contemptuous; hands in pockets, toothpick in mouth, rocking insolently on his heels, he seems to be watching me for some sign.

Most of the time, I am still struggling to establish communication. It is difficult, and I don't know whom to turn to. Dr. Clarke? I don't think he is aware of anything that is going on in his school. All I know about him is that he has a carpet in his office and a private john on the fourth floor landing. Most of the time he secludes himself in one or the other; when he does emerge, he is fond of explaining that education is derived from "e duco," or leading *out* of. He is also partial to such paired pearls as: *aims and goals; guide and inspire; help and encourage*; and *new horizons and broader vistas*; they drop from him like so many cultured cuff links.

And Dr. Bester, my immediate supervisor, Chairman of the English Department, I can't figure out at all. He is a dour, desiccated little man, remote and prissy. Like most chairmen, he teaches only one class of Seniors; the most experienced teachers are frequently promoted right out of the classroom! Kids respect him; teachers dislike him—possibly because he is given to popping up, unexpectedly, to observe them. "The ghost walks" is the grapevine signal for his visits. Bea told me he started out as a great teacher, but he's been soured by the trivia-in-triplicate which his administrative duties impose. I hope he doesn't come to observe me until I get my bearings. I'm still floundering, particularly in my SS class of "reluctant learners." (Under-achievers, non-academic-minded, slow, disadvantaged, sub-paced, non-college-oriented, under-privileged, non-linguistic, intellectually deprived, and laggers—so far, I've counted more than ten different euphemisms for "dumb kids"!)

But I am busiest outside of my teaching classes. Do you know any other business or profession where highly-skilled specialists are required to tally numbers, alphabetize cards, put notices into mailboxes, and patrol the lunchroom?

What a long letter this has turned into! I've quite lost touch with the mainstream, you see, isolated in 304, while bells ring, students come and go, and my wastebasket runneth over.

Write, write! And tell me of the even tenor of your days. If things get too rough here, I might ask you to move over.

Love, *Syl*

P. S. Did you know that in New York City high school teachers devote approximately 100 hours a year to homeroom chores? This makes a grand total of over 500,000 hours that they spend on clerical work. That's official school time only; the number of extracurricular hours spent on lesson plans, records, marking papers, and so on is not estimated.

S.

Oct. 2

Dear Ellen,

Another FTG; another week. Time collapses and expands like an erratic accordion, and your letters bring order, sanity and remembrance of things past to my disheveled present. I envy you your leisure to browse and putter and to enjoy your family in peaceful suburbia. As for me—as for me . . .

The cold war between the Admiral and me is getting warmer; tension between Ferone and me is getting tenser; Miss Finch, the school clerk, floods me with papers from the giant maw of her mimeograph machine, and I'm not at all sure that I will last in the school system.

In my homeroom, I'm lucky if I can get through the D's in taking attendance. Admiral Ass lurks outside in the hall, ready to pounce at the first sign of mutiny. Or perhaps he watches through a periscope from his office.

In my subject classes, we are still juggling books. *Essays Old and New* was changed by the powers that be to *The Odyssey* and *Myths and Their Meaning.* I have only two weeks in which to teach my SS class the mythology of the race and Homer's great epic, since other teachers are waiting for these books, since they must be read before the Midterm Exams, since questions on them will appear on the Midterms, and since the Midterms must be scheduled before Thanksgiving to enable the teachers to mark them during the holidays.

I keep looking for clues in whatever the kids say or write. I've even installed a Suggestion Box in my room, in the hope that they will communicate their feelings freely and eventually will learn to trust me.

So far, most of them are still a field of faces, rippling with every wind, but a few are beginning to emerge.

There is Lou Martin, the class comedian, whose forte is facial expressions. No one can look more crestfallen over unprepared homework: hand clasped to brow, knees buckling, shoulders sagging with remorse, he is a penitent to end all penitents. No one can look more thirsty when asking for a pass: tongue hanging out, eyes rolling, a death-rattle in the throat, he can barely make it to the water fountain. No one can look more horrified at a wrong answer issuing from his own traitor lips; or more humble; or more bewildered; or more indignant. I know it's not in the syllabus, but I'm afraid I encourage him by laughing.

I'm beginning to learn some of their names and to understand some of their problems. I even think I can help them—if they would let me. But I am still the Alien and the Foe; I have not passed the test, whatever it is.

I'm a foe to Eddie Williams because my skin is white; to Joe Ferone because I am a teacher; to Carrie Paine because I am attractive.

Eddie uses the grievance of his color to browbeat the world.

Joe is flunking every subject, though he is very bright. He has become a bone of contention between McHabe and me because I believed in his innocence in the stolen wallet incident. I trust him, and he—he keeps watching me, ready to spring at the first false move I make.

Carrie is a sullen, cruelly homely girl, hiding and hating behind a wall of fat.

Harry Kagan is a politician and apple-polisher. He is running for G.O. president, and I'm afraid he'll be elected.

Linda Rosen is an over-ripe under-achiever, bursting with hormones.

And pretty Alice Blake, pale with love, lost in a dream of True Romances, is vulnerable and committed as one can be only at 16. She feels deeply, I'm sure, but can translate her feelings only into the cheap clichés she's been brought up on.

Then there is Rusty, the woman-hater.

And a quiet, defeated-looking Puerto Rican boy, whose name I can't even remember.

These children have been nourished on sorry scraps, on shabby facsimiles, and there is no one—not at home, not in school—who has not short-changed them.

You know, I've just realized there is not even a name for them in the English language. "Teen-agers," "Youngsters," "Students," "Kids," "Young adults," "Children"—these are inappropriate, offensive, stilted, patronizing or inaccurate. On paper they are our "Pupil-load"; on lecture platform they are our "Youngsters"—but what is their proper name?

The frightening thing is their unquestioning acceptance of whatever is taught to them by anyone in front of the room. This has nothing to do with rebellion against authority; they rebel, all right, and loudly. But it doesn't occur to them to think.

There is a premium on conformity, and on silence. Enthusiasm is frowned upon, since it is likely to be noisy. The Admiral had caught a few kids who came to school before class, eager to practice on the typewriters. He issued a manifesto forbidding any students in the building before 8:20 or after 3:00—outside of school hours, students are "unauthorized." They are not allowed to remain in a classroom unsupervised by a teacher. They are not allowed to linger in the corridors. They are not allowed to speak without raising a hand. They are not allowed to feel too strongly or to laugh too loudly.

Yesterday, for example, we were discussing "The fault, dear Brutus, lies not in our stars/ But in ourselves that we are underlings." I had been trying to relate *Julius Caesar* to their own experiences. Is this true? I asked. Are we really masters of our fate? Is there such a thing as luck? A small boy in the first row, waving his hand frantically: "Oh, call on me, please, *please* call on me!" was propelled by the momentum of his exuberant arm smack out of his seat and fell to the floor. Wild laughter. Enter McHabe. That afternoon, in my letter-box, it had come to his attention that my "control of the class lacked control."

But I had made that little boy think. I started something in him that emerged as an idea. I got him excited by a concept. And that's a lot!

Sometimes, of course, I am misled by their eagerness. There's a girl who never takes her eyes off me. This morning, when I asked a question about Brutus, she flung out her hand, pleading to be recognized. When I called on her, she said: "You wearing contack lens?"

It's a good thing Bester wasn't there to observe me. Yet there's more to that man than meets the eye. I'm impressed by his masterly handling of what's known hereabouts as "a discipline problem." He had stepped into the Early Late Room (don't ask me to explain what it is, nor why I was there) and asked one of the boys for his program card. "Aw, go jump in the lake," said the boy. The class sucked in its breath. With icy courtesy, Bester asked the boy to repeat what he had said, please. The boy did. "What were the first two words?" Bester asked, exquisitely polite. "Aw go." "Would you say that again, please?" "Aw go." "What was it again?" "Aw go." "Would you mind repeating the next word?" "Jump." "Again, please?" "Jump." "Again?" "Jump." Do you know how absurd the word "jump" can begin to sound after a while, when spoken solemnly by a boy standing among his peers? The boy was licked, and he knew it; the snickering class knew it; Bester knew it; and as he left, he said, with the same impeccable courtesy: "I'll be glad to recommend you for a remedial speech class."

I wish I could learn his assurance. It's in my homeroom that I feel such a failure. They are still suspicious of me. They are still trying me out. One girl, shy and troubled, did reach out. She asked to see me after school last Monday. She was apparently afraid to go home. Unfortunately, it was the day of the Faculty Conference, which is sacrosanct; attendance is compulsory. Perhaps I could have helped her. She hasn't been in school since. Truant officer reports she has run away from home.

At the Conference (we're supposed to sit it out for one hour each month; anything less, I believe, is unlawful) I watched my brothers and sisters, resignation or indifference settled like fine dust upon them— except for a few nervous souls who kept stirring up the soup. As a new teacher, I understood the protocol: I was not to speak. I was, however, asked to write up the minutes. I took notes, which I must now type up, and I timed the meeting: 60 minutes to the second!

All our hours and minutes are accounted for, planned for, raced against. Preparations are already afoot for Open School Day and the Xmas Faculty Show, and there are strange portents in the air and on the bulletin board. Only this morning a cryptic notice appeared over the time clock: "Advanced Algebra will be offered next term until further notice." I don't know what it means, either; nor what "minimal standards and maximal goals" means—it's a problem of communication.

Communication. If I knew how to reach them, I might be able to teach them. I asked them to write for me what they had covered so far in their high school English, and what they hoped to achieve in my class. Their papers were a revelation: I saw how barren were the years they brought me; I saw how desperately they need me, or someone like me. There aren't enough of us. Yet—with all my eagerness to teach, teaching is the one thing Calvin Coolidge makes all but impossible.

To the outside world, of course, this job is a cinch: 9 to 3, five days a week, two months' summer vacation with pay, all legal holidays, prestige and respect. My mother, for example, has the pleasant notion that my day consists of nodding graciously to the rustle of starched curtsies and a chorus of respectful voices bidding me good morning.

It's so good to have *you* to write to!

Love, Syl

P. S. Did you know that in New York City there are more than 800 schools, over 86 high schools, and about one million pupils? And that out of every 100 children who start school, only 15 go on to receive a college diploma? For most, this is all the education they'll ever get.

S.

Evan Hunter
(1926–   )

Ever since Aristophanes' satire of Socrates in *The Clouds*, a Greek comedy of 423 B.C., the behavior of teachers has been a vulnerable subject for the critic's ire. Though not a satire (its criticisms are unveiled and humorless), *The Blackboard Jungle* reveals the guises assumed by less than masterful teachers in their attempts to outlast the classes they sit with. A vocational school for dropouts, North Manual Trades may not possess *all* the failed types who pose as teachers. Even suburban schools, protected by parental involvement and the motivations of the middle class, harbor teachers who are strikingly akin to North Manual's Slobberer, Slumberer, and Fumbler. Because large remedies may wait on humble insights, it is good for the inexperienced teacher to learn early the subterfuges resorted to by some of his older colleagues. As Hunter shows, it is one attainment to succeed in a ruse, quite another to fumble toward genuine growth. What are the signs of those teachers brave enough to fumble openly, who shun the illusions of well-being that anyone past puberty can conjure?

A prolific writer, Evan Hunter has published a number of works since the appearance of *The Blackboard Jungle* in 1954, among them *Strangers When We Meet* (1958), *Mothers and Daughters* (1961), *Last Summer* (1968), and *Fathers and Sons* (1969).

THE PEDAGOGUES
OF NORTH MANUAL TRADES

The executive ax began falling the day before Armistice Day, and it dropped finally just before the Thanksgiving vacation. Rick had no idea the ax would fall, nor did he even know it was poised over his head. He considered Stanley's first visit to his classroom a part of normal procedure. He did not know it was the whetting of the ax-blade.

The Department Chairman arrived at Room 206 just before the fifth period began. He entered the room smiling, walked to Rick's desk and said, "Hope you don't mind a little observation, Dadier?"

"Why . . . why not at all," Rick answered, wishing at the same time that Stanley had not chosen this particular class to observe. But then, Stanley undoubtedly knew all about Juan Garza, knew that 55—206 was a class full of disciples, and had purposely chosen it.

"I'll just sit at the back of the room," he said, his lips moving below his now-full mustache. He was dressed impeccably, as always. His not-quite-blond hair was brushed neatly, and his grey eyes had been ordered to attention by a strict drillmaster. There was no doubt that he was the chairman of the English Department. "I'll be very quiet," he added, smiling, assuming the role of a mildly interested observer, giving the lie to his regal bearing and his cold eyes. He walked familiarly to the back of the room, took the last seat in the first row, crossed his legs after lifting the trouser to preserve its crease, and then opened a black notebook on the desk before him.

The class filed in, spotting Stanley instantly, and behaving like choir boys before the Christmas Mass. There'd be no trouble today, Rick knew. It was one thing to badger a teacher, but not when it led to a knockdown-dragout with the Department Chairman. No one liked sitting in the English office under the cold stare of that Stan man.

The cold stare showed no signs of heating up during the lesson. Rick gave it all he had, glad he'd prepared a good plan the night before, able for the first time to actually follow the plan because the kids kept their peace in Stanley's presence. He called primarily on his best students, throwing in a few of the duller kids to show Stanley he was impartial, but he steered away from Miller and West, not wanting to risk any entanglements while Stanley was observing.

At the end of the period, Stanley came to the desk and smiled briefly. "You might watch the distribution of your questions," he said, a bored expression in his eyes. "You seem to favor several students."

"Oh, do I?" Rick asked innocently, cursing Stanley for having seen through his scheme. "I'll watch that."

"Yes, do." He paused and consulted his notes. "Ever call on Morales?"

"Yes," Rick said, a little flustered now. "Yes, I do."

"Nice boy."

"Yes."

"Ever call on Rodriguez?"

"Why, certainly. Yes. Yes, I do."

"Like him?"

Rick shrugged and smiled. "He's all right. Not too bright, but not a bad kid."

"Uh-huh. What about Miller? Notice you didn't call on him once."

"Didn't I? No, I guess I didn't. Oh, he's quite active in the class usually." Rick smiled a fraternal smile. "Oh yes, quite active," hoping Stanley would understand what he meant. Stanley did not return the smile.

"I'll have a report typed up for your guidance, Dadier. I may drop in again sometime."

"Please do," Rick answered politely.

Stanley did not drop in the next day because the next day was Armistice Day and there were no teachers or students present at the high school. But he did drop in on November 12th, this time during Rick's eighth-period class. He took his seat at the back of the room, observed Rick while he taught, made several notes, and then left when the bell rang, not stopping to chat with Rick this time.

Nor was that the last visit. Stanley began stopping by frequently, sometimes remaining for the full period, and sometimes visiting for ten or fifteen minute stretches, and then departing silently.

In the beginning, Rick resented the intrusions. He would watch Stanley scribbling at the back of the room, and he wondered what Stanley was writing, and he felt something like a bug on the microscope slide of a noted entomologist. Why all the secrecy? What the hell was this, the Gestapo?

He began to realize, after a while, that Stanley's visits were probably just what he needed, and he found himself looking forward to the un-announced appearance of the Department Chairman. With painful honesty, he admitted to himself that his students were not entirely to blame for the lack of teaching that went on in his classes. He was not prepared to cope with them, and unless someone told him what he was doing wrong, he'd probably never be prepared to cope with them. Per-haps Stanley's visits were the answer to his problem. Perhaps Stanley would eventually make known the results of his observations, would say, "See here, Dadier, this and this is your trouble. Such and such is fine, but you've got to concentrate more on that and that."

Rick would have appreciated that immensely, and so he was quite pleased with the sudden attention Stanley devoted to him. For the first time in his educational career, he honestly felt that someone was interested in what he did, and in whether or not he was doing it correctly. So where he had made lesson plans carefully before, he now devoted more time to them, enlarged on them, outlined his lessons in the minutest detail. And when Stanley asked to see his plan during one of his visits, Rick felt amply rewarded, even though Stanley made no comment on the outline.

He was grateful, too, for the obedience of his classes whenever Stanley was present. One of his greatest problems had been discipline. With these kids, it was almost impossible to get a word in edgewise and —especially in the beginning—his teaching efforts usually disintegrated into a contest to determine who could shout the loudest. He had never fully licked the discipline problem, and he doubted if he ever would. He had succeeded, though, in forcing some sort of obedience out of the kids, usually by threats of homework or tests or after-school confinement, or visits from parents. There were times when no threat would work, times when the kids were just feeling bastardly and presented a solid, unyielding front that could not be cracked no matter how much he ranted or raved. These times were not infrequent. They were a part of vocational school teaching, a part acknowledged by any teacher who'd ever served in the system.

There were formulas for establishing discipline, Rick learned, and one of these formulas had been succinctly stated by Captain Schaefer during one of his periodic visits to the lunchroom.

"Clobber the bastards," he'd said. "It's the only thing that works. What do you think happens at home when they open their yaps? Pow, right on the noggin. That's the only language they understand."

Perhaps they understood that language in Captain Schaefer's domain, a domain devoted to the physical, a domain of sweating, athletic bodies, a man's world of physical strength. Perhaps they accepted a cuff on the mouth from a man in a tee shirt, a man who was sweating just as they were, a man who was king of this writhing land of bodies unadorned. Perhaps so.

But Rick could not picture Josh Edwards clobbering a kid. Nor could he, in all honesty, picture himself doing that. The urge to do so was always present, of course. You can push someone just so far, and when he finds he can't strike back verbally his first instinct is to inflict some sort of damage, and his only remaining weapons are physical. Especially when these kids did not seem to be kids. The second-termers, yes. They were kids. He could look upon them as kids, and he could feel the superiority of adulthood. There was a difference between his body and their bodies, and a difference between the basic mechanism of his mind and their minds.

Not so with the fifth-termers and certainly not so with the seventh-termers. Perhaps they weren't old enough to vote, and perhaps some of them weren't old enough to be drafted. But their bodies were mature, strong bodies, and they thought—in their own twisted manner—the way adults think, and it was extremely difficult to consider them "kids" when a good many of them outreached you, and outweighed you, and sometimes (only sometimes) outthought you.

So the temptation to clobber was always there, and it was sometimes more difficult not to strike than it would have been *to* strike, and the consequences be damned. Because, despite any edicts about corporal punishment, there were a good many vocational school kids who got clobbered every day, and when the heavy hand of someone like Captain Max Schaefer clobbers, the clobberee knows he's been clobbered, but good.

Clobbering, then, was one accepted means of establishing discipline in a trade school.

Another method was Slobbering, and this worked most efficiently when a female teacher—scarce as such creatures were—used it.

The Slobbering method appealed to the sympathy of the boys, and it took various forms. The most common form (and this is why the method worked best when employed by females) was the one which turned on a touched-to-the-quick expression, and then dolefully complained about the ingratitude of the class.

"After all I've done for you," the Slobberer whined. "You give me this treatment."

When a female used this tactic, unattractive though she might be, there was usually something inside the boys which responded. Perhaps it was their innate chivalry, their desire to come to the rescue of the damsel in distress. Whatever it was, in the hands of a good female Slobberer (and Martha Riley was one of the best at Manual Trades, if not *the* best in the city of New York) an assorted collection of hoodlums could be made to feel like heels, and would indeed hold a respectful silence throughout the remainder of the period, showing their gratitude for all the teacher had done for them, which was usually nothing.

A male Slobberer performed a variation on the theme, and the variations were multiple and many-faceted. The most common form of male Slobbering was the one which appealed to the boys' sense of fraternal spirit. Treating them all like Alpha Beta Tau boys, the male Slobberer would say, "Come on, fellows, give me a break. I'm just a poor slob trying to do a job, that's all."

And the fellows, knowing all about poor slobs trying to do jobs, might or might not respond to the teacher's plea, depending upon how they felt about the proletariat on that particular day.

The Veteran Hook was another variation on the male Slobberer's pitch. The Veteran Hook was not a direct plea; in fact, its effectiveness lay primarily in its quality for understatement. It entailed a dramatic reconstruction of several isolated war experiences, with a few descriptions of the Germans, Italians, or Japanese who had met death at the hands of the male Slobberer. The more dead enemies, the better. The boys loved tales of bashed skulls. But this was not where the Slobbering ended. In fact, had it ended here, it would have accomplished nothing. The Slobberer then went on to tell about the Purple Heart he received, or the steel plate he carried in his head, or the cork leg beneath his trouser, or the way his balls were shot off—none of which things ever happened to him. He then went on to describe the rough time he had rehabilitating, and the rough time he had in college, and the rough time he had finding a teaching job. And now, now that he *is* teaching, he's grateful to the United States and the wonderful people who made all this possible, and he only hoped he could keep his job and continue to teach all these swell kids who helped make all this possible.

And the kids, weaned on the hero legend, unable to tell a cork leg from a cork-tipped cigarette, usually accepted this type of Slobbering and made it a little easier for the teacher to keep this job he fought for, provided they did not kick his leg out from under him some day to see if it really was cork.

Another type of male Slobbering, akin to the fraternal pitch, but different in a degree, was the type Halloran used. Halloran, as he exhibited on the first day of school while introducing the assorted teachers to the assorted students, was "just one of the boys." He'd never been to college. He fulfilled the Board's requirements for becoming a shop teacher in a trade school by:

1) Graduating from Junior High School, and having nine years of trade experience. Or . . .
2) Graduating from Senior High School, and having seven years of trade experience. Or . . .
3) Graduating from a technical or vocational high school, and having five years of trade experience.

He was, as any fool could plainly see, just one of the boys. And so he spoke like the boys, and he joked like the boys, and he even borrowed from the Clobbering approach and sometimes batted the boys around, but all the time just being one of the boys and basing his Slobbering technique upon that single peg.

Oh, the ways of the Slobbering technique were many and varied, and Rick heard about all of them, but he somehow felt all of them were a little degrading, like sucking up to an officer to get a weekend liberty, except that these kids weren't even officers, and there were a good many of them.

If you didn't choose to Clobber or Slobber, you could Slumber. Slumbering, as apart from Slobbering, was an art in itself, and Solly Klein was one of its most ardent practitioners. The Slumberer treated discipline as a non-existent problem. For him, indeed, the problem *was* a non-existent one. He chose to ignore it. He taught, and if no one heard what he was teaching, it was just tough. He taught like a man talking in his sleep. He rattled on and on, and the noises and sounds of the outside world meant nothing to him. If, as occasionally happened, the noises broke into his slumber, the Slumberer would simply step outside the room for a moment, waiting for the class to knock itself out, and keeping an eye open for the Boss at the same time. The Slumberer's philosophy was a simple one: *Let the bastards kill themselves. So long as I'm not hurt.*

So if a fist-fight started in the Slumberer's classroom, the Slumberer allowed the two protagonists to beat themselves silly while he stood by and watched. He then stepped over the pool of blood on the floor and went on with his lesson, not caring if anyone was listening, and having long since realized that no one was listening anyway. No one ever failed a course the Slumberer taught. There were a lot of Slumberers in the New York City system.

The Rumbler was a fellow exactly like the Slumberer, except for one thing. The Slumberer knew there was no discipline in his classes, but he slept soundly at night as well as during the day. The Rumbler, on the other hand, did exactly what the Slumberer did all day long, but then he went home and complained to his wife about the lack of discipline, or he complained to his Department Chairman, or even to the principal. Or when no one else was around to listen, he would rumble silently to himself, cursing everyone responsible, including God, and especially cursing people like the Slumberers who had allowed such a shocking disciplinary problem to develop.

The Fumbler, and Rick classified himself in this broad group of teachers, simply didn't know what the hell to do. The Fumbler kept trying. He tried this way, and he tried that way, and he hoped that some day he would hit upon the miraculous cure-all for the disciplinary problem. Most Fumblers eventually became proponents of one of the other methods of establishing discipline. Some Fumblers really did lick the problem eventually, but they never divulged their secrets—learned after many years of batting their heads against the wall—to the lesser mortals who shared the teaching profession.

So Rick fumbled, and he was immensely grateful for Stanley's visits because there was no disciplinary problems whenever Stanley was present. On those occasions, he was allowed to teach, and he discovered then that there was something other than a lack of discipline to fight at North Manual Trades. The discovery left him feeling a bit defeated, like a man who's purchased an AC television set only to discover that his apartment is wired for DC.

He discovered that the kids simply did not care.

It was as basic as that. They did not want to learn.

He did not know what had planted this attitude inside them, but he suspected it was the vocational school system itself. He was surprised to find out that the kids *knew* they were in a bad school. He'd mentioned something in class about North Manual Trades being a damned fine trade school, and the kids had all but laughed at him. He wasn't kidding them one bit. They knew the school was lousy, and they knew they were here because they'd flunk out of an academic high school within a week. What's more, they knew that *most* vocational high schools were lousy, and they seemed to feel that the lousier the school was, the more desirable it was.

Now that was a strange manner of thinking, Rick felt, and he wondered who was to blame for it. Certainly not the guidance counselors who recommended vocational high schools to students. Certainly not them. They explained patiently and fully that perhaps a vocational school, since you *are* so good in shop, and since your academic grades haven't been so good lately, might be best for you after all. The picture painted *was* a pleasant one, there was no denying that. A school where someone could learn a bread-and-butter trade. A school like that, imagine! The answer to the working-man's prayer. Are there really schools like that? Golly!

But somehow, the secret had leaked, or maybe it just leaked after the kid was in the middle of a trade school for a few days. The picture wasn't as pretty as it had been painted. In fact, the canvas had been slashed with a knife. And if a kid really wanted to learn a trade, see how long he kept his ideals when he was surrounded by other kids who'd have liked to blow up every school in the city.

And the worst part was that when you were in the middle of a bad school, when you were surrounded by kids who were acknowledged problem students, you began to feel bad yourself. The man who goes to a whore house because he likes the magazines in the waiting room is not considered a bibliophile. He's spotted coming out of the red-lanterned doorway, and he's considered a man who has just had a piece of tail. *The Saturday Evening Post* doesn't enter into the observation at all.

So a kid who goes to a vocational school, even if he's going there to learn a trade, is not considered a hard-working, earnest student. He's considered a kid who didn't fit anywhere else in the educational system.

He's considered that, and he senses it, and if he's got the name, he'll have the game, and so he becomes part of the waste product, and he considers the school itself a garbage can.

There are kids who survive, kids who learn trades, kids who maintain their individual goals despite the corrupting stench that surrounds them. Those kids are few and far between.

Those kids were not the problems. Rick had a few of those kids in each of his classes, kids who seemed to want him to say something, who were annoyed when his lesson was interrupted, who did their homework whenever it was assigned, who turned in book reports, who were excellent in the shops of their choice, who wanted to learn, who were eager to learn, and who somehow managed to learn in spite of the opposition.

Those kids were the easy ones to reach. They wanted to be reached, they longed to be reached. It was the others. Those who didn't care, those who were content to wallow in the filth, those who not only didn't want to learn but consciously wanted *not* to learn.

It was those he could not reach, and it was those he tried desperately to reach. It was almost fantastic, and he doubted if he could have explained his problem to anyone but Anne. It was like a man standing on a street corner giving out fifty-dollar bills, and having a tough time finding takers. Why wouldn't they take what he had to give them? He did have something to give them, so much to give them if they would only accept it.

So he tried to reach them, and he tried harder when Stanley was present because he did not have to fight the shouting and the ranting then. Time and again, he found himself remembering Solly Klein's garbage can metaphor, and more and more he began to see himself as the fellow with the fat behind who sat on the lid of the can. He fought against thinking that way because he knew the thought preceded the action, and the instant he conceded the kids were filth and he was a garbage man, he would stop trying to reach them, and he didn't want that to happen.

There were times when he wanted to shout, "Can't you see that I'm trying to help you? Can't you see that?"

There were times when they irritated him so much that he felt like chucking the whole goddamned mess and taking a job as a shoe clerk.

And there were times when he simply did not understand. Like the afternoon four of his seventh-term, eighth-period students stayed after school voluntarily, helping him erase the boards and stack the books away in the closet. They'd asked him if he had a car, said they'd be happy to fix anything that was wrong with it. When he'd told them he didn't own a car, they'd seemed disappointed. They'd chatted with him about their own jalopies, and he'd found himself talking about Anne, and the baby to come, talking to these kids the way he'd talk to anyone else, treating them like the adults he felt they were. When they left him, they all waved and said, "So long, Mr. Dadier. See you tomorrow."

He'd felt a strange inner peace when they'd gone, a feeling of having made some inroad, a feeling of having taken a first wavering step toward breaking through the shell that surrounded them. He'd liked the kids that afternoon, and he couldn't wait to get home and tell Anne about how nice they'd been.

And then the very next day, those same four kids had raised all kinds of hell during the eighth period, creating a havoc he'd never had before in that seventh-term class. The same four kids, the same kids who'd listened sympathetically while he told them about his expected baby, the same kids who'd offered to repair his car if he had one, those same four were the worst bastards imaginable, shouting, yelling, disobedient, not caring for anything he said, not listening to any of his threats.

He could not understand.

He simply could not understand. They didn't even seem like the same boys. What could you do when they ran hot and cold like that? Why even *try* to reach them? Why not throw in the towel and sit with your fat ass tight to the cover of the garbage can? Why not fool the system and fool the kids and fool yourself in the bargain? Why not collect a teacher's salary, and tuck the good vacations into your hip pocket, and all the while be an employee of the DSC?

And you could forget all about being a man in addition.

Oh, so what the hell? Are you supposed to keep banging your head against a stone wall?

Yes.

Are you supposed to try to teach kids who don't want to learn, who aren't interested in learning at all?

Yes.

All right, how? How?

And he had no answer.

He had no answer to why Stanley dropped in so often, either, but he enjoyed the visits, and so he did not probe too deeply into the reasons behind them. He kept teaching in his own fashion, hoping for some miraculous thing to happen, hoping the kids would suddenly realize he was the man with the fifty-dollar bills, hoping he'd break through if he simply kept at it, hoping he'd find the way.

James Herndon

(1926–   )

Set near San Francisco, "The Way It Spozed to Be" describes a junior high school that is typical of ghetto schools throughout the country. Here, a special desolation is felt in the chaos made routine by an institution. Superficially the work of the school gets done. Signs declaim. Bells sound. Classes convene. The payroll is met. Grades are recorded. And scholarship, whether parodied in the classroom or mocked on the auditorium stage by a rigged spelling award, is a mere niggling accessory among too many others. Acts of oppression and near-anarchy pose, respectively, as acts of discipline and creative freedom. But there is no real discipline; the children are intermittently held at bay by a faculty displaying more automatic resolve than courage.

James Herndon, born in Houston, grew up in southern California and later studied at the University of California in Berkeley. After a six-year tenure in Europe he settled with his family in San Francisco and now teaches in a public junior high school nearby. A book-length version of "The Way It Spozed to Be" was published under the same title in 1968.

THE WAY IT SPOZED TO BE

We had come out of the library from our first meeting with the principal, just the new teachers. I walked down the hall with a man named Skates whom I'd just met. It was mid-afternoon; the hall was dark. Suddenly, a trio of girls burst upon us as if they had been lying in ambush. One jumped ahead, pointing a finger at me.

You a new teacher?

Uh-huh. Yes.

What grade?

All of them, it looks like.

You teach the eighth?

Yes. Eighth too.

What you teach to the eighth grade?

English. Social studies. No, only English to the eighth grade.

The other two girls were hanging back, giggling. This girl crowded me, standing right next to me, looking straight up. I kept my head absurdly raised, feeling that if I bent down I'd graze the top of her head with my chin. I kept stepping back in order to get a look at her, and also to get away from her. She kept moving forward. She talked very loudly, smiling and grinning all the time but still almost shouting every word, having a fine time. It was okay with me.

What your name?

Herndon. Mr. Herndon.

Okay, Mr. Herndon, saying Hern-dawn, accent last syllable as I was to hear it spoken from then on by all students. Okay, Mr. Hern-don, you all right. I'm gonna be in your class. You better believe it! I'm in your class!

Well, fine, I said. Good. The two girls giggled in the background. Skates stood around, waiting. The girl ignored all of them; her business was with me.

It seemed to be over. I waved my hand at her and started to move off. She grabbed me by the arm.

I ain't done! Listen you Mr. Hern-don, my name Ruth. Ruth! You'll hear about me, don't worry about it! And what I say, Mr. Hern-don, you don't cause me no trouble and I don't cause you none! You hear?

That suits me, I said. Well, see you later, Ruth, girls. Skates and I started off.

You don't cause me none, and I don't cause you none! she yelled once more, and then the three of them took off, sprinting down the hall away from us, laughing like hell and yelling at the top of their lungs.

The first day, sure enough, there was Ruth in my eighth grade B class. She was absolutely the craziest-looking girl I've ever seen. Her hair was a mass of grease, matted down flat in some places, sticking straight out in several others. Her face was faintly Arabic, and she was rather handsome, and very black. Across her forehead a tremendous scar ran in a zigzag pattern from somewhere above the hairline on her left side across to her right eye, cutting into the eyebrow. The scar was dead white. Her entire figure seemed full of energy and power; she was, every time I saw her, completely alert and ready. She could have been any age from fifteen to twenty-five. I once tried to look up her age, but on every sheet, the space after *Age* was simply left blank. No one knew, and apparently no one knew why it was that no one knew.

True to her word, she didn't cause me any trouble that first day. She sat in the second desk in her row and all she did was grab all the pencils I handed out for that row and refuse to pass them back. The row burst into an uproar, demanding their pencils. The other rows, not having thought of this themselves, yelled derisively, That row ain't gittin' any!

Please pass the pencils back, Ruth, I said, reasonably but loudly, since I wanted to be heard. In the back of my mind I was still wondering how she got in my class, or at least how she knew she was going to be in my class.

Ruth jumped up immediately. Don't go to hollering at me! she yelled. You got *plenty* of pencils! You *spozed* to give 'em all out! They ain't your pencils! You *spozed* to give 'em out! I *need* these pencils!

The class yelled out, Whooooo-eee! Whooo-eee! They all made the same sound. Everyone stood up, laughing and yelling whoo-eee except for the kids in Ruth's row who all screamed, We ain't got no pyenculs!

I advanced on the row. Sit down! I shouted at everybody, I did have plenty of pencils, and I was going to give one to each kid in the row and forget about it. Let her keep the goddam pencils! But as I came toward the row, Ruth suddenly flung the handful of pencils out into the room, screeched No! and launched herself backwards into space. She actually flew through the air and landed on her back on the floor after crashing— some part of her body or head, I couldn't tell—against a desk and a kid or two. Later—as other girls from other classes landed on their heads with a bang—I came to call this the Plop Reflex but all I could think of at the time was getting this damn girl off the floor. As I moved, she jumped up, full of life, and fled for the door.

I'm trying to tell about my year teaching—learning to teach—in a junior high school near San Francisco. It was a Negro school, about 98 per cent Negro they told me downtown in the district office, as if to say not entirely Negro. Its principal, Mr. Grisson, announced candidly that he was new at his job, that he expected to make some mistakes himself and certainly would not be surprised if we made some too. The vice principal, Miss Bentley, likened us to the Army. The Army, she submitted, was an organization of people given certain tasks to perform. So was a school. The school's overall mission was the education of children. "So that learning may take place," Miss Bentley explained, "there must first be order."

Skates had another comparison to suggest. He called our students "The Tribe." Watch out today, he'd yell to me, coming down the hall for lunch, The Tribe's getting edgy! Or, Come into my room; The Tribe's holding a talent show, tap-dancing, strippers, the whole bit. It's a little gift from me, in appreciation of the fact that they didn't eat me up last week.

Still, that was later. On this first day all I knew about my students was that they were divided up into four different groups—a seventh-grade B class which I had twice, an eighth-grade B class, a ninth-grade D class, and a seventh-grade H class. Inquiring around the coffee tables in the teachers' rooms, I learned that the kids were all rated A (high) to H (low) and placed in classrooms together accordingly.

The first day, third period, I pretended to ignore 9D—making out cards and alphabetizing lists while trying to figure out what they might have in mind. They ignored me in turn, steadfastly and actually, roaming the room to try out new seats, applying cosmetics, and listening to transistors. So on the second day, I determined to pass out English books and spellers, to make everything official, and get down to work. The main work, I'd decided, was going to be composition, freely done and at length. The kids were bound to be interested in things they'd written themselves and we could later make some corrections, show up some common faults, use the books to find practical standards for usage and punctuation. The spellers I'd use for regularity; they weren't much good, being just lists of words and a number of rather silly things to do with those words.

Nine D scrambled around for the books and spellers, but then quickly withdrew as soon as it became clear there were enough to go around, which was only when every single person had one of each. Cosmetics came out, kids got up and began searching for new places to sit, a boy took out a transistor radio. I passed out paper; I began to talk about what we were going to do. Cosmetics and conversation continued—not loudly or aggressively, but just as if I weren't addressing them. I began to insist on everyone's attention. Finally a voice said, Teacher, why don't you let us alone?

That stopped it. Oooooh? they all went. The speaker was Verna, a tall, lanky girl, brown, lithe and strong-looking, plain-faced, kinky-haired, without make-up. The tone of the class implied apprehension and excitement; I was now going to throw Verna out. Actually I didn't give a damn. We had everyone's attention; they had momentarily lost. Verna had to say something. I expected an outburst, but instead she said, You should have made us get to work yesterday. All the other teachers made us get to work. If you want us to do work, why didn't you make us yesterday?

She stopped talking and immediately turned around, her back toward me. The class rallied to her support by taking up their conversations where they had left off. Now I was losing. I got ready to start insisting again, wondering what I was going to say if and when they started listening.

Then the door swung open, and a kid walked in, came over and handed me a slip, and found a seat near the back of the room. The class turned around and conversed in a different key. The subject was the new-comer, Maurice, particularly the fact that he had just gotten out of Juvenile Hall in time to make the second day of school. Teacher, Maurice just back from Juvi! shouted somebody, so I wouldn't have any trouble finding out. Maurice himself was subdued, having been warned, I suppose, to be nice or find himself right back in Juvi. But I was winning again; they were so curious about what I was going to say to Maurice that they had to recognize me. I passed a book and speller down the row to him. You spozed to report to the parole officer about Maurice, Teacher! How he do, if he do his work! Do he get in trouble or fighting! . . .

Well now, I said, actually this is not a class about Juvi, but about English. Whoooo-eee! That broke them up. But when they stopped laughing they were attentive enough. I began to talk about how English meant using the language; I was well into my speech about figuring out together what was relatively interesting to do and then figuring out how to do it—which was, naturally, crap since I already had the business of composition in mind—and they were just beginning to get bored (they knew it was crap too) seeing as how I wasn't going either to lecture Maurice about Crime Not Paying or to say anything humorous again, when Bang! Maurice and another boy, locked in each other's arms, fell over their desks and across the desks of the next row and lay there stretched out, struggling. Books, papers, and kids scattered. Whoooo-eee!

Hell! I got over there. Silence. Let go! I shouted, but nothing happened. Maurice was on top, the other kid across a desk, and as I got there Maurice loosed an arm and belted the other kid in the face. Cut it out! I grabbed Maurice. The kid on the bottom let go, but Maurice didn't. I tugged him rather gently. He belted the kid again. I got mad, grabbed Maurice under the arms, and heaved as hard as I could. He flew backwards over the row of desks and landed with a crash on the next row. He landed plenty hard; I imagine it hurt and, also, he must have thought it was all up with him, back to Juvi. He was frantic and mad. He jumped up and started for me. I stood there; he stopped and stood there. He glared. Everybody was frightened. No one in the class looked forward, suddenly, to what was going to happen, which was that Maurice was going to come for me and hit me or I him; the end would be the speedy return of Maurice to Juvenile Hall beaten up by me previously or not. It was inevitable.

We stood there quite a few seconds and then I nodded, turned, and walked swiftly back to my desk and sat down. I hoped I was implying a mutual cease-fire among equals. When I turned around toward the class, Maurice had likewise retreated and was sitting at his desk. We carefully didn't look right at each other, but still in the same general direction, so as not to be accused of avoiding anything either. Maurice had seen the issue—I'd say we saw it exactly alike. We both had something at stake, and we cooperated perfectly.

The class was dumbfounded. They waited, disappointed, but certainly somewhat relieved. The Tribe courted disaster; that doesn't mean they liked it. But they didn't believe the action was over, so they were all attention when I got ready to say something. All right, I said, I guess we can start classwork. The first English assignment is to write a story about what just happened. You can begin writing now, finish it tonight, and have it ready for tomorrow's class.

Whatever they'd expected, that wasn't it. It suddenly seemed like a lousy idea to me, and I decided to admit it and do something else, but before I could Verna said Sh—! loudly and turned around in her seat so her back was to me. The class woke up at that signal and began to yell demands and questions at me. What to write! How we spozed to write without no paper! That ain't no schoolwork, Teacher! You can't make us write about that! I ain't got no pencil! You trying to get us into trouble! No pen! No paper! What to write! What to do!

Shhh—loudly again. This time not from Verna, but from Leon LaTour in the back. None of The Tribe said Shit, only Sh! or, to express extreme disgust, Sheee . . . ! Sh! said Leon LaTour, nobody going to write that. He was addressing the class, not me. He just want to pin it on somebody. He want to find out about it. He want to pull you in on it!

Protestations of innocence and as many accusations and counter-accusations followed that. Finally people's Mamas began to be mentioned, and I had to yell Quiet! again. Well, what if I do want to know? I yelled. Do you know? Something started it didn't it? Here's Maurice pounding on somebody, on Fletcher there, all of a sudden. Do you think he wanted to? So who did start it then?

Accusations, etc. Leon LaTour grinned in the back. Finally Verna jumped up and yelled, Hush up you-all! Sit down big-leg! came an unidentified voice. Forget you! said Verna coldly and everybody hushed. You don't have to get all shook up, said Verna. She was talking to me. Everybody know who start it. Earl he took hold of Maurice's notebook while Maurice writing on them cards you give him for the books, and slip it over onto Fletcher's desk and Maurice look up and find it gone and then he see it on Fletcher's desk and grab it, but Fletcher don't know it Maurice's because he didn't see that Earl put it there so he grab it back and there they go.

No one denied it. Earl was out of his seat and backed up in the corner of the room like John Dillinger facing the FBI. Sit down, Earl, I said. Oooooh? went the class softly. Sh! said Leon La Tour. Verna wasn't convinced. Ain't you sendin' Earl to the office, Teacher? she said flatly.

I was tired of the whole thing. Property. Your Mama. It seemed likely that at the moment Earl was slipping Maurice's notebook over, every other kid in the class was grabbing, poking, pushing, or pulling at some piece of someone else's stuff. I told them so, and looked at the clock; there were only about five minutes left. Okay, I said, now go on and write the assignment, now we all know all about it.

Actually no one wrote the assignment; no one, that is, except for Maurice, who perhaps figured he'd better. The next day all denied any knowledge of its being assigned. I read Maurice's Composition, as it was entitled. A boy took another boy ['s notebook] in the class and so the boy jump [ed] him to beat [him] the teacher broke it up But the teacher didn't send the boys to the office. (*Corrections mine.*)

Teachers are always willing to give advice to new (or old) teachers, and I talked to them all during those first six or seven weeks. The advice was of two kinds. The first kind, useful enough, was about methods and equipment—sets of flash cards, controlled readers, recorders, easy-correcting tests, good films—but after a short time I was already using most of these. My problem was not what to use but how to get the kids to respond in such a way that they learned something. That brought up the other kind of advice, which was also the most common and which was useless to me. It was about a conglomeration of dodges, tricks, gimmicks to get the kids to do what they were spozed to do, that is, whatever the teacher had in mind for them to do. The purpose of all these tricks was to get and keep an aspect of order, which was reasonable enough I suppose. But the purpose of this order was to enable "learning to take place" (so everyone said—not wanting to be guilty of the authoritarian predilection for order for its own sake) and we all knew that most of the kids weren't learning anything. Everyone agreed that our students were on the average a couple of years below grade level, everyone agreed that was because they were "deprived" kids, but no one agreed that simply because their methods weren't working they ought to try something else.

It's not my purpose or even desire to criticize these teachers—they were as good as or better than most and they had a difficult job—but frankly I could never come to terms with their attitude. They knew certain ways to get control of the class, although even these didn't work consistently because the kids were not easily threatened, having little to lose. The material which was so important, which had to be "covered" once order was established, was supposed to lead toward specific understanding and broader knowledge. But actually what was happening was that teachers were presenting the students, every day, with something for them either to do or not-do, while keeping them through "order" from any other alternative. If a kid couldn't or wouldn't copy a paragraph from the board, he had only the choice of not-doing it, of doing nothing. Almost every teacher admitted that this last was the choice of half the class on any given day. Since their teaching methods were right in other schools, they argued, it must be the fact of "deprivation" which was at fault here. If deprivation was the problem, then something should be done about that deprivation. After that, the school program, being essentially right, would work, since the only reason it didn't work now was that the students were of the wrong kind, *i.e.*, they were deprived.

But I began to think something else was the trouble. Long before we met, my wife had worked for Dr. Thomas French at the Institute for Psychoanalysis in Chicago, and during this time I was reading the first volume of his book *The Integration of Behavior*, which he had sent her. In it he noted that the disintegration of reactions in abnormal behavior seemed to show up goals and processes in a kind of relief, and motivational patterns which might be overlooked in normal behavior were clearly shown in the abnormal. It occurred to me that The Tribe's reactions to this teaching were not different, only more overt, violent, and easily seen than those of normal (or nondeprived) children. Where the middle-class kids were learning enough outside of the classroom or accepting conventional patterns of behavior more readily, so as to make it seem that they were actually learning in school, The Tribe was exposing the system as ineffective for everyone.

During Christmas vacation I came across something that did seem effective: Paul Roberts' book *Patterns of English*, the first high-school English text based on modern linguistics or structural grammer. What impressed me about it was that the exercises seemed both practical and extremely interesting. I immediately tried them out on 7B and they were a great success.

Very briefly, the idea was to teach kids the various different kinds of words (the "parts of speech") by the way in which they occurred in sentences, instead of according to the meaning of the word. That is, a word wasn't to be called a noun because it was a person, place, or thing necessarily, but because it occurred in normal sentences in a certain way. If you took a sentence, "The ———— is new," you could see that only certain words would fit that blank, and those words we could call nouns or anything else; whatever we called them, they still were the only kinds of words which would fit there.

This seemed simple and interesting, and 7B was enthusiastic. They learned the various "patterns" easily, and by the time the year was over had gone through about half the book, which was meant for upper-grade high-school kids. I began now to try it out with 9D and 7H and the results were, relatively, quite as good. We did these patterns once a week and almost all the kids enjoyed making up huge lists of words which would fit certain patterns, and became fairly sure of themselves when it came to naming the patterns. The opposite exercise, that of taking a nonsense sentence like *"The groobs fleegled the grinty wilpen-*

tops" and trying to figure out which words were nouns, adjectives, etc., was a great favorite; it had all the virtues, being new, fun, and not difficult. At the same time, Roberts assured the reader, they were learning the signaling devices for the parts of speech in English. This was the only thing I was able to point to to prove I was teaching something, in the ordinary classroom sense, and I was happy about it.

February and March are dull times in the morning sports page—nothing but the interminable scoring of pro-basketball teams and a vague sense of something about minor-league hockey. The season made itself felt at school. It was the beginning of the second semester and although it was impossible to see just why, it was clear that we were pretty stable. We had our schedule of events—reading, library, spellers—so that everyone would know just what they were not-doing, and the interminable and intellectual discussions of the radicals, led by Verna, about what was wrong with everything. Yet even the sports page began to tell us that some baseball team was contemplating a trade, a new manager; and we had a few changes too about this time.

In 9D Leon LaTour stopped coming to my class. In fact, he didn't come to any classes for the rest of the year. He didn't stop coming to school. He came on time, and spent the day roaming the halls or the yard, joining his class at passing periods to talk, going with them, stopping short at the door of whatever classroom they went into, and going on. Kids began to speak of students beaten up by him, of teachers threatened in the halls, of his talk about setting the fires in the big cans in the halls, which now became almost daily events. In the teachers' room it was branded a scandal—something had better be done, was the consensus. Skates told me that a number of his ninth-graders were coming in after lunch half-drunk and the kids all said they were buying wine from Leon LaTour at a nickel a drink. Skates was in favor of the whole thing, both on account of its being a revolutionary act and also because the student-drunks were too sleepy in class to cause any trouble or make any noise.

I began to stop regularly at the Plantation Club after school for a beer or two myself. The Plantation had South Seas decor, a good jukebox, and was dark and warm. There were always several businessmen from the Negro hotel next door, a traveling man's hotel as the bartender said. He often treated me in an extravagant Uncle Tom manner; he would hurry to serve me, wipe the bar over and over, ask me if the beer was cold enough, if I was comfortable, if the music was too loud or not loud enough. At other times he ignored me completely when I came in, until I began to think about getting up to leave, at which instant he would hurry over and become Uncle Tom again. I couldn't see any resemblance between the salesmen here and The Tribe, and indeed whenever I tried to imagine The Tribe grown up I found I couldn't do it. I could only imagine them now. I counted on something happening in my classes and soon, hoping I could hold out long enough for it. I counted on it. It did occur to me now that perhaps it wouldn't; there were too many things against it, the school structure, other teachers, America itself.

But something did. I still have an ordinary yellow-covered notebook which used to belong to Cerise. Open the cover, and there is a page decorated in ink with curlicues and flourishes which enclose a paragraph: "This is the Slambook belonging to Cerise, who says that nobody can read it without her permission and also anyone who steals it is guilty of a crime." It was all spelled correctly and signed with an elegant and unreadable script.

On the next page there is a list, numbered, of the students of 9D, and this is the key to what follows. For on each page afterwards, there is the name of a kid, and on that page other kids have been invited to comment on his or her character, appearance, courage, brains, or wealth, signing themselves only with a number corresponding to the key in the front. The beauty of this system is that the owner of the Slambook may then show the comments to the kid whose name is at the top of the page and have the pleasure of listening to him beg and plead with her to see the first page so that he may identify the commentators, the girl who said he was good-looking or the boy who said he was chicken. The authors of the remarks can also plead for her not to show it, and the owner thus becomes the center of frantic social activity.

I picked this Slambook up from the floor after the class left one period; when I gave it back to Cerise the next day, saying I didn't want to be guilty of a crime, she said it was already out of date and she had another, so I could have it.

Slambooks suddenly took precedence over everything. Charlene, Connie, and Cerise—the Three Cs, we called them—had them one day; everyone else was making them the next. The Three Cs were the prettiest and whitest girls in the class and their lead was bound to be followed. Since making up Slambooks involved doing more work than many kids had done the entire year, I was delighted. Everyone was avidly writing in them, not perhaps in "complete sentences" or the rest of the paraphernalia expected for classwork, but the books were carefully made, the names spelled right, the style of the opening paragraph elegant and complicated and formal. From the appearance and behavior of the class, they might have been involved in some kind of engrossing class project or group work (as of course they were) discussing their progress with each other and writing entries into notebooks to be reported later with the results of their research, discussion, and inquiry.

The whole talk now in the teachers' room was about Slambook season

and voices rose in excited competition about how many had been con-
fiscated or destroyed. Methods for ridding the school of Slambooks forever were discussed and, I guess, tried out. All I could see, though, was
that The Tribe had finally come across something which *needed to be
written down* to be successful or interesting to them, which couldn't
even exist without writing, and they were as enthusiastic about it as
possible.

The next change in 9D began around the same time. It was, I think,
the day I started reading Cerise's book that Geneva came into the room
and, instead of going over to sit down, went to the board and began to
write a list of the Top Forty songs on it. Geneva was a tall, big girl,
middle in the hierarchy of skin-color, hair, features, etc., and middle in
other ways too. This morning, as far as I could tell, she simply felt like
writing tune titles on the board and did it.

The Top Forty, of course, were those forty rock 'n' roll songs played
over and over, all day long, by the disc-jockeys of the local rock 'n' roll
station. Geneva planned to write down only the first twenty—at least
that's all she did write down and later on twenty became established
as the proper number although we all still called it the Top Forty. As
kids noticed Geneva chalking up titles, they began to question spellings,
order, simple correctness; she made a couple of changes. Top Forty soon
became a program, like the pledge of allegiance (or a paragraph on the
board for everyone to copy). Something everyone could expect to start
the class with from now on, except that almost everyone thought it was
something important in itself, which made the difference.

During library periods I kept looking in the back storeroom for anything I could use with my classes and eventually I came across a series of
playbooks. I kept them stacked in a corner of the room, since the librarian
said that no one else ever used them. Occasionally kids from 9D or 7H
would take a look at them.

One day, near the beginning of the period in 9D, with the kids hard
at work or not-work, the Slambooks going through their courses, the
Top Forty being laboriously written on the board under the watchful
eye of Verna and a few critics, I was astonished to see the Three Cs
approaching my desk in a body. They were clutching playbooks and they
asked me why couldn't we read these plays out loud in class, everyone
taking the parts? Why not? I'd already tried to get 9D interested in
play-reading some time before. So I said it was a fine idea, but who was
going to do the reading? It was an idiotic question. With the Three Cs
planning to do something, everyone in the class was suddenly eager to
take part. The Cs' own big table was quickly moved up to the front of
the room—ten boys shoving each other for the honor of grabbing hold

of it—desks shoved out of the way, folding chairs set around it. Trouble began as twenty kids dived for space around the table. I yelled. Everyone finally fell back and, taking the easy way out, I announced that the Three Cs, having introduced the idea, could pick out the players. There followed plenty of threats and counterthreats, some refusals-in-advance-of-expected-rejection, an incipient Plop Reflex or two; the Cs finally extorted enough promises and, with perhaps fifteen minutes left in the period, they began to read the play. That was the first time I realized that the play the Cs were so excited about was *Cinderella.*

It was a terrible reading. Unprepared, the kids stumbled and read too fast, giggled among themselves or argued, forgot their turn in haste to correct someone else, and the audience, prepared at first to listen, soon lost interest and drifted back to their spellers, Slambooks, and cosmetics.

The source of the trouble was the Three Cs. In their haste they had picked *Cinderella* because they saw there was a Prince and a fancy-dress ball and two sisters and a mother who were going to that ball; they saw themselves in starring roles, dancing, dining, diamonds shining and all. They weren't prepared to find Cinderella the heroine and had given that part to a girl named Grace, not concealing the fact that Grace looked, in their opinion, like someone who stayed home and cleaned up all the time. As the play went on and Grace steadily read all the most interesting parts with the fairy godmother and the Prince, the Cs became more and more upset and began to interpose remarks. How could the Prince dance with that ugly old thing? they wanted to know.

By the end of the play they had really become the three jealous women, so much so that they were almost speechless as the Prince began to go around with the glass slipper. When he got to their house and tried the slipper on the first of the mean sisters, he was supposed to read the line, "Oh no! Your foot is much too big for this slipper. You cannot be the lady I seek!" But by the time he got as far as "big," Charlene jumped up in a fury and yelled, Don't you say my feets too big you black monkey! and slammed her book down.

That broke up the play. Everyone began to laugh and yell Whoooo-eee! The other two Cs, having looked ahead now and seen the same fate reserved for them, quit the play too. We ain't playing no part where they get to say our feet too big, Mr. Hern-don! The bell rang about then, and the class rushed out still yelling Whoooo-eee! They left *Cinderella* scattered about the room, the chairs knocked over, the table still up in front.

I left the table there. The next day the Cs tried to recruit someone to move it back for them, but the class objected. A number of them had playbooks out and were planning to read another play. But first, they called out to me, we got to finish that one about Cinderella. They wanted to know how it came out.

Springtime was the rioting season. The Tribe had given up and was becoming violent. By April the story of the year was over—some details, some dramatics left to tell, but the score was already in. All the promises had lost their appeal and The Tribe was busting out. Fights. Fires. Windows. Food thrown all over. Neighborhood complaints about vandalism. And we lost Ruth. She'd remained in the elite 8B all year, getting along well enough, but in the spring she became determined to carry out minor disturbances to the bitter end, insisting on her rights, why she didn't have to give back the other kid's pen or book, what I was spozed to do. One afternoon after school she imprisoned the school nurse, a secretary, and a woman teacher in a room for forty-five minutes, threatening them with an upraised chair if they moved, thereby giving us an idea of what she meant by trouble. Teachers who had kept things in check all year began to have their problems. Oddly enough, the faculty took it in stride. It happens every year, they seemed to say. We try. We hold 'em for as long as we can. . . .

I viewed the daily slaughter with detachment and no little vanity. If they were beginning to lose, I was just starting to win. If their programs were falling apart, we were just starting to move. 9D not only read almost every day, but they were discussing—all right, they were arguing, squabbling, making a lot of noise, using a lot of bad language—certain questions about play-reading. They were discussing who read well and why, they were telling each other what the play was about, they argued about where certain characters should sit at the table. The most important question to them was what relationship the reader should have to the character he was reading. Two solid factions arose, the first arguing that if the character was a giant, a big kid had to read the part. The second disagreed; they thought that, if the character was a beautiful girl, any girl who *read* beautifully, who *sounded* beautiful, should read it. The kids were making it. Rolling. I was enthusiastic, pleased, proud of them.

In this mood I met with Mr. Grisson in April for his official evaluation of my year's work. He opened the interview by stating that it was always painful to him to have to make judgments, but that it was best to be frank. In short, he found my work unsatisfactory on every count; he could not recommend me for rehire in the district. Furthermore he must say that he considered me unfit for the position of junior-high-school teacher in any school, anywhere, now or in the future, and would so state on my evaluation paper.

On the last day of school, Ramona and Hazel told me I was the nicest and best teacher they ever had. I told them I bet they said that to all their teachers; the class agreed loudly that they did.

Grisson had scheduled an assembly for the afternoon. I sat with Skates in the balcony of the auditorium, surrounded by excited students.

On the stage Grisson was giving out awards for the year—for good citizenship, class officers and athletes, and finally for the district-wide spelling contest. He called off the names, waited for the kids to climb up onto the stage, shook their hands, led applause, and frowned into the audience as The Tribe expressed occasional disbelief in the spelling ability of such-and-such a watermelon-head. After it seemed that all the awards had been distributed, Grisson paused significantly. Everyone waited. Then he said, there is one more spelling award which may come as a little surprise. It is my great pleasure now to call up the last winner in the spelling contest—Leon LaTour!

The Tribe went wild, roaring out in what seemed to me equal parts of disbelief, astonishment, glee, and disgust, keeping it up long after Leon LaTour shook Grisson's hand and left the stage. Around us I could see other teachers nodding and smiling; it was another victory—the rebel brought back into the fold, a threat to the system conquered by the carrot. Grisson was leading the way, and everything was okay.

Unfortunately, I was aware that Leon LaTour hadn't ever taken the spelling tests. They were given only in English classes, and Leon LaTour only had one English class—mine; he hadn't been there when I gave it. He hadn't been in any classes then: I suppose Grisson could have called him in and given him the test privately, but it didn't seem likely, nor did it seem likely that Leon LaTour would have come in and taken that test.

In any case Leon LaTour couldn't spell.

So why the award? What the hell? Either Leon LaTour threatened some good-spelling kid to sign his—Leon's—name to his own spelling paper, or else the whole thing was rigged. Like many another event that year there wasn't an answer available, but it was the last day and I didn't have to worry about it. Forget you! I said, talking to myself out loud. Two kids in front of me started to giggle. You hear Mr. Hern-don? one of them said to the other. He say, Forget you!

The movie came on then, something about a Bullfighter and a Kid. The Tribe was restless during it, standing up, talking, scuffling. I was brooding about the position I found myself in. I couldn't remember when I'd worked so hard or concentrated what intelligence and energy I possessed so seriously on a single effort. It seemed unlikely that any kind of work besides teaching was going to satisfy me now, but it seemed even more unlikely that I was going to get another teaching job very soon. It was a kind of bind I wasn't used to.

Around Skates and me the kids stopped scuffling and began to cheer and yell. I looked at the screen. In the movie, the bull had just gored a matador. Two men came out to distract it, and the bull began to chase them around the ring, crashing into the wooden barriers as the men dodged behind them. Time and time again, the bull chased and crashed.

The kids yelled and laughed and stood up and fell down again helpless with laughter. Hey Jim! Skates yelled to me, look, The Tribe likes it! They like it! He was laughing now too, raising his fist and waving it in the air.

Suddenly the lights went on in the auditorium, the film stopped, and Grisson appeared on the stage. He warned them that any further demonstrations of that sort wouldn't be tolerated; if it happened again the film would be stopped and they could return to their classrooms. Sh! said The Tribe.

Let 'em alone! Skates called out loudly from the balcony. Hell, he said to me, it's the first time all year they like something. So let 'em alone . . .

Well, the lights went back out, the bull chased everyone around the ring, the kids yelled. In time the movie was over, the lights came on, the kids dismissed, the season over too, and we all went home.

James Ballard
(1921–   )

A student incorrigibly lost, whose teachers and counselors are helpless to save, embodies a discontent in teaching that is often viewed through the befogging haze of an irresponsible hope. Some wounds lie deeper than our probes and elude suave diagnosis. How often does the counselor or psychiatric social worker spuriously diagnose a student's aberration so that it unjustly conforms to mere present knowledge or to an existing vocabulary? Are there not sicknesses that teachers must struggle to comprehend—though cure may be impossible—simply because each day involves them in an exactitude of suffering, inexactly expressed by the sufferer and imprecisely understood by us all?

In "Man Overboard" a seventeen-year-old drunk named Robert Mercer seems to refute any hope for his rehabilitation, for reasons unknown to his mathematics teacher. Mercer is a dropout still in attendance, a near prodigy who is a casualty of an unknown disaster. The theme of the story is not his malady but its mystery.

Now living in Baltimore, Maryland, James Ballard has studied at St. John's College in Annapolis and served with the Strategic Air Command.

Man Overboard

Randall was opening a bottle of beer when one of the students knocked on his door. He knew it was a student because of the knocking. When any of the other teachers came by, they banged on the door, or kicked on it, or called through to ask if he were busy. He was, this afternoon, or he was thinking about being busy, with test papers from the morning, and he wanted to keep quiet until the boy went away. But that wouldn't do. And he put the bottle down and went to the door.

170

It was Bob Mercer who was knocking. "Captain Randall, sir! How you doing?"

"Hello, Mercer. Come in."

"Well—I could. You sure you're not too busy, Captain?"

Mercer was asking for something. Maybe he wanted to be assured it was all right for him to be here.

"Not too busy. Come on in, man."

"Yessir. Thanks."

But whatever Mercer wanted, that wasn't it. Nor was he here to ask about his test score. There had been a mathematics test that morning, analytic geometry, and most of the papers needed to be graded. Mercer never bothered, though, about his scores. Last week he had got a B instead of the A plus he usually got, but he had still been high man. He was a near prodigy in mathematics, and he was in honors squad in the rest of his classes. Maybe he didn't want anything after all. Maybe he had just dropped around. Then Randall saw his eyes notice the bottle of beer.

"Have a chair, Mercer. What's on your mind?"

"Nothing special, Captain. Just thought I'd stop by for a minute. See how things are going. Grading papers, aren't you?"

"Off and on. I haven't got to yours yet. How do you think you did?"

"Don't know. What did you make it such a hard one for, Captain?"

"I just wanted to be ornery."

"All those problems about hyperbolas? That was a rough test, Captain Randall."

"Did you flunk it?" Mercer was going to ask him for a beer. He considered saying something that would make it easier for him to ask. But if he did that, Mercer might begin hoping he would give him one. Begin thinking he would. He was already hoping.

Mercer smiled. "Won't know till I see the score, Captain." He swallowed. "I don't guess I did. Can I have a bottle of that beer, Captain?"

"No, buddy."

"—Oh. OK."

Danish beer. He had got a case of it, yesterday.

Mercer wanted some. He was hurting for it.

"Well, that's OK, Captain. Thanks anyway." His voice was louder than it had been. It sounded especially friendly. He wanted to show that he had only accidentally in passing thought of suggesting a beer, and it was all right about being turned down. "Uh—OK if I smoke up here, sir?"

"Sure. Go ahead."

Mercer got a cigarette stub out of his shirt pocket. He looked at it and smiled. "Hard times, Captain." When he was lighting it, he had some trouble getting the match pulled out of the folder. He was shaky.

"You out of cigarettes, Mercer?"

"Yessir. Just about."

He got a pack from the carton in his desk. "Here."

"Hey. The whole thing? Thanks a *lot*, Captain."

But it was going to take more than cigarettes. He wished he could have given him a beer. It was against regulations to drink with the students, to allow them to drink at all, but that was not the reason he had said no. Mercer himself was the reason. Then in that case, it was the reason to go ahead and give him one. This was square, to be playing I Know What's Best for You with the boy.

He found Mercer's paper out of the stack. "I'll take a look at how you did on the test. Since you're here."

"Yessir. I tell you who wants to know what their grade is, though, Captain Randall. Gene Pack. You know?"

"Stick around then. I'll see how he came out."

"Yessir." Mercer sat down.

He liked seeing Mercer's mathematics papers. Mercer spent more time with the printing and with drawing the diagrams than he did with working out the problems. He had a fund of solutions, although it didn't appear that he himself realized he did, and matching the appropriate one to a problem was hardly ever any trouble to him. He had learned draftsman's lettering, and he used ballpoint pens with different colors of ink. The other boys, including Gene Pack, needed to do a lot of erasing, and they stuck to pencils.

Mercer got up again. He went over to the window. "It hasn't been so cold lately, Captain Randall."

"It hasn't, has it? Going to be spring before long."

"Yessir. You can always look for it about this time of year."

He heard a bumping sound. When he looked up, Mercer was bumping his forehead against the window frame.

"Cut that out, Mercer."

"Yessir. Sorry, Captain. I'll be glad when it does get to be spring. Birds come out, everything gets green. You like springtime, Captain?"

"It's the best time of the year."

"I think so too. Did you know white-nosed bumblebees can't sting, Captain?"

"Did I know what?"

"White-nosed bumblebees can't sting. Didn't you know that?"

"No, I didn't. I didn't know bees had noses."

"Well, the front end. They call it the nose. I have this book about insects. I'll lend it to you sometime, if you want to see it."

"I'd like to. Bring it around when you think of it."

"Yessir. Hey. I still have your book about thermodynamics."

"I haven't needed it, Mercer. Keep it longer if you want to."

Mercer started to say something else. Instead, he only smiled. "I'm slowing you down, Captain. You want to go ahead with those papers, don't you?" He turned back to the window.

Mercer's paper had two problems missing. It had a wrong answer for another one. The grade came out C-minus. Last week there was a B. Next week it might be an F.

He was working on Gene Pack's paper when the bumping started again. This time it was louder. It was bound to be painful.

"Mercer, will you cut that out?"

"Oh. Yeah. Sorry, Captain. I forgot it bothered you."

"I'd think you're the one it would bother. Smoke, or something. Do some push-ups."

"I'm already smoking, Captain."

"Then do some push-ups. Come on. I'll do some with you."

"I can't, sir. I just can't. But *you* go ahead, if you want to. They say it's good for anybody, once in a while. That is, they say it is."

"Would you like to see your paper, Mercer? I've finished with it now."

"That's not much of a paper to look at, Captain."

"Why did you leave out those two problems?"

"I don't know. I just did."

"Go ahead and work them now. You can if you want to. You didn't use up all your time this morning."

"I— No, sir. I don't want you to think I'm not interested, it isn't that. I just— I've got to cut out, Captain. I think I'll go see what Pack and those others are doing."

"Stick around, Mercer. Work those two problems, and I'll buy you a drink. I'll buy you an ice-cream cone."

"Yessir. I think I'll just check on those others for a minute. I better see what those kids in my squad are doing, too. I'll see you later, Captain Randall. OK?"

"OK, Mercer. You take it easy."

There was something he had meant to do. The bottle of beer. In a minute, he went ahead with it.

He could have done more just now, as to Mercer. They could have listened to some records, or gone over to the gym and boxed awhile. He could have taken Mercer driving for an hour or so. Just about anything besides sit here and let him beat his head against the wall.

It bothered him that Mercer, at the age of seventeen, should be a drunk. There was no reason for it that he had been able to get to. He had read Mercer's personal-history file in the office, and he had had some off-duty acquaintance with him, but he still didn't know how it had come about. Mercer was in his junior year, but this was his first year at this school. This one was called Rampart Ridge Academy. It had a grade school (the Intermediate Battalion) and a high school (the Advanced Battalion). It was a semimilitary school. There was no saluting or drilling, but the students and also the teachers wore uniforms that had a sort of Marine Corps look, and the teachers, the Corps of Instruction, were addressed as Captain.

Mercer had gone to public school before he came here, in Wheeling, West Virginia. He hadn't been in any jam before he got here. A few of the boys had, or they had flunked out of other private schools. Most of them were here, and Mercer was, only because as a private school the Academy had more class than public schools. His father had an automobile agency and a hardware store in Wheeling. Both his parents were living. He had two younger brothers and a younger sister. All his grades in public school had been high, the same as they had been here until lately, and his file had the usual letters of recommendation. He had a buddy here, Gene Pack, and for the first months he had had several other friends. He was a student officer. He was adjutant of a squad of grade-school boys, and he could handle them without having to yell at them. By all evidences, he was an above-average boy from a reasonably sound family. But there was the other. Something had gone wrong.

Randall was sure that Mercer trusted him, but the one time he had tried to get Mercer into a conversation about liquor and drinking, Mercer had closed up about it. Whatever it was that had gone wrong, he was guarding it. Or maybe it was guarding itself, keeping itself from being molested. Before long, he might not even be making C's. Or be knocking on the door anymore.

Mercer's physics teacher was Robbie Roberts. Last fall, Robbie attempted to arrange a psychiatric interview for him. It was only an attempt, since the school's executive officer, the principal, said no. All the Rampart Ridge students were selected carefully before they were matriculated, he said, and in any event the Academy was a school rather than a medical institution. Just before Thanksgiving, Mercer's father visited him, and Robbie undertook then to talk with Mr. Mercer. Nothing came of that either. The man was indignant at the suggestion that his son was drinking, and recommended that Robbie confine his efforts to instruction.

"He had a point," Robbie said. "I guess you've heard about the boy whose teacher gave him a note to take home. For his parents to give him a bath. The boy brought a note back the next day: Don't smell my son, teach him. You see? What I've come to, if they stink, they can stink their way and I'll stink mine. In the meantime, I'll just give them physics lessons. And they'll just learn. They damn well better."

It sounded sensible. It sounded like the right way to look at it. And it was easy to get a bellyful of Robert Mercer. There was nothing anybody could reasonably want that the boy didn't have, that he hadn't had all his life. Certainly nothing material. He was a good-looking boy, he had a good mind. And here he was, whimpering for a beer, smoking butt ends of cigarettes.

But Mercer stayed on Randall's mind. And finally he decided that when he got finished with the papers, he would find him, and go ahead and take him for a drive. It wasn't likely to make any difference if he did; there was no point in imagining that it would. Whatever Mercer was asking for, it would take somebody who had more than he did to have it. Both of them knew it. But even so. He had only a few papers left. Four. They could wait.

While he was putting his shirt on, there was another knock at the door. This time it was Gene Pack. Mercer's roommate.

What Pack had to say, Mercer had already left for town. He had jumped the fence, meaning that he had gone AWOL. The town, Annistown, was twenty miles east, toward Washington. Students could get passes on weekends, or if an instructor accompanied them and there was a special reason, during the week. This was Thursday, and there was no instructor accompanying Mercer.

"Did he have any money, Gene?"

"He sure did, Captain. He had eight bucks. He won it just a little while ago. We were sticking pins in each other."

"What in God's name for?"

"Well, in ourselves. It doesn't hurt."

"All right, but what were you doing it for?"

"Well, the way it is, the one that can stick himself the farthest, without hollering, he wins. Everybody puts up a quarter or fifty cents, and that's the pot."

"If it doesn't hurt, why does anybody holler?"

"It's just the way people think about it, Captain Randall. You see the pin, and you think it's going to hurt, so you yell. Or swear or something. Any kind of noise, you lose. Because it isn't completely the money, you know. It's prestige too, not to make any noise."

"Jesus God."

"Oh, it isn't usually the money. I guess it was this time. With him. Listen, Captain. That is—do you know what he wanted it for?"

"I can guess. He wanted it to get drunk with."

"Yessir. I didn't know if you knew about that or not. He asked me to lend him two bucks. I told him I wouldn't till tomorrow night, when we could go on pass. And then after a while he said he was coming up here. I told him he wouldn't get anywhere with you, either. What he said, he just wanted to talk to you."

"He really said that, Pack?"

"Yessir. That's the exact quotation."

"Did he give you any idea what he wanted to talk about?"

"Not really. He just said he wanted to talk to you."

Mercer had been trying to send him a message. Bumping the wall. When he left out answers on the test.

"Pack, have you and Mercer ever had any serious conversations? The two of you?"

"I guess we have, Captain. Sex, and things like that. He won't talk about drinking, though, if you mean that. He shuts right up."

"And you wouldn't come across with the two bucks."

"I wouldn't today. I told him. I only had three. He could still have two, if he still wanted it, but I just thought he'd go ahead and wait. Till tomorrow. But he wouldn't."

"It looks like he made out better today. Since he found a pin-sticking game. If you can call it a game."

"He didn't find it, Captain. He promoted it. He got it going. You know what he used to get in it? A pack of cigarettes."

"He did, huh? You know where the cigarettes came from? Right here."

"Yessir. That's what he said."

"That's good going, all right. Running a pack of cigarettes into eight dollars. There must have been a bunch of you in it, though. If it starts with just a quarter a person."

"It was just ten of us. I got in so I could win instead of him. I almost did win. And then he offered to make it double or nothing. So that way he got it up to eight bucks. Ten bucks, actually. But he had to pay the referee, so that cut it down. The referee gets paid by the winner."

"Why don't you have teams? We could get some other schools in on this, have a conference."

"It's not anything to get mad about, Captain. Something like yogurt is all it is. Those people that can stretch out on nails."

"That's yoga. Yoga. Have you ever heard of tetanus, Pack? Lockjaw?"

"Well, I've heard of it, yessir."

"You might— All right. All right. When was it Mercer left?"

"Yessir. It was about twenty minutes ago. That's what I came up here about, Captain. We got off the track. What I was thinking, we could go after him. Or you could, you've got the authority and all that. He said he'd be back early, but he won't. I guarantee you he won't. He may not even be back tonight."

"And it was Annistown he was going to?"

"That's where he was starting. He could end up almost anywhere."

Annistown was small, but parts of it were not safe to be in after dark. Especially for a kid, drunk. Mercer probably hadn't reached the highway yet. It took about half an hour to walk to the highway from the school.

"Sir? Couldn't we go see if he'll come on back?"

The Keystone Kops. The Pursuit of Robert Mercer.

"He'll head for that South End part of town, Captain. He'll be lucky to get out without getting knocked in the head or something. We're not supposed to go there at all. When it's two or three of us it's not so bad, but it's going to be just him by himself. What if it was a friend of yours, Captain? What if Robbie—Captain Roberts—was fixing to do something, and you knew it?"

"Settle down, Pack. We'll catch him."

They probably would. If they didn't, the Annistown police could pick him up and hold him for safekeeping. The only thing, it wouldn't especially matter. They were not what Mercer was running from. And he couldn't be held permanently, by the police or here at school.

He hadn't yet got to the highway when they reached him. They rounded a curve, and there he was. Tramping along, and he didn't look back, even when the car slowed. But when the car drew up alongside him, he stopped. And waited.

"Go for a ride, Mercer?"

"Ride where, Captain?"

"Anywhere you want to. Where you headed?"

"Annistown, Captain."

"Where all the beer is, huh?"

"Yessir. Enough of it."

"Think it is enough for you, Mercer?"

"What're you doing, Captain, you trying to be one of the boys? Talking straight from the shoulder or something?"

Pack called over to him. "Cut that out, Mercer. You're being a pain, you know that? You think this is all Captain Randall has to do, is pole up and down the road for you?"

"I didn't ask anybody to pole up and down for me. Let me alone, Pack, how about it?"

"Man, you are a pain. I asked him, if you want to know."

"Then you can go to hell then, will you? The whole bunch of you."

Pack got out and went over to him. "Listen, Mercer. Bob. This ain't any way to be."

"Will you let me alone? You said all you were going to say, back in the room. Why can't you let somebody do something?"

"Mercer baby."

Randall put the car in gear again. "Mercer."

"Yeah? Now what?"

"What is this yeah, Mister?"

Mercer looked away. "Yessir."

So with that, he knew Mercer was coming back with them. "Listen,

Mercer. If you want to go to Annistown, I'll drive you down there, OK? Or if you want to go back, we'll do that."

Mercer was amused. They watched each other for a while. He began walking again. He stopped. He went a little farther. Then he turned, snarled, and went around the front of the car. He kicked the right front tire. Pack was opening the door for him, and he got in. "All right. All right. We might as well go on back if it's going to be all this. Jesus Christ. Get in, Pack, will you? All this just because somebody said they wanted a beer."

Going back, Mercer was holding his left arm close across his chest. Maybe that was the arm he had used the pins on, and it was getting sore now. Maybe it was a defense. Pack reached toward him once, but he drew away quickly. Pack didn't try anymore.

Randall looked at him once or twice in the rearview mirror. Mercer's face looked numb. He was sealing himself off.

"Mercer, are you sure about those white-nosed bumblebees?"

That hadn't been exactly the right thing to say. He wished he had thought before he said it.

For a minute, he and Mercer were looking at each other. A dog he had once, a red setter, it got one of its front legs hurt, the left one, and by the time it got back home it had gnawed that paw off, and green flies were clustered on the end. When it looked at him, its eyes were clouded and too bright at the same time. It got back home, but it never let itself be a pet afterward. He had failed it, and it wasn't able to. Mercer stared back at him, unacknowledging, and then, looked away. Later on, tonight or very likely this afternoon again, Mercer would cut out again. Just possibly he wouldn't, but it was only a small chance. They drove along.

Herbert Gold

(1924–   )

The hardships of teaching derive from any number of collective evils: the antipathy of taxpayers, the fastidious incompetence of a school administration, the thin salaries of the untenured, the defeating student-to-teacher ratios in urban schools. But in the following reminiscence a personal fault, the author's own, festers within the public circumstances of his school. The integrity is there, the author faulting himself for not having for his students "enough love and pressure . . . to open the way through their intentions to the common humanity which remains locked within." As if his own ineffectiveness was a simulacrum of the larger failure, Gold moves narratively between his private disillusionment and the pervasively *public* evils which endangered it. What he remembers "of the formal study of Truth and Beauty, for advanced credit in education, is a great confusion of generalities, committees, conferences, audio-visual importunities, and poor contact."

Invoked by a Brooklyn Great Dane, by a girl named Clotilda Adams, and by Gold's own tenure as a teacher, is a foreboding thesis: American education is failing to weld humanistic knowledge to the personal experiences of its people, to anneal in the heat of that experience a morality that can permit us to survive.

Predominantly a novelist, Herbert Gold is also the author of a collection of stories *Love and Like* (1960), and *The Age of Happy Problems* (1962), a book of essays from which this account is taken. Gold's recent novels are *Fathers* (1968), and *The Great American Jackpot* (1970).

A Dog in Brooklyn,
A Girl in Detroit:
A Life among the Humanities

What better career for a boy who seeks to unravel the meaning of our brief span on earth than that of philosopher? We all wonder darkly, in the forbidden hours of the night, punishing our parents and building a better world, with undefined terms. Soon, however, most of us learn to sleep soundly; or we take to pills or love-making; or we call ourselves insomniacs, not philosophers. A few attempt to define the terms.

There is no code number for the career of philosophy in school, the Army, or out beyond in real life. The man with a peculiar combination of melancholic, nostalgic, and reforming instincts stands at three possibilities early in his youth. He can choose to be a hero, an artist, or a philosopher. In olden times, war, say, or the need to clean out the old west, might make up his mind for him. The old west had been pretty well cleaned up by the time I reached a man's estate, and Gary Cooper could finish the job. Heroism was an untimely option. With much bureaucratic confusion I tried a bit of heroic war, got stuck in the machine, and returned to the hectic, Quonset campus of the G.I. Bill, burning to Know, Understand, and Convert. After a season of ferocious burrowing in books, I was ready to be a Teacher, which seemed a stern neighbor thing to Artist and Philosopher. I took on degrees, a Fulbright fellowship, a wife, a child, a head crammed with foolish questions and dogmatic answers despite the English school of linguistic analysis. I learned to smile, pardner, when I asked questions of philosophers trained at Oxford or Cambridge, but I asked them nonetheless. I signed petitions against McCarthy, wrote a novel, went on a treasure hunt, returned to my roots in the Middle West and stood rooted there, discussed the menace of the mass media, and had another child.

By stages not important here, I found myself teaching the Humanities at Wayne University in Detroit. I am now going to report a succession of classroom events which, retrospectively, seems to have determined my abandonment of formal dealing with this subject. The evidence does not, however, render any conclusion about education in the "Humanities" logically impregnable. It stands for a state of mind and is no substitute for formal argument. However, states of mind are important in this area of experience and metaexperience. However and however: it happens that most of the misty exaltation of the blessed vocation of the teacher issues from the offices of deans, editors, and college presidents. The encounter with classroom reality has caused many teachers, like Abelard meeting the relatives of Eloïse, to lose their bearings. Nevertheless this is a memoir, not a campaign, about a specific life in and out of the Humanities. Though I am not a great loss to the History of Everything in Culture, my own eagerness to teach is a loss to me.

News item of a few years ago. A young girl and her date are walking along a street in Brooklyn, New York. The girl notices that they are being followed by an enormous Great Dane. The dog is behaving peculiarly, showing its teeth and making restless movements. A moment later, sure enough, the dog, apparently maddened, leaps slavering upon the girl, who is borne to earth beneath its weight. With only an instant's hesitation, the boy jumps on the dog. Its fangs sunk in one, then in the other, the dog causes the three of them to roll like beasts across the sidewalk.

A crowd gathers at a safe distance to watch. No one interferes. They display the becalmed curiosity of teevee viewers.

A few moments later a truckdriver, attracted by the crowd, pulls his vehicle over to the curb. This brave man is the only human being stirred personally enough to leave the role of passive spectator. Instantaneously analyzing the situation, he leaps into the struggle—*attacking and beating the boy.* He has naturally assumed that the dog must be protecting an innocent young lady from the unseemly actions of a juvenile delinquent.

I recounted this anecdote in the classroom in order to introduce a course which attempted a summary experience of Humanities 610 for a monumental nine credits. There were a number of points to be made about the passivity of the crowd ("don't get involved," "not my business") and the stereotypical reaction of the truck driver who had been raised to think of man's best friend as not another human being but a dog. In both cases, addicted to entertainment and clichés, the crowd and the trucker could not recognize what was actually happening before their eyes; they responded irrelevantly to the suffering of strangers; they were not a part of the main. This led us to a discussion of the notion of "community." In a closely-knit society, the people on the street would have known the couple involved and felt a responsibility towards them. In a large city, everyone is a stranger. (Great art can give a sense of the brotherhood of men. Religion used to do this, too.) "Any questions?" I asked, expecting the authority of religion to be defended.

An eager hand shot up. Another. Another. Meditative bodies sprawled in their chairs. "Are all New Yorkers like that?" "Well, what can you do if there's a mad dog and you're not expecting it?" "Where does it say in what great book how you got to act in Brooklyn?"

I took note of humor in order to project humorousness. I found my-self composing my face in the look of thought which teevee panelists

use in order to project thinking. I discovered a serious point to elaborate
—several. I mentioned consciousness and relevance and the undefined
moral suggestion implied by the labor which produces any work of art
or mind. A girl named Clotilda Adams asked me: "Why don't people try
to get along better in this world?"

Somewhat digressively, we then discussed the nature of heroism,
comparing the behavior of the boy and the truck driver. Both took
extraordinary risks; why? We broke for cigarettes in the autumn air outside. Then, for fifty minutes more, we raised these interesting questions,
referring forward to Plato, Aristotle, St. Thomas, Dostoevsky, Tolstoy,
William James, and De Gaulle; and then boy, dog, girl, truck driver
and crowd were left with me and the crowned ghosts of history in the
deserted room while my students went on to Phys Ed, Music Appreciation, Sosh, and their other concerns. Having been the chief speaker,
both dramatist and analyst, I was exalted by the lofty ideas floated up
into the air around me. I was a little let down to return to our real life
in which dog-eat-dog is man's closest pal. Fact. Neither glory nor pleasure
nor power, and certainly not wisdom, provided the goal of my students.
Not even wealth was the aim of most of them. They sought to make
out, to do all right, more prideful than amorous in love, more security-
hungry than covetous in status. I saw my duty as a teacher: Through
the Humanities, to awaken them to the dream of mastery over the facts
of our lives. I saw my duty plain: Through the Humanities, to lead them
toward the exaltation of knowledge and the calm of control. I had a
whole year in which to fulfill this obligation. It was a two-semester course.

Before she left the room, Clotilda Adams said, "You didn't answer
my question." Fact.

Outside the university enclave of glass and grass, brick and trees,
Detroit was agonizing in its last big year with the big cars. Automation,
dispersion of factories, and imported automobiles were eroding a precarious confidence. Fear was spreading; soon the landlords would offer
to decorate apartments and suffer the pain. Detroit remembered the war
years with nostalgia. Brave days, endless hours, a three-shift clock, insufficient housing, men sleeping in the all-night, triple-feature movies on
Woodward and Grand River. Though the area around the Greyhound
and Trailways stations was still clotted with the hopeful out of the hill
country of the mid-South and the driven from the deep South—they
strolled diagonally across the boulevards, entire families holdings hands
—some people suspected what was already on its way down the road:
twenty per cent unemployment in Detroit.

The semester continued. We churned through the great books. One
could classify my students in three general groups, intelligent, mediocre,
and stupid, allowing for the confusions of three general factors—background, capacity, and interest. This was how we classified the Humani-

ties, too: ancient, medieval, and modern. It made a lot of sense, and it made me itch, scratch, and tickle. Series of three form nice distinctions. According to Jung and other authorities, they have certain mythic significances. The course was for nine credits. All the arts were touched upon. We obeyed Protagoras; man, just man, was our study. When I cited him—"the proper study of man is Man"—Clotilda Adams stirred uneasily in her seat. "By which Protagoras no doubt meant woman, too," I assured her. She rested.

Now imagine the winter coming and enduring, with explosions of storm and exfoliations of gray slush, an engorged industrial sky overhead and sinus trouble all around. The air was full of acid and a purplish, spleeny winter mist. Most of Detroit, in Indian times before the first French trappers arrived, had been a swamp and below sea level. The swamp was still present, but invisible; city stretched out in all directions, crawling along the highways. Though Detroit was choked by a dense undergrowth of streets and buildings, irrigated only by super-highways, its work was done with frantic speed. The Rouge plant roared, deafened. The assembly lines clanked to the limit allowed by the UAW. The old Hudson factory lay empty, denuded, waiting to become a parking lot. Then the new models were being introduced! Buick! Pontiac! Dodge! Ford and Chevrolet! Ford impudently purchased a huge billboard faced towards the General Motors Building on Grand Boulevard. General Motors retaliated by offering free ginger ale to all comers, and a whole bottle of Vernor's to take home if you would only consent to test-drive the new Oldsmobile, the car with the . . . I've forgotten what it had that year. All over town the automobile companies were holding revival meetings; hieratic salesmen preached to the converted and the hangers-back alike; lines at the loan companies stretched through the revolving doors and out on to the winter pavements. But many in those lines were trying to get additional financing on their last year's cars. The new models were an indifferent success despite all the uproar of display and Detroit's patriotic attention to it. Searchlights sliced up the heavens while the city lay under flu.

Teachers at Wayne University soon learn not to tease the American Automobile. *Lèse* Chrysler was a moral offense, an attack on the livelihood and the sanctity of the American garage. Detroit was a town in which men looked at hub caps as men elsewhere have sometimes looked at ankles. The small foreign car found itself treated with a violent Halloween kidding-on-the-square, scratched, battered, and smeared (another Jungian series of three!). A passionate and sullen town, Detroit had no doubts about its proper business. All it doubted was everything else.

I often failed at inspiring my students to do the assigned reading. Many of them had part-time jobs in the automobile industry or its annexes. Even a Philosopher found it difficult to top the argument, "I couldn't read the book this week, I have to *work*," with its implied reproach for a scholar's leisure. But alas, many of these stricken proletarians drove freshly-minted automobiles. They worked in order to keep up the payments, racing like laboratory mice around the cage of depreciation. Certain faculty deep thinkers, addicted to broad understanding of the problems of others, argued that these students were so poor they *had* to buy new cars in order to restore their confidence. The finance companies seemed to hear their most creative expressions, not me. Deep in that long Detroit winter, I had the task of going from the pre-Socratic mystics all the way to Sartre, for nine credits. Like an audio-visual monkey, I leapt from movie projector to records to slides, with concurrent deep labor in book and tablet. We read *The Brothers Karamazov*, but knowing the movie did not give credit. We studied *The Waste Land*, and reading the footnotes did not suffice. We listened to Wanda Landowska play the harpsichord on records. We sat in the dark before a slide of Seurat's "La Grande Jatte" while I explained the importance of the measles of *pointillisme* to students who only wanted to see life clear and true, see it comfortably. Clotilda Adams said that this kind of painting hurt her eyes. She said that there was too much reading for one course—"piling it on. This isn't the only course we take." She said that she liked music, though. Moses only had to bring the Law down the mountain to the children of Israel; I had to bring it pleasingly.

We made exegeses. I flatly turned down the request of a dean that I take attendance. As a statesmanlike compromise, I tested regularly for content and understanding.

Then, on a certain morning, I handed back some quiz papers at the beginning of class. Out on the street, a main thoroughfare through town, it was snowing; this was one of those magical days of late winter snowfall—pale, cold, clean, and the entire city momentarily muffled by the silence of snow. The room hissed with steam heat; a smell of galoshes and mackinaws arose from the class. "Let us not discuss the test—let us rise above grades. Let us try to consider nihilism as a byproduct of the Romantic revival—" I had just begun my lecture when an odd clashing, lumping noise occurred on Cass Avenue. "Eliot's later work, including *The Four Quartets*, which we will not discuss here. . . ."

But I was interrupted by a deep sigh from the class. A product of nihilism and the romantic revival? No. It was that strange tragic sigh of horror and satisfaction. Out in the street, beyond the window against which I stood, a skidding truck had sideswiped a taxi. The truckdriver had parked and gone into a drugstore. The cab was smashed like a cruller. From the door, the driver had emerged, stumbling drunkenly on the icy road, holding his head. There was blood on his head. There was blood on his hands. He clutched his temples. The lines of two-way traffic, moving very slowly in the snow and ice, carefully avoided hitting him. There were streaks of perforated and patterned snow, frothed up by tires. He was like an island around which the sea of traffic undulated in slow waves; but he was an island that moved in the sea and held hands to head. He slid and stumbled back and forth, around and about his cab in the middle of the wide street. He was in confusion, in shock. Even at this distance I could see blood on the new-fallen snow. Drivers turned their heads upon him like angry Halloween masks, but did not get involved. Snow spit at his feet.

No one in the class moved. The large window through which we gazed was like a screen, with the volume turned down by habit, by snow, by a faulty tube. As the teacher, my authority took precedence. I ran out to lead the cab driver into the building. An elderly couple sat huddled in the car, staring at the smashed door, afraid to come out the other. They said they were unhurt.

I laid the man down on the floor. He was bleeding from the head and his face was a peculiar purplish color, with a stubble of beard like that of a dead man. There was a neat prick in his forehead where the union button in his cap had been driven into the skin. I sent a student to call for an ambulance. The cab driver's color was like that of the bruised industrial sky. "You be okay till the ambulance———?"

Foolish question. No alternative. No answer.

We waited. The class was restless. When they weren't listening to me, or talking to themselves, or smudging blue books in an exam, they did not know what to do in this room devoted to the specialized absorption of ideas. Silence. Scraping of feet, crisping of paper. We watched the slow-motion traffic on the street outside.

The cab driver moved once in a rush, turning over face down against the floor, with such force that I thought he might break his nose. Then slowly, painfully, as if in a dream, he turned back and lay staring at the ceiling. His woollen lumberjack soaked up the blood trickling from one ear; the blood traveled up separated cilia of wool which drew it in with a will of their own. There was a swaying, osmotic movement like love-making in the eager little wisps of wool. An astounded ring of Humanities 610 students watched, some still holding their returned quiz papers. One girl in particular, Clotilda Adams, watched him and me with her eyes brilliant, wet and bulging, and her fist crumpling the paper. I tried by imagining it to force the ambulance through the chilled and snow-fallen city. I saw it weaving around the injured who strutted with shock over ice and drift, its single red Cyclops' eye turning, the orderlies hunched over on benches, chewing gum and cursing the driver. The ambulance did not arrive. Clotilda Adams' eye had a thick, impenetrable sheen over it. She watched from the cab driver to me as if we were in some way linked. When would the authorities get there? When the medics? There must have been many accidents in town, and heart attacks, and fires with cases of smoke inhalation.

Before the ambulance arrived, the police were there. They came strolling into the classroom with their legs apart, as if they remembered ancestors who rode the plains. Their mouths were heavy in thought. They had noses like salamis, red and mottled with fat. They were angry at the weather, at the school, at the crowd, at me, and especially at the prostrate man at our feet. He gave them a means to the creative expression of pique. (Everyone needs an outlet.)

Now Clotilda Adams took a step backward, and I recall thinking this odd. She had been treading hard near the pool of blood about the cab-driver, but when the cops strolled up, she drifted toward the outer edge of the group of students, with a sly look of caution in her downcast, sideways-cast eyes. Her hand still crisped at the returned exam paper. This sly, lid-fallen look did not do her justice. She was a hard little girl of the sort often thought to be passionate—skinny but well-breasted, a high hard rump with a narrow curve, a nervous mouth.

The two policemen stood over the body of the cab-driver. They stared at him in the classic pose—one cop with a hand resting lightly on the butt of his gun and the other on his butt, the younger cop with lips so pouted that his breath made a snuffling sound in his nose. They both had head colds. Their Ford was pulled up on the snow-covered lawn outside, with raw muddled marks of tread in the soft dirt. When the snow melted, there would be wounded streaks in the grass. The cab driver closed his eyes under the finicking, distasteful examination. At last one spoke: "See your driver's license."

The cab driver made a clumsy gesture towards his pocket. The cop bent and went into the pocket. He flipped open the wallet, glanced briefly at the photographs and cash, glanced at me, and then began lip-reading the license.

The cab-driver was in a state of shock. There was a mixture of thin and thick blood on his clothes and messing the floor. "This man is badly hurt," I said. "Can't we get him to the hospital first?"

"This is only your *driver* license," the cop said slowly, having carefully read through Color of Hair: *Brn*, Color of Eyes: *Brn*, and checked each item with a stare at the man on the floor. "Let me see your chauffeur license."

"He's badly hurt," I said. "Get an ambulance."

"Teach'," said the older cop, "you know your business? We know ours."

"It's on the way," said the other. "Didn't you call it yourself?"

"No, one of the students. . . ." I said.

He grinned with his great victory. "So—don't you trust your pupils neither?"

Shame. I felt shame at this ridicule of my authority in the classroom. A professor is not a judge, a priest, or a sea captain; he does not have the right to perform marriages on the high seas of audio-visual aids and close reasoning. But he is more than an intercom between student and fact; he can be a stranger to love for his students, but not to a passion for his subject; he is a student himself; his pride is lively. The role partakes of a certain heft and control. There is power to make decisions, power to abstain, power to bewilder, promote, hold back, adjust, and give mercy; power, an investment of pride, a risk of shame.

Clotilda Adams, still clutching her exam, stared at me with loathing. She watched me bested by the police. She barely glanced, and only contemptuously, at the man bleeding from the head on the floor. She moved slightly forward again in order to participate fully in an action which apparently had some important meaning for her. She had lost her fear of the police when she saw how we all stood with them. The limits were established.

The police were going through the cab-driver's pockets. They took out a folding pocket-knife and cast significant looks at it and at each other. It had a marbled plastic hilt, like a resort souvenir. It was attached to a key ring.

"Hey!" one said to the half-conscious man. "What's this knife for?"

"Where'd you get them keys?" the other demanded, prodding the cabbie with his toe.

"A skeleton key. These cab companies," one of the cops decided to explain to Clotilda Adams, who was standing nearby, "they get the dregs. Hillbillies, you know?"

I said nothing, found nothing to say. I now think of Lord Acton's famous law, which is accepted as true the way it was uttered. The opposite is also true—the commoner's way: Having no power corrupts; having absolutely no power corrupts absolutely.

The bleeding seemed to have stopped. The cab driver sat up, looking no better, with his bluish, greenish, drained head hanging between his knees. His legs were crumpled stiffly. He propped himself on his hands. The police shot questions at him. He mumbled, mumbled, explained, explained.

"How long you been in Detroit? How come you come out of the mountains?"

"Why you pick up this fare?"

"What makes you think Cass is a one-way street?"

Mumbling and mumbling, explaining and explaining, the cab-driver tried to satisfy them. He also said: "Hurt. Maybe you get me to the hospital, huh? Hurt real bad."

"Maybe," said one of the cops, "maybe we take you to the station house first. That boy you hit says reckless driving. I think personally you'd flunk the drunk test—what you think, Teach'?"

I sent one of the students to call for an ambulance again. In the infinitesimal pause between my suggestion and his action, an attentive reluctant expectant caesura, I put a dime in his hand for the call. One of the cops gave me that long look described by silent movie critics as the slow burn. "They drive careful," he finally said. "It's snowing. They got all that expensive equipment."

The snow had started again outside the window. The skid-marks on the lawn were covered. Though the sky was low and gray, the white sifting down gave a peaceful village glow to this industrial Detroit. Little gusts barely rattled the windows. With the class, the cops, and the driver, we were living deep within a snowy paper-weight. I felt myself moving very slowly, swimming within thick glass, like the loosened plastic figure in a paper-weight. The snow came down in large torn flakes, all over the buildings of Wayne University, grass, trees, and the pale radiance of a network of slow-motion super-highways beyond. Across the street a modern building—glass and aluminum strips—lay unfinished in this weather. Six months ago there had been a student boardinghouse on that spot, filled with the artists and the beat, the guitar-wielders and the modern dancers, with a tradition going all the way back to the Korean war. Now there were wheelbarrows full of frozen cement; there were intentions to build a Japanese garden, with Japanese proportions and imported goldfish.

My student returned from the telephone. He had reached a hospital.

The cab driver was fading away. Rootlets of shock hooded his eyes: the lid was closing shut. A cop asked him another question—what the button on his cap stood for—it was a union button—and then the man just went reclining on his elbow, he slipped slowly down, he lay in the little swamp of crusted blood on the floor. You know what happens when milk is boiled? The crust broke like the crust of boiled milk when a spoon goes into coffee. The cop stood with a delicate, disgusted grimace on his face. What a business to be in, he seemed to be thinking. In approximately ten years, at age forty-two, he could retire and sit comfortable in an undershirt, with a non-returnable can of beer, before the color TV. He could relax. He could *start* to relax. But in the meanwhile— nag, nag, nag. Drunk cabbies, goddam hillbillies. The reckless driver on the floor seemed to sleep. His lips moved. He was alive.

Then a puffing intern rushed into the room. I had not heard the ambulance. The policeman gave room and the intern kneeled. He undid his bag. The orderlies glanced at the floor and went back out for their stretcher.

I stood on one side of the body, the kneeling intern with his necklace of stethoscope, and the two meditative cops. On the other side was the group of students, and at their head, like a leader filled with wrath, risen in time of crisis, stood Clotilda Adams, still clutching her exam paper. There were tears in her eyes. She was in a fury. She had been thinking all this time, and now her thinking had issue: *rage*. Over the body she handed me a paper, crying out, "I don't think I deserved a *D* on that quiz. I answered all the questions. I can't get my credit for Philo of Ed without I get a *B* off you."

I must have looked at her with pure stupidity on my face. There is a Haitian proverb: Stupidity won't kill you, but it'll make you sweat a lot. She took the opportunity to make me sweat, took my silence for guilt, took my open-mouthed gaze for weakness. She said: "If I was a white girl, you'd grade me easier."

Guilty, a hundred years, a thousand years of it; pity for the disaster of ignorance and fear, pity for ambition rising out of ignorance; adoration of desire; trancelike response to passion—passion which justifies itself because passionate. . . . I looked at her with mixed feelings. I could not simply put her down. In order to *put down* your own mind must be made up, put down. She had beauty and dignity, stretched tall and wrathful, with teeth for biting and eyes for striking dead.

"But I know my rights," she said, "*mister.* My mother told me about your kind—lent my father money on his car and then hounded him out of town. He's been gone since fifty-three. But you can't keep us down forever, no sir, you can't always keep us down—"

She was talking and I was yelling. She was talking and yelling about injustice and I, under clamps, under ice, was yelling in a whisper about the sick man. She was blaming me for all her troubles, all the troubles she had seen, and I was blaming her for not seeing what lay before her, and we were making an appointment to meet in my office and discuss this thing more calmly, Miss Adams. Okay. All right. Later.

The police, the doctor, the orderlies, and the injured cab-driver were gone. The police car out front was gone and the snow was covering its traces. The janitor came in and swept up the bloodstains with green disinfectant powder. The frightened couple in the cab were released. They all disappeared silently into the great city, into the routine of disaster and recovery of a great city. I dismissed the class until tomorrow.

The next day I tried to explain to Miss Adams what I meant about her failing to respond adequately to the facts of our life together. Her mouth quivered. Yesterday rage; today a threat of tears. What did I mean she wasn't *adequate?* What did I know about adequate anyhow? Nothing. Just a word. Agreed, Miss Adams. I was trying to say that there were two questions at issue between us—her exam grade and her choice of occasion to dispute it. I would like to discuss each matter separately. I tried to explain why putting the two events together had disturbed me. I tried to explain the notions of empirical evidence and metaphor. Finally I urged her to have her exam looked at by the head of the department, but she refused because she knew in advance that he would support me. "White is Right," she said.

"Do you want to drop out of the class?"

"No. I'll stay," she said with a sudden patient, weary acceptance of her fate. "I'll do what I can."

"I'll do what I can too," I said.

She smiled hopefully at me. She was tuckered out by the continual alert for combat everywhere. She was willing to forgive and go easy. When she left my office, this smile, shy, pretty, and conventional, tried to tell me that she could be generous—a friend.

We had come to Thomas Hobbes and John Locke in our tour through time and the river of humanities. I pointed out that the English philosophers were noted for clarity and eloquence of style. I answered this question: The French? Isn't French noted for clarity? Yes, they too, but they were more abstract. On the whole. In general.

The class took notes on the truths we unfolded together. Spring came and the snow melted. There was that brief Detroit flowering of the new season—jasmine and hollyhocks—which, something like it, must have captivated the Frenchman Antoine de la Mothe Cadillac when he paused on the straits of Detroit in 1701. University gardeners planted grass seed where the patrol car had parked on the lawn. The new models, all except the Cadillac, were going at mean discounts.

"The 'Humanities,'" wrote Clotilda Adams in her final essay, "are a necessary additive to any teacher's development worth her 'salt' in the perilous times of today. The West and the 'Free World' must stand up to the war of ideas against the 'Iron' Curtain." This was in answer to a question about Beethoven, Goethe, and German romanticism. She did not pass the course, but she was nevertheless admitted on probation to the student teacher program because of the teacher shortage and the great need to educate our children in these perilous times. Of today.

Humanities 610 provided ballast for the ship of culture as it pitched and reeled in the heavy seas of real life; I lashed myself to the mast, but after hearing the siren song of ground course outlines, I cut myself free and leaned over the rail with the inside of my lip showing.

It would be oversimplifying to say that I left off teaching Humanities merely because of an experience. Such an argument is fit to be published under the title "I was a Teen-Age Humanities Professor." I also left for fitter jobs, more money, a different life. Still, what I remember of the formal study of Truth and Beauty, for advanced credit in education, is a great confusion of generalities, committees, conferences, audio-visual importunities, and poor contact. "Contact!" cried the desperate deans and chairmen, like radio operators in ancient war movies. And much, much discussion of how to get through to the students. How to get through? Miss Adams and Mr. Gold, cab-driver and Thomas Hobbes, policemen and the faceless student who paused an instant for a dime for the telephone—we all have to discover how relevant we are to each other. Or do we *have* to? No, we can merely perish, shot down like mad dogs or diminished into time with no more than a glimpse of the light.

Words fade; our experience does not touch; we make do with babble and time-serving. We need to learn the meaning of words, the meaning of the reality those words refer to; we must clasp reality close. We cannot flirt forever, brown-nosing or brow-beating. We must act and build out of our own spirits. How? How? We continually need new politics, new cities, new marriages and families, new ways of work and leisure. We also need the fine old ways. For me, the primitive appeal to pleasure and pain of writing stories is a possible action, is the way in and out again, as teaching was not. As a teacher, I caught my students too late and only at the top of their heads, at the raw point of pride and ambition, and I had not enough love and pressure as a teacher to open the way through their intentions to the common humanity which remains locked within. As a writer, I could hope to hit them in their bodies and needs, where lusts and ideals are murkily nurtured together, calling to the prime fears and joys directly, rising with them from the truths of innocence into the truths of experience.

The peculiar combination of ignorance and jadedness built into most institutions is a desperate parody of personal innocence, personal experience. Nevertheless, education, which means a drawing out—even formal education, a formal drawing out—is a variety of experience, and experience is the only evidence we have. After evidence comes our thinking upon it. Do the scientists, secreting their honey in distant hives, hear the barking of the black dog which follows them? Will the politicians accept the lead of life, or will they insist on a grade of *B* in Power and Dominion over a doomed race? We need to give proper answers to the proper questions.

Particular life is still the best map to truth. When we search our hearts and strip our pretenses, we all know this. Particular life—we know only what we *know*. Therefore the policemen stay with me: I have learned to despise most authority. The cab-driver remains in his sick bleeding: pity for the fallen and helpless. And I think of Clotilda Adams in her power and weakness; like the cops, she has an authority of stupidity; like the victim of an accident, she is fallen and helpless. But some place, since we persist in our cold joke against the ideal of democracy, the cops still have the right to push people around, Clotilda is leading children in the Pledge of Allegiance. We must find a way to teach better and to learn.

R. V. Cassill
(1919–   )

The reasons for a teacher's cynicism are fathomable and sad. So are the excuses for his evasions. Even his martyrdom, should it occur, can be explained. But the nobility that can muster defeat of his cynicism deserves more than praise. Whereas a martyr may choose prudently in favor of self-sacrifice, for results worth the cost, the man locked in secret combat with himself, where nobility is always bare, may stand to gain nothing by his victory save reaffirmation of his peril. In short, the true idealist explores a wilderness never traversed by the inveterate realist.

Though this story takes place on the campus of a private women's college, the plight of Dr. Cameron is common to all teachers who have come to view their profession as an escape from the ideals that first brought them to it: their days now cohere unvexed by doubts and exhilaration, all campus states having become equal—states of humor, of politics, of stealth, of irony, of cloistering, of bureaucracy, of scholarship. "Larchmoor Is Not the World" describes a school's debasement and a teacher's regeneration. Dr. Cameron sheds the illusion adored by many of his nonfictional colleagues, that teachers can somehow salvage this world without ever, by act or influence, having to enter it.

A native of Iowa, R. V. Cassill is the author of *Clem Anderson* (1961), *The Father and Other Stories* (1965), and *La Vie Passionée of Rodney Buckthorne* (1968).

192

LARCHMOOR IS NOT THE WORLD

In the winter the glassed arcade between Thornton and Gillespie Halls was filled with potted flowers so it smelled and looked like a greenhouse. Last night's storm, blowing in across the athletic fields of the Northwest campus, had left a shape of frozen snow like a white boomerang in the corner of each pane behind the rows of geraniums and ferns.

The first time Dr. Cameron walked through the arcade on this particular day he stopped to point with his pipestem at the ranked greenery so slightly and perilously separated from the outside cold. "There," he rumbled to Mr. Wilks of History, "is your symbol for this young women's seminary. There is your Larchmoor girl cut off by a pane of glass from the blast of your elements. A visible defiance of the nature of things, made possible by a corrupt technology."

Mr. Wilks grimaced and chuckled, weighed this illustration of their common attitude toward the college in which they taught, finally amended, "The glass is wrong. Glass they could see through. See the world in which they don't live even though. . . ." His thought trailed off in a giggle. At Larchmoor Mr. Wilks seemed to spend most of his energy looking behind him to see if he had been overheard.

"True," Dr. Cameron said. As they loitered through the arcade, the music and the rumble of the student lounge rose to them from the floor below. It rose mixed inextricably with the smell of baked goods from the dining hall and the moist smell of steam from laboring radiators. Now and then a cry, barbaric, probably happy but otherwise meaningless, punctuated the noise. "The analogy breaks down, true. Listen to them down there. One gets to be like an animal trainer. Sensitive to their noises. If I had no calendar I could tell by their tone that Christmas vacation started this afternoon."

"Then there's an identifying noise that distinguishes Christmas Vacation from the beginning of—say—Spring Vacation?"

"Hmm. Yes, that's right. In seven years my ear has become acutely attuned to it. You'll pick it up eventually. Unhappily in learning their mass sound you'll become unable to distinguish one of them from the others. Compensation at work. They will seem to you one single enormous female juvenile named Shirley or whatever the name would happen to be of the child movie star ascendant in the year of their birth." Dr. Cameron's baby-pink face grew almost radiant. "Tomorrow," he said, "the sonsofbitches will all be gone home and we'll have three weeks of peace. Shantih."

The second time he went through the arcade that day he met Sandra White, dressed for her journey with high heels now and a fur coat, looking like the ads in the fashion magazines with the good sharp empty Nordic shape of her head an appurtenance to the excellent clothes— looking five years older than she had looked that morning in his American Literature class. Her manner, too, had been changed with her clothes so that she spoke to him as a young matron patronizing an old and crotchety, really lovable, duck who had "made his lah-eef out of literature."

"Dr. Cameron. Thank *you* for the list of books," she said. "I don't think I'll give any presents this Christmas except books and I. . . ." Yet because this was so obviously a statement coined to please him, both became momentarily embarrassed. It was the girl who first recovered and went on, "I think I'll get Daddy the Dos Passos *USA*."

"Hmmm." He chewed his pipestem and stared at the glass roof of the arcade, then smiled.

"Well," she said in defense, "Daddy is really searching . . . for . . . *that* kind of Americanism. He's not just a businessman. He's really. . . ."

"Yes," he said. "I understood you to say you wanted this list of books for yourself, not just for presents."

"Oh. I'm going to ask for the Yeats for myself," she said. Her tone, demanding that this would please him, produced from the efficient catalog of his memory the image of her eyes becoming feminine-dramatic in that class hour a week before when he had quoted "An aged man is a paltry thing . . . unless soul clasp its hands and sing and louder sing for every tatter in its mortal dress." Well, the quotation had been an indulgence for him and not intended for the class at all. It had been a parade before their innocent minds of a conscious expression of his own dilemma. He had spoken the lines to his class with the motives that lead a man to confess to his dog the sentiments for which he has no human confidant. But this little female, Sandra, whatever those words may have meant to her, had caught something of their importance to him and trapped him now into paying for the indulgence with a compliment to her taste.

"Fine," he said, "that's fine."

With a still doubtful look she said "Merry Christmas" and let him go on to his office.

Here was the sanctuary which he had been seven years in building. A desk barred off one corner of the room. When students came in he sat behind it like a magistrate at the bar. Three walls, excepting door and window spaces, were lined to the ceiling with books. "I bought them," he once told Wilks, "but only for insulation and display. It's fatuous to assume that anybody can own books. I think that President Herman is pleased to find them there when he brings down parents and the prospective customers to exhibit me as a mechanism of the English department."

His swivel chair took most of the space behind the desk. It made of the corner an efficient nest, for he could swing to any of the cabinets and drawers in which he filed themes. Also within reach were the two material items he needed for his intellectual life. One was a bolt tied on a length of wrapping cord that he sometimes swung as a pendulum. The other was a motto that he had lettered painstakingly on colored paper. Originally it had come from an examination paper handed in to him during his first year at Larchmoor. "Shelley's main purpose was to write a lot of poems," it said. "This it came easy for him to do." Sometimes when he was alone he would place the inscription before him on his desk and sit laughing crazily at it until all the stains of teaching at Larchmoor were washed away. Then purified, without moving except to throw his shoulders back, he would watch that fraction of the campus where the pendulum of seasons appeared before his window.

This afternoon the sunlight was a strange and clamorous orange that moved on the black tree trunks and the snow. Here nature dramatized the quality of a Beckman painting, black cedars over water, it might have been, or such a landscape as the horns in Sibelius presented with not so much art as longing, such a landscape as might contain a golden mute princess called out by Death—that central myth that all the Romantics had exploited.

The embroidered, death-bidden, golden will-o'the-wisp (and Sandra White now drifted on his mind's screen in a role that would have surprised her. Not as an intellect that shared his understanding of poetry but, wrapped in a rich cocoon of fur, wool, and silk that protected her delicacies from the blowing cold, as the image itself which the poets had conceived and desired—the figure on the Grecian urn, the witch-lady on the mead, or that which Malraux's Dutchman saw on the Shanghai sidewalks, proud and strutting beyond the reach of the pro-letariat desire) which like Shelley's Beatrice must be the fairest, youngest, purest of flesh to satisfy the snowy mouth of the Death the Romantics had imagined.

The peacefulness of snow is pure commercial folklore, he speculated, and in art the cold North always somehow emerged as the symbol of hungry frenzy—like the glacid and perfect tyranny which Plato described as the worst disaster of all that society can manage. The disorder of cold which had wrought the counter disorder of Northern art—the wind-whipped fires in the snowfield—with its load of desire protesting too much.

If Dr. Cameron had moved closer to his window, he would neces-sarily have seen more than this private landscape of a few trees, snow, and sun in which his mind pursued the lost girl. He would have seen more than twenty Larchmoor girls standing in the slush in front of the Kampus Kabin while they waited for taxis. They bounced, giggled, sang ("a woman, a woman, a woman without a man, teedlededum, bumph"), chewed gum, shifted packages or suitcases from hand to hand, stamped their fur-topped boots in the muck of the road. He knew they were there, not five degrees outside the arc of vision which the window gave him. "But I have the right not to look."

With the arrival of each Christmas Vacation since he had come to Larchmoor he had discovered himself confronted with a particular crisis of fatigue and depression. The beginning of yet another school year and the first exacting months hollowed him emotionally, and the pleasures of intellect had lost their recreational power. While the girls went off to whatever indulgences the society provided for its most expensive and pampered stock, he went to his bachelor rooms to read and smoke incessantly, and considered how he might get a job elsewhere until always, with the passing of the actual and figurative solstice, the change of renewal occurred. What was compounded of hatred and contempt for Larchmoor led him first to review the other places he had taught—the two big universities where the younger assistants whinnied like mares around the head of the department and the religious college where he had been forbidden to smoke on campus and required to attend chapel daily—then led through a couple of drinking bouts with some one of his friends, like Mr. Wilks. There had always been younger men like Mr. Wilks coming and going as Larchmoor instructors. Just out of graduate school they regarded Larchmoor as a stepping stone to bigger schools, but while they stayed—one or two each year succeeding those who had gone—they formed a fit audience though few for such occasions as the Christmas drunks. Those times gave him the chance to elaborate with perverse brilliance on the attractions Larchmoor had for him.

They would be sitting in the easy chairs of his rooms with a litter of crackers and cheese on a card table between them, the black windows frosting over, and in the late hours the monologue would pause only when one or another went unsteadily to the bathroom. "Do you remember reading about that Jap general on Iwo Jima . . . said 'I will die here' . . . the component of all the forces of his life . . . so that even the melodrama was right for the bandy-legged little bastard. Fitting. The answer is a kind of balance—not balance—but that second in the pendulum's swing when all the forces are composed so there must be an instant of harmony that the eye isn't quick enough to catch when one reasons that there must be no motion. Still. . . . The effort of the mind to perpetuate that second by selection out of all the comic and vicious flux in us and around us is the same as the slave's impulse to show off his ropes. . . . Larchmoor locks up kids that should be out and doing things. Their bad luck is good for me. There are different ages, and for me freedom doesn't exist in the world. It's an asylum growth. . . . I've got my office for asylum like a rat's nest in the corner of a busy house. I don't huddle there because I'm interested in the house. Nobody but a damn fool would be concerned with Larchmoor as Larchmoor. . . . It gives me a stable place to sit and watch the 'pismires'" here he smiled "'and the stars.' And don't you know, Wilks, that a man has to actually utter his ideas? Your gloomy newspapers tell you that. It's such an undeniable premise of the search for freedom. Here I can say whatever I please to my classes. Elsewhere, in these days, I might be quickly apprehended as a Communist or an atheist, but when I say something to my girls they put it in their notebooks and there's an end to it. Oh, I have my disguises here. On another level I can talk to the vermin Herman"—Larchmoor's president—"the same way. As far as that goes. When he asked me what I thought of the new dormitory with the air-conditioned bedsprings I made same trivial remark about painting 'our outward walls so costly gay.' And he thought it was my stamp of approval, yes he did. . . . And then we mustn't fool ourselves. Where else could I go? I'm not a scholar in the sense that I've ever felt a mission to get my name in *PMLA* or write a book on Chaucer's cook's mormal. I'm a reader, that's all I amount to. 'Whatever games are played with us, we must play no games with ourselves, but deal in our privacy with the last honesty and truth.' Larchmoor not only lets but forces me to be honest with myself. The games it plays with me are not much bother. To them I'm just an old gaffer that talks like Bartlett's quotations. I have a place here. They pay me as a fixture. . . . The girls are pretty. Like old David's my bones need the warmth provided by a moderate proximity of young female flesh. My disguises . . . I look too old to notice them. I am too old to letch for any of them, but by God they're pleasant furniture. . . . At Larchmoor I come close to balancing. If it were any better I'd get involved with it. No doubt I've searched subconsciously for Larchmoor all my life. I'm preoccupied with how I die. Like the Jap general. That isn't morbid at my age. More natural. I want to die in this moral Iwo Jima . . . and be buried under the hockey field."

II

He had put on his overcoat to go home when he passed through the glassed arcade for the third time that day. This time a clatter of heels on the tile floor rang behind him. There was a hand on his arm and Shirley Bridges' face suddenly thrust so close to his own that he jumped back. At first the circles of white around her eyes and the chalky strip on either side of her mouth struck him as an antic fashion culled from the pages of *Vogue* and destined to become a part of the fluctuating uniform of Larchmoor. But even as he began to smile her hand clawed down his sleeve until she had hold of his bare wrist and he understood that her face was marked with some girlish emotion. Her hand on his wrist was wet and cold. He felt pain in the back of his skull and then a release of anger. "What's the trouble, Miss Bridges?" He lifted her fingers one at a time from their hysterical grasp. "Are you ill?"

To his exasperation she said, "No. My grade. You. . . ."

"I understand," he said. He cleared his throat the better to snarl. "In spite of your studious industry, I, I, I have so seriously misprized you that I reported you to the Dean, who maliciously put you on academic probation. Now you're going to be forbidden the delights of the juke-box and the downtown dance hall for the rest of the semester." The tonic of anger had blurred away any distinctions he might have tried to make between her and The Larchmoor Girl in a more temperate season. "Every coercion will be applied to force you to the unreasonable humiliation of reading your books. I am committed to the belief that you will live through it. Now, if you will excuse me, may I bid you a Merry Christmas?"

"Please," she said. In the blue expanse of her eyes the pupil diminished nastily like an insect pulling its wings to its body.

He felt the burning of his face. She'd better not put her hands on me again, he thought. "Don't take all this so intensely. There really isn't any reason you can't make up your work. Weren't you the one last fall who was, well—so sublimely confident of her ability? You sometimes make interesting comments in class. I think you just need to decide to do some work."

"No," she said. "Talk to me." Her mouth hung loose like a bright ribbon, and her tongue arched against her lower teeth.

"You're *not* well."

She nodded. "Talk to me in your office. Please."

One hall on their way led past the president's office and reception rooms. She would not go this way. Without quite knowing why, he let her guide him down a roundabout stairway.

While he lit his pipe and rocked squeaking in his swivel chair, he looked at the girl's hands. The lacquered nails were broader than they were long and the fingers were tapered like a child's from the palm. How do they manage to look like *women?* he asked himself. What corruption and tampering with mortality in the flesh is it that lets them or makes them look generally the same from fifteen to thirty-five, brushed and painted and girdled to a formula that here across his desk was breaking down into its sodden components. He noted that two beads of spittle had stuck in the corners of Shirley's mouth.

What would be the effect, he wondered, if he should announce at once that he had reconsidered her case and had already decided to give her an A for the semester?

"You restore my faith," he said. "In seven years of teaching here I have never seen a Larchmoor girl who spent the day before a vacation even thinking about the college, let alone the grades she might get in one class in Biblical literature."

"They're going to kick me out," she said.

"Oh nonsense. No final grades go in for six weeks yet."

"They are," she insisted. "They sent for Daddy. He's in President Herman's office now. I know they sent for him to take me out of school."

"Because of your grades? Not because of your grades, surely."

"Oh. I thought if I could get my grades straightened out that would help."

"You mean you've got in some kind of trouble. If your grades were good you might get by with it?"

The note of sarcasm was heavy enough to warn her of a trap. She said, "No, I don't think there would be any trouble if my grades were all right. I could work everything else out, I know."

"If you're in difficulty you ought to have gone to your housemother, not to me."

"Honest it's the grades and my classes and things."

Dr. Cameron shook his head. His white mustache dipped at the ends as he made a face. "I'm guilty of many things, but I have never given any grades I didn't think were deserved; so there isn't much use to talk about that. Nevertheless I might tell you something that will reassure you. Among other things Larchmoor is a commercial institution. I have even heard President Herman speak of it as a business. You pay a considerable tuition here which would have to be refunded if you were dropped before the end of the semester. I have no doubt that the administration will find some way to avoid that unpleasant necessity." This will end the interview, he thought. She can understand that better than anything. Coin is the sea that bore them hither and will bear them hence. It is the direct communication, the basis of knowledge on which whatever they might get from the library or classroom would only be fluff. "Does that explain exactly why they aren't going to kick you out?"

"It isn't that way, is it?"

He grinned like a devil. "Undoubtedly." Less because she demanded it than because of the habit of explanation he went on, "There's much more to it than that. I have simply given you a short cut to understanding why you won't be expelled. From your side of the fence everything seems to be an absolute. Every rule, every pronouncement, perhaps. I'm old enough to know there are no absolutes. Everyone here who has anything to do with your case lives in a tangle of confusions and opinions not so different from your own. Out of these will come some compromise that won't be too hard on you. That's the truth. That's the way the world goes. Compromise, compromise. President Herman's decrees and judgments may seem absolute and final to a freshman. They're not really. He's not God Almighty."

"They're all God Almighty," the girl said. "My father is God Almighty too." He was not sure whether she meant this as a joke or as an attempt at philosophy, but whichever it was it seemed to amuse her. "That's why it's so goofy. They say I destroyed their faith. Didn't you hear about that, Dr. Cameron? It happened in your Biblical Lit class so I guess you knew about it. It's so funny because I think there is God Almighty. Lots of them. You're another one because remember at the first of the year you told us to use our minds and question things and then I was the only one that argued and you're going to give me an F."

"You haven't handed in any work," he said irrelevantly. He turned the swivel chair sharply sideways so the old bearings screamed. So the other little ones had sat in class all semester being careful to hear nothing, read nothing before their open eyes except what confirmed those memories of Sunday school they liked to call "their faith." All right. He had known that and had remarked on it caustically. But here was the other twist—that they were leagued, each little monster with her shining braids, to smell out differences within the herd which had not been apparent to him. He labored his memory for images of the class from which this one girl would appear standing like a martyr among the Philistian mob. She said that she had "argued." He could remember nothing of the sort. Each day she had seemed as impersonal as a ninepin in a row of her classmates. Her eyes had been as blue as theirs, her hair more blonde than some; the courtesy of her bored attention had been the same though she had not taken notes so assiduously as a few. Somehow, on a level of intuition that he could only guess at they had found the intolerable difference in her. He remembered the wetness of her hand on his wrist and wondered if it had been fear they smelled.

"I thought you got along all right with the girls," he said.

"I will try. I will get along if they'll let me stay. I think I was just beginning to make some friends." She drew in her upper arms against her breasts and shivered.

"That sort of thing has to happen. I don't suppose it's possible to *make* friends."

The idea, with her own interpretation, had not helped. "I know I could," she said.

"Don't you have any—well, people, girls you run around with here?"

"Oh, yes. My roommate. And there's lots of others. I know how to make them like me if I could stay."

If there had been someone impartial with them—Mr. Wilks perhaps—to whom he could have rationalized the abyss he glimpsed, letting orderly words mount like a steel bridge over it, he might still have kept himself from involvement. "One must not seek the contagion of the herd," he would have said. "God knows what conformities they may exact from her once she has kissed the rod. Whatever it may cost to maintain even the fear, if it's only the fear that distinguishes one. . . ." If he could have found the words on which he depended.

"'Larchmoor, calm and serene on thy hill,'" he muttered. "Now Miss Bridges, Shirley, maybe we ought to look at this another way. Suppose they . . . suppose you leave Larchmoor now. There are bigger schools you might go to where you'd have a better chance to be yourself."

"Bigger?" she said. "Oh no."

"You mustn't forget that there is time for anything you want to do."

"Not if I go home," she said.

"But you're wrong. There will be fifty years ahead of you"—realizing that she could not believe this—"Larchmoor is not the world. Every possibility is open at your age."

"Would you go to the president and tell him I'm a good student? Could you give me any kind of a good grade if I'd work all through vacation?" She rose and came round the desk and stood just in front of him, just beyond arm's length from him. She stood very straight facing him and neither swaying nor looking at him. "Please," he said. "Sit down. I'm afraid I don't understand at all. I can't understand why it's so important for you to stay here. You have so many years ahead of you. There is plenty of time. Go home for a while."

She sighed like a child, heavily. "I guess I ought to tell you why they sent for Daddy. It was because when the railroad agents came out to sell tickets home I was the only girl in school who wasn't going. I would have stayed here if they would have let me. Then I got scared and rented a hotel room downtown."

He was afraid to ask any further questions. Once again his necessary refuge was not in forty years of the poor scholar's study but only in the pipe which he could chew and smoke and scrape ostentatiously as he did now. His eyebrows arched as though to admonish her to say no more.

"I can't go home. I'm afraid of Daddy. That was the reason."

"Now, now. You could surely explain to him. . . . Grades aren't that important."

"He fought me last summer with his fists. I'm not quite as strong as he is. He knocked me down and was choking me when mother came and made him stop." The words were rushing from her throat like a foul torrent heaved up by the convulsions of her body as she writhed from side to side. "Don't know what he'll do to me now. Now. Now."

The revelation of pain, however confused, was not to be doubted.

(So Shelley's Beatrice would have said, "Reach me that handkerchief—My brain is hurt.")

Then as though she was rid of it, she quieted. "I hit him first and cut his face with my ring." She held up her right hand, showing the ring and for the first time that afternoon laughed shortly.

Resentment mixed with his bewilderment and horror. All around about them, he thought, on the walls and towers of Larchmoor, on the stubblefields and highways for unimaginable miles lay the snow. It's as if she's trying to drag me with her into elements that neither of us, teacher or student, should ever have to face. She's trying to elect me not just her father, but as she said, God Almighty.

"Why?" he asked. His voice seemed to boom.

"I don't know why he did it," she said with crazy slyness, her face weird.

> (Oh, icehearted counsellor . . .
> If I could find a word that might make known
> The crime of my destroyer. . . .)

"Are you sure you're well? Have you told anybody else about this?"

She shook her head. "They sent me downtown to see the psychiatrist when they found out I wasn't going home. I told him. He said he'd help me. I think he's the one that told them to send for Daddy to come and get me. I'm in trouble so they're afraid I'll dirty up their college. But I would be good and everybody would get to like me if I could stay."

III

The president's secretary knocked on his door and put her head in. "Oh, good," she said seeing them both and then bobbing her head as though to confirm a suspicion that they were both quite real. "Can I speak to you privately, Dr. Cameron?" She pulled the door tight behind him and whispered, "Wheeeew, what a relief. The whole campus has been upside down looking for Shirley Bridges. Her father wants her upstairs. We couldn't find her in her room and they thought she might have done away with herself."

"Who thought that?" he demanded angrily.

"I don't know. We were all worried."

"But why should anyone think such a thing?"

"We've been having a lot of trouble with her. Her father says she gets in trouble wherever she goes. He just can't seem to do anything with her. He's going to take her home. I guess it's a good thing he came when he did. We had to send her to the psychiatrist last week."

"Oh that's nonsense. Anyone can go to a psychiatrist."

"Well," she said. "Well, don't pick on me. Will you send her right up to the president's office?"

Instead he went himself. The noise in the halls was faint and infrequent now. Buses and taxis had carried most of the students to the depot. He passed one of the maids locking her mops into a closet and slowed his angry, absorbed march to say Merry Christmas to her.

A little man whose mouth protruded as though he were deciding whether or not to whistle sat in the president's reception room. He looked as sleek and innocent as a little dachshund perched on the edge of an overstuffed lounge. Dr. Cameron nodded stiffly to him. So this is the fist-fighter, he thought. The champ.

"Go right in," the secretary said.

The hand in which President Herman held his glasses dangled over a chairback. He gestured with the glasses to indicate that Dr. Cameron should sit down.

"I'm glad you've come, Arthur," he said. "I understand from Miss Lee that Shirley Bridges has been in your office all afternoon. We've been very much concerned with Shirley today."

"As well we might be."

"Yes. Oh yes."

"She's in a very tight spot. You might call it a kind of snare that tightens the more she struggles."

"She's not well. Upset mentally. There are always the few who can't adjust to Larchmoor. Her father is very much concerned with her, poor fellow." He sighed. His eyes rolled up under their thick lids.

"The girl has a rather different interpretation of him."

"You mean about her father's beating her? That's an unsavory story for her to tell, isn't it?" He looked challengingly across his desk like a lawyer requiring a Yes or No answer. He's no fool, Cameron thought. This is going to be difficult. The president continued, "Shirley is quite an actress. Her talent should find its outlet on the stage. She's told that story to several people around here. Did she just tell you today? She seems to have fled to you as a last resort. If I'm not mistaken, she told the same story to the housemother before she'd been here two weeks. With different embellishments, I suppose. She'd broken this or that rule and seemed to think the story would be a kind of excuse. Don't you think a less unpleasant story might have served her better?"

"And what if it is true?"

"Do you believe it?"

"Suppose I did not. Why did Miss Lee say to me 'they thought she might have done away with herself'? Whether you believe the story or not, you seem to recognize a terrible situation there."

"I'm sure that I have no idea what Miss Lee may have meant." There was a clock on President Herman's desk with ornate bronze scrolls representing the tails of mermaids. With a lead pencil's point he traced out first one then the other of these scrolls. "I have, just as an assumption, gone so far as to assume that Shirley's story with all its—its morbid implications—might have some foundation. I have a psychiatrist's report in which such possibilities are examined. Inconclusively anyway. I don't put much stock in psychiatry. It's best not to. But if they had any basis, I would say they were the best of reasons why Shirley—and her father—ought to scamper away from Larchmoor, wouldn't you, Arthur?"

"I would not. She needs something to hang on to. Let her stay, Dr. Herman."

"Mr. Bridges has decided, I think, that he'll take her home. That was all settled before you came up, Arthur."

"Are you going to let him? Whatever else is true, that girl's afraid of him."

"Is she? Maybe she's been up to something that ought to make her afraid of him." He sighed deeply for Larchmoor's sake. "That kind of thing has happened here before. Another good reason she shouldn't be here. Arthur, do you imagine that I am going to tell a parent—a *parent*—that Larchmoor forbids him to take his daughter home?" He chuckled at the impossibility.

("Think of the offender's gold, his dread hate,
And the strange horror of the accuser's tale
Baffling belief and overpowering speech.")

"Larchmoor isn't a hospital, Arthur. If Shirley is having mental troubles and her father isn't, ah, just the one to see that she's taken care of properly, some of the family will surely handle it."

"They will? How do we know? 'O that the vain remorse which must chastise crimes done had but as loud a voice to warn. . . .' "

President Herman tapped his pencil impatiently on the desk top. "That's all very well," he said.

"It means, in the language of the Rotary Club, 'Don't expect George to do it.' "

"You think I might understand the language of the Rotary Club?"

"In the situation that's what it means. It's from a play. *The Cenci.* By Shelley. He was an English poet." He had seen the warning glitter in President Herman's eyes but he could not now stop his sarcasm.

Yet President Herman maintained the reserve which had helped him greatly in administering a school so old and prosperous as Larchmoor for so many years.

"Arthur, do you realize the scandal we narrowly missed? Seems she had rented a hotel room downtown and told her roommate she was going to stay there and 'get soused.' Can you imagine?"

"So her roommate told you that? My God, my God. Doesn't Larchmoor ever produce anything but little stoolies? I don't understand that girl, but I believe she needs help. And as soon as there is some suspicion that she might, every student and old maid housemother and the administration itself set on her. Did you ever see a flock of chickens go after one with a broken leg?"

Now President Herman's face had grown faintly red. "I must say, Arthur, that I'm considerably interested in hearing your opinion of Larchmoor. You've always seemed rather reticent and noncommittal. All these years. I'm glad to know what you think of us."

The two old men glared at each other. "I apologize," Dr. Cameron said. "That was an unfortunate outburst. Let me begin again and appeal to you in the name of the Christian principles which guide Larchmoor."

"I resent your sneering when you say 'Christian principles.'"

Both of them stood up. "If I sneered," said Dr. Cameron, "the intonation was superfluous. I told that girl. . . ." Compromise, compromise were the words he had in mind. He could see no reason now for saying them.

Blinded by his feeling—the whole compounded hate for Larchmoor, which must gloss over everything—he stumbled against a little mahogany coffee table as he turned to leave. This little and inconsequential piece of reality that had tripped him up was, finally, his undoing. President Herman might have forgiven him or forgotten the hot things he had said. But when he felt the table strike his shins, he stood for just one second watching it: then he kicked it with all his might. It flew against the wall, its glass top tinkling, and lay on its side.

He threw his hands above his head in a terrible gesture. "You dull, criminal, unperceiving bastards," he shouted and rushed from the room.

If Mr. Bridges had been still outside in the waiting room, he would have struck the man, seen how good he was with his fists at anything besides beating up his daughter. The little dachshund man had gone. No one was there but Miss Lee, the secretary. She was watching him with terror, and it did him good to see her cringe.

Without beginning to think what he would say to Shirley, only aware that it was now he who must and would protect her, he went to his office with all the speed his old legs could manage.

She was not there. He hunted, ridiculously, in the offices next his own and in the nearby classrooms, almost dark now. He had a tremendous fear for the girl. His head began to ache as he trotted from room to room.

There is a long hall in the buildings at Larchmoor, beneath the glassed arcade and extending through the principal structures as an evidence that Larchmoor girls not only don't have to go out in the weather as they pass from bedroom to dining room to classroom, but that they need not even veer from a luxuriously straight path. After the classrooms, Dr. Cameron went to the end of this hall. There, far off, down a long perspective of windows and doors, he saw Shirley and her father. They were talking, and as he watched, the dachshund man took her coat from the rack outside the student lounge and held it for her while she put her arms into it and flipped her hair up over the collar. They went out the front door together.

He got his coat and overshoes. He took from his desk the gloves which he had been almost ready to put on two hours ago. He walked down the hall toward the door from which Shirley and her father had left, but slowly, reluctantly. Was it all a lie that she had told him? If he were going to come back at the end of vacation, would he have heard that one of the busybodies on the Larchmoor payroll had unearthed the plot—"she just tried to fix it so she could stay in the hotel with her boy friend. Got caught at it." No, no, it couldn't be just that. Whatever it was, though, however muddled and sordid, the walls of Larchmoor—that were bigger, much bigger than Larchmoor; as big as money and complacency—were going to enclose it gently in indestructible steam heat. He was the only one who had been projected, tossed, into the cold, where an old scholar had to worry about rent.

The lights along Larchmoor's main walk had a festive air. Each one had been wreathed in red and green for holiday. At the bases of the lampposts and in the trees overhead, driven back only a little, lurked the blue shadows of the absolute snow. It was not Shirley who had lured him out of his warm corner into this, not any real Shirley that he had been protecting or that had determined he would die in the real cold, he thought, defending himself against self-ridicule, self-obloquy. The realer Beatrice, the gold-embroidered princess, the beautiful lady without mercy and without hope had brought him out of the door.

Part Four

Environments: The City, The Suburb, The Slum

The tragedy of life is not so much what men suffer, but rather what they miss.

Thomas Carlyle

Environment is formally defined as a complex of biotic, climatic, and edaphic forces that influences an organism, or entire culture, and determines to a considerable extent its form and survival. Though respectable, this definition is a bit icy and fails to measure the emotional vicinity, the inner sensations and convictions, that a person feels in his own environment. Though it *happens* in public, environment is most privately sensed, and feared, and cherished, and borne. As mood is to feeling, so environment is to action—an enclosure of our lives that is variously stable, fickle, neurotically versatile, idyllic, suppressive, or free as space.

Whether belittled by defenders of heredity or celebrated out of all reason by behaviorists, the reality of one's environment is both personal and objective and, as such, does have a life apart from its physical handiwork. It should never be studied, ignorantly, by academicians who treat it solely as a detached oddity rather than as a participant in the sensibilities of its people. How can human environment ever be known apart from its inhabitants, through whose perceptions its milieu *exists*?

More than amassing facts about the external surroundings out of which their students appear each day, teachers must sense the *inner* environment that insinuates itself. A teacher may know the data of his school's neighborhood—the income averages, the rate of divorce, the racial composite—and still be pedagogically impotent because he is blind to the interior worlds of his children that are stimulated by observable conditions. Knowledge of these interiors teaches, for example, that the horror of a slum derives not so much from what it is as from what it is not; a slum, for all its pungency and varied refuse, lacks *place* and substance; it vitiates in the way described by Wallace Stevens when he wrote,

The greatest poverty is not to live
In a physical world, to feel that one's desire
Is too difficult to tell from despair.

Of the stories that compose Part Four, two are set in urban neighborhoods, two in suburbia, and one in that utterly stranded area of America, the *rural* ghetto. The narratives range in time from Alfred Kazin's New York City during the 1920s, through the 1930s depression in rural Alabama, to the contemporary slum depicted by Carol Sturm and the suburban cultures described by Richard Yates and Robert Paul Smith.

The people portrayed here are not case histories. They are not caricatured or simplified. More of their environments is drawn than local habitation and name. The denser circumstances of their lives are viewed—the bands of accident and human motive and natural force, whose matrix holds the world.

Alfred Kazin

(1915–   )

This part of *A Walker in the City*, Alfred Kazin's account of his New York youth, bares the intensity of a child's environment in the first line: "All my early life lies open to my eye within five city blocks." The ensuing description of his neighborhood does not invite but rather subjects readers to an urban memory that may differ in kind from newer childhoods but not from some of the sentiments held by them. Neighborhoods change, educational doctrines change; but the feelings they engender seem capable of endless adaptation and investiture, seem at times awesomely interchangeable.

A critic of literature and society, Alfred Kazin was formerly an editor of the *New Republic* and is now a teacher at the State University of New York at Stony Brook. In addition to *A Walker in the City* (1951), his major works are *On Native Grounds* (1942), and *Contemporaries* (1962).

SCHOOL DAYS IN BROWNSVILLE

All my early life lies open to my eye within five city blocks. When I passed the school, I went sick with all my old fear of it. With its standard New York public-school brown brick courtyard shut in on three sides of the square and the pretentious battlements overlooking that cockpit in which I can still smell the fiery sheen of the rubber ball, it looks like a factory over which has been imposed the façade of a castle. It gave me the shivers to stand up in that courtyard again; I felt as if I had been mustered back into the service of those Friday morning "tests" that were the terror of my childhood.

It was never learning I associated with that school: only the necessity

211

to succeed, to get ahead of the others in the daily struggle to "make a good impression" on our teachers, who grimly, wearily, and often with ill-concealed distaste watched against our relapsing into the natural savagery they expected of Brownsville boys. The white, cool, thinly ruled record book sat over us from their desks all day long, and had remorselessly entered into it each day—in blue ink if we had passed, in red ink if we had not—our attendance, our conduct, our "effort," our merits and demerits; and to the last possible decimal point in calculation, our standing in an unending series of "tests"—surprise tests, daily tests, weekly tests, formal midterm tests, final tests. They never stopped trying to dig out of us whatever small morsel of fact we had managed to get down the night before. We had to prove that we were really alert, ready for anything, always in the race. That white thinly ruled record book figured in my mind as the judgment seat; the very thinness and remote blue lightness of its lines instantly showed its cold authority over me; so much space had been left on each page, columns and columns in which to note down everything about us, implacably and forever. As it lay there on a teacher's desk, I stared at it all day long with such fear and anxious propriety that I had no trouble believing that God, too, did nothing but keep such record books, and that on the final day He would face me with an account in Hebrew letters whose phonetic dots and dashes looked strangely like decimal points counting up my every sinful thought on earth.

All teachers were to be respected like gods, and God Himself was the greatest of all school superintendents. Long after I had ceased to believe that our teachers could see with the back of their heads, it was still understood, by me, that they knew everything. They were the delegates of all visible and invisible power on earth—of the mothers who waited on the stoops every day after three for us to bring home tales of our daily triumphs; of the glacially remote Anglo-Saxon principal, whose very name was King; of the incalculably important Superintendent of Schools who would someday rubberstamp his name to the bottom of our diplomas in grim acknowledgment that we had, at last, given satisfaction to him, to the Board of Superintendents, and to our benefactor the City of New York—and so up and up, to the government of the United States and to the great Lord Jehovah Himself. My belief in teachers' unlimited wisdom and power rested not so much on what I saw in them—how impatient most of them looked, how wary—but on our abysmal humility, at least in those of us who were "good" boys, who proved by our ready compliance and "manners" that we wanted to get on. The road to a professional future would be shown us only as we pleased *them. Make a good impression the first day of the term, and they'll help you out. Make a bad impression, and you might as well cut your throat.* This was the first article of school folklore, whispered around the classroom the opening day of each term. You made the "good impression" by sitting firmly at your wooden desk, hands clasped; by silence for the greatest part of the live-long day; by standing up obsequiously when it was so expected of you; by sitting down noiselessly when you had answered a question; by "speaking nicely," which meant reproducing their painfully exact enunciation; by "showing manners," or an ecstatic submissiveness in all things; by outrageous flattery; by bringing little gifts at Christmas, on their birthdays, and at the end of the term—the well-known significance of these gifts being that they came not from us, but from our parents, whose eagerness in this matter showed a high level of social consideration, and thus raised our standing in turn.

It was not just our quickness and memory that were always being tested. Above all, in that word I could never hear without automatically seeing it raised before me in gold-plated letters, it was our *character*. I always felt anxious when I heard the word pronounced. Satisfactory as my "character" was, on the whole, except when I stayed too long in the playground reading; outrageously satisfactory, as I can see now, the very sound of the word as our teachers coldly gave it out from the end of their teeth, with a solemn weight on each dark syllable, immediately struck my heart cold with fear—they could not believe I really had it. Character was never something you had; it had to be trained in you, like a technique. I was never very clear about it. On our side *character* meant demonstrative obedience; but teachers already had it— how else could they have become teachers? They had it; the aloof Anglo-Saxon principal whom we remotely saw only on ceremonial occasions in the assembly was positively encased in it; it glittered off his bald head in spokes of triumphant light; the President of the United States had the greatest conceivable amount of it. Character belonged to great adults. Yet we were constantly being driven onto it; it was the great threshold we had to cross. *Alfred Kazin, having shown proficiency in his course of studies and having displayed satisfactory marks of character* . . . Thus someday the hallowed diploma, passport to my further advancement in high school. But there—I could already feel it in my bones—they would put me through even more doubting tests of character; and after that, if I should be good enough and bright enough, there would be still more. *Character* was a bitter thing, racked with my endless striving to please. The school—from every last stone in the courtyard to the battlements frowning down at me from the walls—was only the stage for a trial. I felt that the very atmosphere of learning that surrounded us was fake—that every lesson, every book, every approving smile was only a pretext for the constant probing and watching of me, that there was not a secret in me that would not be decimally measured into that white record book. All week long I lived for the blessed sound of the dismissal gong at three o'clock on Friday afternoon.

I was awed by this system, I believed in it, I respected its force. The alternative was "going bad." The school was notoriously the toughest in our tough neighborhood, and the dangers of "going bad" were constantly impressed upon me at home and in school in dark whispers of the "reform school" and in examples of boys who had been picked up for petty thievery, rape, or flinging a heavy inkwell straight into a teacher's face. Behind any failure in school yawned the great abyss of a criminal career. Every refractory attitude doomed you with the sound "Sing Sing." Anything less than absolute perfection in school always suggested to my mind that I might fall out of the daily race, be kept back in the working class forever, or—dared I think of it?—fall into the criminal class itself.

I worked on a hairline between triumph and catastrophe. Why the odds should always have felt so narrow I understood only when I realized how little my parents thought of their own lives. It was not for myself alone that I was expected to shine, but for them—to redeem the constant anxiety of their existence. I was the first American child, their offering to the strange new God; I was to be the monument of their liberation from the shame of being—what they were. And that there was shame in this was a fact that everyone seemed to believe as a matter of course. It was in the gleeful discounting of themselves—what do we know?— with which our parents greeted every fresh victory in our savage competition for "high averages," for prizes, for a few condescending words of official praise from the principal at assembly. It was in the sickening invocation of "Americanism"—the word itself accusing us of everything we apparently were not. Our families and teachers seemed tacitly agreed that we were somehow to be a little ashamed of what we were. Yet it was always hard to say why this should be so. It was certainly not—in Brownsville!—because we were Jews, or simply because we spoke another language at home, or were absent on our holy days. It was rather that a "refined," "correct," "nice" English was required of us at school that we did not naturally speak, and that our teachers could never be quite sure we would keep. This English was peculiarly the ladder of advancement. Every future young lawyer was known by it. Even the Communists and Socialists on Pitkin Avenue spoke it. It was bright and clean and polished. We were expected to show it off like a new pair of shoes. When the teacher sharply called a question out, then your name, you were expected to leap up, face the class, and eject those new words fluently off the tongue.

There was my secret ordeal: I could never say anything except in the most roundabout way; I was a stammerer. Although I knew all those new words from my private reading—I read walking in the street, to and from the Children's Library on Stone Avenue; on the fire escape and the roof; at every meal when they would let me; read even when I dressed in the morning, propping my book up against the drawers of the bureau as I pulled on my long black stockings—I could never seem to get the easiest words out with the right dispatch, and would often miserably signal from my desk that I did not know the answer rather than get up to stumble and fall and crash on every word. If, angry at always being put down as lazy or stupid, I did get up to speak, the black wooden floor would roll away under my feet, the teacher would frown at me in amazement, and in unbearable loneliness I would hear behind me the groans and laughter: *tuh-tuh-tuh-tuh.*

The word was my agony. The word that for others was so effortless and so neutral, so unburdened, so simple, so exact, I had first to meditate in advance, to see if I could make it, like a plumber fitting together odd lengths and shapes of pipe. I was always preparing words I could speak, storing them away, choosing between them. And often, when the word did come from my mouth in its great and terrible birth, quailing and bleeding as if forced through a thornbush, I would not be able to look the others in the face, and would walk out in the silence, the infinitely echoing silence behind my back, to say it all cleanly back to myself as I walked in the streets. Only when I was alone in the open air, pacing the roof with pebbles in my mouth, as I had read Demosthenes had done to cure himself of stammering; or in the street, where all words seemed to flow from the length of my stride and the color of the houses as I remembered the perfect tranquility of a phrase in Beethoven's *Romance in F* I could sing back to myself as I walked—only then was it possible for me to speak without the infinite premeditations and strangled silences I toiled through whenever I got up at school to respond with the expected, the exact answer.

It troubled me that I could speak in the fullness of my own voice only when I was alone on the streets, walking about. There was something unnatural about it; unbearably isolated. I was not like the others! I was not like the others! At midday, every freshly shocking Monday noon, they sent me away to a speech clinic in a school in East New York, where I sat in a circle of lispers and cleft palates and foreign accents holding a mirror before my lips and rolling difficult sounds over and over. To be sent there in the full light of the opening week, when everyone else was at school or going about his business, made me feel as if I had been expelled from the great normal body of humanity. I would gobble down my lunch on my way to the speech clinic and rush back to the school in time to make up for the classes I had lost. One day, one unforgettable dread day, I stopped to catch my breath on a corner of Sutter Avenue, near the wholesale fruit markets, where an old drugstone rose up over a great flight of steps. In the window were dusty urns of colored water floating off iron chains; cardboard placards advertising hairnets, Ex-Lax; a great illustrated medical chart headed

THE HUMAN FACTORY, which showed the exact course a mouthful of food follows as it falls from chamber to chamber of the body. I hadn't meant to stop there at all, only to catch my breath; but I so hated the speech clinic that I thought I would delay my arrival for a few minutes by eating my lunch on the steps. When I took the sandwich out of my bag, two bitterly hard pieces of hard salami slipped out of my hand and fell through a grate onto a hill of dust below the steps. I remember how sickeningly vivid an odd thread of hair looked on the salami, as if my lunch were turning stiff with death. The factory whistles called their short, sharp blasts stark through the middle of noon, beating at me where I sat outside the city's magnetic circle. I had never known, I knew instantly I would never in my heart again submit to, such wild passive despair as I felt at that moment, sitting on the steps before THE HUMAN FACTORY, where little robots gathered and shoveled the food from chamber to chamber of the body. They had put me out into the streets, I thought to myself; with their mirrors and their everlasting pulling at me to imitate their effortless bright speech and their stupefaction that a boy could stammer and stumble on every other English word he carried in his head, they had put me out into the streets, had left me high and dry on the steps of that drugstone staring at the remains of my lunch turning black and grimy in the dust.

In the great cool assembly hall, dominated by the gold sign above the stage KNOWLEDGE IS POWER, the windowsills were lined with Dutch bulbs, each wedged into a mound of pebbles massed in a stone dish. Above them hung a giant photograph of Theodore Roosevelt. Whenever I walked in to see the empty assembly hall for myself, the shiny waxed floor of the stage dangled in the middle of the air like a crescent. On one side was a great silk American flag, the staff crowned by a gilt eagle. Across the dry rattling of varnish-smelling empty seats bowing to the American flag, I saw in the play of the sun on those pebbles wildly sudden images of peace. *There* was the other land, crowned by the severe and questioning face of Theodore Roosevelt, his eyes above the curiously endearing straw-dry mustache, behind the pince-nez glittering with light, staring and staring me through as if he were uncertain whether he fully approved of me.

The light pouring through window after window in that great empty varnished assembly hall seemed to me the most wonderful thing I had ever seen. It was that thorough varnished cleanness that was of the new land, that light dancing off the glasses of Theodore Roosevelt, those green and white roots of the still raw onion-brown bulbs delicately flaring up from the hill of pebbles into which they were wedged. The pebbles moved me in themselves, there were so many of them. They rose up around the bulbs in delicately strong masses of colored stone, and as the sun fell between them, each pebble shone in its own light. Looking across the great rows of empty seats to those pebbles lining the window-sills, I could still smell summer from some long veranda surrounded by trees. On that veranda sat the family and friends of Theodore Roosevelt. I knew the name: Oyster Bay. Because of that picture, I had read *The Boy's Life of Theodore Roosevelt*; knew he had walked New York streets night after night as Police Commissioner, unafraid of the Tenderloin gangsters; had looked into *Theodore Roosevelt's Letters to His Children*, pretending that those hilarious drawings on almost every page were for me. *There* was America, I thought, the real America, *his* America, where from behind the glass on the wall of our assembly hall he watched over us to make sure we did right, thought right, lived right.

"Up, boys! Up San Juan Hill!" I still hear our roguish old civics teacher, a little white-haired Irishman who was supposed to have been with Teddy in Cuba, driving us through our Friday morning tests with these shouts and cries. He called them "Army Navy" tests, to make us feel big, and dividing the class between Army and Navy, got us to compete with each other for a coveted blue star. Civics was city govern-ment, state government, federal government; each government had functions; you had to get them out fast in order to win for the Army or the Navy. Sometimes this required filling in three or four words, line by line, down one side of the grimly official yellow foolscap that was brought out for tests. (In the tense silence just before the test began, he looked at us sharply, the watch in his hand ticking as violently as the sound of my heart, and on command, fifty boys simultaneously folded their yellow test paper and evened the fold with their thumbnails in a single dry sigh down the middle of the paper.) At other times it meant true-or-false tests; then he stood behind us to make sure we did not signal the right answers to each other in the usual way—for true, nodding your head; for false, holding your nose. You could hear his voice barking from the rear. "*Come on now, you Army boys! On your toes like West Point cadets! All ready now? Get set! Go! Three powers of the legislative branch? The judiciary? The executive? The subject of the fifteenth amend-ment? The capital of Wyoming? Come on, Navy! Shoot those land-lubbers down! Give 'em a blast from your big guns right through the middle! The third article of the Bill of Rights? The thirteenth amend-ment? The sixteenth? True or false, Philadelphia is the capital of Penn-sylvania. Up and at 'em, Navy! Mow them down! COME ON!!!*" Our "average" was calculated each week, and the boys who scored 90 per cent or over were rewarded by seeing *their own names* lettered on the great blue chart over the blackboard. Each time I entered that room for a test, I looked for my name on the blue chart as if the sight of it would decide my happiness for all time.

Down we go, down the school corridors of the past smelling of chalk, lysol out of the open toilets, and girl sweat. The staircases were a gray stone I saw nowhere else in the school, and they were shut in on both sides by some thick unreflecting glass on which were pasted travel posters inviting us to spend the summer in the Black Forest. Those staircases created a spell in me that I had found my way to some distant, cool, neutral passageway deep in the body of the school. There, enclosed within the thick, green boughs of a classic summer in Germany, I could still smell the tense probing chalk smells from every classroom, the tickling high surgical odor of lysol from the open toilets, could still hear that continuous babble, babble of water dripping into the bowls. Sex was instantly connected in my mind with the cruel openness of those toilets, and in the never-ending sound of the bowls being flushed I could detect, as I did in the maddeningly elusive fragrance of cologne brought into the classroom by Mrs. B., the imminence of something severe, frightening, obscene. Sex, as they said in the "Coney Island" dives outside the school, was like going to the toilet; there was a great contempt in this that made me think of the wet rings left by our sneakers as we ran down the gray stone steps after school.

Outside the women teachers' washroom on the third floor, the tough guys would wait for the possible appearance of Mrs. B., whose large goiterous eyes seemed to bulge wearily with mischief, who always looked tired and cynical, and who wore thin chiffon dresses that affected us much more than she seemed to realize. Mrs. B. often went about the corridors in the company of a trim little teacher of mathematics who was a head shorter than she and had a mustache. Her chiffon dresses billowed around him like a sail; she seemed to have him in tow. It was understood by us as a matter of course that she wore those dresses to inflame us; that she *was* tired and cynical, from much practice in obscene love-making; that she was a "bad one" like the young Polish blondes from East New York I occasionally saw in the "Coney Island" dives sitting on someone's lap and smoking a cigarette. How wonderful and unbelievable it was to find this in a teacher; to realize that the two of them, after we had left the school, probably met to rub up against each other in the faculty toilet. Sex was a grim test where sooner or later you would have to prove yourself doing things to women. In the smell of chalk and sweat and the unending smirky babble of the water as it came to me on the staircase through my summer's dream of old Germany, I could feel myself being called to still another duty—to conquer Mrs. B., to rise to the challenge she had whispered to us in her slyness. I had seen pictures of it on the block—they were always passing them around between handball games—the man's face furious, ecstatic with lewdness as he proudly looked down at himself; the woman sniggering as she teased him with droplets from the contraceptive someone had just shown me in the gutter—its crushed, filmy slyness the very sign of the forbidden.

They had never said anything about this at home, and I thought I knew why. Sex was the opposite of books, of pictures, of music, of the open air, even of kindness. They would not let you have both. Something always lingered to the sound of those toilets to test you. In and out of the classroom they were always testing you. *Come on, Army! Come on, Navy!* As I stood up in that school courtyard and smelled again the familiar sweat, heard again the unending babble from the open toilets, I suddenly remembered how sure I had always been that even my failures in there would be entered in a white, thinly ruled, official record book.

Carol Sturm

Certain details make two interpretations of this story possible. One must decide whether Ernest Hemingway McGworski is an idiot savant, a genetic joke; or a child victimized by a slum milieu, an ignorant mother, and by unperceptive school personnel. Pertinent to either interpretation is the onus thrust on classroom teachers to cope with the separate pulls of heredity and environment at work within their slow learners.

If Ernest's fate is truly deserved, if he is actually an idiot savant, the story's force is wholly dependent on the dramatic and verbal ironies created by Rose McGworski's illusions. But if the boy is a victim of the slum and of adult misjudgment, the story holds a pathos that releases sharper implications of loss.

Carol Sturm is a native of Indiana and a graduate of St. Louis University. Her stories have appeared in *The Minnesota Review, Phylon,* and *Prairie Schooner.*

The Kid Who Fractioned

From far down the block Rose McGworski spotted the church spire tall against the dusky sky. She plodded toward it eagerly, leaning backward a bit to offset her unaccustomed weight. Maybe I shouldn't be goin' if it's gonna mark the baby, she thought, frowning at the bulge beneath her maternity jacket. But I just *had* to get outta that apartment and watchin' Gus drinkin' beer all the time!

In front of the old red brick church, Rose drew a hurried breath, then picked her way over the cracked sidewalk, past the scrawny rose bushes and lilacs to the side door. Above it hung a bare light bulb and a hand-lettered sign: BING. Inside the building it was dim and hot. She stood on the landing listening to the sounds from the basement while her eyes gradually made out the stone stairway. In her throat she felt the same queasy tremblings that always came when she went to a place for the first time. She swallowed once and followed the stone steps down to the basement.

The large room was crowded with women drinking grape soda, smoking filter-tipped cigarettes, and talking to no one and everyone simultaneously. Toddlers chased each other around crying infants in strollers. At last Rose's eyes settled on a table loaded with lamps, steak knives with imitation bone handles, toilet bowl brushes, home hair-cutting sets, and fluffy throw rugs. At least they got good stuff for prizes! she thought, her eyes lingering long on the assortment.

At the head of the farthest table Rose noticed a man whirling a wire cage of dice. Faster and faster he whirled the cage as Rose watched in growing fascination. At the peak of his frenzy, a woman in a pink linen sheath yelled, "Let's go already," and instantly the room's noises drifted down to murmurings.

Then one of the women spotted Rose. "Come on in and grab a chair, honey."

Rose waddled over eagerly.

"My God, kid, you're preg!" The woman shoved the green-visored cap farther back on her perspiring forehead.

Rose giggled as she sat down on the wooden folding chair next to the woman.

"I'm Mary Murphy." The woman shot a blast of smoke over Rose's head. "But everybody here calls me Fat Mary. Guess you can see why." She nudged Rose and chortled once. "Lemme get ya started."

Fat Mary shoved a handful of corn kernels to Rose and thumped the table for someone to bring over the bingo cards.

"You gotta be careful ya pick lucky ones," she hissed confidentially to Rose, alternately squinting and grunting at the cards. "Here. These are sure shots for four corner wins."

Rose looked at the three dog-eared cards before her and faltered. "I don't know if I can—I ain't never—"

"That's okay, kid," Fat Mary grinned benevolently. "I know ya ain't never been here before. I'll keep 'em in the corner of my eyes."

Rose blinked at the solid block of cards stacked in front of Fat Mary. "Okay, but I don't wanna make you miss your—"

Fat Mary laughed hoarsely. "That's okay, kid. Tell ya the truth, that's why I called ya over when I seen ya come in the door. 'Beginner beside ya, luck won't deride ya.'" She cackled again.

Rose said, "Well, I—" But a boy with a canvas money pouch tapped her on the shoulder.

"Lemme get 'em this game for ya," Fat Mary rasped. "You can get 'em next game for both of us. 'Even Steven,' huh?" She grabbed a quarter from her wallet and tossed the wallet back onto the table. "Smart to play three," she confided in a hoarse whisper, "'cause you're gettin' one for a nickel. Ten cents apiece, three for a quarter."

Rose said, "I—" But the man at the front of the room started calling bingo numbers.

All evening Rose lost herself in the bingo cards, the shouts of the winners, and Fat Mary's rasping commentary. When the lights on the stage flicked on, she looked up at the wall clock in surprise. My gosh, I been happy all night, she marveled. I ain't even thought about Gus once!

"Sure goes fast, don't it, kid?" Fat Mary hollered over the din. "Father always talks at the end."

Rose turned toward the stage. A priest she thought looked like Tyrone Power stood in the center of the stage. Behind him a canvas curtain made up of flashy square advertisements for the local drugstores, meat markets, and insurance agencies swayed lightly in the gentle summer breeze, making Rose feel a little dizzy.

The priest gripped the microphone. "Good ladies," he intoned with obvious sincerity. The loudspeaker shrilled once and from then on Rose could only watch the priest's lips moving.

"Don't worry, kid," Fat Mary consoled. "Father's just tellin' us how glad he is we had us a good time. Tells us every time." She turned and noticed Rose's flushed face. "You like bingo, kid? You want me to tell ya the other places?"

Rose nodded.

"Mondays and Fridays at St. Ben's, Holy Angels on Tuesdays and Saturdays, and Wednesdays and Sundays here."

Rose silently rehearsed the nights as she left the church basement arm-in-arm with her new friend.

"You wanna come home with me and—have a beer?" Rose dared ask once they were outside. "'Course if Gus is still there the beer'll all be inside him!" She laughed nervously.

"Who's Gus?" Fat Mary inquired suspiciously.

"I married him," Rose said simply.

"A drinker, huh?" Fat Mary asked indignantly.

"Yeah. Some people might think Gus ain't so much, but when I first met him he looked sorta like this here picture of Ernest Hemingway I seen in a magazine once. I thought Gus was really something." She snorted, remembering how Gus had courted her by waiting until she left work and tapping on his auto horn from half-way down the block until she gradually worked up enough courage to speak when she passed his gray Chevvy coupe. "Looked like Ernest Hemingway on account of he don't shave most days."

"God!" said Fat Mary.

Then, afraid lest she had given the impression she had married blindly, Rose sought to convey some of the magic of her husband. "Before we were married, Gus used to tell me about the water tanks he painted and the ceilings and all the high dangerous places, and I could just see the faces of all them ladies where I work when I said I was married to the guy who done all that." Rose sighed, remembering how she had imagined all the good things that marrying Gus had never brought.

Fat Mary seemed to understand. "Where ya workin'?" she asked.

"The Beauty Nook on North Michigan," Rose said proudly. "It ain't bad, with all them classy ladies comin' in for washes and sets and all that." Rose smiled mysteriously, failing to mention that her chores were restricted to shampooing customers' daughters, cleaning the brushes and combs, and sweeping up after haircuts.

"I guess when I started workin' there I figured I'd get to be like them ladies, all with fancy clothes and stuff, if I was with 'em enough," she said soberly. "They sure got class! I can spot a dentist's wife a block away. But you know, after bein' with 'em, I found somethin' out. They're all stuck-up! I wouldn't even *wanna* be like 'em!"

"God, ain't it the truth!" Fat Mary exploded.

"I'm thinkin' of gettin' me another job. I just haven't decided where yet," Rose said mysteriously.

"You been to college?"

"Well, not exactly. Who'd want to go, anyway?"

"God, I know what you mean," Fat Mary grunted.

"High school was bad enough. Always hearin' about stuff that nobody cared about, or sittin' in some dark auditorium watchin' them stuck-up ones gettin' called on the stage to get awards that nobody'd care about havin'."

Fat Mary pursed her lips and nodded knowingly.

"After a while I left high school and started working. That was right after my father died and my mother and sister went to New Jersey to live with my aunt. Then Gus and me got married. Right after that, Gus falls off a ladder on to this here radiator and now he says it hurts him to lift a paint brush." Rose made a face. "So all I do now is work and evenings watch him drink beer."

"My God, kid," Fat Mary said, "you've sure had it."

"No," Rose said seriously. "I learned about life and people. I know what the whole thing's about now. Sure, I had me some rough times, but *now* things are gonna be different. The baby'll make everything better. You wait and see."

"My God, kid, you're a good one!" Fat Mary thumped Rose across the butt.

They reached Rose's apartment building and Rose led Fat Mary up the narrow stairs.

"Watch them loose pieces of stuff," Rose warned. "Them pieces is always comin' off the stairs."

Rose opened the apartment door. Gus was sprawled on the couch staring at the television, a beer can balanced on his bare chest.

Fat Mary sat down at the kitchen table and looked around at the two-room efficiency.

"Gus got some paint wholesale and done the walls when he first moved in here with me," Rose said in a loud voice, jerking her head significantly toward the battleship-gray enamel paint. "That's *all* he's done since the honeymoon." She turned away from Fat Mary suddenly, still having to choke down disgust about her honeymoon, when she had had to cash her own paycheck their first night away.

Gus turned his large, bristle-haired head toward them and waved a twenty-dollar bill. "See this? Won it today bettin' some guys I could make a cat pick up a beer bottle."

"That tavern again," Rose said scornfully, sliding the porcelain sugar bowl deftly over the tear in the oilcloth on the kitchen table. "Always that tavern. And me gettin' close to my time."

"Say," said Fat Mary. "Why don't I see if I can get Gus workin' nights at the place I work at days?"

Rose brightened. "Hey Gus, ya hear that?"

Without looking away from the TV, Gus touched his forearm and winced.

The following week Rose quit the Beauty Nook and Gus started bartending nights at the Pennsylvania Bar and Grill.

To show her gratitude to Fat Mary, Rose missed only six nights of bingo when the baby came.

Gus first saw his son the night Rose arrived home from the hospital.

"I picked him out a name already," she told him proudly.

Later that week Rose took the skinny infant to church and had him christened Ernest Hemingway McGworski.

At last Rose fancied the tide of her fortunes had truly changed. No longer an observer of life's benefits, she felt herself beginning to be a participant, and at times, even a star. Now that she no longer worked at the Beauty Nook, she slept late each morning, got up and got herself dressed and her face put on extra special. Then she tended little Ernest, cooing over him: "You gotta wear somethin' different and cute every day, honey, so's the people will notice us."

Things ain't never been like this before, she thought triumphantly while she paraded the streets with her new son. I'm *somebody* now! These people look at me and even *smile*. Everybody notices me when I tell 'em Ernest's name!

Rose sometimes went back to the Beauty Nook to show Ernest to the ladies. Sometimes she pretended to examine merchandise so she could talk about Ernest to the clerks in stores. But always on Fridays she attended the matinee at the Ritz.

Now I can see all the first-run movies in town, she thought happily. Babies are *sure* good to have. Only I just wish Ernest didn't pee on me so much at the movies.

At night Rose and the baby met Fat Mary at the church basement. Soon Ernest graduated from the secondhand baby buggy to the floor around Rose's feet, and spent his evenings mouthing corn kernels and sucking on the ends of Rose's sandal straps.

One night after bingo while Rose plucked corn kernels from her son's mouth, she saw that the bows on her black patent leather flats had something else on them besides the usual slobber. Teeth marks!

"Hey, look," Rose shouted. "Ernest Hemingway's got teeth!"

Fat Mary stuck her finger into Ernest's mouth and found out for herself. "By God, he sure does!"

In the midst of this unique attention, Ernest spoke his first word. He looked up at Rose, drooled from both corners of his mouth, and gleefully bubbled, "B—in—ingo!"

"God, ain't that cute! Hi, ya little Bingo," Fat Mary burst out.

"Bingo, bingo, bingo," he repeated.

Nothing else distinguishable passed over his lips until he was nearly three.

Untroubled by his bumbling gushes of sounds, Rose continued showing Bingo off unceasingly.

"This is *my* boy," she beamed. "*My* boy. And he's good and smart and's gonna be *somebody*. I *know* it."

Rose repeated it so often that she came to fully believe it herself, and her unfaltering belief served as reason enough to say it many more times.

Things, indeed, had never seemed better to her.

Then one night when she returned from the church basement with little Bingo, she found a note from Gus saying his arm hurt him so bad that he was going to California because he heard that was where the best doctors were.

After the first shock, Rose brooded about Bingo. "How'm I gonna tell poor Bingo he ain't got no more Daddy?"

But the four-year-old reacted calmly to her explanation of Gus's departure, merely questioning, "Man go bye-bye?" whenever he saw a beer can.

Now I gotta go back to work, Rose thought. She left Bingo with a lady in the same apartment building and returned to the Beauty Nook.

"Why, my kid's so smart he knows more in his little finger than them other kids in their whole head," she told the customers.

She swept away her disappointments about Gus with the fallen wisps of hair. She daydreamed about her son constantly while she washed the hard-rubber combs. Someday Bingo'll *build* water towers like Gus *said* he painted. Or maybe he'll write books better'n the other Ernest Hemingway.

When it came time for Bingo to start school, Rose's pride knew no bounds. Imagine, she marveled. Me! Me! The mother of a first-grader!

She bought Bingo the best clothes she could afford, slicked down his straight yellow hair with perfume, pinned his name onto the front of his shirt, and proudly sent him off to school with four unsharpened colored pencils.

The phone call came during the second week of school. It didn't surprise Rose. She had been impatiently waiting for the school to recognize Bingo's talents.

"Don't be alarmed," the voice said. "But Dr. Higgins, our school psychologist, examined Ernest yesterday, following the request of his first-grade teacher. He would like to discuss Ernest's abilities with you."

Rose considered this a minute. "Sure. Fine. I could come talk to him." Imagine! she thought after she had hung up. My Ernest being promoted *so soon!*

She triumphantly told her news to Fat Mary that night at the church basement.

"Bernice Hatenburg had a conference about her kid, too," Fat Mary said glumly. "Somethin' about him bein' ready to read and all that. He went three years to the first grade."

Rose frowned. "I'd just *die* if Bingo wasn't *somebody*, and *me* bein' his mother."

"Don't worry, kid," Fat Mary assured her. "Bingo's a good boy."

Thus assured, Rose traveled through the week before her conference with the school psychologist. Rather a good week, too, she concluded. Three money wins and a porcelain lamp with blue violets.

She got to school early on Friday. Outside Dr. Higgins' door she stopped and made sure her seams were straight. For herself, it didn't matter, but she wanted the school people to know Bingo had a good mother.

"Dr. Higgins?" she asked. The young man behind the gray metallic desk arose.

"Mrs. McGworski, I asked you to come in today because the first-grade teacher isn't sure Ernest belongs in her room," Dr. Higgins said as Rose sat down.

Sure Bingo's real smart, she thought, swelling proudly and looking around her at all the books.

"Since testing Ernest I can say I heartily agree with her. Do you have any idea of Ernest's I.Q.? I mean, do you realize he's—"

"Well, no," she interrupted him modestly. "If you mean, do I *know* about him, all my lady friends say he's a real good boy."

"Yes, I'm sure he must be an obedient child," Dr. Higgins said gingerly.

Rose watched him impatiently while he toyed with a pencil. Just tell me what grade you want Bingo to be in and let me go back at the Beauty Nook, she thought.

"Did he do good for you in the tests?" she asked finally to break the silence.

"The truth of the matter," said Dr. Higgins in a rush, "is that Ernest's I.Q. is about 47. Now I know that this might come as a—

"Forty-seven!" exclaimed Rose. "Imagine that! And him bein' only six years old!"

Dr. Higgins opened his mouth and closed it without speaking. "I don't think you quite understand what I'm trying to say," he said, swallowing several times. He pointed to a sheet of paper in front of him. "Listen to this. I asked Ernest to name four colors. He said: 'Yellow goes to orange, orange goes to red, red goes to blue, blue goes to green.' I must confess I don't see what—"

"He's right!" Rose laughed delightedly. "Fat Mary, she's at bingo after she gets through work at the tav—the sal—the place where she works, and she tells Ernest about the juke box. It goes just like he said. Yellow, orange, red, blue, green. Then the yellow again. He's right!"

"Oh," said Dr. Higgins. He pushed aside the papers, laid his chin in his hands, and stared at the woman facing him. "Mrs. McGworski, sometimes there are certain aberrations—" He stopped as soon as he saw the woman's expression cringe. He pulled the papers back in front of him and reread a line. He tried again, "The child doesn't seem to know the same things that the rest of the first-graders know. For example, numbers."

Rose half-stood in her excitement. "Oh, then you know about his fractioning?"

"His WHAT?"

"His fractioning. He fractions real good. He—" Her sentence stopped midway as a young lady opened the door, rolled her eyes ceilingward, and pushed Bingo into the room.

"That," said Dr. Higgins reverently after the woman had left, "was Ernest's first-grade teacher."

Bingo ignored Dr. Higgins and trotted over to Rose.

"Hi, honey," she said, giving him an affectionate pat on the head. "Let's show the man how good you fraction."

She scooped Bingo up onto her lap and faced him around toward the psychologist. "Now Bingo," she said sweetly, "listen to Mama. He's real good at fractioning," she confided to Dr. Higgins. "Now Bingo, if me and this other lady the both of us goes to bingo and wins the same game, and the winner's s'posed to get fifteen dollars, you tell the man here how much Mama'd get."

Bingo's eyes glistened. "Seven-fifty."

"That's good, honey. *Real* good." She gave him another pat on the head. "Now you see, Dr. Higgins, he's real good at fractioning."

Dr. Higgins recovered from choking and asked, "Could you have him do another? I mean, is he getting tired?"

"Tired! F'heaven sakes, no! He fractions all night at the church basement, don't you, honey? Let's do another one, okay? Now, if me and two of them other ladies all shouted at the same time, and they had the jackpot a hundred dollars, you tell the man here how much we'd take home."

Bingo gurgled once and slid off Rose's lap. "Thirty-three dollars and thirty-three cents and one for the beer can."

Rose laughed. "What he means, if the money's not even, we put the extra in this little can, sorta like a beer can."

The psychologist cleared his throat, his eyes wide. "Mrs. McGworski, I suppose the term 'idiot savant' is strange to you?"

"I never learned no foreign tongues," Rose admitted.

The psychologist waited a moment. "Then let me explain. I know you want Ernest to be happy."

Rose nodded enthusiastically.

The psychologist drew a deep breath and plunged. "I think, in view of Ernest's—his fractioning—that he would be very happy at the State Training School."

"The what?" Rose asked.

"A Training School. They have boys living there who are his same age. Boys who are slower learners, ones who need special help in their—their academ—their fractioning."

Rose hesitated. The memories of the combs she had cleaned, the never-realized promises of Gus, the hopes of Ernest—but her own selfishness must not stand in the way of Ernest's happiness—all merged into a generous certitude. She pulled herself up erectly. "Sure. Sure, doctor." She nodded rapidly, ignoring the tears that formed automatically in her eyes. "Sure, I'd let Ernest go there and live with them other kids. He'd be glad to go there and live." She jabbed Bingo with her elbow. "Wouldn't you go live there, honey?"

Bingo sat down on the floor, drew the soles of his shoes together, and fingered the fly on his pants.

"Good," said Dr. Higgins. "Ernest can enter the school as soon as we make certain arrangements."

Rose beamed. "Sure, doctor." She stood up. "But with Bing—Ernest at this other school, the money—I work, but—"

"Don't let money bother you. We'll work out satisfactory arrangements."

Rose left his office glowing, with Bingo tagging after her.

That night she bought a bottle of Mogan David and invited Fat Mary to the apartment. "This here's a celebration," she said, waving toward the bottle of wine. "Bingo's goin' to a special school."

"God!" Fat Mary gasped.

"Yeah," said Rose modestly. "That doctor at school didn't say too much about it, but I figured out that them boys at the school *need* Bingo to teach 'em fractioning."

"God!" Fat Mary gasped again.

"Them boys are 'slow learners,' " Rose said in a reverential whisper.

"Really, kid?"

Rose smiled serenely. "Yeah. I wouldn't have to work, what with Bingo's money from teachin'. But I'm thinkin' of goin' ahead and workin' anyway, so's I don't miss him too much."

Fat Mary nodded emphatic agreement.

In the days before Bingo was to leave, Rose sang delightedly through the two-room efficiency. "This is even better'n what I thought," she grinned at Bingo. "You on the stage, fractioning, the other boys sittin' there watchin' you." She could almost hear the boys stomping and whistling as Bingo fractioned for them. Bingo tellin' them how he fractioned, learnin' them all to fraction. Other schools wantin' Bingo—

Saturday morning Rose trimmed Bingo's hair and dressed him and tied his new shoes and gave him a new little blue school bag with a magazine in it to carry. She called a cab to take him to the bus depot, and told the driver how to put him on the right bus.

When at last she saw Bingo leaving, tears slipped down her face. She hugged her son hard against her, then slammed the cab door and waved until he was out of sight.

"*My* son," she excitedly began improvising the conversation with the lady who always acted so high and mighty about *her* children. "*My* son—"

Richard Yates

(1926–   )

Vincent Sabella is a boy deprived by two environments that are grossly dissimilar. For Miss Price, Vincent's teacher, the boy is a challenge, a mission, a case, a tender metabolism. He is never seen by her as a boy, real, in his bifurcated world of suburb and slum. Whatever the cruelties she commits in the name of therapeutic decency, Miss Price emerges, in her own way, as pathetic a figure as her pupil. She has the show of empathy without its feeling. The Miss Prices of this earth survive, accepted as progressive workers for the newer world. The Vincent Sabellas may or may not survive, depending on their grit, their resourcefulness, and their luck.

Richard Yates is the author of *Revolutionary Road* (1961) and *Eleven Kinds of Loneliness* (1962), a book of short stories which includes "Dr. Jack-o'-lantern."

DOCTOR JACK-O'-LANTERN

All Miss Price had been told about the new boy was that he'd spent most of his life in some kind of orphanage, and that the gray-haired "aunt and uncle" with whom he now lived were really foster parents, paid by the Welfare Department of the City of New York. A less dedicated or less imaginative teacher might have pressed for more details, but Miss Price was content with the rough outline. It was enough, in fact, to fill her with a sense of mission that shone from her eyes, as plain as love, from the first morning he joined the fourth grade.

He arrived early and sat in the back row—his spine very straight, his ankles crossed precisely under the desk and his hands folded on the

230

very center of its top, as if symmetry might make him less conspicuous—and while the other children were filing in and settling down, he received a long, expressionless stare from each of them.

"We have a new classmate this morning," Miss Price said, laboring the obvious in a way that made everybody want to giggle. "His name is Vincent Sabella and he comes from New York City. I know we'll all do our best to make him feel at home."

This time they all swung around to stare at once, which caused him to duck his head slightly and shift his weight from one buttock to the other. Ordinarily, the fact of someone's coming from New York might have held a certain prestige, for to most of the children the city was an awesome, adult place that swallowed up their fathers every day, and which they themselves were permitted to visit only rarely, in their best clothes, as a treat. But anyone could see at a glance that Vincent Sabella had nothing whatever to do with skyscrapers. Even if you could ignore his tangled black hair and gray skin, his clothes would have given him away: absurdly new corduroys, absurdly old sneakers and a yellow sweatshirt, much too small, with the shredded remains of a Mickey Mouse design stamped on its chest. Clearly, he was from the part of New York that you had to pass through on the train to Grand Central—the part where people hung bedding over their windowsills and leaned out on it all day in a trance of boredom, and where you got vistas of straight, deep streets, one after another, all alike in the clutter of their sidewalks and all swarming with gray boys at play in some desperate kind of ball game.

The girls decided that he wasn't very nice and turned away, but the boys lingered in their scrutiny, looking him up and down with faint smiles. This was the kind of kid they were accustomed to thinking of as "tough," the kind whose stares had made all of them uncomfortable at one time or another in unfamiliar neighborhoods; here was a unique chance for retaliation.

"What would you like us to call you, Vincent?" Miss Price inquired. "I mean, do you prefer Vincent, or Vince, or—or what?" (It was purely an academic question; even Miss Price knew that the boys would call him "Sabella" and that the girls wouldn't call him anything at all.)

"Vinny's okay," he said in a strange, croaking voice that had evidently yelled itself hoarse down the ugly streets of his home.

"I'm afraid I didn't hear you," she said, craning her pretty head forward and to one side so that a heavy lock of hair swung free of one shoulder. "Did you say 'Vince'?"

"Vinny, I said," he said again, squirming.

"Vincent, is it? All right, then, Vincent." A few of the class giggled, but nobody bothered to correct her; it would be more fun to let the mistake continue.

"I won't take time to introduce you to everyone by name, Vincent," Miss Price went on, "because I think it would be simpler just to let you learn the names as we go along, don't you? Now, we won't expect you to take any real part in the work for the first day or so; just take your time, and if there's anything you don't understand, why, don't be afraid to ask."

He made an unintelligible croak and smiled fleetingly, just enough to show that the roots of his teeth were green.

"Now then," Miss Price said, getting down to business. "This is Monday morning, and so the first thing on the program is reports. Who'd like to start off?"

Vincent Sabella was momentarily forgotten as six or seven hands went up, and Miss Price drew back in mock confusion. "Goodness, we do have a lot of reports this morning," she said. The idea of the reports— a fifteen-minute period every Monday in which the children were encouraged to relate their experiences over the weekend—was Miss Price's own, and she took a pardonable pride in it. The principal had commended her on it at a recent staff meeting, pointing out that it made a splendid bridge between the worlds of school and home, and that it was a fine way for children to learn poise and assurance. It called for intelligent supervision—the shy children had to be drawn out and the show-offs curbed—but in general, as Miss Price had assured the principal, it was fun for everyone. She particularly hoped it would be fun today, to help put Vincent Sabella at ease, and that was why she chose Nancy Parker to start off; there was nobody like Nancy for holding an audience.

The others fell silent as Nancy moved gracefully to the head of the room; even the two or three girls who secretly despised her had to feign enthrallment when she spoke (she was that popular), and every boy in the class, who at recess liked nothing better than to push her shrieking into the mud, was unable to watch her without an idiotically tremulous smile.

"Well—" she began, and then she clapped a hand over her mouth while everyone laughed.

"Oh, *Nancy*," Miss Price said. "You *know* the rule about starting a report with 'well.'"

Nancy knew the rule; she had only broken it to get the laugh. Now she let her fit of giggles subside, ran her fragile forefingers down the side seams of her skirt, and began again in the proper way. "On Friday my whole family went for a ride in my brother's new car. My brother bought this new Pontiac last week, and he wanted to take us all for a ride—you know, to try it out and everything? So we went into White Plains and had dinner in a restaurant there, and then we all wanted to go see this movie, 'Doctor Jekyll and Mr. Hyde,' but my brother said it was too horrible and everything, and I wasn't old enough to enjoy it—oh, he made me so mad! And then, let's see. On Saturday I stayed home all day and helped my mother make my sister's wedding dress. My sister's engaged to be married, you see, and my mother's making this wedding dress for her? So we did that, and then on Sunday this friend of my brother's came over for dinner, and then they both had to get back to college that night, and I was allowed to stay up late and say goodbye to them and everything, and I guess that's all." She always had a sure instinct for keeping her performance brief—or rather, for making it seem briefer than it really was.

"Very good, Nancy," Miss Price said. "Now, who's next?"

Warren Berg was next, elaborately hitching up his pants as he made his way down the aisle. "On Saturday I went over to Bill Stringer's house for lunch," he began in his direct, man-to-man style, and Bill Stringer wriggled bashfully in the front row. Warren Berg and Bill Stringer were great friends, and their reports often overlapped. "And then after lunch we went into White Plains, on our bikes. Only we *saw* 'Doctor Jekyll and Mr. Hyde.'" Here he nodded his head in Nancy's direction, and Nancy got another laugh by making a little whimper of envy. "It was real good, too," he went on, with mounting excitement. "It's all about this guy who—"

"About *a man* who," Miss Price corrected.

"About a man who mixes up this chemical, like, that he drinks? And whenever he drinks this chemical, he changes into this real monster, like? You see him drink this chemical, and then you see his hands start to get all scales all over them, like a reptile and everything, and then you see his face start to change into this real horrible-looking face—with fangs and all? Sticking out of his mouth?"

All the girls shuddered in pleasure. "Well," Miss Price said, "I think Nancy's brother was probably wise in not wanting her to see it. What did you do *after* the movie, Warren?"

There was a general "Aw-w-w!" of disappointment—everyone wanted to hear more about the scales and fangs—but Miss Price never liked to let the reports degenerate into accounts of movies. Warren continued without much enthusiasm: all they had done after the movie was fool around Bill Stringer's yard until suppertime. "And then on Sunday," he said, brightening again, "Bill Stringer came over to *my* house, and my dad helped us rig up this old tire on this long rope? From a tree? There's this steep hill down behind my house, you see—this ravine, like?—and we hung this tire so that what you do is, you take the tire and run a little ways and then lift your feet, and you go swinging way, way out over the ravine and back again."

"That sounds like fun," Miss Price said, glancing at her watch.

"Oh, it's *fun*, all right," Warren conceded. But then he hitched up his pants again and added, with a puckering of his forehead, " 'Course, it's pretty dangerous. You let go of that tire or anything, you'd get a bad fall. Hit a rock or anything, you'd probably break your leg, or your spine. But my dad said he trusted us both to look out for our own safety."

"Well, I'm afraid that's all we'll have time for, Warren," Miss Price said. "Now, there's just time for one more report. Who's ready? Arthur Cross?"

There was a soft groan, because Arthur Cross was the biggest dope in class and his reports were always a bore. This time it turned out to be something tedious about going to visit his uncle on Long Island. At one point he made a slip—he said "botormoat" instead of "motorboat"— and everyone laughed with the particular edge of scorn they reserved for Arthur Cross. But the laughter died abruptly when it was joined by a harsh, dry croaking from the back of the room. Vincent Sabella was laughing too, green teeth and all, and they all had to glare at him until he stopped.

When the reports were over, everyone settled down for school. It was recess time before any of the children thought much about Vincent Sabella again, and then they thought of him only to make sure he was left out of everything. He wasn't in the group of boys that clustered around the horizontal bar to take turns at skinning-the-cat, or the group that whispered in a far corner of the playground, hatching a plot to push Nancy Parker in the mud. Nor was he in the larger group, of which even Arthur Cross was a member, that chased itself in circles in a frantic variation of the game of tag. He couldn't join the girls, of course, or the boys from other classes, and so he joined nobody. He stayed on the apron of the playground, close to school, and for the first part of the recess he pretended to be very busy with the laces of his sneakers. He would squat to undo and retie them, straighten up and take a few experimental steps in a springy, athletic way, and then get down and go to work on them again. After five minutes of this he gave it up, picked up a handful of pebbles and began shying them at an invisible target several yards away. That was good for another five minutes, but then there were still five minutes left, and he could think of nothing to do but stand there, first with his hands in his pockets, then with his hands on his hips, and then with his arms folded in a manly way across his chest.

Miss Price stood watching all this from the doorway, and she spent the full recess wondering if she ought to go out and do something about it. She guessed it would be better not to.

She managed to control the same impulse at recess the next day, and every other day that week, though every day it grew more difficult. But one thing she could not control was a tendency to let her anxiety show in class. All Vincent Sabella's errors in schoolwork were publicly excused, even those having nothing to do with his newness, and all his accomplishments were singled out for special mention. Her campaign to build him up was painfully obvious, and never more so than when she tried to make it subtle; once, for instance, in explaining an arithmetic problem, she said, "Now, suppose Warren Berg and Vincent Sabella went to the store with fifteen cents each, and candy bars cost ten cents. How many candy bars would each boy have?" By the end of the week he was well on the way to becoming the worst possible kind of teacher's pet, a victim of the teacher's pity.

On Friday she decided the best thing to do would be to speak to him privately, and try to draw him out. She could say something about the pictures he had painted in art class—that would do for an opening— and she decided to do it at lunchtime.

The only trouble was that lunchtime, next to recess, was the most trying part of Vincent Sabella's day. Instead of going home for an hour as the other children did, he brought his lunch to school in a wrinkled paper bag and ate it in the classroom, which always made for a certain amount of awkwardness. The last children to leave would see him still seated apologetically at his desk, holding his paper bag, and anyone who happened to straggle back later for a forgotten hat or sweater would surprise him in the middle of his meal—perhaps shielding a hard-boiled egg from view or wiping mayonnaise from his mouth with a furtive hand. It was a situation that Miss Price did not improve by walking up to him while the room was still half full of children and sitting prettily on the edge of the desk beside his, making it clear that she was cutting her own lunch hour short in order to be with him.

"Vincent," she began, "I've been meaning to tell you how much I enjoyed those pictures of yours. They're really very good."

He mumbled something and shifted his eyes to the cluster of departing children at the door. She went right on talking and smiling, elaborating on her praise of the pictures; and finally, after the door had closed behind the last child, he was able to give her his attention. He did so tentatively at first; but the more she talked, the more he seemed to relax, until she realized she was putting him at ease. It was as simple and as gratifying as stroking a cat. She had finished with the pictures now and moved on, triumphantly, to broader fields of praise. "It's never easy," she was saying, "to come to a new school and adjust yourself to the—well, the new work, and new working methods, and I think you've done a splendid job so far. I really do. But tell me, do you think you're going to like it here?"

He looked at the floor just long enough to make his reply—"It's awright"—and then his eyes stared into hers again.

"I'm so glad. Please don't let me interfere with your lunch, Vincent.

Do go ahead and eat, that is, if you don't mind my sitting here with you." But it was now abundantly clear that he didn't mind at all, and he began to unwrap a bologna sandwich with what she felt sure was the best appetite he'd had all week. It wouldn't even have mattered very much now if someone from the class had come in and watched, though it was probably just as well that no one did.

Miss Price sat back more comfortably on the desk top, crossed her legs and allowed one slim stockinged foot to slip part of the way out of its moccasin. "Of course," she went on, "it always does take a little time to sort of get your bearings in a new school. For one thing, well, it's never too easy for the new member of the class to make friends with the other members. What I mean is, you mustn't mind if the others seem a little rude to you at first. Actually, they're just as anxious to make friends as you are, but they're shy. All it takes is a little time, and a little effort on your part as well as theirs. Not too much, of course, but a little. Now for instance, these reports we have Monday mornings—they're a fine way for people to get to know one another. A person never feels he has to make a report; it's just a thing he can do if he wants to. And that's only one way of helping others to know the kind of person you are; there are lots and lots of ways. The main thing to remember is that making friends is the most natural thing in the world, and it's only a question of time until you have all the friends you want. And in the meantime, Vincent, I hope you'll consider *me* your friend, and feel free to call on me for whatever advice or anything you might need. Will you do that?"

He nodded, swallowing.

"Good." She stood up and smoothed her skirt over her long thighs. "Now I must go or I'll be late for *my* lunch. But I'm glad we had this little talk, Vincent, and I hope we'll have others."

It was probably a lucky thing that she stood up when she did, for if she'd stayed on that desk a minute longer Vincent Sabella would have thrown his arms around her and buried his face in the warm gray flannel of her lap, and that might have been enough to confuse the most dedicated and imaginative of teachers.

At report time on Monday morning, nobody was more surprised than Miss Price when Vincent Sabella's smudged hand was among the first and most eager to rise. Apprehensively she considered letting someone else start off, but then, for fear of hurting his feelings, she said, "All right, Vincent," in as matter-of-fact a way as she could manage.

There was a suggestion of muffled titters from the class as he walked confidently to the head of the room and turned to face his audience. He looked, if anything, too confident: there were signs, in the way he held his shoulders and the way his eyes shone, of the terrible poise of panic.

"Saturday I seen that pitcha," he announced.

"Saw, Vincent," Miss Price corrected gently.

"That's what I mean," he said; "I sore that pitcha. 'Doctor Jack-o'-lantern and Mr. Hide.'"

There was a burst of wild, delighted laughter and a chorus of correction: "Doctor *Jekyll!*"

He was unable to speak over the noise. Miss Price was on her feet, furious. "It's a *perfectly natural mistake!*" she was saying. "There's no reason for any of you to be so rude. Go on, Vincent, and please excuse this very silly interruption." The laughter subsided, but the class continued to shake their heads derisively from side to side. It hadn't, of course, been a perfectly natural mistake at all; for one thing it proved that he was a hopeless dope, and for another it proved that he was lying.

"That's what I mean," he continued. "'Doctor Jackal and Mr. Hide.' I got it a little mixed up. Anyways, I seen all about where his teet' start comin' outa his mout' and all like that, and I thought it was very good. And then on Sunday my mudda and fodda come out to see me in this car they got. This Buick. My fodda siz, 'Vinny, wanna go for a little ride?' I siz, 'Sure, where yiz goin'?' He siz, 'Anyplace ya like.' So I siz, 'Let's go out in the country a ways, get on one of them big roads and make some time.' So we go out—oh, I guess fifty, sixty miles—and we're cruisin' along this highway, when this cop starts tailin' us? My fodda siz, 'Don't worry, we'll shake him,' and he steps on it, see? My mudda's gettin' pretty scared, but my fodda siz, 'Don't worry, dear.' He's tryin' to make this turn, see, so he can get off the highway and shake the cop? But just when he's makin' the turn, the cop opens up and starts shootin', see?"

By this time the few members of the class who could bear to look at him at all were doing so with heads on one side and mouths partly open, the way you look at a broken arm or a circus freak.

"We just barely made it," Vincent went on, his eyes gleaming, "and this one bullet got my fodda in the shoulder. Didn't hurt him bad— just grazed him, like—so my mudda bandaged it up for him and all, but he couldn't do no more drivin' after that, and we had to get him to a doctor, see? So my fodda siz, 'Vinny, think you can drive a ways?' I siz, 'Sure, if you show me how.' So he showed me how to work the gas and the brake, and all like that, and I drove to the doctor. My mudda siz, 'I'm prouda you, Vinny, drivin' all by yourself.' So anyways, we got to the doctor, got my fodda fixed up and all, and then he drove us back home." He was breathless. After an uncertain pause he said, "And that's all." Then he walked quickly back to his desk, his stiff new corduroy pants whistling faintly with each step.

"Well, that was very—entertaining, Vincent," Miss Price said, trying to act as if nothing had happened. "Now, who's next?" But nobody raised a hand.

Recess was worse than usual for him that day; at least it was until he found a place to hide—a narrow concrete alley, blind except for several closed fire-exit doors, that cut between two sections of the school building. It was reassuringly dismal and cool in there—he could stand with his back to the wall and his eyes guarding the entrance, and the noises of recess were as remote as the sunshine. But when the bell rang he had to go back to class, and in another hour it was lunchtime.

Miss Price left him alone until her own meal was finished. Then, after standing with one hand on the doorknob for a full minute to gather courage, she went in and sat beside him for another little talk, just as he was trying to swallow the last of a pimento-cheese sandwich.

"Vincent," she began, "we all enjoyed your report this morning, but I think we would have enjoyed it more—a great deal more—if you'd told us something about your real life instead. I mean," she hurried on, "for instance, I noticed you were wearing a nice new windbreaker this morning. It *is* new, isn't it? And did your aunt buy it for you over the weekend?"

He did not deny it.

"Well then, why couldn't you have told me about going to the store with your aunt, and buying the windbreaker, and whatever you did afterwards. That would have made a perfectly good report." She paused, and for the first time looked steadily into his eyes. "You do understand what I'm trying to say, don't you, Vincent?"

He wiped crumbs of bread from his lips, looked at the floor, and nodded.

"And you'll remember next time, won't you?"

He nodded again. "Please may I be excused, Miss Price?"

"Of course you may."

He went to the boys' lavatory and vomited. Afterwards he washed his face and drank a little water, and then he returned to the classroom. Miss Price was busy at her desk now, and didn't look up. To avoid getting involved with her again, he wandered out to the cloakroom and sat on one of the long benches, where he picked up someone's discarded overshoe and turned it over and over in his hands. In a little while he heard the chatter of returning children, and to avoid being discovered there, he got up and went to the fire-exit door. Pushing it open, he found that it gave onto the alley he had hidden in that morning, and he slipped outside. For a minute or two he just stood there, looking at the blankness of the concrete wall; then he found a piece of chalk in his pocket and wrote out all the dirty words he could think of, in block letters a foot high. He had put down four words and was trying to remember a fifth when he heard a shuffling at the door behind him. Arthur Cross was there, holding the door open and reading the words with wide eyes. "Boy," he said in an awed half-whisper. "Boy, you're gonna get it. You're really gonna *get* it."

Startled, and then suddenly calm, Vincent Sabella palmed his chalk, hooked his thumbs in his belt and turned on Arthur Cross with a menacing look. "Yeah?" he inquired. "Who's gonna squeal on me?"

"Well, nobody's gonna *squeal* on you," Arthur Cross said uneasily, "but you shouldn't go around writing—"

"Arright," Vincent said, advancing a step. His shoulders were slumped, his head thrust forward and his eyes narrowed, like Edward G. Robinson. "Arright. That's all I wanna know. I don't like squealers, unnastand?"

While he was saying this, Warren Berg and Bill Stringer appeared in the doorway—just in time to hear it and to see the words on the wall before Vincent turned on them. "And that goes fa you too, unnastand?" he said. "Both a yiz."

And the remarkable thing was that both their faces fell into the same foolish, defensive smile that Arthur Cross was wearing. It wasn't until they had glanced at each other that they were able to meet his eyes with the proper degree of contempt, and by then it was too late. "Think you're pretty smart, don'tcha, Sabella?" Bill Stringer said.

"Never mind what I think," Vincent told him. "You heard what I said. Now let's get back inside."

And they could do nothing but move aside to make way for him, and follow him dumfounded into the cloakroom.

It was Nancy Parker who squealed—although, of course, with someone like Nancy Parker you didn't think of it as squealing. She had heard everything from the cloakroom; as soon as the boys came in she peeked into the alley, saw the words and, setting her face in a prim frown, went straight to Miss Price. Miss Price was just about to call the class to order for the afternoon when Nancy came up and whispered in her ear. They both disappeared into the cloakroom—from which, after a moment, came the sound of the fire-exit door being abruptly slammed—and when they returned to class Nancy was flushed with righteousness, Miss Price very pale. No announcement was made. Classes proceeded in the ordinary way all afternoon, though it was clear that Miss Price was upset, and it wasn't until she was dismissing the children at three o'clock that she brought the thing into the open. "Will Vincent Sabella please remain seated?" She nodded at the rest of the class. "That's all."

While the room was clearing out she sat at her desk, closed her eyes and massaged the frail bridge of her nose with thumb and forefinger, sorting out half-remembered fragments of a book she had once read on the subject of seriously disturbed children. Perhaps, after all, she should never have undertaken the responsibility of Vincent Sabella's loneliness. Perhaps the whole thing called for the attention of a specialist. She took a deep breath.

"Come over here and sit beside me, Vincent," she said, and when he had settled himself, she looked at him. "I want you to tell me the truth. Did you write those words on the wall outside?"

He stared at the floor.

"Look at me," she said, and he looked at her. She had never looked prettier: her cheeks slightly flushed, her eyes shining and her sweet mouth pressed into a self-conscious frown. "First of all," she said, handing him a small enameled basin streaked with poster paint, "I want you to take this to the boys' room and fill it with hot water and soap."

He did as he was told, and when he came back, carrying the basin carefully to keep the suds from spilling, she was sorting out some old rags in the bottom drawer of her desk. "Here," she said, selecting one and shutting the drawer in a businesslike way. "This will do. Soak this up." She led him back to the fire exit and stood in the alley watching him, silently, while he washed off all the words.

When the job had been done, and the rag and basin put away, they sat down at Miss Price's desk again. "I suppose you think I'm angry with you, Vincent," she said. "Well, I'm not. I almost wish I could be angry—that would make it much easier—but instead I'm hurt. I've tried to be a good friend to you, and I thought you wanted to be my friend too. But this kind of thing—well, it's very hard to be friendly with a person who'd do a thing like that."

She saw, gratefully, that there were tears in his eyes. "Vincent, perhaps I understand some things better than you think. Perhaps I understand that sometimes, when a person does a thing like that, it isn't really because he wants to hurt anyone, but only because he's unhappy. He knows it isn't a good thing to do, and he even knows it isn't going to make him any happier afterwards, but he goes ahead and does it anyway. Then when he finds he's lost a friend, he's terribly sorry, but it's too late. The thing is done."

She allowed this somber note to reverberate in the silence of the room for a little while before she spoke again. "I won't be able to forget this, Vincent. But perhaps, just this once, we can still be friends—as long as I understand that you didn't mean to hurt me. But you must promise me that you won't forget it either. Never forget that when you do a thing like that, you're going to hurt people who want very much to like you, and in that way you're going to hurt yourself. Will you promise me to remember that, dear?"

The "dear" was as involuntary as the slender hand that reached out and held the shoulder of his sweatshirt; both made his head hang lower than before.

"All right," she said. "You may go now."

He got his windbreaker out of the cloakroom and left, avoiding the tired uncertainty of her eyes. The corridors were deserted, and dead silent except for the hollow, rhythmic knocking of a janitor's push-broom against some distant wall. His own rubber-soled tread only added to the silence; so did the lonely little noise made by the zipping-up of his windbreaker, and so did the faint mechanical sigh of the heavy front door. The silence made it all the more startling when he found, several yards down the concrete walk outside, that two boys were walking beside him: Warren Berg and Bill Stringer. They were both smiling at him in an eager, almost friendly way.

"What'd she do to ya, anyway?" Bill Stringer asked.

Caught off guard, Vincent barely managed to put on his Edward G. Robinson face in time. "Nunnya business," he said, and walked faster.

"No, listen—wait up, hey," Warren Berg said, as they trotted to keep up with him. "What'd she do, anyway? She bawl ya out, or what? Wait up, hey, Vinny."

The name made him tremble all over. He had to jam his hands in his windbreaker pockets and force himself to keep on walking; he had to force his voice to be steady when he said "Nunnya *business*, I told ya. Lea' me alone."

But they were right in step with him now. "Boy, she must of given you the works," Warren Berg persisted. "What'd she say, anyway? C'mon, tell us, Vinny."

This time the name was too much for him. It overwhelmed his resistance and made his softening knees slow down to a slack, conversational stroll. "She din say nothin'" he said at last; and then after a dramatic pause he added, "She let the ruler do her talkin' for her."

"The *ruler*? Ya mean she used a *ruler* on ya?" Their faces were stunned, either with disbelief or admiration, and it began to look more and more like admiration as they listened.

"On the knuckles," Vincent said through tightening lips. "Five times on each hand. She siz, 'Make a fist. Lay it out here on the desk.' Then she takes the ruler and *Whop! Whop! Whop!* Five times. Ya think that don't hurt, you're crazy."

Miss Price, buttoning her polo coat as the front door whispered shut behind her, could scarcely believe her eyes. This couldn't be Vincent Sabella—this perfectly normal, perfectly happy boy on the sidewalk ahead of her, flanked by attentive friends. But it was, and the scene made her want to laugh aloud with pleasure and relief. He was going to be all right, after all. For all her well-intentioned groping in the shadows she could never have predicted a scene like this, and certainly could never have caused it to happen. But it was happening, and it just proved, once again, that she would never understand the ways of children.

She quickened her graceful stride and overtook them, turning to smile down at them as she passed. "Goodnight, boys," she called, intending it as a kind of cheerful benediction; and then, embarrassed by their three startled faces, she smiled even wider and said, "Goodness, it *is* getting colder, isn't it? That windbreaker of yours looks nice and warm, Vincent. I envy you." Finally they nodded bashfully at her; she called goodnight again, turned, and continued on her way to the bus stop.

She left a profound silence in her wake. Staring after her, Warren

Berg and Bill Stringer waited until she had disappeared around the corner before they turned on Vincent Sabella.

"Ruler, my eye!" Bill Stringer said. "Ruler, my eye!" He gave Vincent a disgusted shove that sent him stumbling against Warren Berg, who shoved him back.

"Jeez, you lie about *everything*, don'tcha, Sabella? You lie about *everything!*"

Jostled off balance, keeping his hands tight in the windbreaker pockets, Vincent tried in vain to retain his dignity. "Think *I* care if yiz believe me?" he said, and then because he couldn't think of anything else to say, he said it again. "Think *I* care if yiz believe me?"

But he was walking alone. Warren Berg and Bill Stringer were drifting away across the street, walking backwards in order to look back on him with furious contempt. "Just like the lies you told about the policeman shooting your father," Bill Stringer called.

"Even *movies* he lies about," Warren Berg put in; and suddenly doubling up with artificial laughter he cupped both hands to his mouth and yelled, "Hey, Doctor Jack-o'-lantern!"

It wasn't a very good nickname, but it had an authentic ring to it—the kind of a name that might spread around, catch on quickly, and stick. Nudging each other, they both took up the cry:

"What's the matter, Doctor Jack-o'-lantern?"

"Why don'tcha run on home with Miss Price, Doctor Jack-o'-lantern?"

"So long, Doctor Jack-o'-lantern!"

Vincent Sabella went on walking, ignoring them, waiting until they were out of sight. Then he turned and retraced his steps all the way back to school, around through the playground and back to the alley, where the wall was still dark in spots from the circular scrubbing of his wet rag.

Choosing a dry place, he got out his chalk and began to draw a head with great care, in profile, making the hair long and rich and taking his time over the face, erasing it with moist fingers and reworking it until it was the most beautiful face he had ever drawn: a delicate nose, slightly parted lips, an eye with lashes that curved as gracefully as a bird's wing. He paused to admire it with a lover's solemnity; then from the lips he drew a line that connected with a big speech balloon, and in the balloon he wrote, so angrily that the chalk kept breaking in his fingers, every one of the words he had written that noon. Returning to the head, he gave it a slender neck and gently sloping shoulders, and then, with bold strikes, he gave it the body of a naked woman: great breasts with hard little nipples, a trim waist, a dot for a navel, wide hips and thighs that flared around a triangle of fiercely scribbled pubic hair. Beneath the picture he printed its title: "Miss Price."

He stood there looking at it for a little while, breathing hard, and then he went home.

Robert Paul Smith

(1915–   )

Derelict in a welter of riches is one way to describe the child of suburbia
whose parents have forgotten the requisites of childhood. Robert Paul Smith
remembers the ways a child can be alone, and not lonely, for the inventions
of the mind to dream themselves. Less harrowing than the threats of the
ghetto, but just as importunate, are teachers and parents who bind the lives
of their children in girdles of supervisory zeal. Though the author confines his
attack to parents and PTA followers, the implications of his ire apply as well
to teachers, counselors, and administrators.

Some questions remain. How much *can* the school do for children who
have little? How much *should* it do for children who have enough, or too much?
Put another way, why should educators blithely exhaust whatever energies
they possess on the very children who may need them least?

Other works by Robert Paul Smith are *So It Doesn't Whistle* (1941),
Where Did You Go? Out. What Did You Do? Nothing. (1957), and *Transla-
tions from the English* (1958).

LET YOUR KIDS ALONE

When I was a kid, the way we got to play baseball was this: school was
out, we ran home and hooked a handful of cookies, hollered, "I'm home,
goin' out on the block," grabbed a beat-up fielder's glove, went out on
the block and met a friend who had an old first baseman's mitt and a
ball, went down the block a little and hollered at the kid who had the
bat. So we proceeded until we had rounded up all those kids who were

not chained to piano practice, making model airplanes, lying on their backs studying the ceiling, feeding their rabbits or writing out one thousand times, "I will not put blotting paper in the inkwell." We went to the vacant lot and played a game resembling major league baseball only in that it was played with a bat and bases. It was fun.

My kid went to play soccer the other day. The way you play soccer now is this: you bring home from school a mimeographed schedule for the Saturday morning soccer league. There are six teams, named after colleges, and the schedule is so arranged that at the end of the season, by a mathematical process of permutations and combinations that would take me six weeks to figure out, every team has played every other team and every kid has shown up at the right hour the right number of times. There are always exactly eleven men on each team, the ball is regulation size, the games are played on a regulation-size field with regulation-size soccer goals, and there is a regulation-size adult to referee.

After the game I asked my kid, "Was it fun?" "Yes," he said, but he didn't sound sure. "We lost 3–0." When I was a kid, we lost 3–0 too— and also 16–2 and 135–3 at soccer or baseball or kick-the-can—but by the time we had fought about where the strike zone was, what was out of bounds and who was offside, we could wind up winning the argument, if not the game.

Because, you see, it was *our* game. I think that my kid was playing someone else's game. I think he was playing Big Brother's game.

Big Brother, in this case, is all the parents who cannot refrain from poking their snoots into a world where they have no business to be, into the whole wonderful world of a kid, which is wonderful precisely because there are no grownups in it. In come today's parents, tramping down the underbrush, cutting down the trees, driving away the game, making the place hideous with mimeographed sheets and names and regulations. They are into everything. They refuse to let anything alone if there is a kid connected with it. They have invented a whole new modern perversion: child-watching.

There are two main groups of child-watchers. The first, which includes the PTA's and the child study leagues and the children's mental hygiene groups, watches but does not touch. These are the peepers through one-way glass, the keepers of notebooks, the givers of tests.

The second group watches *and* touches—and also coaches and uniforms and proliferates rulebooks. This group manages such things as the soccer leagues and the Little Leagues and the Cub Scouts and the Boy Scouts and the Girl Scouts and the Brownies and the Sea Scouts and the Explorer Scouts and, I'd bet, the Satellite Scouts. These are the getters down on all fours, the spies in the children's world, the ones who cannot be sure whether they wish the kids to be as grownup as themselves, or wish themselves to be as childish as the kids.

All this child-watching and child-helping and child-pushing has made it tough for the kids to do anything without a complete set of instructions. Of course, once in a while they do break through the instruction barrier. The afternoon following the soccer game, my kid went off on his own business. This consisted of assembling an arrangement of batteries and resistors and what I have learned are called capacitors (not condensers), which makes five tiny neon tubes blink in a manner I can only describe as infuriating. Obviously this was fun for him. There are no plans for constructing such a machine. Indeed, it may be the first time such a machine has been built. So he built it. But he did not go outside and do the idle footling of a soccer ball which I used to do because the kid next door happened to have a soccer ball, and he did not play one-o-cat or throw a football around or even watch squirrels.

He did not do this because, although Big Brother has organized every league known to man and issued a rule book therefor, he has not yet put out a mimeographed sheet of instructions on watching squirrels. There are no books on how to be a lousy right fielder (it came to me natural), and in no book does it say that when you go to make a tackle, of course you shut your eyes and lie about it later. No doubt these books are being written.

Perhaps the finest single example of an organization that is devoted to not leaving the kids alone is the Scouts. It is not my intention to knock the Scouts as a whole. It is a well-meaning organization devoted to salutary works. I am sure that its officials are high-principled, admirable people. I merely wish to point out that the name of the organization is the *Boy* Scouts. It is for *boys.* And yet there is a small, wallet-sized card printed by the Boy Scouts of America entitled "The Scout Parent's Opportunity." Among the exhortations on this card are these:

"Be a companion to your own son." "Weave Cub Scouting into home-life pattern." "Use the program to draw the family closer." "Be with your son at all pack meetings." "Work closely with the Den Mother."

The day an organization, *any* organization, tells me how to be a companion to my son is the day I am going to take a good hard look at that organization, and if they mean it for real, I am going to prepare to mount the barricades. I find "The Scout Parent's Opportunity" a terrifying document, but it is as nothing compared to another communiqué from the same organization. This is a sheet of yellow paper headed HERE ARE THE THINGS YOU DO TO BECOME A BOBCAT.

Well, the very first thing you do to become a Bobcat is learn and take the Cub Scout promise: "I promise to DO MY BEST to do my DUTY to GOD and my COUNTRY, to be SQUARE, and to OBEY the Law of the Pack." (The capital letters are *not* mine.) Only after you have said you will OBEY the Law of the Pack do you find out what the Law of the Pack is. The very first article of the Law is, "The Cub

Scout FOLLOWS Akela." Then you hear that "Akela means 'Good Leader'—your mother and father, your teacher, your Cubmaster, and many other people who have shown that they are the kind of people who are able and willing to help you." Follow this reasoning carefully: first you say you will do something; then you find out what it is that you have promised to do; and then you find out what the thing you have promised to do means.

Before I let my kid subscribe to this, he is going to have a little talk with OLD FATHER, who is going to HOLLER at him GOOD AND LOUD. And what OLD FATHER is going to TELL him is never sign a BLANK CHECK, and before he goes off following Akela, he better take a GOOD HARD LOOK at all these people who have shown that they are "able and willing" to help him and find out where they are able and willing to lead him TO.

Bobcats, I have news for you. I know who Akela is, and he is not all those people. He is the old leader of the wolves in Kipling's Mowgli stories, and during wolf meetings he lies quietly on the Council Rock, interpreting the law and keeping order by means of dignity and aloofness. He spends a great deal of time keeping his mouth shut and he spends absolutely no time at all down in the grass with the young cubs playing Pin the Tail on the Hartebeest or Ring Around the Cobra.

I know a father in Connecticut whose kid FOLLOWED Akela to a Den, and after several sessions the kid wanted out. He did not know how to convey this horrible intelligence to Akela, so instead he went to his father. Apparently he thought quitting the Scouts was like breaking with the Communist party, or trying to get away from George Raft and being cut down by a machine gun at the corner of Fifth and Main.

The thing that drove this boy away from the Cub Scouts grew out of the little joker in one corner of the Bobcats' contract. It is called the "Parents' O.K." and it says: "We have had an active part in our son's first Cub Scout experience—becoming a Bobcat. We have tried to see things through his eyes and not expect too much. On the other hand, we haven't been too easy. We have helped him complete all the Bobcat requirements and we are satisfied that he has done his best."

This sounds mawkish but fairly harmless. The way my friend from Connecticut tells it, it isn't harmless at all. "Your kid brings you a book called the Wolf Cub Scout Book. If, Lord help us, you're a Good Scout Dad, you read a little of the book. On page 18 is something called 'Feats of Skill,' and your kid has to do any three of them to pass. He can choose a frontward, backward and falling somersault, or playing catch with someone twenty feet away, or climbing at least twelve feet up a tree, or swimming thirty feet in shallow water, or walking a two-by-four forward, sideways and backward. Now I'm for this, so I watch my kid practice. He tries and he doesn't get anywhere near twelve feet up the tree. I say, 'No, that's about five feet. You didn't do it.' When he tries to walk backward on the two-by-four, he falls off, so I say, 'Give it a little more work.' After all, I'm the one who's got to sign a paper saying he passed the test."

I could see why my friend was concerned: when he signs contracts, he fulfills them.

"So there's this pack meeting," my friend continued, "and they start giving kids badges because they have done their feats of skill. After a while, my boy and I see this one kid from our block who we *know* can't find his bottom with both hands in the dark, and he's getting a badge because he did the feats of skill. It's 'proven.' His mother signed the pledge. My kid looks at me. Something is very fishy here, is what he is thinking. That goof climbed twelve feet up a tree? Then why can't he climb stairs very good? It didn't take my kid long to figure it out: mothers lie and scoutmasters believe them. So he quit.

"That summer my kid took a look at an island in the middle of a lake at a kind of farm he goes to. He was the littlest kid there. He swam out and back and wrote a letter home, and in the envelope was a weed from the island. I didn't have to tell him it was a feat of skill and the weed was a badge. He knew it."

I suggested to my friend that he tell his kid that Akela—Mr. Kipling's Akela—would have known it, too, and so would Dan Beard, whose concern in helping found the Boy Scouts was to get kids out on their own in the country where they could learn to be independent.

I hear that things are bad in the Brownie world too. One Boston mother complains that she was required to learn to do everything her daughter had to learn to do to become a Brownie. At what cost to her self-esteem she cannot say, she even had to learn to sing, with gestures, the "Brownie Smile Song," which includes the words, "I have something in my pocket." And what mother has in her pocket is a smile, which she takes out and puts on her face. I ask you.

A New York City mother swears that when her daughter was "invested" in the Brownies, all the mothers had to be invested too. "I went to the investiture," this mother says, "and before I knew it, I and all the other mothers were standing up in a line, reciting the Brownie oath and having badges pinned on us."

Well, what's the point? The real point is that this kind of jazz doesn't fool anyone but the parents. The kids know that any grownup who gets down on all fours and makes mudpies with them is either a spy or a fool. Not that kids don't like spending time with grownups, but what they want is for the grownup to take them into his world. They are familiar with the child's world, they can handle themselves there. But a grownup can take them to a new place, an exciting world of cigars and restaurants with linen napkins and automobiles and tall people. But do parents do this today? No, they are too busy being Real Dandy Scout Dads and True Blue Brownie Moms.

The Scouts, of course, are only an example. This same attitude is found everywhere that parents and children get together. Anybody who thinks that the kids don't understand what is going on is living in a dream. These kids watch their parents making spectacles of themselves, and they reach conclusions. All parents who are now, or ever have been, down on all fours should give careful thought to the conclusions that they invite their kids to reach.

It seems to me that we are doing things we do not really want to do for kids who do not really want to have them done. Perhaps the saddest proof of all is provided by the town of Proctor, Minnesota, where members of the Duluth, Missabe and Iron Range Railway Employees Association actually go out on the street to try to get kids to use their bowling alleys, golf course, ball park, football field, rifle range, skating rink and tennis courts. No sale. The Proctor Moose Lodge offered to give away quarters to all the children of its 450 members on the Fourth of July. All the kids had to do was show up and hold out their hands. The first year only 50 kids bothered to show and the next year fewer than 25. The project was abandoned. And when Proctor sponsored a safety contest open to all the school kids in town, only one boy entered. Naturally he won first prize, a watch, but since he already had a watch he asked for $10 instead.

For reasons of their own the kids of Proctor don't want to use the bowling alleys, don't want to walk that far for a quarter, don't care very much about safety. I suspect that the main reason is that they never asked for any of these things and would rather be left alone. What is true for the kids of Proctor is going to be true for the kids of San Francisco and Chicago and New York and Ashtabula. The thing to do, I think, is for us to stop pestering them.

To this end I have formed an organization called Modern Parents Anonymous, or MPA (not under any circumstances to be confused with a recently formed Seattle organization known as PPPTA, or Proud Papas of the Parent-Teachers Association). MPA got its start one night when four supposedly adult persons—my wife and I and another couple —were sitting in moderately comfortable chairs in our moderately well-heated, well-lighted living room. All four of us read books and magazines, we have minds to think with and an enormous world to think about. So for two hours we talked about—children.

The actions of our children seemed more sensible to me than our own. They had looked into the living room some time before, seen that grownups were in tedious conclave, said hello and good-by and left. They were not wasting their time talking about us. The moment I realized this, MPA was born.

The principal goal of MPA is to encourage parents to think and worry and talk about something other than their own offspring. I have a list of things that might be talked about: freedom, liberty, the mating habits of Eskimos, the difference between Conté crayon and charcoal, the difference between voltage and amperage, religion, Ralph De Palma, the inflation of a basketball, the principle of a two-stroke engine, money, marbles and chalk. These intelligent areas of discourse I obtained from my kids. The care and handling of parents is not, of course, on their list. They stay away from this topic with consummate ease.

Last year I wrote a book which suggested, in the mildest possible ways, that if people remembered what a nuisance grownups were when they were kids, perhaps now that they were in turn presumably grownups they might like to get off the kids' backs. The mail has been fantastic, all in agreement, and most fantastic of all have been the communications from PTA groups asking me to come and holler at them.

I am booked for one such PTA talk in the near future, and I have a letter on the subject from the program chairman. "We need you, Mr. Smith," the letter says. "We want to stimulate our parents to think seriously about the probable risk of too many set designs for living and about the possible triumphs of unstressed, unconformist ways of growing."

Translating from the PTA-ese, I take this to mean that they want me to tell them how to leave their kids alone to grow up in peace. Well, I will go, and if I do not lose my nerve I will tell them that the way to leave kids alone is to leave them alone.

James Agee
(1910–1955)

James Agee was born in Knoxville, Tennessee, and his early life there is re-flected in two novels, *The Morning Watch* (1951) and *A Death in the Family*, which received the Pulitzer Prize when published posthumously in 1957. After graduation from Harvard, Agee wrote a book of verse, *Permit Me Voyage*, and in 1932 went to work for *Fortune Magazine*, transferring to *Time* in 1939.

Critical opinion is unanimous: Agee's early death by heart failure was an extreme loss both to American journalism and to American literature. Agee's prose, its style so matched to intent, its meanings so held by its rhythms, has the authority to startle honorably and to compel in readers a deeper return to their own minds.

"Education" is part of *Let Us Now Praise Famous Men* (1942), a study of the rural South prepared in collaboration with photographer Walker Evans. After admitting that his research on the Alabama public schools was "thin, indirect, and deductive," Agee reveals what he directly saw and felt. Though his indignation is fed by particular evils, his compassion is general. As sum-moned by Agee, the shacks and schools of the depressed South invoke a past that is still upon us. Without charts he allows us still to see. Without statistics he leads us through a time within our age, into a land within our country.

EDUCATION

In every child who is born, under no matter what circumstances, and of no matter what parents, the potentiality of the human race is born again: and in him, too, once more, and of each of us, our terrific responsibility towards human life; towards the utmost idea of goodness, of the horror of error, and of God.

Every breath his senses shall draw, every act and every shadow and thing in all creation, is a mortal poison, or is a drug, or is a signal or symptom, or is a teacher, or is a liberator, or is liberty itself, depending entirely upon his understanding: and understanding,[1] and action proceeding from understanding and guided by it, is the one weapon against the world's bombardment, the one medicine, the one instrument by which liberty, health, and joy may be shaped or shaped towards, in the individual, and in the race.

This is no place to dare all questions that must be asked, far less to advance our tentatives in this murderous air, nor even to qualify so much as a little the little which thus far has been suggested, nor even either to question or to try to support my qualifications to speak of it at all: we are too near one of the deepest intersections of pity, terror, doubt and guilt; and I feel that I can say only, that "education," whose function is at the crisis of this appalling responsibility, does not seem to me to be all, or even anything, that it might be, but seems indeed the very property of the world's misunderstanding, the sharpest of its spearheads in every brain: and that since it could not be otherwise without destroying the world's machine, the world is unlikely to permit it to be otherwise.

In fact, and ignorant though I am, nothing, not even law, nor property, nor sexual ethics, nor fear, nor doubtlessness, nor even authority itself, all of which it is the business of education to cleanse the brain of, can so nearly annihilate me with fury and with horror; as the spectacle of innocence, of defenselessness, of all human hope, brought steadily in each year by the millions into the machineries of the teachings of the world, in which the man who would conceive of and who would dare attempt even the beginnings of what "teaching" must be could not exist two months clear of a penitentiary: presuming even that his own perceptions, and the courage of his perceptions, were not a poison as deadly at least as those poisons he would presume to drive out: or the very least of whose achievements, supposing he cared truly not only to hear himself speak but to be understood, would be a broken heart.[2]

For these and other reasons it would seem to me mistaken to decry the Alabama public schools, or even to say that they are "worse" or "less good" than schools elsewhere: or to be particularly wholehearted in the regret that these tenants are subjected only to a few years of this education: for they would be at a disadvantage if they had more of it, and at a disadvantage if they had none, and they are at a disadvantage in the little they have; and it would be hard and perhaps impossible to say in which way their disadvantage would be greatest.

[1] Active "understanding" is only one form, and there are suggestions of "perfection" which could be called "understanding" only by definitions so broad as to include diametric reversals. The peace of God surpasses all understanding; Mrs. Ricketts and her youngest child do, too; "understanding" can be its own, and hope's, most dangerous enemy.

[2] It may be that the only fit teachers never teach but are artists, and artists of the kind most blankly masked and least didactic.

School was not in session while I was there. My research on this subject was thin, indirect, and deductive. By one way of thinking it will seem for these reasons worthless: by another, which I happen to trust more, it may be sufficient.

I saw, for instance, no teachers: yet I am quite sure it is safe to assume that they are local at very least to the state and quite probably to the county; that most of them are women to whom teaching is either an incident of their youth or a poor solution for their spinsterhood; that if they were of much intelligence or courage they could not have survived their training in the State Normal or would never have undertaken it in the first place; that they are saturated in every belief and ignorance which is basic in their country and community; that any modification of this must be very mild indeed if they are to survive as teachers; that even if, in spite of all these screenings, there are superior persons among them, they are still again limited to texts and to a system of requirements officially imposed on them; and are caught between the pressures of class, of the state, of the churches, and of the parents, and are confronted by minds already so deeply formed that to liberate them would involve uncommon and as yet perhaps undiscovered philosophic and surgical skill. I have only sketched a few among dozens of the facts and forces which limit them; and even so I feel at liberty to suggest that even the best of these, the kindly, or the intuitive, the so-called natural teachers, are exceedingly more likely than not to be impossibly handicapped both from without and within themselves, and are at best the servants of unconscious murder; and of the others, the general run, that if murder of the mind and spirit were statutory crimes, the law, in its customary eagerness to punish the wrong person,[3] might spend all its ingenuity in the invention of deaths by delayed torture and never sufficiently expiate the enormities which through them, not by their own fault, have been committed.

Or again on the curriculum: it was unnecessary to make even such search into this as I made to know that there is no setting before the students of "economic" or "social" or "political" "facts" and of their situation within these "facts," no attempt made to clarify or even slightly to relieve the situation between the white and negro races, far less to explain the sources, no attempt to clarify psychological situations in the individual, in his family, or in his world, no attempt to get beneath and to revise those "ethical" and "social" pressures and beliefs in which even a young child is trapped, no attempt, beyond the most nominal, to interest a child in using or in discovering his senses and judgment, no attempt to counteract the paralytic quality inherent in "authority," no attempt

[3] This is not to suggest there is a "right person" or that punishment can ever be better than an enhancement of error.

beyond the most nominal and stifling to awaken, to protect, or to "guide" the sense of investigation, the sense of joy, the sense of beauty, no attempt to clarify spoken and written words whose power of deceit even at the simplest is vertiginous, no attempt, or very little, and ill taught, to teach even the earliest techniques of improvement in occupation ("scientific farming," diet and cooking, skilled trades), nor to "teach" a child in terms of his environment, no attempt, beyond the most suffocated, to awaken a student either to "religion" or to "irreligion," no attempt to develop in him either "skepticism" or "faith," nor "wonder," nor mental "honesty" nor mental "courage," nor any understanding of or delicateness in "the emotions" and in any of the uses and pleasures of the body save the athletic; no attempt either to relieve him of fear and of poison in sex or to release in him a free beginning of pleasure in it, nor to open within him the illimitable potentials of grief, of danger, and of goodness in sex and in sexual love, nor to give him the beginnings at very least of a knowledge, and of an attitude, whereby he may hope to guard and increase himself and those whom he touches, no indication of the damages which society, money, law, fear and quick belief have set upon these matters and upon all things in human life, nor of their causes, nor of the alternate ignorances and possibilities of ruin or of joy, no fear of doubtlessness, no fear of the illusions of knowledge, no fear of compromise:—and here again I have scarcely begun, and am confronted immediately with a serious problem: that is: by my naming of the lack of such teaching, I can appear too easily to recommend it, to imply, perhaps, that if these things were "taught," all would be "solved": and this I do not believe: but insist rather that in the teaching of these things, infinitely worse damage could and probably would result than in the teaching of those subjects which in fact do compose the curriculum: and that those who would most insist upon one or another of them can be among the deadliest enemies of education: for if the guiding hand is ill qualified, an instrument is murderous in proportion to its sharpness. Nothing I have mentioned but is at the mercy of misuse; and one may be sure a thousand to one it will be misused; and that its misuse will block any more "proper" use even more solidly than unuse and discrediting could. It could be said, that we must learn a certitude and correlation in every "value" before it will be possible to "teach" and not to murder; but that is far too optimistic. We would do better to examine, far beyond their present examination, the extensions within ourselves of doubt, responsibility, and conditioned faith and the possibilities of their more profitable union, to a degree at least of true and constant terror in even our tentatives, and if (for instance) we should dare to be "teaching" what Marx began to open, that we should do so only in the light of the terrible researches of Kafka and in the opposed identities of Blake and Céline.

All I have managed here, and it is more than I intended, is to give a confused statement of an intention which presumes itself to be good: the mere attempt to examine my own confusion would consume volumes. But let what I have tried to suggest amount to this alone: that not only within present reach of human intelligence, but even within reach of mine as it stands today, it would be possible that young human beings should rise onto their feet a great deal less dreadfully crippled than they are, a great deal more nearly capable of living well, a great deal more nearly aware, each of them, of their own dignity in existence, a great deal better qualified, each within his limits, to live and to take part toward the creation of a world in which good living will be possible without guilt toward every neighbor: and that teaching at present, such as it is, is almost entirely either irrelevant to these possibilities or destructive of them, and is, indeed, all but entirely unsuccessful even within its own "scales" of "value."

Within the world as it stands, however, the world they must live in, a certain form of education is available to these tenant children; and the extent to which they can avail themselves of it is of considerable importance in all their future living.

A few first points about it:

They are about as poorly equipped for self-education as human beings can be. Their whole environment is such that the use of the intelligence, of the intellect, and of the emotions is atrophied, and is all but entirely irrelevant to the pressures and needs which involve almost every instant of a tenant's conscious living: and indeed if these faculties were not thus reduced or killed at birth they would result in a great deal of pain, not to say danger. They learn the work they will spend their lives doing, chiefly of their parents, and from their parents and from the immediate world they take their conduct, their morality, and their mental and emotional and spiritual key. One could hardly say that any further knowledge or consciousness is at all to their use or advantage, since there is nothing to read, no reason to write, and no recourse against being cheated even if one is able to do sums; yet these forms of literacy are in general held to be desirable: a man or woman feels a certain sort of extra helplessness who lacks them: a truly serious or ambitious parent hopes for even more, for a promising child; though what "more" may be is, inevitably, only dimly understood.

School opens in middle or late September and closes the first of May. The country children, with their lunches, are picked up by busses at around seven-thirty in the morning and are dropped off again towards the early winter darkness. In spite of the bus the children of these three families have a walk to take. In dry weather it is shortened a good deal;

the bus comes up the branch road as far as the group of negro houses at the bottom of the second hill and the Ricketts children walk half a mile to meet it and the Gudger children walk three quarters. In wet weather the bus can't risk leaving the highway and the Ricketts walk two miles and the Gudgers a mile and a half in clay which in stretches is knee-deep on a child.

There was talk during the summer of graveling the road, though most of the fathers are over forty-five, beyond road-age. They can hardly afford the time to do such work for nothing, and they and their negro neighbors are in no position to pay taxes. Nothing had come of it within three weeks of the start of school, and there was no prospect of free time before cold weather.

Southern winters are sickeningly wet, and wet clay is perhaps the hardest of all walking. "Attendance" suffers by this cause, and by others. Junior Gudger, for instance, was absent sixty-five and Louise fifty-three days out of a possible hundred-and-fifty-odd, and these absences were "unexcused" eleven and nine times respectively, twenty-three of Junior's and a proportionate number of Louise's absences fell in March and April, which are full of work at home as well as wetness. Late in her second year in school Louise was needed at home and missed several consecutive school days, including the final examinations. Her "marks" had been among the best in her class and she had not known of the examination date, but no chance was given her to make up the examinations and she had to take the whole year over. The Ricketts children have much worse attendance records and Pearl does not attend at all.

School does not begin until the children shall have helped two weeks to a month in the most urgent part of the picking season, and ends in time for them to be at work on the cotton-chopping.

The bus system which is now a routine of country schools is helpful, but not particularly to those who live at any distance from tax-maintained roads.

The walking, and the waiting in the cold and wetness, one day after another, to school in the morning, and home from schools in the shriveling daylight, is arduous and unpleasant.

Schooling, here as elsewhere, is identified with the dullest and most meager months of the year, and, in this class and country, with the least and worst food and a cold noonday lunch: and could be set only worse at a disadvantage if it absorbed the pleasanter half of the year.

The "attendance problem" is evidently taken for granted and, judging by the low number of unexcused absences, is "leniently" dealt with: the fact remains, though, that the children lose between a third to half of each school year, and must with this handicap keep up their lessons and "compete" with town children in a contest in which competition is stressed and success in it valued and rewarded.

The schoolhouse itself is in Cookstown; a recently built, windowy, "healthful" red brick and white-trimmed structure which perfectly exemplifies the American genius[4] for sterility, unimagination, and general gutlessness in meeting any opportunity for "reform" or "improvement." It is the sort of building a town such as Cookstown is proud of, and a brief explanation of its existence in such country will be worth while. Of late years Alabama has "come awake" to "education," illiteracy has been reduced; texts have been modernized; a good many old schools have been replaced by new ones. For this latter purpose the counties have received appropriations in proportion to the size of their school population. The school population of this county is five black to one white, and since not a cent of the money has gone into negro schools, such buildings as this are possible: for white children. The negro children, meanwhile, continue to sardine themselves, a hundred and a hundred and twenty strong, into stove-heated one-room pine shacks which might comfortably accommodate a fifth of their number if the walls, roof, and windows were tight.[5] But then, as one prominent landlord said and as many more would agree: "I don't object to nigrah education, not up through foath a fift grade maybe, but not furdern dat: I'm too strong a believah in white syewpremcy."

This bus service and this building the (white) children are schooled in, even including the long and muddy walk, are of course effete as compared to what their parents had.[6] The schooling itself is a different matter, too: much more "modern." The boys and girls alike are subjected to "art" and to "music," and the girls learn the first elements of tap dancing. Textbooks are so cheap almost anyone can afford them: that is, almost anyone who can afford anything at all; which means that they are a stiff problem in any year to almost any tenant. I want now to list and suggest the contents of a few textbooks which were at the Gudger house, remembering, first, that they imply the far reaches of the book-knowledge of any average adult tenant.

> *The Open Door Language Series: First Book: Language Stories and Games.*
> *Trips to Take.* Among the contents are poems by Vachel Lindsay, Elizabeth Madox Roberts, Robert Louis Stevenson, etc.

---

[4] So well shown forth in "low-cost" housing.

[5] Aside from discomfort, and unhealthfulness, and the difficulty of concentrating, this means of course that several "grades" are in one room, reciting and studying by rotation, each using only a fraction of each day's time. It means hopeless boredom and waste for the children, and exhaustion for the teacher.

[6] Their parents would have walked to one-room wooden schoolhouses. I'm not sure, but think it more likely than not, that many of the white children still do today.

Also a story titled: "Brother Rabbit's Cool Air Swing," and sub-headed: "Old Southern Tale."

Outdoor Visits: Book Two of *Nature and Science Readers.* (Book One is *Hunting.*) Book Two opens: "Dear Boys and Girls: in this book you will read how Nan and Don visited animals and plants that live outdoors."

Real Life Readers: New Stories and Old: A Third Reader. Illustrated with color photographs.

The Trabue-Stevens Speller. Just another speller.

Champion Arithmetic. Five hundred and ten pages: a champion psychological inducement to an interest in numbers. The final problem: "Janet bought 1¼ lbs. of salted peanuts and ½ lb. of salted almonds. Altogether she bought ? lbs of nuts?"

Dear Boys and Girls indeed!

Such a listing is rich as a poem; twisted full of contents, symptoms, and betrayals, and these, as in a poem, are only reduced and diluted by any attempt to explain them or even by hinting. Personally I see enough there to furnish me with bile for a month: yet I know that any effort to make clear in detail what is there, and why it seems to me so fatal, must fail.

Even so, see only a little and only for a moment.

These are books written by "adults." They must win the approval and acceptance of still other "adults," members of school "boards"; and they will be "taught" with by still other "adults" who have been more or less "trained" as teachers. The intention is, or should be, to engage, excite, preserve, or develop the "independence" of, and furnish with "guidance," "illumination," "method," and "information," the curiosities of children.

Now merely re-examine a few words, phrases and facts:

The Open Door: open to whom. That metaphor is supposed to engage the interest of children.

Series: First Book. Series. Of course The Bobbsey Twins is a series; so is The Rover Boys. *Series* perhaps has some pleasure associations to those who have children's books, which no tenant children have: but even so it is better than canceled by the fact that this is so obviously not a pleasure book but a schoolbook, not even well disguised. An undisguised textbook is only a little less pleasing than a sneaking and disguised one, though. *First Book:* there entirely for the convenience of adults; it's only grim to a child.

Language: it appears to be a *modern* substitution for the word "English." I don't doubt the latter word has been murdered, the question is, whether the new one has any life whatever to a taught child or, for that matter, to a teacher.

Stories and Games: both, modified by a school word, and in a school context. Most children prefer pleasure to boredom, lacking our intelligence to reverse this preference: but you must use your imagination or memory to recognize how any game can be poisoned by being "conducted": and few adults have either.

Trips to Take. Trips indeed, for children who will never again travel as much as in their daily bus trips to and from school. Children like figures of speech or are, if you like, natural symbolists and poets: being so, they see through frauds such as this so much the more readily. No poem is a "trip," whatever else it may be, and suffers by being lied about.

The verse. I can readily imagine that "educators" are well pleased with themselves in that they have got rid of the Bivouac of the Dead and are using much more nearly contemporary verse. I am quite as sure, knowing their kind of "knowledge" of poetry, that the pleasure is all theirs.

These children, both of town and country, are saturated southerners, speaking dialects not very different from those of negroes. *Brother* Rabbit! *Old Southern Tale!*

Outdoor Visits. Nature and Science. Book One: *Hunting.* Dear Boys and Girls. In this book you will read (oh, I will, will I?). Nan and Don. Visit. Animals and Plants that Live Outdoors. Outdoors. You will pay formal calls on Plants. They live outdoors. "Nature." "Science." Hunting. Dear Boys and Girls. Outdoor Visits.

Real Life. "Real" "Life" "Readers." Illustrated by *color* photographs.

Or back into the old generation, a plainer title: *The Trabue-Stevens Speller.* Or the *Champion Arithmetic*, weight eighteen pounds, an attempt at ingratiation in the word champion, so broad of any mark I am surprised it is not spelled *Champeen.*

Or you may recall the page of geography text I have quoted elsewhere: which, I must grant, tells so much about education that this chapter is probably unnecessary.

I give up. Relative to my memory of my own grade-schooling, I recognize all kinds of "progressive" modifications: Real Life, color photographs, Trips to Take (rather than Journey, to Make), games, post-kindergarten, "Language," Nan and Don, "Nature and Science," Untermeyer-vintage poetry, "dear boys and girls"; and I am sure of only one thing: that it is prepared by adults for their own self-flattery and satisfaction, and is to children merely the old set retouched, of afflictions, bafflements, and half-legible insults more or less apathetically submitted to.

Louise Gudger is fond of school, especially of geography and arithmetic, and gets unusually good "marks": which means in part that she has an intelligence quick and acquisitive above the average, in part that she has learned to parrot well and to respect "knowledge" as it is presented to her. She has finished the third grade. In the fourth grade she will learn all about the history of her country. Her father and much more particularly her mother is excited over her brightness and hopeful of it: they intend to make every conceivable effort by which she may continue not only through the grades but clear through high school. She wants to become a teacher, and quite possibly she will; or a trained nurse; and again quite possibly she will.

Junior Gudger is in the second grade because by Alabama law a pupil is automatically passed after three years in a grade. He is still almost entirely unable to read and write, and is physically fairly skilful. It may be that he is incapable of "learning": in any case "teaching" him would be a "special problem." It would be impossible in a public, competitive class of mixed kinds and degrees of "intelligence"; and I doubt that most public-school teachers are trained in it anyhow.

Burt and Valley Few are too young for school. I foresee great difficulty for Burt, who now at four is in so desperate a psychological situation that he is capable of speaking any language beyond gibberish (in which he has great rhythmic and syllabic talent) only after he has been given the security of long and friendly attention, of a sort which markedly excludes his brothers.

Pearl Woods, who is eight, may have started to school this fall (1936); more likely not, though, for it was to depend on whether the road was graveled so she would not have the long walk to the bus alone or within contamination of the Ricketts children. She is extremely sensitive, observant, critical and crafty, using her mind and her senses much more subtly than is ever indicated or "taught" in school: whether her peculiar intelligence will find engagement or ruin in the squarehead cogs of public schooling is another matter.

Thomas is three years too young for school. As a comedian and narcist dancer he has natural genius; aside from this I doubt his abilities. Natural artists, such as he is, and natural craftsmen, like Junior, should not necessarily have to struggle with reading and writing; they have other ways of learning, and of enlarging themselves, which however are not available to them.

Clair Bell is three years young for school and it seems probable that she will not live for much if any of it, so estimates are rather irrelevant. I will say, though, that I was so absorbed in her physical and spiritual beauty that I was not on the lookout for signs of "intelligence" or the lack of it, and that education, so far as I know it, would either do her no good or would hurt her.

Flora Merry Lee and Katy are in the second grade. Katy, though she is so shy that she has to write out her reading lessons, is brighter than average; Flora Merry Lee, her mother says, is brighter than Katy; she reads and writes smoothly and "specially delights in music." Garvrin and Richard are in the fourth grade. Garvrin doesn't take to schooling very easily though he tries hard; Richard is bright but can't get interested; his mind wanders. In another year or two they will be big enough for full farm work and will be needed for it, and that will be the end of school.

Margaret quit school when she was in the fifth grade because her eyes hurt her so badly every time she studied books. She has forgotten a good deal how to read. Paralee quit soon after Margaret did because she was lonesome. She still reads fairly easily, and quite possibly will not forget how.

The Ricketts are spoken of disapprovingly, even so far away as the county courthouse, as "problem" children. Their attendance record is extremely bad; their conduct is not at all good; they are always fighting and sassing back. Besides their long walk in bad weather, here is some more explanation. They are much too innocent to understand the profits of docility. They have to wear clothes and shoes which make them the obvious butts of most of the children. They come of a family which is marked and poor even among the poor whites, and are looked down on even by most levels of the tenant class. They are uncommonly sensitive, open, trusting, easily hurt, and amazed by meanness and by cruelty, and their ostracism is of a sort to inspire savage loyalty among them. They are indeed "problems"; and the "problem" will not be simplified as these "over"-sexed and anarchic children shift into adolescence. The two girls in particular seem inevitably marked out for incredibly cruel misunderstanding and mistreatment.

Mrs. Ricketts can neither read nor write. She went to school one day in her life and her mother got sick and she never went back. Another time she told me that the children laughed at her dress and the teacher whipped her for hitting back at them, but Margaret reminded her that that was the dress she had made for Flora Merry Lee and that it was Flora Merry Lee and Katy who had been whipped, and she agreed that that was the way it was.

Fred Ricketts learned quickly. He claims to have learned how to read music in one night (he does, in any case, read it), and he reads language a little less hesitantly than the others do and is rather smug about it—"I was readn whahl back na Pgressive Fahmuh—" He got as far as the fifth grade and all ways was bright. When his teacher said the earth turned on a axle, he asked her was the axle set in posts, then. She said yes, she reckoned so. He said well, wasn't hell supposed to be under the earth, and if it was wouldn't they be all the time trying to chop the axle post out from under the earth? But here the earth still was, so what was all this talk about axles. "Teacher never did bring up nothn bout no axles after that. No sir, she never did bring up nothin about no durn axles after that. No sir-ree, she shore never did brang up nufn baout no dad blame axles attah dayut."

Woods quit school at twelve when he ran away and went to work in the mines. He can read, write, and figure; so can his wife. Woods understands the structures and tintings of rationalization in money, sex, language, religion, law, and general social conduct in a sour way which is not on the average curriculum.

George Gudger can spell and read and write his own name; beyond that he is helpless. He got as far as the second grade. By that time there was work for him and he was slow minded anyway. He feels it is a terrible handicap not to be educated and still wants to learn to read and write and to figure, and his wife has tried to learn him, and still wants to. He still wants to, too, but he thinks it is unlikely that he will ever manage to get the figures and letters to stick in his head.

Mrs. Gudger can read, write, spell, and handle simple arithmetic, and grasps and is excited by such matters as the plainer facts of astronomy and geology. In fact, whereas many among the three families have crippled but very full and real intelligences, she and to a perhaps less extent her father have also intellects. But these intellects died before they were born; they hang behind their eyes like fetuses in alcohol.

It may be that more are born "incapable of learning," in this class, or in any case "incapable of learning," or of "using their intelligences," beyond "rudimentary" stages, than in economically luckier classes. If this is so, and I doubt the proportion is more than a little if at all greater, several ideas come to mind: Incapable of learning what? And capable of learning what else, which is not available either to them or, perhaps, in the whole field and idea of education? Or are they incapable through incompetent teaching, or through blind standards, or none, on the part of educators, for measuring what "intelligence" is? Or incapable by what pressures of past causes in past generations? Or should the incapability be so lightly (or sorrowfully) dismissed as it is by teachers and by the middle class in general?

But suppose a portion are born thus "incapable": the others, nevertheless, the great majority, are born with "intelligences" potentially as open and "healthful," and as varied in pattern and in charge, as any on earth. And by their living, and by their education, they are made into hopeless and helpless cripples, capable exactly and no more of doing what will keep them alive: by no mean so well equipped as domestic and free animals: and that is what their children are being made into, more and more incurably, in every year, and in every day.

"Literacy" is to some people a pleasing word: when "illiteracy" percentages drop, many are pleased who formerly were shocked, and think no more of it. Disregarding the proved fact that few doctors of philosophy are literate, that is, that few of them have the remotest idea how to read, how to say what they mean, or what they mean in the first place, the word literacy means very little even as it is ordinarily used. An adult tenant writes and spells and reads painfully and hesitantly as a child does and is incapable of any save the manifest meanings of any but the simplest few hundred words, and is all but totally incapable of absorbing, far less correlating, far less critically examining, any "ideas" whether true or false; or even physical facts beyond the simplest and most visible. That they are, by virtue of these limitations, among the only "honest" and "beautiful" users of language, is true, perhaps, but it is not enough. They are at an immeasurable disadvantage in a world which is run, and in which they are hurt, and in which they might be cured, by "knowledge" and by "ideas": and to "consciousness" or "knowledge" in its usages in personal conduct and in human relationships, and to those unlimited worlds of the senses, the remembrance, the mind and the heart which, beyond that of their own existence, are the only human hope, dignity, solace, increasement, and joy, they are all but totally blinded. The ability to try to understand existence, the ability to try to recognize the wonder and responsibility of one's own existence, the ability to know even fractionally the almost annihilating beauty, ambiguity, darkness, and horror which swarm every instant of every consciousness, the ability to try to accept, or the ability to try to defend one's self, or the ability to dare to try to assist others; all such as these, of which most human beings are cheated of their potentials, are, in most of those who even begin to discern or wish for them, the gifts or thefts of economic privilege, and are available to members of these leanest classes only by the rare and irrelevant miracle of born and surviving "talent."

Or to say it in another way: I believe that every human being is potentially capable, within his "limits," of fully "realizing" his potentialities; that this, his being cheated and choked of it, is infinitely the ghastliest, commonest, and most inclusive of all the crimes of which the human world can accuse itself; and that the discovery and use of "consciousness," which has always been and is our deadliest enemy and deceiver, is also the source and guide of all hope and cure, and the only one.

I am not at all trying to lay out a thesis, far less to substantiate or to solve. I do not consider myself qualified. I know only that murder is being done, against nearly every individual in the planet, and that there are dimensions and correlations of cure which not only are not being used but appear to be scarcely considered or suspected. I know there is cure, even now available, if only it were available, in science and in the fear and joy of God. This is only a brief personal statement of these convictions: and my self-disgust is less in my ignorance, and far less in my "failure" to "defend" or "support" the statement, than in my inability to state it even so far as I see it, and in my inability to blow out the brains with it of you who take what it is talking of lightly, or not seriously enough.

Part Five

The Rites
of Prejudice

Dark is the Heaven above, and cold and hard the earth beneath:
And, as a plague-wind, fill'd with insects, cuts off man and beast,
And, as a sea o'erwhelms a land in the day of an earthquake,
Fury, rage, madness, in a wind swept through America. . . .

from *America, a Prophecy*, 1793
William Blake

A future historian might venture the observation that in the ripe years of the twentieth century the disparagement of prejudice had at last become fashionable for all but a few Americans. Apparently the bigot is now reviled in an ecumenical way. He is publicly loathed. We grieve competitively for his victims. The question, obviously, is whether our announced unanimity about his evil has abetted his obsolescence. Probably not. For prejudice includes motives beyond the literal sin of bigotry, motives of guilt, arrogance, fear, candid pride, and cynicism. Perhaps because most strongholds of prejudice lie exposed to any binge of our self-righteousness, we should suspect our virtue. For to understand only the prejudice of an oppressor is to know little about bigotry. Such recognition of obvious villains is cheap, fastidiously defensible, and shirks wisdom; for prejudice, rarely as callow as we would have it, can infiltrate any perception we have about the world and can work itself into any crevice of the will not sealed by a wary sophistication or by an unearthly innocence.

Assuming, then, that fair-minded men may discern the blatant encampments of prejudice, can they detect commensurately the habits of prejudice that are groomed furtively by all faiths, nationalities, and races?

These habits, these rites, beg for satire, for a Rabelaisian latitude, for a fresh *Don Quixote* (or a universal reading of the original), or for a new *Travels* with a cycle-mounted Gulliver. The characters await their author: White Franchot of Duluth, who swears to a tolerance that he refuses to test; White Thea of Radcliffe, who won't patronize black businesses because she cannot, in her enlightenment, encourage any incipient Uncle Neo-Tomism. Then of course there is Sir Robert of Midcult, who piously reads his *Harper's*, then lets his Chicano maid go, then writes a check for twenty dollars to the California Farm Workers Relief Fund. Emil Feinberg writes a check too, his to the Anti-Defamation League. Emil knows. The jingoism of the fascist Wasps must be quelled. Meanwhile, Sass Blackmale proves his manhood by burning down a headquarters of the Students for Democratic Society. Sass knows, too. The last stronghold of White Bourgeois Revisionism must be obliterated. Meanwhile, we are diverted, we the hip audience, by the New Comedians of the mass media, emancipists all, who snugly bait the Establishment that underwrites them. Conventional nonconformity is the rage. Interchangeable rebels harbor intolerances inherently as common as the candid bigotries of a quieter age.

Their fashion in the larger world dictates that rites of prejudice must also infect American education, the underbelly of the democratic Leviathan. The times, at least when men debate, seem to require the strident phrase, the calculated threat, the grotesque charity. In education we discover instant revolutions at every turn that are precipitously opposed by a motley of critics, some deserving, some unworthy of notice. Black and white evangelists, those who are verbose if nothing else, demand utter change or instant consequences. In response, mossy administrators nod condescendingly, or shrink in fear, or committee their opponents to death, or resign. Saviors of curriculum mature in a day, nightride the routes of controversy, and defer to newer prophets. The federal government, blessed and damned by strategists of woefully unequal talents, wields subsidy programs which when moderately successful must still live in the shadow of yearly appropriational threats.

Given the complexities of our educational crises, particularly those of urban school systems, the entries in Part Five may seem inconclusive. Irrelevant they are not. To offer stories that are merely inclusively topical (even should they exist) is to pander to obsolescence and to third-rate writing as well. There is surely enough loose rhetoric dispursed on the subject of prejudice without resorting to bad fiction.

Regarding the habits of bigotry depicted in the following stories, the trick of one applies: to perceive *one* habit in all its wily craft is to know one's own potential for detecting other rites. The special gift of these stories by William Saroyan, Delmore Schwartz, and Joanne Greenberg is that each renders men and women in their singularity rather than as *members, types, advocates,* or *causes.* In their particularity of attitude and deed these characters move to recover those insights that our abstractions lose for us, or have lost.

William Saroyan
(1908–   )

One of the special traits of literature is its power to render universal meanings through concrete portrayals. In *Gulliver's Travels*, for example, the faults and values of post-Renaissance England and Continental Europe, indeed of all mankind, were satirized by Jonathan Swift through the means of Gulliver's journey. Centuries later, George Orwell assembled pigs, dogs, horses, and Farmer Jones, wrote of them incisively, and gave us *Animal Farm*, a fable that dramatized the ironies of a fallen-away Marxism. William Faulkner, in America, caught up a world and delivered it whole within the fictional patch of Mississippi earth named Yoknapatawpha County.

This technique of compression, further condensed for the demands of the short story, is used in "Citizens of the Third Grade." Here a universal vice, the bigotry of chauvinism, is reached through the particular, in this instance a classroom of youngsters. Perhaps more to be lamented than the acrimony of the children is the effete goodwill of their teacher Miss Gavit. The effects of spurious pride and real ostracism are staged on this private battleground of World War II, California's valley of the San Joaquin.

The author of more than thirty books and plays, William Saroyan is noted for such works as *The Daring Young Man on the Flying Trapeze and Other Stories* (1934), the play *The Time of Your Life* (1939), the novels *The Human Comedy* (1943) and *My Name Is Aram* (1940), and for his recent book, *One Day in the Afternoon of the World* (1964).

CITIZENS OF THE THIRD GRADE

Tom Lucca was incredible. Only eight years old, he was perhaps the brightest pupil in the third grade, certainly the most alert, the most intellectually savage, and yet the most humane. Still, his attitude seemed sometimes vicious, as when Aduwa was taken and he came to class leering with pride, the morning newspaper in his pants pocket, as evidence, no doubt, and during recess made the Fascist salute and asked the colored Jefferson twins, Cain and Abel, what they thought of old King Haile Selassie now.

Same as before, Miss Gavit heard Abel say. You got no right to go into Africa.

And Tom, who wouldn't think of getting himself into a fist-fight since he was too intelligent, too neat and good-looking, laughed in that incredible Italian way that meant he knew everything, and said, We'll take Addis Ababa day after tomorrow.

Of course this was only a gag, one of Tom Lucca's frequent and generally innocent outbursts, but both Abel and Cain didn't like it, and Miss Gavit was sure there would be trouble pretty soon no matter what happened.

If General Bono *did* take Addis Ababa and Tom Lucca forgot himself and irritated Cain and Abel, there would surely be trouble between the colored boys in the Third Grade and the Italian boys, less brilliant perhaps than Tom Lucca, but more apt to accept trouble, and fight about it: Pat Ravenna, Willy Trentino, Carlo Gaeta, and the others. Enough of them certainly. And then there were the other grades. The older boys.

On the other hand, if Ras Desta Demtu, the son-in-law of Emperor Haile Selassie, turned back the Italian forces at Harar, Cain and Abel, somewhat sullenly, would be triumphant without saying a word, as when Joe Louis, the Brown Bomber of Detroit, knocked out and humiliated poor Maxie Baer, and Cain and Abel came to class whistling softly to themselves. Everybody, who normally didn't dislike the boys, quiet and easy-going as they were, deeply resented them that morning. No matter what happened, Miss Gavit believed, there would be trouble at Cosmos Public School, and it seemed very strange that this should be so, since these events were taking place thousands of miles away from the school and did not concern her class of school-children, each of whom was having a sad time with the new studies, fractions and English grammar.

Tom Lucca was impossible. He had no idea how dangerous his

nervous and joyous behavior was getting to be. It was beginning to irritate Miss Gavit herself who, if anything, was in favor of having the ten million Ethiopians of Abyssinia under Italian care, which would do them much less harm than good and probably furnish some of the high government officials with shoes and perhaps European garments.

It was really amazing that many of the leaders of Abyssinia performed their duties bare-footed. How could anybody be serious without shoes on his feet, and five toes of each foot visible? And when they walked no important sound of moving about, as when Americans with shoes on their feet moved about.

Of course she hated the idea of going into an innocent and peaceful country and bombing little cities and killing all kinds of helpless people. She didn't like all the talk about poison gases and machine guns and liquid fire. She thought it was very cruel of the Italians to think of killing people in order to gain a little extra land in which to expand, as Mussolini said.

Miss Gavit just bet ten cents the Italians could do all the expanding they needed to do right at home, in the 119,000 square miles of Italy. She just bet ten cents with anybody that Mussolini didn't really need more land, all he wanted to do was show off and be a hero. It was dreadful the way some people wanted to be great, no matter how many people they killed. It wasn't as if the people of Abyssinia were pagans; they were Christians, just like the Italians: their church was the Christian church, and they worshiped Jesus, the same as Pope Pius.

(The Pope, though, was a man Miss Gavit didn't like. She saw him in a Paramount News Reel, and she didn't like his face. He looked sly for a holy man. She didn't think he was really holy. She thought he looked more like a scheming politician than like a man who was humble and good and would rather accept pain for himself than have it inflicted upon others. He was small and old and cautious. First he prayed for peace, and then Italy went right ahead and invaded Abyssinia. Then Pope Pius prayed for peace again, but it was war just the same. Who did he think he was fooling?)

She guessed every important man in the world was afraid, the same as the Pope. Poor loud-mouthed Huey got his, and for what? What did poor Huey want for the people except a million dollars for every family? What was wrong with that? Why did they have to kill a man like that, who really had the heart of a child, even if he did shout over the radio and irritate President Roosevelt by hinting that he, Huey Long of Louisiana, would be the next President of the United States? What did they want to invent guns for in the first place? What good did guns do the people of the world, except teach them to kill one another? First they worried about wild animals, and then Indians, and then they began worrying about one another, France worrying about Germany, Germany worrying about France and England and Russia, and Russia worrying about Japan, and Japan worrying about China.

Miss Gavit didn't know. She couldn't quite understand the continuous mess of the world. When it was the World War she was a little girl in grammar school who thought she would be a nun in a convent, and then a little later, a singer in opera: that was after the San Carlo opera troupe came to town and gave a performance of *La Bohème* at the Hippodrome Theatre and Miss Gavit went home crying about poor consumptive Mimi. Then the war ended and the parades ended and she began to forget her wilder dreams, like the dream of some day meeting a fine man like William Farnum and being his wife, or the still more fantastic dream of suddenly learning from authoritative sources that she was the true descendant of some royal European family, a princess, and all the other wild dreams of sudden wealth and ease and fame and importance, sudden surpassing loveliness, the most beloved young lady of the world. And sobering with the years, with the small knowledge of each succeeding grade at school, she chose teaching as her profession, and finally, after much lonely studying, full of sudden clear-weather dreaming of love, she graduated from the normal school, twenty-two years old, and was a teacher, if she could get a job.

She was very lucky, and for the past five years had been at Cosmos Public School, in the foreign section of the city, west of the Southern Pacific tracks, where she herself was born and lived. Her father was very happy about this good luck. The money she earned helped buy new furniture, a radio, and later on a Ford, and sent her little sister Ethel to the University of California. But she didn't know. So many things were happening all over the world she was afraid something dangerous would happen, and very often, walking home from school, late in the afternoon, she would suddenly feel the nearness of this danger with such force that she would unconsciously begin to walk faster and look about to see if anything were changed, and at the same time remember poignantly all the little boys and girls who had passed through her class and gone on to the higher grades, as if these young people were in terrible danger, as if their lives might suddenly end, with terrific physical pain.

And now, with this trouble between Italy and Abyssinia, Benito Mussolini, Dictator of Italy, and Haile Selassie, the Lion of Judah, Miss Gavit began, as Tom Lucca's joyousness increased, to feel great inward alarm about the little boy because she knew truthfully that he was very kind-hearted, and only intellectually mischievous. How many times had she seen him hugging Mrs. Amadio's little twenty-month-old daughter, chattering to the baby in the most energetic Italian, kissing it, shouting at Mrs. Amadio, and Mrs. Amadio guffawing in the loudest and most delightful manner imaginable, since Tom was such a wit, so full of innocent outspokenness, sometimes to the extent even of being almost vulgar. The Italians. That's the way they were, and it was not evil, it was a virtue. They were just innocent. They chattered about love and passion and child-birth and family quarrels as if it were nothing, just part of the day's experience. And how many times had she seen Tom Lucca giving sandwiches from his lunch to Johnny Budge whose father had no job and no money? And not doing it in a way that was self-righteous. She remembered the way Tom would say, Honest, Johnny, I can't eat another bite. Go ahead, I don't want this sandwich. I already ate three. I'll throw it away if you don't take it. And Johnny Budge would say, All right, Tom, if you're sure you don't want it. That was the strange part of it, the same little Italian boy being fine like that, giving away his lunch, and at the same time so crazy-proud about the taking of Aduwa, as if that little mud-city in Africa had anything to do with him, coming to class with the morning paper and leering at everybody, stirring the savage instincts of the Negro twins, Cain and Abel Jefferson.

Miss Gavit believed she would do something to stop all the nonsense. She wouldn't sit back and see something foolish and ugly happen right under her nose. She knew what she would do. She would keep Tom Lucca after school.

When the last pupil had left the room and the door was closing automatically and slowly, Miss Gavit began to feel how uneasy Tom was, sitting still but seeming to be moving about, looking up at her, and then at the clock, and then rolling his pencil on the desk. When the door clicked shut, she remembered all the little boys she had kept in after school during the five years at Cosmos and how it was the same with each of them, resentment at accusation, actual or implied, and dreadful impatience, agonized longing to be free, even if, as she knew, many of them really liked her, did not hate her as many pupils often hated many teachers, only wanting to be out of the atmosphere of petty crime and offense, wanting to be restored to innocence, the dozens and dozens of them. She wondered how she would be able to tell Tom why she had kept him after school and explain how she wanted his behavior, which was always subtle, to change, not in energy, but in impulse. How would she be able to tell him not to be so proud about what Mussolini was doing? Just be calm about the whole business until Italy annexed Abyssinia and everything became normal in the world again, at least more or less normal, and Cain and Abel Jefferson didn't go about the school grounds apart from everybody, letting their resentment grow in them.

What's the matter now? Tom said. He spoke very politely, though, the inflexion being humble, implying that it was *he* who was at fault: he was ready to admit this, and if his offense could be named he would try to be better. He didn't want any trouble.

Nothing's the matter, Miss Gavit said. I want to talk to you about the war, that's all.

Yes, ma'am, he said.

Well, said Miss Gavit, you've got to be careful about hurting the feelings of Cain and Abel Jefferson.

Hurting their feelings? he thought. Who the hell's hurting whose feelings? What kind of feelings get hurt so easily? What the hell did I ever say? The whole world is against the Italians and *our* feelings ain't hurt. They want to see them wild Africans kick hell out of our poor soft soldiers, two pairs of shoes each. How about our feelings? Everybody hates Mussolini. What for? Why don't they hate somebody else for a change?

He was really embarrassed, really troubled. He didn't understand, and Miss Gavit noticed how he began to tap the pencil on the desk.

I don't know, he began to say, and then began tapping the pencil swifter than before.

He gestured in a way that was very saddening to Miss Gavit and then looked up at her.

You are an American, said Miss Gavit, and so are Cain and Abel Jefferson. We are all Americans. This sort of quarreling will lead nowhere.

What quarreling? he thought. Everybody in the world hates us. Everybody calls us names. I guess Italians don't like that either.

He could think of nothing to say to Miss Gavit. He knew she was all right, a nice teacher, but he didn't know how to explain about everybody hating the Italians, because this feeling was in Italian and he couldn't translate it. At home it was different. Pa came home from the winery and sat at the table for supper and asked Mike, Tom's big brother in high school, what the afternoon paper said, and Ma listened carefully, and Mike told them exactly what was going on, about England and the ships in the Red Sea, and France, and the League of Nations, and Pa swallowed a lot of spaghetti and got up and spit in the sink, clearing his throat, and said in Italian, All right, all right, all right, let them try to murder Italy, them bastards, and Ma poured more wine in his cup and Pa said in American, God damn it, and Tom knew how the whole world was against Italy and he was glad about the good luck of the army in Africa, taking Aduwa, and all the rest of it, but now, at school, talking with Miss Gavit, he didn't know what to say.

Yes, ma'am, he said.

Miss Gavit thought it was wonderful the way he understood everything, and she laughed cheerfully, feeling that now nothing would happen.

All right, Tom, she said. Just be careful about what you say.

You may go now.

Jesus Christ, he thought. To hell with everybody.

He got up and walked to the door. Then he began walking home, talking to himself in Italian and cussing in American because everybody was against them.

Tom was very quiet at the supper table, but when Pa asked Mike how it was going in Abyssinia and Mike told him the Italians were moving forward very nicely and it looked like everything would turn out all right before the League would be able to clamp down on Italy, Tom said in Italian, We'll show them bastards. His father wondered what was eating the boy.

What's the matter, Tom? he said in American.

Aw, Tom said, they kept me in after school just because I talked about taking Aduwa. They don't like it.

His father laughed and spit in the sink and then became very serious.

They don't like it, hey? he said in Italian. They are sorry the Italian army isn't slaughtered? They hate us, don't they? Well, you talk all you like about the army. You tell them every day what the army is doing. Don't be afraid.

The next day Cain Jefferson swung at Tom Lucca and almost hit him in the eye. Willy Trentino then challenged Cain Jefferson to a fight after school, and on her way home Miss Gavit saw the gang of Italian and colored and Russian boys in the empty lot behind Gregg's Bakery. She knew for sure it was a fight about the war. She stood in the street staring at the boys, listening to their shouting, and all she could think was, This is terrible; they've got no right to make these little boys fight this way. What did they want to invent guns for in the first place?

She ran to the crowd of boys, trembling with anger. Everybody stopped shouting when Miss Gavit pushed to the center of the crowd where Willy Trentino and Cain Jefferson were fighting. Willy's face was bloody and Cain was so tired he could barely breathe or lift his arms. Miss Gavit clapped her hands as she did in class when she was angry and the two boys stopped fighting. They turned and stared at her, relieved and ashamed.

Stop this nonsense, she said, panting for breath from excitement and anger. I am ashamed of you, Willy. And you, Cain. What do you think you are fighting about?

Miss Gavit, said Cain Jefferson, they been laughing at us about the Ethiopians. All of them, teasing us every day.

How about you? said Willy. How about when Joe Louis knocked out Max Baer? How about when it looked like Abyssinia was going to win the war?

Then three or four Italian boys began to talk at once, and Miss Gavit didn't know what to think or do. She remembered a college movie in which two football players who loved the same girl and were fighting about her were asked to shake hands and make up by the girl herself, and Miss Gavit said, I want you boys to shake hands and be friends and go home and never fight again.

Miss Gavit was amazed when neither Willy Trentino nor Cain Jefferson offered to shake hands and make up, and she began to feel that this vicious war in Abyssinia, thousands of miles away, was going to bring about something very foolish and dangerous in the foreign section. In the crowd she saw Abel Jefferson, brooding sullenly and not speaking, a profound hate growing in him, and she saw Tom Lucca, his eyes blazing with excitement and delight, and she knew it was all very horrible because, after all, these were only little boys.

And then, instead of shaking hands and making up as she had asked them to do, Willy Trentino and Cain Jefferson, and all the other boys, began to move away, at first walking, and then, overcome with a sense of guilt, running, leaving the poor teacher standing in the empty lot, bewildered and amazed, tearing her handkerchief and crying. They hadn't shaken hands and made up. They hadn't obeyed her. They had run away. She cried bitterly, but not even one small tear fell from her eyes. When old Paul Gregg stepped from the bakery into the lot and said, What's the trouble, Miss Gavit? the little teacher said, Nothing, Mr. Gregg. I want a loaf of bread. I thought I would come in through the back way.

When she got home she took the loaf of white bread out of the brown paper bag and placed it on the red and blue checkered table-cloth of the kitchen table and stared at it for a long time, thinking of a thousand things at one time and not knowing what it was she was thinking about, feeling very sorrowful, deeply hurt, angry with everybody in the world, the Italians, the Pope, Mussolini, the Ethiopians, the Lion of Judah, and England.

She remembered the faces of the boys who were fighting, and the boys who were watching. She breathed in the smell of the bread, and wondered what it was all about everywhere in the world, little Tom Lucca kissing Mrs. Amadio's baby and giving Johnny Budge his sandwich and leering at everybody because of the taking of Aduwa, the Negro twins joyous about Joe Louis and sullen about Abyssinia. The bread smelled delicious but sad and sickening, and Abel Jefferson watching his brother fighting Willy Trentino, and the *Morning Chronicle* with news of crime everywhere, and the *Evening Bee* with the same news, and the holy Pope coming out on the high balcony and making a holy sign and looking sly, and somebody shooting poor Huey Long, and none of her pupils being able to understand about English grammar and fractions, and her wild dreams of supreme loveliness, and her little sister at the University of California, and the day ending. She folded her arms on the table and hid her head. With her eyes closed she said to herself, They killed those boys, they killed them, and she knew they were killing everybody everywhere, and with her eyes shut the smell of the fresh loaf of bread was sickening and tragic, and she couldn't understand anything.

Delmore Schwartz
(1913–1967)

The farce in this story is ubiquitous and covert, an open secret for the reader to intercept. Mr. Fish, the teacher, is personable, intellectually modish, and, until the end of the story, painlessly liberal. He is for all the right ideas, this gentleman teacher who wants the world nice. He is so critically mindful of his students' prejudices, of bigotries and stratagems that are candid compared to his own. Mr. Fish enacts a notion that pretends modernity but was old in Dante's time—that we are the woods we wander in.

Delmore Schwartz was born in Brooklyn and educated at New York University, Harvard, Columbia, and the University of Wisconsin. A teacher at Harvard and later at Syracuse, Schwartz also served as poetry editor for the *Partisan Review* and *New Republic*. His principal works are *In Dreams Begin Responsibilities* (1938), *Shenandoah* (1941), *The World Is a Wedding* (1948), and *Vaudeville for a Princess* (1950).

A BITTER FARCE

The summer was a very difficult summer for Mr. Fish, youthful teacher of composition and author of promise. He had never before taught in the wet heat of summer, and now he was teaching Navy students, some of whom had been in action in the Pacific. He also taught a class of girls which differed in no way from his former classes in composition.

It was soon clear to Mr. Fish that the students of the Navy must be taught elementary things carefully and clearly. Yet such was the heat and the difficulty of teaching during the summer that he was quickly drawn from discussions of spelling and grammar to other matters, matters which are sometimes referred to as topics of the day.

Soon the two Navy classes regarded Mr. Fish as an authority. The reason or reasons for this view were obscure both to Mr. Fish and his students. It was a view vague, strong and general; and Mr. Fish thought that perhaps his worn indifference had entered into his tone when he expressed opinions, and thus impressed the boys as authoritative.

This was the second summer of America's part in the war. The feeling of mid-war was everywhere because no one was able to see how the war might end very soon. Hence it was that Mr. Fish was asked by his students to express his opinions as to the establishment of a second front, the existence of a secret weapon, and Hitler's generalship.

Had he been cooler and more energetic, he would often have refused the seductions of such discussion or his replies would have been of a different character. As it was, he was worn and warm enough to state both sides of every question so that they both appeared to be very true. The boys were charmed by the somersaults of dialectic and did not mind in the least. They begged Mr. Fish to begin a discussion at the least pretext.

Thus he was asked about when the second front would be launched and if it would be successful.

"The question of opening a second front will be fully understood in a hundred years, very little will be understood until the end of the war," he observed, before beginning a new discussion of grammar and spelling. "The war, however, will be over long before some members of the Navy learn how to spell. But let us make an effort."

These judicious evasions and quick transitions delighted the Navy students.

And when the Detroit race riots occurred during the second summer of the war, the Navy's students wished to know what Mr. Fish thought of the Negro problem.

"It can't be stated in black and white," he said, and the students groaned as he had known they would, although on the other hand he had little idea that he was about to fall into a pun when he began the sentence.

"What do you think ought to be done?" asked one of the students, inspired in part by interest and in part by a desire to avoid the serious drill in grammar.

"What I think can be done or ought to be done," said the withdrawn Mr. Fish, touched somewhat by the interest of the boys in his opinion, "cannot conceivably have much effect on anyone. Yet, for the little that it is worth, which is probably nothing, I will say this: that nothing at all can be done in the South, except for the Negroes to depart from the South. Any other course would result in a resumption of the Civil War. On the other hand, this is a very big country, and it is as yet largely unsettled. There is no reason why some region cannot be chosen where a strict equality would be enforced. Yet equality cannot be dictated merely by signing a bill. The process would take a hundred years. By that time all of us will be dead and you will have no way of knowing if this is a good idea——"

At least half of the students in the Navy were from the South, as Mr. Fish knew very well. One of them raised his hand and waved it like a baseball bat, being excited.

"Where will this region be?" he asked in a hurry.

"Don't be disturbed," said Mr. Fish. "This is merely the idle idea of a teacher of composition who plays no part in the fabulous destiny of the aging republic——"

He knew that this student feared that the imaginary region might be near his own home, which was Missouri, one of the border states.

Another boy raised his hand. This boy's name was Murphy, and he had often been disturbed by Mr. Fish. Tall, strong, broad-shouldered, and black-haired, his face often wore an expression of anger.

"It's just like a dog show, sir," he said, speaking of the race riots. "The thoroughbred dogs will always fight with the mongrels."

"Mr. Long," said Mr. Fish, speaking to a student who came from Texas, "Mr. Murphy has just called all Southerners dogs: are you going to let him get away with that?"

The class laughed and Mr. Murphy looked disgusted. He felt that he had made a serious point and the instructor had dismissed it with a play on words.

"Now," said Mr. Fish, "we had better return to the difference between the use of the semicolon and the comma. It is possible, as I said the other day, that the absence of a comma may result in the death of a man——"

"Sir," said one of the boys in the back of the classroom, a Mr. Kent, who had not awaited the recognition of his raised hand, "I want to ask just one more question about your idea about the blacks: would you marry a Negro woman?"

Mr. Fish had anticipated the possibility of this question the moment that the question of the Negroes had arisen. And from previous conversations in very different circumstances, he had derived an answer, which was to be uttered in the mock-grand style. He was going to say that he would marry any woman to whom he made love because otherwise his children might be illegitimate. He felt that this might touch both the sense of honor and the memory of experience in some of them.

(Mr. Fish felt that in this way he turned the tables on his questioners and put them on the defensive. In the same way, when the war began, he was prepared to be asked why he was not in uniform and he was going to reply, "That is a very good question. Why don't you write to my draft board? I will give you the address." But the question was never asked, a significant silence.)

So, as these thoughts passed quickly through the teacher's head, he decided that it would be ill-advised to make such an answer, for any reference to sexual intercourse brought about an unfortunate period in the classroom, a period in which the giggle and the smirk entered like English horn and flute.

"Your question is an old one," said Mr. Fish, to gain time, "and an interesting one."

Mr. Fish knew very well that if he confessed a willingness to marry a Negro woman, he would lose face with his students. They would not forgive him the admission. On the other hand, if he said that he would not marry a black woman, his students would regard him as having admitted that he believed in social inequality, just as they did. And this would be a betrayal of the principles he supposed himself to believe with his whole mind and heart.

"The fact is," continued Mr. Fish, speaking to the waiting and troubled boys, "I don't know any Negroes. I don't know why I don't, certainly I have not been avoiding them: it just happens that I have not been introduced to any of them. Hence the question is one which in a sense has no meaning for me——"

The students groaned in a species of triumph, for they regarded this as an obvious evasion and confession.

Prompted by the groan, Mr. Fish felt that he must go further. Self-contained and constricted was his appearance; but his inner being was suddenly full of fear and trembling.

"I would not marry a Negro woman," he said having decided quickly, "but there are many white women whom I would not marry for the same reasons that I would not marry a Negro woman. Thus it is not a question of discrimination against the Negro race. Enough now of this discussion of my private life and marriage——"

The class relaxed. The boys from the South were relieved to hear that Mr. Fish would not marry a black woman. Some of the students did not really understand what Mr. Fish had answered. Mr. Fish at the moment was wondering just what he meant, although he had no doubt about the success of his answer. Most of the students felt then that Mr. Fish would not marry many white women as well as Negro women because he was a Jew. And this pleased them very much; they were pleased to the depths of their being. However, they had misunderstood him.

After teaching the students of the Navy at the University, Mr. Fish went to get his lunch. He ate in a state of abstraction, thinking of all the remarks he might have made and had not made about the problem of race prejudice. He said to himself that he was only a teacher of the ways to use the powerful English language. But language was involved in all things, and he felt now a sense of insufficiency and withdrawal. He had turned aside, as often before; he had side-stepped a matter about which he felt that he ought to be direct, blunt and frank as to his conviction and belief. Soon, in less than an hour, he was going to meet some of the students in his class of girls. For two years now he had taught a class of boys and then walked across the campus to teach a class of girls, and at times it seemed to him that it was as if he went to teach in another country when he taught the girls, or at least as if he taught another subject. For the girls were unlike the boys as students in many ways. They did not like to argue, but the boys argued at the drop of a hat. They were passive, polite and docile, the antithesis of the boys in each of these things. And this made it necessary that the teacher be more active. It was often useful to use the method of asking questions and discussing the answers, so that instead of the oppression of passive listening, the students participated in the hour as if they played a game.

To some extent it was possible to make more progress with female students when they came to what was termed conference, a period of half an hour during which the teacher conversed privately with the student, either reviewing themes which had already been corrected, or trying to help the student in thinking about the subject of a new theme. The girls were often self-conscious and constrained then, for they were still adolescent and to be alone with a young man summoned up such feelings in them. But on the whole, this part of teaching, which was very like tutoring, was interesting and useful so far as Mr. Fish was concerned. It was for him a way of coming to know human beings with whom otherwise he would never have had much acquaintance.

The girls had of late been asked to keep a journal in which each night they made observations of the interesting things they had seen or heard during the day. The purpose of this journal was to create the habit of articulating one's perceptions, of moving in mind habitually from thing to word; and then also the improvised and informal character of the journal was intended to free the student from the inhibitions overpowering them when they had to write a formal theme. This task of the journal had proved to be a very successful one when introduced during the previous year.

When Mr. Fish came to his office, Miss Lucy Eberhart awaited him. She was a tall blonde and blue-eyed girl, who looked as if she might become pretty at some later date. Now, at eighteen, she looked somewhat gawky, and she was both nervous and self-conscious, a fact which expressed itself in unwieldy movements of her limbs. As she sat down in the chair which faced the teacher's desk, she pulled down the skirt over her bare legs with an unnecessary emphasis; she pulled it down as if it had been up too high and as if the instructor had been glancing at her legs. But he had not; he had begun to read the first entry of her journal, which was entitled, for that day:

Just Some Thoughts

At lunch today, two of my friends and I had a most interesting discussion. One of the girls suddenly asked: "If you had to marry one of them, which of these three would you choose, a Chinaman, a Jew, or a Negro?" We all immediately agreed that we wouldn't marry at all! But for the sake of argument we agreed that we had to marry one, and that all of them were intelligent, well-educated, and also good-looking for their respective races. Each of the three was a native of his particular home country, although all could speak English and were refined gentlemen. I, for one, positively could not make up my mind. My two pals, after pondering the situation for several minutes, guessed that they would choose the Chinaman, certainly not the Negro. "And why would you marry the Chinaman? Why not the Jew?" I asked. "Even if he were from Syria, I think he would be more like us physically than the China-man." My friends were not very definite. They pointed out that there is something about Jews that other races can't stand. It always comes out sooner or later. Some Jews are charming people, but even the best simply are not liked, because, well, they are demanding, grasping, almost un-scrupulous about the way they get what they want. On the other hand according to my friends, the Chinese are very friendly, and the educated ones seem unusually intelligent.

But I wonder if there is not another reason for their choice. Although perhaps there is less prejudice here against the races than in some other countries, America has its share of intolerance. Because the Negroes were once our slaves, it is easy to see that even now we consider them distinctly inferior. There is certainly prejudice against the Jews as well. Possibly some of it is jealousy because the Jews have managed to wangle themselves into good positions and make money. But it seems that every-where they go, they make enemies by their attitude, and barbarous methods of reaching their goals. Ah! but the Chinamen! For years we have been trying to help the Chinese—today they are our allies in war! We have no bone to pick with them, and we are sorry for them.

If the choice of my two friends was influenced by these factors, in my mind their selection was not quite just. Therefore, I think if I were placed in that horrible position, and must marry one of the three men, I would choose the one who was the fairest and most honest, the kindest, and he whose ideas most nearly coincided with mine.

"This is very interesting, Miss Eberhart," said Mr. Fish, amazed to such an extent that for the moment his only emotion was amazement. He asked the student if the other two girls were also in the same English class, and he was told that one of them was, and the one who was had told her not to make the conversation about marriage the subject of her journal entry, but she had decided to do so anyway.

"O no, Miss Eberhart," said Mr. Fish, "to say what you think and to be sincere, to use what is in your own mind is the purpose of this kind of assignment. Your writing improves if you draw directly upon your feelings. However, there are faults in expression here. As I have pointed out before, you ought not to use such a colloquialism as 'wangled' in a piece of writing. And then, to speak of 'refined gentlemen' is a redundancy, since the idea of gentleman includes the idea of refinement. You make an error in idiomatic usage also when you write 'in my mind,' and not 'to my mind.' Be careful with prepositions especially, for most errors in idiom occur in the use of prepositions. As for the content of your entry, I don't think that it is necessary for me to make any comment upon it."

"I didn't mean to take a crack at anybody," said Miss Eberhart to Mr. Fish's surprise, for nothing in his tone seemed to him to express resentment or distaste.

Mr. Fish was silent for a moment. He was seeking to consult his feelings, and he felt only that certain feelings were absent which perhaps should be present.

Miss Eberhart gazed at him and waited for a final word before she departed from the conference.

"Apart from the errors I have mentioned, Miss Eberhart," said Mr. Fish at last, "this is a satisfactory piece of work, and a fulfillment of the assignment. I believe there are some Chinese at the university at present——"

He paused. I don't want to say that, he said to himself, for Miss Eberhart's nostrils had flared as he spoke.

"But," he continued, compelled, "I am told that on the Pacific Coast, the Chinese are disliked very much too, or were for a time, until the Exclusion Act was passed.

"However, I can speak with authority only on matters of the choice of words, sentence structure, and clear thought. If you have no questions, that will be all for today." He had become more and more formal as he continued, formality being his only recourse when worn out.

"No crack was intended," said Miss Eberhart, perplexed and nervous.

"Miss Eberhart, to use words like crack or words like wangle is to succumb to slang usages. You can be simple, natural, and direct without using slang."

"Thank you very much, Mr. Fish," said Miss Eberhart, departing because Mr. Fish had given her her notebook in a way that meant that the conference was concluded.

It would be hard to say why Mr. Fish did not think more of this incident after it was concluded. Perhaps the concerns of his private life were such that his mind had no time to be occupied with it. Certainly he did not like the occurrence. Yet it provoked in him few strong feelings.

Two days after, when he went to teach his students of the Navy, the classroom work was supposed to be based upon a reading assignment in the textbook especially prepared for the Navy boys. The assignment on this day was an essay on the immigrant in America by Louis Adamic. The essay was fitly entitled "Plymouth Rock and Ellis Island," and its gist, made with many careful qualifications, was that America's power and glory had been made possible by immigrant labor, by the acceptance of differences among human beings, by the diversity of many racial strains. The hope of the world, said Adamic, was here just because of this diversity of peoples; and this made the possibility of a universal culture, a pan-human culture, such as had never before existed on the globe. And this was the American Dream and the American Tradition. Adamic made his argument specific by speaking of the Germans, the Jews, and the Negroes especially as peoples who might be subjected to race-prejudice, to the hatred of those who are different from oneself. And he observed that if the German people had produced Hitler, they had also produced Thomas Mann.

Mr. Fish revolved the essay in his mind as he walked to the classroom. It was natural that he should be reminded of his conference with Miss Eberhart, and his classroom discussion of the Negroes. He resolved to review the essay quickly and not permit the hour to be wasted in a general discussion which would accomplish nothing at all but the expression of dark opinions.

And yet, since Mr. Fish had as a matter of habitual method often expressed grave doubts as to the assigned reading, he found himself criticizing Adamic too. It was a matter of method with him because he had often told his students never to accept anything printed without rigorous examination. And as he drew forth by means of questions a summary of Adamic's argument, he said:

"What Adamic has to say is true, in part; but we ought also to remember that if America has always been the land of liberty, it has also been the land of the witch-hunt and the lynching party, the land of persecution and the land where everyone feared that he was a stranger or was conscious of a fear of the stranger. That this is true does not in the least deny or contradict the truth of what Adamic says. This has been the land of liberty and of persecution from the days when witches were burned in Salem until the day four weeks ago when the race riot occurred in Detroit, or the riot in May in Los Angeles when the sailors beat up the zoot suit boys. These riots, riots of just this kind, would not occur if this were not also the land of liberty."

The instructor's criticism of Adamic emboldened the black-haired Mr. Murphy who also disagreed with the text.

"Take the Jews, sir," said Mr. Murphy, "Adamic says that there is [and now he read from his book] 'a tendency among the Jews in many parts of the country to suppress their talents, and to draw apart.' That's not true. And not only that, there is something wrong with a lot of Jews. Some of them are all right. But a lot of them are not. I know from personal experience because I worked for a couple of them——"

There were three Jewish students in this Navy class, and Mr. Fish's glance took in their responses. One of them made believe that he was intent upon his textbook, and one of them turned white. The third looked stolidly ahead at the blackboard, and Mr. Fish was unable in a quick glance to make out what his feelings were. But the dead white face of one of the Jewish boys made Mr. Fish feel that something must be said; or perhaps he spoke for a deeper reason of which he was unaware; or perhaps he was merely feeling fluent and argumentative on that day; or perhaps he had in mind Miss Eberhart's journal.

"You say," he said to the black-haired Murphy, "that you know from personal experience that some Jews, indeed many Jews, are no good. Are you Irish?" He knew very well that Murphy was Irish.

Murphy affirmed that both his mother and his father were Irish.

"Do you know what is said of the Irish very often in this city? It is said that the Irish are drunken and truculent. Now I know from personal experience that the man who lives next door to me, who is Irish, gets drunk on Saturday nights and beats up his wife. Does that mean that I have justification for hating most of the Irish or condemning them as drunken and truculent?"

"I know the Irish," said Murphy, "and I know that that's not true of most of them."

"I know the Jews, I might say to you," said Mr. Fish, "and I know that what you say of them can be shown to be untrue in many instances. On the other hand, there are instances which prove the truth of what is said of both the Jews and the Irish. It is true that the Jews, since they have engaged for centuries in financial dealings, practice some of the methods which make the commercial world infamous. You're a Catholic: do you know why the Jews have been more a commercial people than anything else?"

"I don't know," said Murphy with the tone of one who is judicious enough to admit his own ignorance when it is true that he is ignorant.

"They have been a commercial people," said Mr. Fish, "because that is all they were permitted to be by the decree of the Catholic Church. Do you know why the Pope decreed that the Jews might be usurers?

Because usury was a sin against nature; and one which led to the damnation of the soul. It was all right for Jews to be usurers because they were damned in any case, in view of the Holy Father. Thus by civil and theological decree, the Jews were prevented from doing that which is right and condemned to do that which is a mortal sin. Do you think that that is a good, noble or religious way to treat a people?"

"Well, why did they do it?" asked Murphy.

"They had no choice: and I might ask you why the Holy Apostolic Church behaved in this way? To get others to do your usurious banking for you is no less a sin than to get another man to do your murdering for you, or is it?" said Mr. Fish, carried away by his own rapid association of ideas, for he had never thought of the matter in this way before this particular occasion, and knew nothing of usury.

"The Jews seem to have taken it pretty well," said Murphy. "They were suited for it."

"How did they get to be suited for it?" said Mr. Fish, feeling in himself the rise of a flood of rhetoric.

"I don't know," said Murphy pensively. His face wore the look of one who was involved in much more than he had intended or expected. He hesitated. "They are traitors by inheritance, I guess."

"How can you be a traitor by inheritance?" asked Mr. Fish, rising to a pitch of intensity in tone. "Can a moral act be inherited? Can anyone be condemned to death as a murderer because his father is a murderer?"

To this surprising question there was no answer.

By now the classroom was silent and electrified.

"No," said Mr. Fish, "among the civilized nations, no man is by law responsible for the crimes of another man. Hence, even if the worst that is said of the Jews were true, it is illegal (and it is also immoral) to blame any Jew in advance——"

(By this time Mr. Fish was anticipating in his own mind objections and questions which would never have occurred to his students.)

"For even if we grant that there are inherited patterns of behavior, like inherited diseases and inherited features, no one can be sure in advance that any person, starting from the moment of his birth, is bound to have a certain kind of character. How many great men have had great sons? Very few. Nonetheless, even if we grant a certain tendency to behave as one's parents, it is an abomination to condemn any man before he has committed a crime. And this is exactly what race prejudice does: it is a denial of the freedom of the will and of moral responsibility. How many in this class are Irish?"

Half the class raised hands, including a boy named Cohan, who looked very Jewish or Irish. Mr. Fish thought that he was joking, but this was untrue.

"Let me state at this point," said Mr. Fish, pleased by what he took to be Cohan's wit and the class's good humor, "that some of my best friends are Irish——"

He awaited laughter, but the boys did not understand.

"——and some of my best friends are anti-Semitic: what can I do?"

Again the boys were perplexed, though interested.

"Two of the modern authors I admire most of all are Irish, and it might be maintained that if they had not been Irish but English, they might not have been great authors——"

This meant nothing to the boys. Mr. Fish decided to use a new argument.

"Let us consider," said Mr. Fish, "the proposition Mr. Murphy stated just before, that the Jews were traitors by inheritance."

Quickly Mr. Fish drew a crude map of Ireland upon the blackboard. He was inspired at the moment by James Joyce.

"If we wish to indulge in prejudice, then this map shows how the Irish are traitors visibly upon the map. That author I spoke of a moment ago once wrote that all Ireland was battling against the rest of Ireland. He referred to the division between Ireland and Ulster."

Mr. Fish pointed to the map. "The Irish to one who does not like them may be said to be traitors by tradition. Their efforts at liberation have often been weakened or betrayed by renegade Irishmen."

"I myself," said Mr. Fish, after a rhetorical silence, "am of Russian-Jewish distraction. I mean detraction. I feel very proud of my ancestors, who wrote the Bible and other great works of aspiration, morality and fiction which have been the basis of Western culture for the past two thousand years at least. My ancestors, in whom I take pride, but not personal pride, were scholars, poets, prophets and students of God when most of Europe worshipped sticks and stones: not that I hold that against any of you, for it is not your fault if your forbears were barbarians grovelling and groping about for peat or something.

"Nonetheless I must confess a great shame to you, an ancestor of mine who was also a barbarian."

Mr. Fish told the class to observe his high cheek bones and wide-set eyes.

"My face bears the mark of some Mongolian rapist. Some Mongolian barbarian raped one of my greatgrandmothers. In the Jewish community a man was honor bound to accept such a child of rape as his own; thus I am, alas, as the mirror repeats to me often, a mongrel Mongol.

"But here a very important question presents itself: it appears to be likely that the Mongolians are the ancestors of the American Indians, who are the only true natives of this country of ours, America. Thus I may say that from the point of view of race I am of Indian distraction or destruction. I am a hundred and fifty per cent American. Hence I may say to you, Mr. Murphy, why don't you go back where you came from, if you don't like the class of people here?"

It was difficult to say whether the teacher and the class were more pleased or appalled by this formulation.

The bell rang, concluding the hour. Four excited students of the Navy stood at Mr. Fish's desk to discuss the whole matter with him. Everyone was in good spirits. Mr. Murphy also waited to speak to Mr. Fish.

"It is better in the Southwest," said a boy from Texas, "there Jews and white people intermarry and no one thinks anything about it———"

"I am olive-skinned myself," said Mr. Fish, "but I know just what you mean" (for the Texan had intended to be amiable and condemn the wicked decadent East).

"Another wasted hour," said Mr. Fish as he took up books and papers, and prepared to depart from the classroom in the company of the four students.

"Do you know," he said to one of them, "a good many of the things I have just said to the class were merely verbalism—ratiocination—" (he searched for the word which would be clear to them, gazing at their perplexed looks)—"I was just playing a game with facts and with words, after a time."

Then Mr. Fish saw that Murphy still waited apart to speak to him.

He bade the other boys goodbye and Murphy made his approach.

"Sir," said Murphy, "they shouldn't have put such essays in the textbook. They're troublemakers."

Now they walked upon the campus, crowded with the students of changing classes.

"Mr. Murphy," said Mr. Fish, "I don't really care what you say. But you ought not to say such things. It is foolish of you. Even if it is true, it is a foolish thing to say and if you said it in another class, you might get into trouble. I don't know what the rules about such expressions of race feeling are, but I suspect that it is forbidden to bring such feelings into the open air of the classroom."

"I have nothing against you," said Murphy, "you always give me a square deal."

"I am glad that you think so," said Mr. Fish, "an interesting thought just entered my mind: if I reported you to your commanding officer, then you might get into trouble, for as an officer-to-be you have shown an extraordinary lack of tact and discretion. Perhaps it is my duty to report this incident to your commanding officer, although I certainly will not report you."

"Thanks a lot," said Murphy, his brows contracted with concern, "they certainly ought to be more careful about what they put in these textbooks."

"There is nothing wrong with the textbook," said Mr. Fish. "I must go now, but I want to ask you one more question, which is, since I am a Jew and since you have publicly insulted my own people, why don't I report you?"

"I told you I knew that some Jews are all right," said Murphy.

"Answer my question," said Mr. Fish, "why don't I report you, since perhaps I ought to report you?"

"I don't know why," said Mr. Murphy.

"Neither do I," said Mr. Fish as he returned to his home to await the arrival of innumerable anxiety feelings which had their source in events which had occurred for the past five thousand years.

Joanne Greenberg

The truths of this story are often ignored by the controversialists who most reflect them. A black woman, an embittered martinet, prevails as a necessary heroine. A circumspect librarian learns that progress often arranges itself in devious yet inspiring patterns. The enemy, race bigotry, is challenged by black women whose best strength lies in the unself-conscious audacity of their innocence.

The central character, a librarian, uncovers her courage, a bravery that matures after its declaration in act. Her "greetings" from the Tugwell jail denote the bond between topical issue (in this case the citizen's right to read) and historical comprehension, which alone makes any social issue truly intelligible.

"Gloss on a Decision of the Council of Nicaea" is taken from Joanne Greenberg's *Summering*, a book of short stories (1966). She is the author of two previous works of fiction, *The King's Persons* (1963) and *The Monday Voices* (1965).

GLOSS ON A DECISION
OF THE COUNCIL OF NICAEA

The major schisms of the Church. A list of the Bishops of Sarum. She knew a great deal about medieval church politics. With luck and God's help, knowledge would save her. Because the jail was so terrifying.

She had seen the demonstrators out there in front of the library, and she had watched them for a few minutes, unemotionally, and then she had gone into her little office and scratched out some words on a piece of cardboard for a sign. Then she had walked out of the library and down the steps to stand with the demonstrators. She had made no conscious decision to do this. Her heart was exploding its blood in rhythmic spasms of panic, but she paid no attention to it; and this frightened Myra, because she had always weighed her choices carefully and measured feeling against propriety.

Now she was standing in a jail cell. What was there to be afraid of? Jails haven't changed much since the Middle Ages; the properties of a jail—the dirt, discomfort, lack of privacy, and ugliness—were the same. Being a student of history, she had pondered many imprisonments. Except for the electric lights, Tugwell's county jail might have been anywhere at any time; and for Myra, who had always respected fighters for a cause, prison had meant Boethius' great hour, Gottschalk, the Albigensian teachers, and John of the Cross. She now understood that the worst, the most horrifying feature of their imprisonment had eluded her; and in her own moment, its sudden presence was almost too much to stand. Captors hate. How could she have missed so plain a fact? Captors hate. When the sheriff had come to "protect" them from the hecklers, she had started forward, trying to get to him. "These Negroes and I are protesting an unjust . . ."

But he had turned, reaching to take her and the girl next to her, and he had looked at them with a look that stopped the words in her mouth. At the jail, as they went past him into the cell, she saw the look again, a loathing, an all-pervading contempt. Before the wave of fear and sickness had passed, the door was closed and he was gone.

There were no statements taken, no charges made. She had wasted the first hours mustering answers from an array of imprisoned giants, the brilliant, searing words of men whose causes, once eclipsed and darkened, were now the commonplace truths of our civilization.

After a while Myra had looked around and counted. There are eight of us. The young men had been taken somewhere else. Eight girls, two beds—an upper and lower bunk—one spigot, two slop buckets, one bare wall, and two square yards of floor to sit on. That was all. The girls had gone to the bunks in an order that seemed natural: two rested or slept on the lower, four sat on the upper bunk, leaving the floor for the remaining two. When anyone had sat or rested enough, she would move and a girl on the floor would take her place.

She had expected choices. There were none, not even a list of rules that they could obey or refuse to obey. It underlined the sheriff's look. One doesn't give choices to an animal; the sheriff, giving such choices, would be recognizing the humanity of his prisoners and their right to make some disposition of their own lives. So, Miss Myra, the careful librarian of Tugwell, who walked in the crosswalks and did not spit where it said *No Spitting*, was forced to put her own boundaries to her day. She decided to spend the mornings mentally recounting history, braiding popes and synods and the heresies they sifted. Perhaps they would shed light on the evolution of secular law, in which she had done a good deal of reading. In the afternoon she would have to find a way to get some exercise, to get a letter out, to wash her clothes. . . . The girls talked a little now and then, the random exchanges of people waiting. Myra sensed that they didn't have her need for formed, measured bits of time, for routines and categories. They seemed to hang free within the terms of imprisonment, simply waiting.

On the evening of the second day Matilda Jane asked her, "Miss Myra, how you come to be with us?"

The others looked over at her, some smiling, no doubt remembering the scene of themselves as they stood and sang in front of the library, hoping they could keep their voices from quavering. They had watched the door, certain of the nose of a gun or the tip of a firehose as it slowly opened. Instead, there had grown only the tiny white edge of Myra's quickly lettered sign, giving them a word at a time: OPEN LIBRARY TO ALL! IGNORANCE IS NOT BLISS. Then, Myra herself had come, slowly, very much alone. It was as if in the expectation of a cannon, they had been shocked by a pop gun. Some of them had even laughed.

"I'd never thought about it, I mean about colored people not using the library, not until Roswell Dillingham came. After that, I had to—well—to protest."

"*Roswell?*" And the other girls sat up, surprised, interested, waiting for something rich. "Heber's little brother?"

"Hey, she mean Sailor."

They laughed.

"What Sailor done now?"

"I didn't know his nickname," Myra said, and Lalie, who was sitting on the bed beside her, guffawed. "Lord, yes! Great big mouth, blowin' an' goin' all the time, two big ears a-flappin', ma'am; you be with Sailor, you ain' need no boat!" And they all wanted to know what Sailor had done now. They were all eager to hear Roswell's latest, all except Delphine, who was stretched out on the bed dozing.

"Well," Myra said, "there's not much to tell, really. You see, when Mrs. Endicott left and I took over as county librarian, she simply told me that you—I mean that Negroes—just didn't use the library, but that when a Negro needed to look something up, why he would come to me and I would take the book out myself. I know it will seem odd to you—it does to me now—but before that it had never occurred to me that there were no Negroes coming into the library. Anyway, one day this spring, I was locking up and Roswell came and asked me for a book. I just followed Mrs. Endicott's instructions—I got it for him on my card. In three days he was back. Soon he started asking me to recommend books for him to read. Two or three books every week. I started combing lists for things I thought he would like, and the more he read, the more foolish it seemed not to have him come and browse around and pick out the books for himself. When I told him to come, he looked at me as if I had told him to fly like a bird. Negroes were forbidden to use the library.

"*The library!* That business of my getting the books for him had been designed to make me ask him why he wanted them, and then to decide that he wasn't responsible! I wrote an inquiry to the county commission and never got an answer. I never dreamed of demonstrating. I have to be honest and say that, but *the library*—well—I just couldn't consent to that. So, I suppose it was Roswell who got me to come out."

M.J. looked away and there was silence while everyone groped for a new, less dangerous subject.

Loretta whistled softly and said, "Kin you beat that damn Roswell?"

No getting away now; there it was. "What's the trouble?" Myra asked.

"You in here with us, Miss Myra," M.J. said, "so I'm gonna tell you truly what Roswell been doin'. He been makin' money offa them books."

"I don't see how. They were returned on time and in good shape."

"Ma'am, he been liftin' offa them books."

"I'm sorry, M.J., I just don't understand . . ."

"I'm in here in this jail, an' I got to be ashame' for that bigmouth! He takes them books, an' he reads 'em, an' then he take an' make 'em into a play. Then he go an' puts up a sign down to Carters' store an' he an' Fernelle an' one or two of 'em, they acts it out, see. Ten cents a person. He get almost everyone to come an' bring the kids an' make a night out. He ain' stop there. I know there's whole parts of the play that he have just graff right out of the book. I could tell it. Don't shake your head, Lalie, you know good as I do, ain' no words like that come out o' Roswell bigmouth! He lays them words down so nice—an' *powerful!* Miss Myra, he been gettin' maybe five, six dollars clear every Saturday, just showin' *your* books in the meetin' hall of the Hebron Funeral Home!"

Echo of Boethius, calling out of a sixth century cell, "Come, Goddess Wisdom, Come, Heart-ravishing Knowledge . . ." Roswell Dillingham, bootlegger of knowledge, echoed that day when knowledge was an absolute and its conquest as sure as the limits of a finite heaven. Myra wished she could tell them about Boethius, broken and condemned, and crying in his agony "Earth conquered gives the stars!" It would only embarrass them. She said, "Do the people like the plays?"

"Well—yes, they do. See, Roswell's plays—they're about us, about colored people. It's a' interestin' play, an' folks don' have to go all the way in to Winfiel' Station, sit in the balcony. My granmaw say, she gets to see a play she understan', an' they's nobody drinkin', swearin', runnin' aroun' in they underwear. Roswell plays—I mean *your* plays—they about what happen to our people. Like las' week, he had one call *Oliver Twiss*. Everybody cry in that one. Before that he had one call *Two Cities*."

Myra heard Dickens' story about how Sydney Carton gave himself up to the sheriff, back in the thirties, when the K.K.K. rode patrol out of Tugwell.

"Kite my books, will he . . . I wish I'd known. There's a fine one about a Civil Rights worker who got too rich and comfortable, name of Julius Caesar; one about a girl named Antigone, the freedom play of all time."

There was a snort from the bed. Delphine stretched and then swung her legs over the side and grunted again. "*Miss* Myra, we don't need white stories made over for black people."

"I wasn't patronizing. The books I gave Roswell were good books. They weren't 'white' stories. They were about people—any people . . ."

"No, *ma'am*, Miss Myra, *ma'am*, not while you got 'em piled up and stored away in the white-only library."

"That's why I was glad about Roswell." Myra looked down at Delphine. The two girls on the floor shifted a little, ready to use their bed places. Delphine got up slowly, and Myra got down, and they stood together in the cell.

From the beginning Delphine was the only one with whom Myra knew she could have no more than an armed truce. Delphine knew it too, probably. They seldom spoke to one another directly; when they had to speak, they used an agonizingly elaborate etiquette, which Myra noted had just gone over into parody. Delphine had a hard, absolute way of speaking that Myra found irritating; but Myra knew that Delphine must find life in the cramped cell more difficult with her there. Delphine was their leader. She had been in protests and sit-ins, and jailed four times. She spoke with hard-won, frightening knowledge.

"Next time, wear pedal-pushers like I got on, plaid or check. They hold up good an' they don't show the dirt."

"When they're going to hit you, the muscles by their eyes cinch up. You can always tell. Never take the smack, let the smack take you. Go with it."

If she had been an Albigensian under the Question, Myra knew that Delphine would wake great admiration in her. She was strong and intelligent; she could duck a blow, parry a question, and make her silence ring with accusation. Somehow, the heroine was also an arrogant bitch. Myra wondered if some straying grain of her own prejudice made Delphine's virtues seem so much like faults. As the pressures built up in the shares of water, slop bucket, and stench, Myra could see, from her neatly labeled and scheduled mental busy-work, that Delphine was trying to separate her from the rest of the girls.

They waited for three days. On the morning of the fourth, the sheriff came around with his notebook. As he stopped on the other side of the bars, Myra spoke to him. They had been arrested and jailed without being given their legal rights, she said. Would this be remedied?

The sheriff looked up slowly from his book, feigning a courteous confusion. "Why you're the little lady works over to the library, ain't you?" Then he let his gaze sift slowly over the others in the cell and come back to her, the expression now one of sympathetic reproof (Now, look at what you have caused to happen to you.)

She had a sudden, terrifying vision of him in all his genial Southern courtesy cutting away their justice, their law, their lives.

"Oh, ma'am, it's a shame! The commissioners only decided last week that we got to do Comminists the same as we do niggers. Comminist wants to live with niggers, why we ain' gonna stop 'em. But, ma'am, I seen you over in church on Sunday, an' all the bazaars, an' you was servin' donuts at the Legion parade." He looked at her earnestly. "It must be a mistake. I'm sure you ain' one of them Comminists."

Myra had never thought of herself as being a perceptive person. A narrow and careful life had never made it a necessity. Sensitivity can be a frightening gift. It was better to depend on more tangible things: hard work, reasonableness, and caution. Now, in the quiet, fear-laced minute, she suddenly knew that this contemptuously play-acting man was offering her a way out. She had only to weep and tell him how confused she was, to ask for his protection. (Lonely spinster-woman—everybody knows how notional they get. A woman, being more took up with the biological part of things, why, if she don't get to re-lize that biological part of her nature, it's a scientific fact she'll go to gettin' frusterated. Women, why they're *cows!*) It was as if she heard his mind form words. When he did speak, the words were so close that she was dumfounded.

"I guess you kinda got turned around here, all this niggers rights business. I guess you just got confused for a bit. I sure hate to see you in here like this. It sure is a pity." White women are ladies, the code said. You crush ladies not with violence but with pleasant contempt.

She didn't want to leave the girls in the cell. She looked at the sheriff, but she did not speak. The "lady" dealt with, he turned his attention to the others, and his voice hardened and coarsened as the code demanded when speaking to Them.

"We got a list here. You answer to your name when I call it." Then he read the names, stopping between each syllable to allow for their slow black wits to apprehend his meaning. The girls answered in the way Delphine had taught them: their voices cool and level, their eyes straight on him. Myra had been in Tugwell for only three years, having come in answer to a wildly exaggerated ad in the *Library Journal*, and staying because she had liked the town. She had never had any dealings with Tugwell's Negroes, except for Roswell; but she knew somehow that this was not the usual way for Negroes to react to authority in Tugwell. She couldn't trace this knowledge—she had never seen it directly or heard mention of it—it was just there, a certitude that their look was treason and would damn them. She also knew that from that judgment anyway, she was exempt. She might face down the sheriff and be called an old-maid eccentric, but she wouldn't be hurt. Another line of difference had been drawn, excluding her; and for a long moment of the sheriff's passing by, she was overwhelmed with a loneliness so keen that she found herself shivering and on the verge of tears.

She tried to close this separation. To do it, she had to appeal to Delphine. "Four days!" she said. "There must be a way we can get hold of a lawyer . . ."

But Delphine stepped back from the line that the sheriff had helped to set between them. "You aren't Miss Myra here; you aren't ma'am. Not with us. Not for giving us white-man heroes or white-man lawyers either. *You* get *your* lawyer. Let him get *you* out."

"Look, Delphine, I don't know anything about the struggle between the races. I know about the library and the books that are in the library; and I know that it is wrong for the library to deny its treasures to those who want them. I know about books and reading. That's what I know about, where I am strong and where I will fight."

But Delphine had turned her back and gone toward a space on the bed which Myra realized shouldn't have been there. It was there for Delphine. She was the complete leader now. She would always have a seat on the bed or a space to lie down on the bed when she wanted it. Having measured the sheriff, the others had chosen his adversary— tyrant for tyrant. Delphine went to rest on "her" bunk, to claim her compensation. "Her" places would now be offered to others only at her discretion. It was wrong. Myra saw it denying the very equality for which they were risking so much; because Myra now knew that her cellmates were facing the sons of the men who had broken Gottschalk's bones. If only she could give them some of his or Boethius' passionate and simple poetry to have when the time came. They might be strengthened by the words of great prisoners whose causes had been so much like their own. They would need grandeur. That sheriff was one who, to the end, would follow the Customs of the Country.

Later, she was sitting next to M.J. on the floor and they were talking quietly about wonderful food they had eaten. After Myra had dismembered a large, delicately broiled lobster and dipped the red claw carapace full of its vulnerable meat into a well of butter, M.J. leaned close and whispered, "Hey, Myra—uh—you ain' a Comminist or nothin', are you?"

Myra turned in wonder from the fading lobster. "What? Whatever gave you that idea?" Some words scurried across her mind in a disorderly attempt to escape being thought.

"I didn' mean to hurt your feelin's," M.J. murmured, "but see, Delphine don' trust you, because if you was another kind of different person —well—it wouldn' be like it was one of the regular whites comin' over to our side; it would be like you was arguin' for your own difference, see?"

"M.J., you tell Delphine that all I want is to have the Tugwell library open to everybody, regardless of race, creed, color, or national origin."

"I don' think Delphine is really agains' you."

"Where does she come from?" Myra asked, and M.J. said quickly, "Oh, she from here . . ." And then she looked down. "It's the schoolin' make her talk so much nicer, that's all. Her folks don't live but a street away from us. Her daddy work on the railroad, though, made steady money."

"It's not the way she talks," Myra said, stumbling over that other barrier between them. How could she have read the sheriff so well that his predicted words followed like footprints, and yet not be able to show herself to this girl who had the face and voice of a friend? "Delphine is different from you other girls, she . . ."

"It's the same with us as with the white," M.J. said, and she fingered her torn sleeve in a little nervous gesture that Myra had seen her begin to use after the sheriff's visit. "Some people, you fit 'em in with the rest; it don't bother 'em none. Some, they got to be just one an' the mold broke. Delphine, she like that. She always did feel sharp for things that was done wrong to her. I think she felt hurts more, say, than me. It's cause she's smarter; she got more person to hurt. You know, she went up North to the college."

"I didn't know that."

"I can remember her sayin' all the time how learnin' and education was goin' to get her free. Our grade school here in Tugwell, it ain' hardly one-legged to the white school; an' our high school ain' but a butt-patch to the white. Oh, Myra, an' we didn' know it! Delphine come out of Booker T. Washington High all proud an' keen. She made the straight A. Then she went up North to the college. An' all of a sudden, here she was, bein' counted by white folks measure—an' put down, put way low. It shamed her. The white-school diploma she got cost her a extra year just to fill in on what ol' Booker T. High didn' think a Negro had to know."

"But she did succeed . . ."

"That's what I wonder at—why she come back afterward, here to

Tugwell, where she ain't no different from any of us that never done what she did. I can't see how anybody that got the college degree would come back here to be put down low again."

"The fight and the fighter have to be close to each other," Myra murmured.

"What?"

Myra felt a gnawing in her mind that was strange to her. She had to wait until it became plain, and then she recognized that it was her mind moving, feeling blindly toward one of its own motives. It came bumping against something, won the shape from the darkness, and with the shape, a meaning. "Not pretty or smart or gifted, but I had one thing that was mine. The pretty and smart ones had the future; the rich ones had the present. I had the past. In a way, in 'having,' I 'owned.' The history and literature were mine to give when I opened that library door every morning. . . . When Roswell told me that Negroes couldn't use the library, I was mad because the town had no right, no right to deny what wasn't theirs to give or withhold. In a way, Delphine and I are alike." Then she said to M.J., "Delphine has a calling; there's no doubt about that."

Why can't I like her? Myra looked at the leader over the soggy bread in her dinner plate. She has everything I've always reverenced. Watching Delphine at the spigot. . . . not running away, standing, as Boethius stood, and Gottschalk and John. The courage is in knowing exactly what will happen, where the wound will gall most cruelly, and still, standing. . . . But the arrogance in Delphine, who was beginning to posture like Savonarola silhouetted by the light of his own fire, made Myra wince. Delphine's arrogance reached into Myra's thoughts and began to move toward all of the heroes Myra had stored there. She began to worry for the giants she venerated, for years of her pity and love. Was courage only the arrogance used to an enemy?

The next morning the sheriff began.

Tactical blunder: He took Delphine first. She came back sick, the brown color of her face grayed. She was bloody and puffy-faced and harder than ever. Now, anyone who followed would have to come to Delphine before and after, and would be judged. When Loretta went in the afternoon and returned still retching, she was greeted by Delphine's wry smile and the slow unfolding of Delphine's bones, one by one, to make a place for her on the bunk throne of honor. The next day Dilsey and Lalie went. They came back trembling and exhausted, embarrassed at where their hurts were, and with a rumor that things were going to be speeded up because the legal machinery was slowly lumbering in to help. In the night, counting the heretics she knew, burned between 890 and 1350 in France, Myra could hear M.J. quietly sobbing with fear.

It had been hardest for M.J., who had seen all the hurts and heard the accumulating voices in their nightmares. Now the untried ones had the floor all the time. Myra crawled over to M.J. and put a hand on her thin back in a forlorn gesture of comfort. M.J.'s back stopped heaving and the crying stopped or, rather, retreated inward. Myra began to feel that someone was observing her; another silence was there, one that seemed to fill its space instead of being there by default of sound. She turned and saw Delphine looking at them from a seat on the top bunk, her face showing nothing in the dimness. She was awake, all right, watching, listening, as if she were waiting to pounce. It made Myra feel guilty of something. She looked down at M.J., who hadn't moved and was pretending to be asleep, and then she stood up. It was painfully slow; she grunted with the effort and the pain; her legs had been bent against the concrete floor for a long time. When she finally stood, her eyes were at the level of Delphine's kneecaps.

"Help M.J. You know, Delphine, we can't all be as tough as you." She realized immediately that such a plea for M.J. was wrong and stupid.

Crying weakness to Delphine was like asking sympathy from a tornado. Were all heroes so frighteningly impersonal? Damn her! Why couldn't that precious martyrs' firelight extend its warmth and radiance to cover M.J., who had waited all these days while the terror grew?

"Listen, Delphine, I know something about you."

Delphine's impassive face did not move. Damn her, I'll make it move.

"I know, for instance," she continued slowly, whispering a word at a time, "that whatever you took from the sheriff, it didn't hurt as much as theirs did . . ." And she gestured around the cell at the sleepers who were shielding their ugly dreams from the forty-watt light that burned in the corridor outside the cell. "Maybe you didn't feel it at all."

"How come?" Delphine said, fastidiously disinterested.

"You knew it before you went in," Myra went on. "It's a nice secret, too, Delphine, because the welts are real and no one can prove they didn't hurt. Maybe they don't even hurt now."

"No!" Delphine hissed. "Nothing hurts! It's the black skin. Makes you immune. Tougher than the white! Less sensitive!"

"Come off it. It's the anger or the hate that makes you immune. Your anger and hate are better than morphine for shielding you from pain. You were dressed up to the eyes in hate, and you walked in with it to the sheriff and took your licks and came back bleeding. You didn't even have to lie. Did it make you feel superior to the other girls who had to take it raw, without hate?

That hit. Myra could see it going in to burn behind Delphine's slowly blinking eyes. She was standing close to Delphine, whispering, but they were both aware that M.J. and maybe others were awake and would hear them if their voices got any louder.

Delphine began to negotiate. "What are you going to do about it?"

"You help M.J. to take what she's going to have to take or I'll tell what I know about you."

Delphine laughed, a silent mouth-laugh, whose mirth died long before it reached her eyes.

"I know they won't believe me," Myra said, "but maybe there'll be a minute of doubt, just enough to force you to come right out and claim that bed space and that first drink in the morning."

Delphine sat there, surprised, and Delphine's surprise was a source of pain to Myra. She had no style and she knew it. Her courage looked silly. Nevertheless, she had gotten to Delphine, and Delphine wasn't used to being gotten to.

"I don't want you here!" she hissed. "I don't want what you have to give us! Get your white face out of this cell and let us, for once, do something all by ourselves!"

"I'm here and my white face is here, and you can either like it or lump it."

Where had the words and the strength come from? She had always been a sheltered person, and three years as Miss Myra, the toy librarian in this toy white town of antimacassars and mint tea hadn't done any more than confirm her opinion. Who had she been a week ago that she could be so far from that self right now? Like a rocket, she thought, that had veered a millionth of a degree from the center of its thrust. She had, on the 14th of April, asked a question of a boy named Roswell Dillingham. It was only the smallest shift, a millionth of a degree, and that smallest change was measuring her path at tangent, thousands of miles into strange darkness, to end lost, perhaps, in uncharted spaces that she could not imagine.

Delphine was muttering curses, and Myra turned back to her place on the floor and sat down. Delphine didn't want her, and she had said so. Why not? What did Myra, and by extension white people, have that Delphine couldn't accept? If Delphine hadn't been to college up North, it might have been a falsely exalted picture of American history, a Parson Weems history that no Negro in slave-holding country could take seriously. It wasn't that. Delphine had read enough and learned enough to know that white men also searched their souls occasionally. Myra knew that she had to get at it, whatever it was, because she needed everything she could use against Delphine's arrogance. She found herself staring at the slop bucket, riveted on it. Exhausted, she thought.

Hard floors and groping, needs and angers, mine and hers, and barely knowing where to separate mine and hers. Why is *she* in this cell? Then she found herself staring at Lalie's back as if to bore through it, and Lalie shifted and moaned so that Myra pulled her eyes away. I have the past. . . . I have the past and two enemies, who both seem to say "nothing personal." It really isn't, I suppose. They are enemies to my history. What a couple they would make: the sheriff, with his fake past, and Delphine, with her fake . . .

It was there, somewhere near, elusive but near, in Delphine's idea of a future. She became alert, groping to more purpose now. It was in a future of which Delphine dreamed, a world that made "white" history irrelevant and Myra a danger. She looked over the sleeping girls. Delphine had given up too, and was curled in a ball, her arm protectively over her face. The only ones who merely pretended to sleep were the two whose turn it would be to go with the sheriff tomorrow. Myra knew that she would not be beaten, and that the law was slowly lumbering toward her. If only Delphine had let it happen, she might have given them a thousand years of prison humor and two thousand years of resistance to the tyrant, eloquent, proud resistance, face to face, as Delphine would have liked it.

And *I* wanted to be in the history too! she thought. Oh, my God, it was as simple as that! I wanted to be in the history even more than I wanted to fight over Roswell's reading. I wanted to come forward where the fire was, feeling that in the fire, I would not be so alone. . . . The thoughts that she had sent out walking for Delphine's weakness had found hers instead. Does it hurt and sear and shatter, that thought? Is it as hard as the sheriff's blows? No, not so hard as that. She wasn't going to be in the history, even though she was in the fire. In the fire, but no less alone. Delphine had fixed that. A segregated fire. She would have to work at not hating Delphine. This cause was right and the cause should take precedence over its leaders. Heaven knows it was an old argument. It showed up as the Montanist Controversy; and it was put to a rule in 325 A.D.: Decision of the Nicene Council, valid sacraments by a lapsed bishop. Very good. It was a comfort to know that the early Church had ruled on Delphine's case.

M.J. rolled over, but her eyes were closed, and she was still pretending to be asleep. She was a nice girl. If Delphine had allowed it, they could have been, all of them, friends together in this cause. Her mind yearned toward M.J. in the night. There were thousands of men and women before you in that room, a thousand rooms, acts, moments. Don't be afraid. You are neighbored all around by people who have screamed or been silent, wept or been brave—all the nations are represented, all the colors of man. Don't be afraid of pleading, of weeping. You are with some shining names.

At the window there was a little gray light coming. The window was almost hidden by the bunks which had been pushed against its bars, but from where Myra sat on the floor, she could see up into a tiny square of the changing sky. The cell looked even worse in the muddy yellow of the electric bulb.

I suppose I shouldn't stop at the heroes of the Middle Ages. There are more recent slaves and conquerers. Dachau and Belsen—they, too, had men who stood in their moment and said, "I am a person; you must not degrade me." Her eye wandered around the cell and fixed on the slop bucket again, and she tried to ease her aching body on the floor. Dachau and Belsen.

In 1910, technology was going to make everybody free and freedom was going to make everybody good. The new cars had rolled up to the gates of death camps. Dreams of the perfecting of man ended in the gas chambers and behind the cleverly devised electric fences. Didn't everybody dream that dream? Didn't we *all?*

Maybe all but one. Is man imperfect by nature? Maybe only white man? There it was. Delphine was answering to everyone who had ever told her that she and hers were outside the elm-street-and-steeple dream of democracy. If the black heroes weren't in the history books, then they were also not included in the Albigensian Crusade and the ride to Belsen. The possibility of perfection—that was being girded, all right. If Delphine took her blows in hate and in the belief that *her* people could be perfect, not in some millennium but soon, and by her own good efforts, what would be, could be given her, what pain could she endure that wasn't worth it? Not for freedom, not for friendship, certainly not for the right of ingress to the Tugwell library. Oh, God, who will help M.J. take her hurting now, when all that M.J. wants is to include in her God-blesses before bed all the misery-running, sorrow-spawning world of white and black?

It was morning. M.J. was trembling quietly on the floor. She looked exhausted and ill, and she hadn't even gone yet. Myra got up, and the aching numbed to her every bone. She went to where Delphine was perched, sleeping.

"Delphine?"

"What-do-you-want?" It was the too-clear enunciation of an educated Negro to a white who will call him Rastus if he slurs a letter.

"You've got to do something to help M.J."

"I bet you're happy, white gal. If it wasn't for your people putting us down, she wouldn't *be* scared now!"

So it was true. The blind would see and the halt would rejoice. No cowards, no sinners, no wrongs. In the jubilee. In the great jubilee. "Help her, Delphine. The sheriff is looking for weakness. If he finds it, he might kill her with his hands or with her own shame. Help her, or I'm going to start talking about you, Delphine. I'm going to start asking questions that the others have never asked."

Myra could see the gains and losses ticking off in Delphine's head. Her eyes were clinical and her expression detached as an Egyptian funerary statue. Delphine, at the height of her concentration, was intensely, breathtakingly beautiful. She stayed in her place for a minute,

two. Then she stretched and the odds and possibilities arranged themselves before her. With elaborate, lithe ease she swung down to the
floor, yawning, and bent to where M.J. lay. They began to whisper. Myra
was glad she couldn't hear them. For a moment her eye strayed to the
vacant place, Delphine's place on the bed. She had a sudden urge to
climb up and take it and make Delphine fight to get it back. The place
would be comfortable for a little nap; she was sore all over from the floor.
The place would be dark against the back wall; she could sleep for a
while.

No, Delphine was the leader, the place was her place. Only Delphine,
however fanatical and blind, could lead the girls through all the questions, the licks and the lawyers. She found her eyes fixed again. What
was so fascinating about the slop bucket! We're both on the floor, she
thought.

"I wish to record an opinion," she said to it quietly. "In 325 the
Council of Nicaea decided that sacraments at the hands of a lapsed
bishop were valid where the intent of the communicant was sincere. The
baptisms of these bishops stood. I always wondered about that decision.
It smacked too much of ends justifying means. I hereby make my statement to the estimable theologians of the Council of Nicaea: 'Avé, fellas,
Salvé, fellas, Congratulations and greetings from the Tugwell jail.'"

Part Six

Scenes
from Childhood

Spring, of all seasons most gratuitous,
Is fold of untaught flower, is race of water,
Is earth's most multiple, excited daughter;

And those she has least use for see her best,
Their paths grown craven and circuitous,
Their visions mountain-clear, their needs immodest.

Philip Larkin

In an essay entitled "The Darlings at the Top of the Stairs," James Thurber observed that the "worried psychologists, sociologists, anthropologists, and other ologists, who jump at the sound of every backfire or slammed door, have called our present jeopardy a 'child-centered culture.'" Dissatisfied with this diagnosis, Thurber goes further, christening our society a "child-overwhelmed culture." It would seem that couples who might just as artfully keep dogs, now keep children, and for motives no more glorious. With a resolve not entirely characteristic, Thurber chooses not to surrender to our hordes of infancy. Instead he opts to support that part of The Inevitable which shows a civil brevity in its judgments on the world, like the small girl who reviewed a volume with the remark, "This book tells me more about penguins than I wanted to know." As for the unbrief, the savants of prolixity, Thurber hazards: "More has been written about the child than about any other age of man, and it is perhaps fortunate that the literature is now so extensive a child would have become twenty-one before its parents could get through half the books on how to bring it up."

Alloyed to Thurber's indictment and to the predicted effects, all dire, of our too slowly declining birthrate is the question of *quality* in the childhoods of our children. Assuming the best contingency, or in Thurber's terms the worst, that we really do aspire to a culture dominated by those members least sophisticated in the ways of life, then how are these heralded beings to thrive in an atmosphere that must deny the amenities now deemed an American child's birthright: the privacy of mind that inspires imagination; the privacy of place that a sufficiency of land protects; and the privacy of relationship whereby a child and his parents may engage one another as special beings?

Educators who are aware of the population terror have been pre-

307

dictably reluctant to broadcast what their insight urges, namely that many solutions to educational problems wait simply for a reduction in family size, particularly in the families of the middle class, whose statistics are vastly the most culpable. So brazenly obvious, this solution risks sarcasm from those forces with interests in humanity as consumer and from varsity casuists who would deem it simplistic. Moreover, suburban schoolmen, employees of the middle class, must speak warily of matters close to their employers. Discussions of population, even among school board members, have been tentative to the extreme, if not furtive. Meanwhile, the enervating effects of overpopulation continue to infect the curricula, the quality of teaching, and the daily atmospheres of the schools. Within easy reach, however, is a query of self interest: Who stands to profit *more* from a sizeable reduction of school population than the children of the middle class? The upper class gets along. Parents of the lower class who will not eventually "elevate" to the middle class can be helped perennially by intensive birth control programs yet to be realized. The middle class, however, for motives various and transparent, *wants* children: a pretense of immortality is granted the father through his children; in an age of emasculating comforts, a virility of sorts is witnessed (though not measured) through a man's progeny; and the vapidity of life common to many suburbs obscures the external horizons of its citizens, forcing them to turn inward to the nest in hopes that its spawn will live a dynamism lost to themselves. Other motives conspire too. But even should an unlikely and early diminution in family size occur, our perversions of natural environment must be quelled and ecological aims improved if scenes of childhood are not to be nightmarish landscapes.

The title of Part Six may imply a bucolic, perhaps nineteenth-century milieu—Robert Schumann's version, or Wordsworth's—surely not James Thurber's Columbus, Ohio, or Muriel Resnik's New York City. Such an expectation carries its own pathos. Why should not our children, now, have the secure opulence of variety, the sensuousness of place, indeed the *scenes*, the tableaus of first experience that display themselves mortally in the rememberer's mind? *Skēnē*, the ancient Greek word for scene, meant a covered place, and now, as apt metaphor, a bower where the innocent may grow supple enough to lose themselves to nature and to art and to their own humanity when the world opens up.

When this world opens to bestow the larger view of things, of visions too richly random and diverse for any unalterable frame, is when our experience, in its immediacy, needs the perspective that alone can order it. Just so, these stories by James Thurber, Mark Schorer, and Muriel Resnik lend perspective—three hindsights that are the remorse and recompense of maturity.

James Thurber

(1894–1961)

This reminiscence answers some questions and refuses others. Everything taken on is resolved. Thurber's tone is reportorial, at times brushing understatement, and never softened by emotive interference. Thurber trusts his readers, permitting them to take his language and to create from its art the experience he intends they have.

Those Sullivant Schools that are still with us may have changed in architecture (belated remodelings), or in grading philosophy (compulsory-pass systems), or in disciplinary ploys (the police, not janitors, are called). But have the values of the students changed commensurately? Have their primal emotions become outworn? Primitive terror sensed within the groves of civilization is, in fact, a frequent quality of Thurber's tone, which somehow adds to the humor implicit in it.

James Thurber's cartoons, sketches, and stories were, for many years, featured in *The New Yorker*. His books include *My Life and Hard Times* (1933), *Let Your Mind Alone* (1937), the play *The Male Animal* (1940), *The Thurber Carnival* (1945), *Alarms and Diversions* (1957), the autobiographical *The Years with Ross* (1959), and *Lanterns and Lances* (1961).

I Went to Sullivant

I was reminded the other morning—by what, I don't remember and it doesn't matter—of a crisp September morning last year when I went to the Grand Central to see a little boy of ten get excitedly on a special coach that was to take him to a boys' school somewhere north of Boston. He had never been away to school before. The coach was squirming with youngsters; you could tell, after a while, the novitiates, shining and

309

tremulous and a little awed, from the more aloof boys, who had been away to school before, but they were all very much alike at first glance. There was for me (in case you thought I was leading up to that) no sharp feeling of old lost years in the tense atmosphere of that coach, because I never went away to a private school when I was a little boy. I went to Sullivant School in Columbus. I thought about it as I walked back to my hotel.

Sullivant was an ordinary public school, and yet it was not like any other I have ever known of. In seeking an adjective to describe the Sullivant School of my years—1900 to 1908—I can only think of "tough." Sullivant School was tough. The boys of Sullivant came mostly from the region around Central Market, a poorish district with many colored families and many white families of the laboring class. The school district also included a number of homes of the upper classes because, at the turn of the century, one or two old residential streets still lingered near the shouting and rumbling of the market, reluctant to surrender their fine old houses to the encroaching rabble of commerce, and become (as, alas, they now have) mere vulgar business streets.

I remember always, first of all, the Sullivant baseball team. Most grammar-school baseball teams are made up of boys in the seventh and eighth grades, or they were in my day, but with Sullivant it was different. Several of its best players were in the fourth grade, known to the teachers of the school as the Terrible Fourth. In that grade you first encountered fractions and long division, and many pupils lodged there for years, like logs in a brook. Some of the more able baseball-players had been in the fourth grade for seven or eight years. Then, too, there were a number of boys, most of them colored (about half of the pupils at Sullivant were colored), who had not been in the class past the normal time but were nevertheless deep in their teens. They had avoided starting to school—by eluding the truant officer—until they were ready to go into long pants, but he always got them in the end. One or two of these fourth-graders were seventeen or eighteen years old, but the dean of the squad was a tall, husky young man of twenty-two who was in the fifth grade (the teachers of the third and fourth had got tired of having him around as the years rolled along and had pushed him on). His name was Dana Waney and he had a mustache. Don't ask me why his parents allowed him to stay in school so long. There were many mysteries at Sullivant that were never cleared up. All I know is why he kept on in school and didn't go to work: he liked playing on the baseball team, and he had a pretty easy time in class, because the teachers had given up asking him any questions at all years before. The story was that he had answered but one question in the seventeen years he had been going to classes at Sullivant and that was "What is one use of the comma?" "The commy," said Dana, embarrassedly unsnarling his long legs from beneath a desk much too low for him, "is used to shoot marbles with." ("Commies" was our word for those cheap, ten-for-a-cent marbles, in case it wasn't yours.)

The Sullivant School baseball team of 1905 defeated several high-school teams in the city and claimed the high-school championship of the state, to which title it had, of course, no technical right. I believe the boys could have proved their moral right to the championship, however, if they had been allowed to go out of town and play all the teams they challenged, such as the powerful Dayton and Toledo nines, but their road season was called off after a terrific fight that occurred during a game in Mt. Sterling, or Piqua, or Zenia—I can't remember which. Our first baseman—Dana Waney—crowned the umpire with a bat during an altercation over a called strike and the fight was on. It took place in the fourth inning, so of course the game was never finished (the battle continued on down into the business section of the town and raged for hours, with much destruction of property), but since Sullivant was ahead at the time 17 to 0 there could have been no doubt as to the outcome. Nobody was killed. All of us boys were sure our team could have beaten Ohio State University that year, but they wouldn't play us; they were scared.

Waney was by no means the biggest or toughest guy on the grammar-school team; he was merely the oldest, being about a year the senior of Floyd, the colored centre-fielder, who could jump five feet straight into the air without taking a running start. Nobody knew—not even the Board of Education, which once tried to find out—whether Floyd was Floyd's first name or his last name. He apparently only had one. He didn't have any parents, and nobody, including himself, seemed to know where he lived. When teachers insisted that he must have another name to go with Floyd, he would grow sullen and ominous and they would cease questioning him, because he was a dangerous scholar in a school-room brawl, as Mr. Harrigan, the janitor, found out one morning when he was called in by a screaming teacher (all our teachers were women) to get Floyd under control after she had tried to whip him and he had begun to take the room apart, beginning with the desks. Floyd broke into small pieces the switch she had used on him (some said he also ate it; I don't know, because I was home sick at the time with mumps or something). Harrigan was a burly, iron-muscled janitor, a man come from a long line of coal-shovellers, but he was no match for Floyd, who had, to be sure, the considerable advantage of being more aroused than Mr. Harrigan when their fight started. Floyd had him down and was sitting on his chest in no time, and Harrigan had to promise to be good and to say "Dat's what Ah get" ten times before Floyd would let him up.

I don't suppose I would ever have got through Sullivant School alive if it hadn't been for Floyd. For some reason he appointed himself my protector, and I needed one. If Floyd was known to be on your side, nobody in the school would dare be "after" you and chase you home. I was one of the ten or fifteen male pupils in Sullivant School who always, or almost always, knew their lessons, and I believe Floyd admired the mental prowess of a youngster who knew how many continents there were and whether or not the sun was inhabited. Also, one time when it came my turn to read to the class—we used to take turns reading American history aloud—I came across the word "Duquesne" and knew how to pronounce it. That charmed Floyd, who had been slouched in his seat idly following the printed page of his worn and pencilled textbook. "How you know dat was Dukane, boy?" he asked me after class. "I don't know," I said. "I just knew it." He looked at me with round eyes. "Boy, dat's sump'n," he said. After that, word got around that Floyd would beat the tar out of anybody that messed around me. I wore glasses from the time I was eight and I knew my lessons, and both of those things were considered pretty terrible at Sullivant. Floyd had one idiosyncrasy. In the early nineteen-hundreds, long warm furry gloves that came almost to your elbows were popular with boys, and Floyd had one of the biggest pairs in school. He wore them the year around.

Dick Peterson, another colored boy, was an even greater figure on the baseball team and in the school than Floyd was. He had a way in the classroom of blurting out a long deep rolling "beee—eee—ahhhh!" for no reason at all. Once he licked three boys his own size single-handed, really single-handed, for he fought with his right hand and held a mandolin in his left hand all the time. It came out uninjured. Dick and Floyd never met in mortal combat, so nobody ever knew which one could "beat," and the scholars were about evenly divided in their opinions. Many a fight started among them after school when that argument came up. I think school never let out at Sullivant without at least one fight starting up, and sometimes there were as many as five or six raging between the corner of Oak and Sixth Streets and the corner of Rich and Fourth Streets, four blocks away. Now and again virtually the whole school turned out to fight the Catholic boys of the Holy Cross Academy in Fifth Street near Town, for no reason at all—in winter with snowballs and iceballs, in other seasons with fists, brickbats, and clubs. Dick Peterson was always in the van, yelling, singing, beeee-ahing, whirling all the way around when he swung with his right or (if he hadn't brought his mandolin) his left and missed. He made himself the pitcher on the baseball team because he was the captain. He was the captain because everybody was afraid to challenge his self-election, except Floyd. Floyd was too lazy to pitch and he didn't care who was captain, because he didn't fully comprehend what that meant. On one occasion, when Earl Battec, a steam-fitter's son, had shut out Mound Street School for six innings without a hit, Dick took him out of the pitcher's box and went in himself. He was hit hard and the other team scored, but it didn't make much difference, because the margin of Sullivant's victory was so great. The team didn't lose a game for five years to another grammar school. When Dick Peterson was in the sixth grade, he got into a saloon brawl and was killed.

When I go back to Columbus I always walk past Sullivant School. I have never happened to get there when classes were letting out, so I don't know what the pupils are like now. I am sure there are no more Dick Petersons and no more Floyds, unless Floyd is still going to school there. The play yard is still entirely bare of grass and covered with gravel, and the sycamores still line the curb between the schoolhouse fence and the Oak Street car line. A street-car line running past a schoolhouse is a dangerous thing as a rule, but I remember no one being injured while I was attending Sullivant. I do remember, however, one person who came very near being injured. He was a motorman on the Oak Street line, and once when his car stopped at the corner of Sixth to let off passengers, he yelled at Chutey Davidson, who played third base on the ball team, and was a member of the Terrible Fourth, to get out of the way. Chutey was a white boy, fourteen years old, but huge for his age, and he was standing on the tracks, taking a chew of tobacco. "Come ahn down offa that car an' I'll knock your block off!" said Chutey, in what I can only describe as a Sullivant tone of voice. The motorman waited until Chutey moved slowly off the tracks; then he went on about his business. I think it was lucky for him that he did. There were boys in those days.

Mark Schorer
(1908–   )

"What We Don't Know Hurts Us" describes a father's self-wrought isolation and the consequent decay of family rapport. The father's dereliction is routine in its rationalizations and addicted to ploys that are by turns subtle, crass, and indecisive. The armor of Charles Dudley's estrangement, his ignorance of the actuality of other selves, is well forged. He knows neither the depths of his self-centeredness nor the motives that drift there, that break to the surface and ward off his son and his wife.

Goethe warned that the distinct great evil of ignorance is that it loves; whereas knowledge can distinguish itself simply by action, being. Accordingly in this story the ignorance depicted is not a dormant not-knowing. It is importunate.

A writer of short stories, novels, and literary criticism, Mark Schorer is Professor of English at the University of California, Berkeley. His principal works are *William Blake: The Politics of Vision* (1946), a collection of short stories, *The State of Mind* (1947), the critical essay "Technique as Discovery" (1948), the novel *The Wars of Love* (1953), and a critical biography, *Sinclair Lewis: An American Life* (1961).

WHAT WE DON'T KNOW HURTS US

The mid-afternoon winter sun burned through the high California haze. Charles Dudley, working with a mattock in a thicket of overgrowth, felt as steamy and as moldy as the black adobe earth in which his feet kept slipping. Rain had fallen for five days with no glimmer of sunshine, and now it seemed as if the earth, with fetid animation like heavy breath, were giving all that moisture back to the air. The soil, or the broom which he was struggling to uproot, had a disgusting, acrid odor, as if he were tussling with some obscene animal instead of with a lot of neglected vegetation, and suddenly an overload of irritations—the smell, the stinging sweat in his eyes, his itching skin, his blistering palms—made him throw the mattock down and come diving out of the thicket into the clearing he had already achieved. "Jesus!" he said, panting.

"Is it hard?"

He looked up and saw Josephine, his wife, sitting on the railing of the balcony onto which the French doors of their bedroom opened. She was holding a dustmop, and a tea towel was wrapped round her head, and her face seemed pallid and without character, as it always did, to Charles, when she neglected to wear lipstick.

He snorted instead of replying, and wiped his muddy hands on the seat of his stiff new levis. Then he walked over to the short flight of steps that led up to the balcony from the garden, and lit a cigarette.

"It looks as though the ground levels out up there where you're working," Josephine said.

"Yes, it does. Somebody once had a terrace up there. It's full of overgrown geraniums that are more like snakes, and a lot of damned rose vines."

"You've got the pepper tree almost free."

He looked up at the pepper tree, with its delicate, drooping branches and the long gray tendrils that hung down from the branches to the ground. He had chopped out the broom as far up the incline as the tree, and now he could see that a big branch of the eucalyptus at the very edge of the property had forced the top of the pepper tree to grow out almost horizontally from the main portion of its trunk. 'Look at the damned thing!' he said.

"It's charming, like a Japanese print."

"I'm going to hate this house long before it's livable," he said.

"Oh, Charles!"

"I didn't want to buy a house. I never wanted to own any house. I certainly never wanted to own a miserable, half-ruined imitation of a Swiss chalet built on an incline that was meant for goats." Vehemently he flipped his cigarette up into the pile of brush he had accumulated.

Josephine stood up and shook out the dustmop. "Let's not go into all that again. There was no choice. It's no pleasure for me, either, living the way we are, nor is it for the children." She paused, and then she added a cold supplement. "I sometimes think that your disinclination to own anything is a form of irresponsibility." She turned swiftly and went into the house.

He stood staring after her, frowning a little, for it seemed momentarily that with studied intent she had cracked the bland habit of her amiability. But in a minute she reappeared in the doorway and said matter-of-factly, "I heard on the radio that Boston has had eighteen inches of snow." Then she went back inside.

"Are you trying to make me homesick?" he asked of no one as he started back up the incline, and he remembered the frozen river, snow blowing over the Esplanade, and city lights faint in a blizzard.

He began again to chop at the roots of the broom. All right, he told himself, so he was being unpleasant. He did not like the idea of being pinned down by a mortgage to a place his firm had picked for him. He did not even like the idea of being pinned down by a mortgage. To own something was, to that extent, to be owned, and he did not like the feeling. His idea of a good way to live was in a duplex apartment owned by someone else, in Charles River Square, or, better than that but always less likely, in a duplex apartment owned by someone else, on the East River. He connected happiness with a certain luxury, and, probably, sexuality with elegance and freedom. These were not noble associations, he was aware, and he knew that it was foolish to let impossibilities, as they faded, become forms of minor torture. This knowledge made him chop more angrily than ever at the broom.

It was vegetation with which Charles felt that he had a peculiar intimacy, perhaps the only thing in California which, in the several weeks they had lived there, he had really come to know. And he loathed it with a violence which he recognized as quite undue, and which, now, made him feel childish and curiously guilty. Yet he could not laugh away his loathing. The stuff was ubiquitous, and sprang up anywhere at all the minute the ground was neglected. If it grew up in a patch, it began a foolish competition with itself, and the thin, naked stalks shot ten and twelve and fourteen feet into the air, all stretching up to the sun for the sake of a plume of paltry foliage at the top. Then the foliage tangled together in a thatch, and when you had managed to chop out the shallow roots of the tree, you still had to extricate its trivial but tenacious branches from those of all its neighbors to get it out of the clump. Once it was out, the wood was good for nothing, but dried up into a kind of bamboo stalk so insubstantial that it did not make even decent kindling. As a tree it was a total fraud, and in spite of the nuisance of its numbers, and of its feminine air of lofty self-importance, it was, with its shallow roots in this loose soil, very vulnerable to attack. Charles beat away at it in an angry frenzy, as if he were overwhelming, after a long struggle, some bitter foe.

He did not hear his son come up the incline behind him, and the boy stood quietly watching until his father turned to toss a stalk up on the pile in the clearing. Then the boy said, "Hi." He said it tentatively, almost shyly, as though his father's responses were unpredictable.

"Hi, Gordon."

"What're you doing?"

"Can't you see? How was school?"

"It stinks," he answered doggedly, his dark eyes half-averted and sorrowful.

Charles felt a twinge of pain for him. "Cheer up. Give it time. You'll get to like it after a while."

"I'll never like it," Gordon said stubbornly.

Charles took up his mattock again. "Sure you will," he said as he began to swing it.

"Nobody likes me."

Charles let the mattock come to rest and, turning once more to the boy, he spoke with an impatient excess of patience. "You say that every day. I've told you it isn't true. You're a new boy in the school, and you came in the middle of the term, and there's never yet been a new boy who entered a school late who made friends right away. You're nearly nine, Gordon, and you can understand that. Anyway, I'm tired of explaining it to you."

"When can I get a paper route?"

Charles laughed without humor. "My God, boy! Give us a chance to get settled."

"I need money."

"You get an allowance."

"I need more money," the boy insisted. "I want a paper route. How do kids get them?"

"You can work for me. You can get in there with a hedge shears and cut out all those vines."

The boy looked at his father despairingly and shook his head. "No, I need a lot of money."

"You can earn a lot of money working for me," Charles said, swinging his mattock.

"I need a dollar," Gordon said faintly.

His father did not hear him, and he did not turn from his work again until presently he heard his daughter calling him shrilly from the foot of the hill on which the house stood.

"What is it?" he called back. She was climbing the path, and he saw that she had a white envelope in her hand.

Then Gordon broke into rapid, desperate speech. "I need a dollar. I'll pay it back out of my allowance. Remember yesterday I told you about that dollar I found? I have to pay it back."

Charles stared at him. "What dollar?"

Gordon glanced wildly over his shoulder. His sister, holding the menacing white envelope in one hand and her workman's tin lunchbox in the other, was halfway up the hill, coming along the side of the house. Pleadingly, Gordon looked back up to his father. "The dollar. Remember? I told you I found it. You wanted to know what I did with it."

"What dollar?"

He sighed. "You didn't listen! You never listen!"

Charles patted his shoulder. "Now take it easy. Don't get excited. Tell me again. I don't think you told me anything about a dollar yesterday."

"The dollar I found. You asked me what I did with it, and I told you I gave it to Crow, and you said I should have brought it home to you."

"That Crow! I thought you were joking."

Penelope, the six-year-old, was behind him now, and Gordon's shoulders sagged in despair. "I wasn't joking," he said almost wearily as Penelope handed his father the letter. "You never really listen."

Charles read the precise handwriting on the envelope. "Mr. or Mrs. Dudley," it said, and in the lower left-hand corner, "Courtesy of Penelope." He opened the envelope and read the message:

> Dear Mr. and Mrs. Dudley:
>   Gordon became involved in some difficulty about a dollar today, and I wish you would help me. The dollar was lunch money belonging to a girl who says she left it deep in her coat pocket, in the cloak room, yesterday. When I brought it up with Gordon, he immediately said that he did not steal it. He says that he found it on the floor, and he also says that he told his father about it yesterday and that his father said he should have brought it home to him, and now he is fixed in his confusions. He gave it to an older boy named Will Crow, who spent it, and I have told Gordon that he will have to return a dollar to the girl tomorrow. Gordon is a very worthwhile little personality, but I do not think he has been entirely happy here at the Crestview School, and therefore, if you can help me straighten this out to his own best interest, I will be ever so grateful.
>
>   Sincerely yours,
>   Gertrude Grandjent, *Principal*

Charles groaned in exasperation. "My God, why did you have to drag me into it? What will that woman think?"

Gordon's lips were trembling. "You remember? I did tell you, didn't I?"

"Yes, I remember now. I remember very clearly that you told me you found it on the way to school, and when I asked you what you did with it, and you said you gave it to Crow, naturally I said you should have brought it home. *Listen,* Gordon——" The very simplicity of the boy's strategy infuriated Charles, and it was with an effort that he controlled his temper. He said, "Penny, you go in now and tell your mother you're home."

Penny was staring at her brother. "What did Gordon do?"

"Run along, Penny, as I told you."

She went down the incline reluctantly, staring back over her shoulder, and when she had gone into the house, Charles turned to Gordon again and said, "Sit down."

They sat down side by side on the damp slope. Gordon said, "Will you lend me a dollar and keep my allowance until it's made up? I have to take it back tomorrow."

"We'll talk about that later." Charles tapped the letter with his muddy hand. "Why did you tell me you found it in the street?"

Gordon looked away but answered promptly. "I knew if I told you I found it in school, you'd have said I should have taken it to the office."

"So you lied to me instead. That was better?"

Gordon did not answer.

"Answer me."

"Yes."

"Yes, what?"

"I lied."

That was that. Charles started over. "Why did you tell Miss Grandjent that you did not steal it when she hadn't even said that you had?"

"I knew that's what she thought."

"How did you know?"

"I just knew."

Charles hesitated. When he spoke again, his voice was warmer, friendly, almost confidential. "What's the little girl's name, Gordon?"

"She's not little. She's in high fourth."

"What's her name?"

"I don't know. Joan, I guess."

"What color is her coat?"

Gordon glanced at his father sharply. "I don't know. I never noticed it."

Charles bit his lip in exasperation and stood up. "Let's go inside." He led the way in.

Josephine was standing on a chair in the middle of the living room. She was dusting the hideous chandelier of dark metal and colored glass which hung from the center of the ceiling. It was only one of many distasteful features in the house which the Dudleys hoped to rid it of, but it was hard to find men to do all the necessary work, and none would promise to do it quickly. An electrician had torn away a good deal of plaster and lathing, and a carpenter had ripped out some bookshelves and ugly mantels and taken down most of a wall between the dining room and a useless hallway, but neither had returned, and painters, plasterers, paperhangers had not yet come at all. The Dudleys had decided to leave most of their belongings in storage until the work was done, and to bring nothing out of storage that they cared about. The result was that the house was almost fantastically disordered and bleak and squalid, and while Josephine managed to keep an even temper under these conditions, Charles, who found them very trying, did not.

He stood in the doorway of the living room now and said to her, "Why do you bother?"

"The light was so dim," she said, and then, seeing his expression, asked quickly, "What's wrong?"

"Another problem." He came heavily into the living room and gave her the letter. She read it standing on the chair, her face expressionless. Then she stepped down and went out into the hall where Gordon was lurking and said, "Come in, dear."

There was one old sofa in the room, and Josephine sat down there with Gordon. Charles sat facing them on the single straight chair. Josephine took Gordon's hands and said, "Now tell me everything, Gordon, just the way it happened."

The boy's face was composed in a kind of stolid determination, but when he raised his moody eyes from the bare floor to his father, his chin began to tremble, his eyelids fluttered, and suddenly the dogged expression broke in despair, his body sagged, his head fell back against the sofa, and he burst into harsh sobs. Josephine put her arm around his shoulders and held him close while he cried, and she shook her head sharply at Charles as he jumped up impatiently. He sat down again. Finally Gordon stopped crying, almost as abruptly as he had begun.

"How did it happen, Gordon?" his mother asked.

He straightened up and stared at the floor again. "Nothing happened. I just came in the cloak room and saw it on the floor. I took it and put it in my pocket, and at recess I gave it to Crow."

"Didn't anyone see you pick it up?"

"There wasn't anyone else there."

"In the cloak room? Before school? Why not?"

"I was late."

"Late? But why? You left here in plenty of time."

"I stopped on the way and played with a cat."

Josephine frowned. "So there was no one else there at all to see you?" she asked meaningfully.

"No."

Josephine glanced at Charles. He drew his lips apart and, with a heavy satiric edge, said, "Well, Gordon, that's too bad! If there'd been someone else there, you could prove that you hadn't——"

Josephine broke in. "Tell me just where the dollar was, Gordon," she said softly, and her voice had no relation to the look in her eyes as she glared at Charles.

"On the floor."

"But exactly where. Was it near the little girl's coat?"

"She isn't little."

"Was it near her coat?"

"I don't know which coat is hers."

"Was it near any coat?"

"It was on the floor, near all of them. They hang on a rack, and it was on the floor near them."

Josephine paused, and Gordon wriggled his shoulders out from under her arm and slumped in the corner of the sofa, away from her. "When can I get out of here?" he asked.

"When you start answering our questions," his father said sharply. "You insist that you didn't steal it?"

Gordon raised his lids slowly, as if they were very heavy, and stared out at his father from under his brows. "I found it on the floor."

Josephine spoke brightly. "Very well. We have settled that. But Gordon, surely you don't think that because you found it on the floor, it belonged to you? Don't you see that it was just as much stealing it as if you had really taken it from the pocket of the person it belonged to?"

"Not as much," Gordon said.

"But it wasn't *yours!* You knew that."

The boy nodded.

"Well, then——"

"Someone else would have found it!"

"But would someone else have kept it?"

"I didn't keep it."

Charles leaped up from his chair. "That's the point! Why in God's name did you give it to that Crow rat?"

"He's my friend," Gordon said with simple defiance, and then he slid off the sofa and lay on the floor.

"Your friend! A fine friend!" Charles shouted in disgust, standing over him. "Get up!"

Gordon did not make any effort to move, and Josephine grasped Charles's arm. "Let me," she said quietly. "Sit down."

"Nonsense!" he cried angrily at her, and pulled his arm free of her touch. "I'll take over now." He seized the boy by the shoulders and pulled him up on the sofa. The jerk which he gave his body made the boy's head bob back and forward like a doll's, and he slumped against the sofa back almost as if he had been injured, dull eyes staring out of his pale face. "Now listen to me, Gordon. I don't know if you took that money out of someone's pocket or not, but it looks, from the way you're behaving, as if you did. Anyway, you took it. It didn't belong to you, you knew that, and yet you took it. Do you see that there is no difference between the floor and the pocket as long as you kept it?"

"I didn't keep it," Gordon repeated, but almost listlessly. "Oh, my God!" Charles ran his hand through his hair, and the rumpled hair gave him a sudden wild look. "Listen," he said as quietly as he could, "we are all having a very hard time here. We are trying to live in a house that isn't fit to live in. I am trying to get used to a new office. Your mother——"

Josephine said, "Don't bother about me."

"I will bother! We are all having a tough time, and Gordon can't think of anything better to do than to get into this mess at school. Of all the friends you could pick, you pick that nasty Crow brat, who is too old for you by three years and is a snide little—"

"Charles!"

Gordon lay back in the sofa. He looked ill and defeated.

"Will you admit that you stole that dollar? That taking it from the floor was just as much stealing it as if you had taken it from the pocket?"

"Yes," he answered faintly.

"Speak up!"

"Yes, I *do!*" Gordon cried, and turned his face away.

Then the room was very still. Josephine stood stiffly beside the couch, her eyes fixed on Charles with dismay. Charles sagged a little, as if he, too, were defeated. And Gordon might have been asleep or dreaming, so remote had he suddenly become. Then they all heard a sly noise at the door, and Charles and Josephine swung toward it. Penelope stood there, embarrassed to have been caught. She giggled and said, "Why did Gordon steal money?"

"Go away," Charles said.

"Go to your room, dear," Josephine said, "or go outside."

"But why did Gordon steal money?"

Charles walked to the girl, gave her a little push, and closed the door on her face. Then he came back to the sofa. He sat down next to Gordon, and when he spoke, his voice was nearly lifeless. "You want to earn that dollar. All right, you can, Gordon. First go to your room and write your five sentences. Do them quickly for a change, and then go out into that patch of broom with the hedge shears and cut down all the vines you can find in it. You have an hour left before it gets dark."

Gordon's eyes dreamed over his father's face, and then he slowly got up and left the room. His parents watched him go, and when he had closed the door softly behind him, Charles broke out. "What is it, what stubbornness, that makes that boy so impenetrable? Did he steal that money or not? I haven't the slightest idea. All I could do was force him to admit that there was no difference between the two things."

Josephine was looking at him with studious appraisal.

"Well?" he challenged her.

"You forced his admission. Did that gain anything? And what did it lose? How much did it hurt him? Is it of very great importance whether he stole it or not?"

"I don't know what's more important."

"No, I really think you don't."

"Well?"

"What's more important is why he took it, and what he did with it, and why he did that. What's more important is that he's a miserable little boy, and that you haven't made the slightest effort to understand *that*. All you've done is played the heavy parent, shown him that you don't trust him or believe him, and left him with a nice new layer of solidified guilt, and what is he supposed to do with *that?*"

"Let's skip the psychology for a change," Charles said. "There is an old-fashioned principle of honesty and dishonesty."

"There's a more old-fashioned one of simple perception!" Josephine's face was red with anger. She stood in the middle of the bare room and looked rapidly around her, as if she felt a sudden desperate need, a hunger, for objects. But there was only the sofa, the chair, and Charles. Her eyes came back to him.

"Have you thought of his difficulties at all? Just the simple matter of his writing, for example? He came from a school where the children printed, and he printed as well as anyone. He comes here where the children do cursive writing, and of course he's made to feel like a fool, and he has to practice at home to learn it when other boys are playing. Or have you once helped him with that? Have you even suggested a sentence he might write? No. All you've done is given him the extremely comforting bit of information that new boys, especially if they enter school late, have a hard time making friends! The one friend he has made, you deride. No, don't interrupt. I know he's a horrid boy. I don't want Gordon playing with him either. But you haven't the sense to see that what has brought them together is that they are both pariahs. I think Gordon's giving that dollar to that dreadful boy is one of the most touching things I've ever heard of!"

"If what you've told me about Crow is true," Charles said quietly, "I won't have Gordon playing with him, and that's that."

"Because Crow taught him some nasty words and told him some nasty, mistaken things about sex? You're perfectly right. But you can't just stand there and say *no* to him! If you were half a father, you would have told him yourself. *You* should be his friend! You're the one who should be giving him a decent attitude toward those things. You *are* his father, after all."

"Oh, listen—He's not even nine!"

"All right. But he's getting it, isn't he? And all wrong?" And then, without warning, she sat down heavily on the single chair and began to sob, her reddened face lifted, her mouth twisted in sorrow, tears streaming down over her cheek. "All *wrong!*" she wailed.

Charles went to her quickly and, half standing, half kneeling beside the chair, awkwardly put his arms around her. "Josephine, listen——"

"Oh, I know!" she sobbed. "We all get in your way. We're all a nuisance that you're saddled with! We all just *bother* you. I know. It just isn't your idea of the way to live. You really *hate* it, don't you?"

His arms tightened. "Darling," he said, "don't be a damned fool. Listen, I love you, I love the kids. Why, little Penny, I——"

"Oh, yes. Penny, sure! She's tractable! She doesn't raise any problems. That's different!"

"You're crazy. Gordon, too. You. Maybe I'm not much good with him, but that doesn't mean—And listen—I'll try. I'll go out there now."

She dug in her pocket for a piece of kleenex. She blew her nose and wiped her eyes. She pulled the tea towel off her head and shook out her hair. Then she blew her nose again. "I'm all right now," she said, getting up. She picked up the dustcloth which she had flung over the back of the chair, and she said, "It's probably just this awful house, the way we have to camp. I'm going to get cleaned up and dress and I'm going to find a tablecloth, and we'll have dinner at a table tonight, instead of sitting on the floor with plates in our laps."

He said, "Good girl!" I'll go and fix it up with Gordon."

Charles went into Gordon's room. It was empty. He glanced at the table where Gordon worked and saw that there was a sheet of writing there. Then he looked out of the window and saw the boy on his hands and knees in among the remaining broom. He crossed the hall to the bedroom where Josephine was dressing. "I may not be very subtle with him, but I seem to get results," he said. She merely glanced up at him, and as he went out on the balcony, down the steps, and up the slippery incline, he felt no satisfaction whatever in his remark.

"How's it going?" he asked the boy.

Gordon glanced over his shoulder. "All right," he said, and turned at once to his job. The hedge shears made a busy, innocent sound.

Charles found his mattock where he had dropped it and began to chop at the edge of the overgrowth again. Immediately his nostrils filled with the poisonous smell he had noticed before, his hands began to chafe, and even though the heat of the sun had gone in the late afternoon, sweat broke out with a prickling sensation all over his face and body. Once more he was tense with irritation, and he said, "That awful smell! What is it?"

"I don't know," Gordon replied without looking up.

"Like something decaying."

The boy did not answer, and Charles chopped angrily away at a root. When it came free, he shook the earth off and tossed the slim tree down the slope. "This crazy, piddling stuff!" he shouted, and then reminded himself that it was only a kind of exaggerated weed, a thing that grew everywhere, so futile that it could not even send down a decent root, and was hardly designed as a personal affront to him. Or was it? He laughed and started to chop at the next root, but stopped at once. "I'm quitting for today," he said. "Come on, let's go in."

Gordon said, "No, I'll work a while. I want to earn the money."

"Oh, let it go. We'll fix that up."

Gordon stared at him. "I want to earn it," he said, and went on clipping at the rose vines.

"All right," Charles said, "but come in soon. You'll have to wash up thoroughly to get that muck off."

He went back into the house by way of the bedroom, but Josephine was no longer there. He went into Gordon's room, but she was not there, either. On the table lay the white sheet of ruled paper covered with the boy's writing, his five sentences in their hasty, uncertain, and very large cursive characters. Charles picked it up. The first sentence was, "I am going to cut vins." The second was, "I am going to ern mony." The third was, "The sun is shining." The fourth was, "When it rains here it rains hard." The last, which seemed to have been written with greater care, with a kind of precision and flourish which his writing had never shown before, was, "You hate me and I hate you."

Charles took a sharp breath and held it, then sagged. After a moment he walked to the window and put his forehead against the cool glass. He stared out into the desolate garden, at the bare earth and the darkening tangle, and tried to think. When he heard Josephine moving on high heels somewhere in the rugless house, he began to fold the sheet of paper, and he folded it again and again, until it was a small hard square. This he stuffed deep into his pocket.

He came into the hall and saw Josephine standing in the center of the barren living room. She looked tall in an old but still handsome black housecoat, a straight, severe garment which hung from the tightly belted waist in heavy folds and was without ornament or color anywhere. Her hair was pulled tautly away from her face, and her face was smooth and white, and her mouth was painted dark red.

She was detached from the room, from the house, and utterly from him—remote and beautiful, cold in a resolution. Never in the ten years he had known her had she appeared so wonderfully in possession of herself. And helplessly, his scheme irrelevant, absurd, Charles turned away.

He went into the boy's room again, and looked out to see the boy. But twilight obscured the garden now, shadows hung about it like veils, and Charles could hardly see into the trees. Then he thought he saw the boy's shape, hunched on the ground among the slim trunks; and he went quickly out to find him. Perhaps, even now, after everything, it was the boy who, somehow, could help.

Muriel Resnik

Excerpted from Muriel Resnik's autobiographical *Life without Father*, this account depicts an urban progressive school where a teacher, a kindergartner, and a beleaguered mother wrestle with a theory that is at odds with circumstances. Prepossessions are allowed to obscure what would otherwise be obvious truths. At least two questions are raised here: Whatever became of the educator's candid respect for common sense? And how many quandaries might we elude simply by paying them no obeisance?

Muriel Resnik is also the author of two plays, *Any Wednesday* and *The Unnatural State*.

A SLIGHT CASE OF ADJUSTMENT

In the fall of 1943 I moved with my two small sons from a tiny fishing village in Connecticut to midtown New York. I anticipated long, happy days shopping for clothes, absorbing culture, and exploring the city, while my offspring were constructively occupied at a good school, returning to me at the end of the day newly able to share their toys and ready for a night of unbroken sleep.

Before we moved I conscientiously investigated several schools, finally choosing the one I felt to be properly sympathetic with my ideas on child training—which had been formed by studying the works of a master of a certain psychological school of thought on the subject.

Mike, the older boy, was then five years old, with a wistful face that belied his strong will. Hank, at three, was quite rotund and solemn, his owl-like quality accentuated by spectacles worn soiled and askew at the tip of his button nose. He was to enter the advanced nursery group. Mike was found to be eligible for the kindergarten. Advanced nursery, by the way, differed from primary nursery in that its members were expected to stand by themselves and "remain dry" a good part of the time. The school hours were the same for both boys, nine until three, with hot lunch, nap, and afternoon milk included.

The first day of school was brilliantly sunny and comfortably crisp. The park foliage was golden, the sky free of clouds, and a brisk little wind blew us along the street. The schoolhouse was five stories high, limestone outside, marble inside. Great double doors of brass and iron and glass clanged behind us and we entered the hall rather timidly. The shrill voices of children greeting each other after the long holiday, the wailing of the little ones, the scolding, soothing mother voices, the pot-pourri aroma of chalk dust and soap, furniture polish and Lysol, woolens and vegetable soup, the dankness of the mausoleum-like marble walls and floor, produced in me that long forgotten first-day-of-school sinking in the pit of the stomach. My sons hung on my hands, clasping them convulsively.

I had been told by the billowing chatelaine of the establishment to be prepared to "stay with them" for a short time the first day. It was a difficult time for all of them, she told me, but particularly for mine. She impressed upon me the grave dangers of the move from our established home to a new environment so completely different, and added that this plus a new school and routine might result in great fears and insecurities. I felt like the next of kin who has authorized an operation that is 90 per cent fatal.

We climbed the winding marble stairs and found Mike's room at the top. It was a large room with a fireplace, wide windows overlooking a garden, and a clean bare floor. Against the walls were open shelves filled with a variety of fascinating toys. A blackboard covered one wall, original drawings were tacked on the others, and small chairs stood in friendly groups around the low tables. The kindergarten students were busy hanging up jackets, donning smocks, and looting the shelves with a grim single-mindedness. Mike dropped my hand, grabbed his smock, and with a hurried "g'by" to us, wrested a large steam shovel from a bewildered child seated flat on the floor with legs straight out before him. "See?" said Mike, manipulating the shovel.

Mike's teacher told us that Hank's group had gone to the roof, so we stepped into the little elevator and rode haltingly to the top. We emerged from the darkness of the hall into the brilliant sunlight. The floor of this playground was covered with gravel and the entire area was enclosed in chicken wire like a large cage. Two of the group sat solidly on tiny chairs. Three were crying on their mother's laps. One small individualist was busily engaged in throwing pebbles onto the street below, aiming at passers-by.

Hank's teacher, a pleasant young woman who asked us to call her Joan, suggested that she tell a story. We drew our little chairs and stools into a circle around her. Joan was a spellbinding storyteller. In a short time the three mothers were able to slip away, unnoticed by their off-spring. I unfolded slowly, only to have a small hand dart out to grab my skirt. I caught Joan's eye. She shook her head at me and smiled at Hank. "Mother's here just as long as you want her," she cooed. "Now you just listen to the rest of the story." I settled myself as comfortably as possible on my little stool, staring at the fresh run in my stocking. My back was beginning to ache.

After what seemed to me an interminable time, we all went downstairs to the classroom. Here Hank obligingly draped himself in his little blue smock, smoothed it over his round front and sat down in a small chair, gesturing me into the one next to him. I glanced hopefully at Joan. "That's right," she smiled, "Mommy will sit next to Hank. Isn't that nice?" I looked at my watch. It was ten-thirty. I sat down.

The group sang a little morning song. The group did a little dance of falling leaves. The group beat out a little rhythm on drums, cymbals, a tambourine, and a triangle. Then the group spread themselves around with great sheets of paper and pots of finger-paints. During all this activity Hank and I sat quietly in our chairs. When the mid-morning juice was served he roused from his torpor for a moment. I rose only to be stopped by the tug on my skirt. I sat down, shifting restlessly from haunch to haunch. My legs were numb, my stocking was ruined, New York was waiting. Finally I raised my hand. "Joan, I've got to go home," I said. "I have so much to do. I can't stay here any longer."

"All right," she said smoothingly, "you go home now, Mother, and Hank will stay with us—"

Hank rose.

"—and have lots to tell you when you call for him this afternoon—"

Hank hurled his smock to the floor and reached for my hand.

"No?"

Hank had reached the door, dragging me with him.

"Perhaps tomorrow then. We'll see." Joan waved and laughed unconcernedly. "Byeeee. See you tomorrow."

We trudged down the marble steps and strolled out into the street. A week later Joan suggested that perhaps if I showed an interest in the group activities.

Two weeks later I knew all the songs, had developed a definite flair for fingerpaints, had made an excellent adjustment to the group, cooperated well with my classmates, always shared my toys, and was by far the most graceful falling leaf. My son observed me with delight as he sat still as a little Buddha.

We went to school each morning and stayed until lunchtime. (That was as long as *I* was willing to stay.) We went directly back to our apartment where we had lunch and a brief rest period. Then we walked to the park where I perched restlessly on the working end of a seesaw.

My dreams of renewed culture were necessarily in abeyance, and I was uncomfortable when seated more than ten inches off the floor. I intimated to Joan that perhaps there might be another method of handling the problem. She murmured something vague about adjustment periods and how some took longer than others and The Move . . . but on my insistence she agreed that I could leave my child in the morning with the promise that if he were "unhappy" the school would call me and I would hasten to retrieve him.

I explained the new system to Hank. "Now that you're accustomed to school," I said, "beginning Monday I will leave you there in the morning and I will come home."

He dropped to the floor like a wounded bird and turned blue.

"If you are not happy at school," I continued rapidly, "Joan will call me on the telephone and I will come back for you. But you will be happy. Your group has such fun."

He released his breath slowly. His expression was thoughtful.

As soon as the big doors closed behind them that Monday morning I skipped lightheartedly down the street, loitering in front of shop windows to scrutinize their contents. I did some marketing, browsed my way through the neighborhood rental library for something to occupy my newly found leisure, and went home humming happily. As I put my key in the door I heard the phone ringing. I crossed the room slowly and picked it up. It was Joan. I think it was Joan. I could barely hear her voice over Hank's roars of grief and indignation.

"All right, all right," I said. "I'll be right there. Tell him I'll be right there."

When I arrived at the school Hank was seated comfortably in the reception room. He seemed calm enough. As soon as he saw me he slid off his chair and took my hand, pulling toward the door. The teacher on duty smiled understandingly. "He was unhappy," she said, "so we thought . . ."

I nodded.

We went home, had lunch and rest period, and again I found myself in the park, bouncing viciously on the seesaw while Hank sat stolidly across from me. This became the pattern of my days. I would leave the boys at school each morning and, returning home, would find my phone ringing. I then retraced my steps to the school, exchanged a few bitter quips with the teacher guarding Hank, and took him home.

It was well on to November when I succeeded in cornering Joan. I suggested that it was up to her ingenuity to find some way to keep this child happily at school. We had made no progress, since, contrary to her expectations but not to mine. Hank refused to increase his waiting period. The duration of his school day was still approximately one half-hour.

Joan and I finally agreed to hold an after-hours conference.

Three days later we met at school in a small office. Joan assured me that Hank was everything charming, bright, unusual, and endearing, and I agreed, wondering how she knew anything of the child, having spent so little time with him.

I leaned back in my chair studying the dust on the files and the sweet potato growing rampant in the window, wondering about dinner . . . could anything attractive be done with leftover boiled cabbage? . . . listening absently to Joan weave her way in and out of the facts. The move, uprooting . . . young plants . . . tender care and nurturing . . . slowly. . . . The little room was warm and the late afternoon sun beat upon my head. I was fighting to keep my eyes open when I realized that she was waiting for me to reply to something she had just said about Stamford.

"Stamford," I repeated fuzzily.

Joan looked at me archly. "Hank has told me all about it, Mrs. Resnik."

"About what?"

"About the Stamford incident."

I straightened. "I'm sorry. I don't think I understand."

"I do feel quite certain," she continued after a moment, "that careful treatment will gradually eradicate the memory of the Stamford thing and that Hank will regain his feeling of security and faith in you."

I giggled nervously. "But what *are* you talking about? What Stamford—?"

"Mrs. Resnik." She leaned toward me and patted my knee. "My dear, Hank has told me everything. Everything. That you took him to Stamford and left him there promising to return for him, then you didn't and he became so very frightened. You see, his behavior pattern now is the result of your error at that time. Wherever you take him now and attempt to leave him, he will fight you, for he becomes frightened and does not believe that you will come back for him. Now if you will just—"

"Joan, this is incredible," I interrupted. "Hank has never been to Stamford. He's never been there. Hank has *never been* to Stamford."

Her eyes were accusing, fixed on mine.

"I've never gotten off the Parkway . . . we go right past it. I don't know anyone in Stamford." I could feel the warmth rising over my neck and my face was burning. I knew that I looked guilty. She continued to gaze at me with that "out of the mouths of babes" look. I felt even warmer. "But Joan," I faltered. Her expression was sympathetic, even kind, and disappointed. I knew she would never believe me. I stopped and waited for the blush to fade, studying the toe of my right shoe.

"This is not irrevocable," Joan remarked. "You have done harm, thoughtlessly perhaps, but we will be able to repair the damage. You must believe me, however, that the way back is a slow one. We will create a new behavior pattern. You *must* return to the school for him again and again and again until the child feels, eventually, that his faith in his parent is well-founded and he finds security once more. Until he *knows* that if you tell him you will return for him that you will be here. Therefore, that anything you say you will do, you will do, and that anything you say is so, *is* so."

I could hear someone running down a flight of steps with a great echoing clatter. A door opened, a snatch of song burst out, to be hushed when the door swung heavily to. I raised my eyes from my shoe to Joan. "How long"—I cleared my throat. "Excuse me. How long do you think this will take?"

"I really couldn't say. Maybe a month, two months, three"—she waved her hand expansively—"maybe right till the very end of the year."

I swallowed.

"But even if it does take right up to the very last school day, it will be a year well spent," she added enthusiastically, "if we accomplish nothing else. How much more important it is for a youngster to re-establish his faith in his parent than to become proficient in finger-painting or blocks . . . hummm?"

I returned her smile weakly. I thanked her and walked home slowly, thinking. When I closed the door quietly behind me I could hear Mike's voice in the boys' bedroom being very definite about something with the middle-aged sitter I had hired for the occasion. I hung up my coat and rubbed my numbed hands together. Hank came shuffling into the room, redolent of Johnson and Johnson, cheeks scarlet, light blue bathrobe belted tight across his fat middle, stepping on the feet of his dun-colored sleepers. He stopped dead and peered at me, gauging my mood. I studied his bland face. He whipped his glasses out of his bathrobe pocket, placed them atilt on the end of his nose, and stared up at me. I sat down in a large chair.

"Come here," I said.

He approached me willingly enough and leaned upon my knee, head on hand, fat cheeks pushed out of shape.

"You told Joan I took you to Stamford and left you there."

A small smile played fleetingly with the corners of his mouth.

"Hank, how could you? You know very well you've never been to Stamford. And when did I ever break my word to you? Never."

He remained immobile.

"What ever made you say such a thing?" I waited for his answer. His lips were sealed but there was a gleam in the back of his eyes.

"All right," I said, finally. "It was not nice of you to tell Joan something that wasn't true. Not nice at all. You embarrassed me, but that's beside the point. It wasn't true and you know it and I know it."

He leaned harder.

"Now you listen to me. I am going to take you to school on Monday and leave you there. And I am not coming home. I will not be here if the telephone rings. It can ring and ring and ring and ring, but I will not be here to answer it."

He looked deep into my eyes.

"But I will come to school in the afternoon and bring you home when I bring Mike home and when all the other mothers and nurses bring the children home. It won't do you any good to say that you're unhappy, because I won't be around to *bring* you *home*."

He tried to stare me down but I refused to lower my eyes. He pulled himself erect with a sigh and stumbled into his room.

We spent a quiet weekend with no mention of the new routine. Monday morning I took my sons to school, fled back to my apartment. I jammed my key in the lock, burst inside, slammed the door, and leaned against it. There was no sound but the pounding of my heart. I sat down and waited. The phone didn't ring.

That afternoon when I called for the children at school I was quiet, relaxed, and content. I had spent the entire day window-shopping Madison Avenue.

Joan smiled at me over the heads of her class. She pushed toward me and whispered, "It worked."

I looked at her, startled.

"I told you," she said, "if you'd only be patient . . . and it happened much sooner than I had expected. Remember I told you it might take months? I am really amazed. Really. No trouble at all this morning. He seemed to be quite happy all day. Not terribly active, but happy." She put her arm around my shoulders. "Happy in his security, Mommy. His faith in you has been restored."

I smiled enigmatically and reached for Hank's hand. He placed it trustingly in mine.

Part Seven

The Rites
of Adolescence

*Far more often is it that in adolescence we experience
the stultifications we associate with old age.*

Malcolm Lowry

The American adolescent is to some an invention of the times, to others a necessity of nature. Whatever his origins, he has accepted over the past thirty years the homage of ceaseless observation. He has borne this scrutiny conservatively, for his best aspirations are now no less sublime than before, his outrages no less predictable, his contempt for the rubrics of his elders no less versatile. Deified, excoriated, and shunned by disparate groups within the adult world, the adolescent controls a sizable portion of the gross national product, an unwitting investor in the adult establishment he may officially deplore. He is both the victim and the guardian of fad. He is selfless. He is boorish. He can own an unself-conscious integrity that finds a miniature truth and names it, while his elders befog a larger truth and shirk it.

If adolescence, as psychologists would have it, is the roiled time between puberty and adulthood, then it would seem that this period has undergone progressive extension. A quarter-century ago, adolescence was considered coeval with the teen years, a time ample for the *finding* of oneself. A decade ago, this time of search had lengthened to include the post-high school years: one's early twenties became the time for founding an identity. Today, the period of quest spans the post-college years, the late twenties of life. Conceivably, in another decade, with longevity aided by sophisticated medicine, the adolescent could forgo to the now untrusted age of thirty-five his debut into self-admitted adulthood, Roughshod reasons have been advanced for this progressive delay, but the one most handy exploits the complexity of our civilization: choices must be pondered longer in an intricate age; options are too fateful and too numerous; annihilatory hints are everywhere; doubt is the lonely certitude; and, after all, the era bewilders even those who have long since staked their mortal claims to vocation, matrimony, and political allegiance.

Another explanation issues smoothly from the foregoing assumptions, namely that a society unnervingly complex requires of its people an education equally intricate and long termed. But lamentably the intricate often becomes the inane when the school curriculum balloons to affect a relevance to the motley of claims laid on it by commerce, politics, various reforms, and pedagogical fashions of the day. A question persists: Does such "pluralism" result in bright diversity or in a chaos of aims that is unintelligible to the public at large and unclear even to the schoolmen who fashion them?

Implicit in our dedication to Relevance and Intricacy is a grotesque analogy that we seem unable to refute—the comparison of a desperate race with the life of man. A voracity for facile accomplishment, for automated sensations, for painless victories consumes our days. Even the children are contaminated.

Consider the not so humorous irony of language which lurks in the Latin meaning for the word *curriculum*. To the Romans a curriculum was a racecourse, not a mild term of pedagogy. But it could be wryly argued that the old meaning still lives in current usage. The youngster in elementary school is urged to develop study skills, not for the intrinsic benefits of knowledge but as preparation for high school, the next lap of the race. In turn, the high school student learns to view his own classes as a mere prelude to college. And the freshman adolescent respectfully inquires of his biology professor, "What must I do to get through your course?" Our freshman already anticipates his vocational race, or his military stint, or his tenure in VISTA or the Peace Corps, or dilatory travel, for which the college curriculum seems, at best, inchoate training. Must the race wear on, lap after dutiful lap?

However harried and intricate the milieu of the adolescent, it fosters behaviors and ambitions that are legible, actually patterned, and not new. Though somewhat different in execution, the rites of today's adolescents, considering all forms of worship and all priests held in favor, are remarkably akin to the rites of past generations. Youth's touted "revolution" in manners and aspirations pleads originality; but measured by the long arc of human motives (even adolescent motives) this novelty shrinks to imitation, to an unwitting mimicry. These recurrences of motive are witnessed in the writings of Willa Cather, Arthur Koestler, and Malcolm Cowley, whose scenes of adolescence derive from their own generations yet strike to the heart of today's attitudes. No condescension lurks in our recognition of such recurrences. Every generation imitates. Proper questions ask about the kind of imitation pursued, for what real motives, and by how many converts.

The writers assembled in Part Seven are not agents of an adult conspiracy; nor are they sentimentalists in the thrall of youth cults. They write of experience, not of sociologisms, and their cumulative point of view is not content with its own authority. Like so many writers before them (like Turgenev, Mark Twain, Shakespeare, Henry James, Jane Austen, James Joyce, and André Gide), they write about the *audacity* peculiar to adolescence and the *intrepidity* essential to adulthood.

The audacity of adolescence suspects import of everything, despairs of every human flaw, and demands that all things be possible. The intrepidity of adulthood has a rangy valor that seethes in the worst of times, refutes despair and capricious hope, learns of limits and the freedoms found therein, and is not resigned. Both attributes spring from conviction, not from circumstance. There is wonder in both certitudes.

Malcolm Cowley
(1898–   )

In one sense nostalgia is the memory of remembrance. When it is not betrayed by sentimentality, our nostalgia chooses memories that enable us to identify large meanings in the minutiae of former experience. For example, in the poem "Ars Poetica," Archibald MacLeish summons "all the history of grief" by confronting us with "an empty doorway and a maple leaf," an image that excites an order, a relation between separated events, so that a vaster appreciation can be grasped.

Malcolm Cowley, in similar fashion, describes in "Blue Juniata" and "Big-Town High School" the factual and emotional territories of his youth in Pennsylvania: landscapes of long autumns, pine squirrels, urban Pittsburgh, and a well-equipped high school; then, the inner landscapes of flamboyant idealism, preciosity, derivative cynicism, and hope. Like Henry Adams, Cowley measures his education graphically, with the seasons, smells, camaraderies, and rivalries that prevailed.

The following chapters are taken from *Exile's Return*, Cowley's account of the expatriate movement in American arts and letters during the post-World War I years. Revealing a nostalgia that is tender but uncloyed, the author extracts from ephemeral scenes some enduring habits of adolescence: the status seeking, the menageries of class, the "bashful veneration for everything illicit," and the protests more publicized today but no more fiercely felt than then.

Translator, editor, poet, and critic, Malcolm Cowley is known chiefly for *Exile's Return* (1934), for the editing of an influential book of Faulkner's writing, *The Portable Faulkner* (1946), for an account of American writing during the 1950s entitled *The Literary Situation* (1954), and for his *Collected Poems* (1968).

BLUE JUNIATA

Somewhere the turn of a dirt road or the unexpected crest of a hill reveals your own childhood, the fields where you once played barefoot, the kindly trees, the landscape by which all others are measured and condemned. Here, under the hemlocks, is a spring. Follow the thread of water as it winds downward, first among moss, then lost in sweetfern or briers, and soon you will see the bottom lands, the scattered comfortable houses, the flat cornfields along the creek, the hillside pastures where the whitetop bends in alternate waves of cream white and leaf green. The Schoharie Valley in August . . . or perhaps what we find is an Appalachian parade of mountains rank on rank: the first ridge is a shadowy green, the second a deep blue; the ridges behind it grow fainter and fainter, till the last is indistinguishable from the long cloud advancing to hide and drench the mountains, flood the parallel creeks, and set the millwheels turning in the hollows and coves. Or perhaps— our childhoods differ—we are on a low bluff overlooking the Cumberland. Northward into Kentucky, south into middle Tennessee, the river lands continue with their bluffs, their bottoms, their red-clay gullies, their cedars dotting the hillsides like totem poles. It is November: smoke rises from lonely tobacco barns; a hound bays from the fields where corn stands yellow in the shock.

Perhaps our boyhood is a stream in northern Michigan, Big Two-Hearted River, flowing through burned-over lands dotted with islands of pine into a tamarack swamp. The water is swift and chill in July; a trout lurks in a hollow log, ready to take the grasshopper floating toward him at the end of your line. Perhaps we remember a fat farm in Wisconsin, or a Nebraska prairie, or a plantation house among the canebrakes. Wherever it lies, the country is our own; its people speak our language, recognize our values, yes, and our grandmother's eyes, our uncle's trick of pausing in a discussion to make a point impressive. "The Hopkinses was alluz an arguin' family," they say, and suddenly you laugh with a feeling of tension relaxed and pretenses vanished. This is your home . . . but does it exist outside your memory? On reaching the hilltop or the bend in the road, will you find the people gone, the landscape altered, the hemlock trees cut down and only stumps, dried tree-tops, branches and fireweed where the woods had been? Or, if the country remains the same, will you find yourself so changed and uprooted that it refuses to take you back, to reincorporate you into its common life? No matter: the country of our childhood survives, if only in our minds, and retains

our loyalty even when casting us into exile; we carry its image from city
to city as our most essential baggage:

> Wanderers outside the gates, in hollow
> landscapes without memory, we carry
> each of us an urn of native soil,
> of not impalpable dust a double handful
>
> anciently gathered—was it garden mold
> or wood soil fresh with hemlock needles, pine
> and princess pine, this little earth we bore
> in silence, blindly, over the frontier?
> —a parcel of the soil not wide enough
> or firm enough to build a dwelling on,
> or deep enough to dig a grave, but cool
> and sweet enough to sink the nostrils in
> and find the smell of home, or in the ears,
> rumors of home, like oceans in a shell.

BIG-TOWN HIGH SCHOOL

I was born in a farmhouse near Belsano, in Cambria County, Pennsylvania, on the western slope of the Alleghenies. All my summers were
spent there, and sometimes the long autumns too—fishing, shooting
cottontails and pine squirrels, or simply wandering through the woods
by myself; I thought of Belsano as my home. But my father was a doctor
in Pittsburgh and I attended a big-town high school.

It must have been like two hundred other high schools west of the
mountains. It was new, it was well equipped, it was average in size,
having in those days about a thousand pupils. In retrospect it seems that
all sorts of people went there—I can remember the daughter of a mil-
lionaire coal operator, a future All-American halfback, a handsome
Italian who later became a big-time mobster, a tall, serious and stupid
Negro boy, two girls who wore cotton-print dresses all year round and
whom we suspected of being sewed into their winter underwear—but
the atmosphere of the school was prosperous and middle class. Everyone
was friendly. There were, on the other hand, all sorts of separate crowds,
the football crowd, the social crowd, the second-best social crowd, and
the literary crowd composed of boys who made good marks in English

Composition, read books that weren't assigned for reading, were shy, noisy, ill dressed and helped to edit the school magazine.

That of course was the crowd to which I belonged—with Kenneth Burke and Jimmy Light (who later became a theatrical director), Russell Farrell (the valedictorian of the class, who changed his mind and didn't become a priest), Jake Davis and three or four others. In the high schools west of the mountains there must have been, at that time, scores of these groups of adolescent writers. Let us see what we were like at seventeen.

I suppose we had all the normal aberrations of our age and type. We were wholly self-centered, absorbed in our own personalities, and appalled by the thought that these would some day be obliterated. We brooded often on death, often on slights to our timid vanity. We yearned: pimpled and awkward we yearned for someone to accept our caresses, be conquered by our cleverness, our real distinction, our reserves of feeling hidden from the world. We dreamed of escape, into European cities with crooked streets, into Eastern islands where the breasts of the women were small and firm as inverted teacups. We felt a bashful veneration for everything illicit, whether it was the prostitute living in the next block or the crimes of Nero or the bottle of blackberry cordial we passed from hand to hand on Sunday afternoons. We felt that we were different from other boys: we admired and hated these happy ones, these people competent for every situation, who drove their fathers' cars and led the cheers at football games and never wrote poems or questioned themselves.

Symptoms much like these have recurred in the adolescence of writers for at least two centuries; they could probably be traced much farther into the past. But we had other symptoms too, more characteristic of our time and nation.

Thus, we felt a certain humility in the face of life, a disinclination to make demands on the world about us. Art and life were two realms; art was looked down upon by the ordinary public, the "lifelings," and justly so, since it could never have any effect on them. Art was uncommercial, almost secret, and we hoped to become artists. That was our own concern. An artist, a poet, should not advertise his profession by his clothes, should not wear a black cloak or flowing tie or let his hair grow over his collar. The artist had a world of his own: his ambitions in the real world should be humble. One of my friends confided to me that he wanted to earn seven thousand dollars a year and go to a symphony concert every week: I thought he showed presumption. Another friend, like Somerset Maugham's hero in *Of Human Bondage*, wanted to be a ship's doctor and visit strange ports; another would be satisfied to enter his father's business. For my part I was determined to be the dramatic critic of a newspaper, metropolitan or provincial: I should earn about three thousand dollars a year and have a mistress. Meanwhile I should be writing; all my friends would be writing—but about what?

Every new generation has its own sentimentality, its symbols that move it to compassion or self-compassion. For early Romantic writers beginning with Byron, the favorite symbol was the Haunted Castle— inaccessible, lonely, dwelled in by a young aristocrat of fabulous lineage, a Manfred seeking absolution for an inner sense of guilt, but wholly contemptuous of human-kind. For the socially minded writers who followed Ibsen, the stock situation was that of the misunderstood reformer, the Enemy of the People, who tries to help his neighbors and is crucified for his good intentions. The situation of the artist frustrated by society has been popular with the late Romantics. All these symbols seemed foreign to ourselves, even slightly ridiculous. Our sensibilities were touched by older situations—girls mourning their lost lovers, men crippled in battle, death, the longing for home, prostitutes weeping at songs about marriage and babies. . . . Those were the themes we should normally have employed, but our sensibility, at that point, was checked by our ideas.

In describing the ideas I run the danger of making them seem too reasoned and definite. Essentially they were not ideas at all: they were attitudes or emotions, persistently but vaguely felt and often existing only in germ. They are important because they help to explain what followed —because, after a period of imitation and before a period of change, they reappeared in what we wrote, and because what we felt at seventeen is an explanation and criticism of what we should later believe.

At seventeen we were disillusioned and weary. In the midst of basketball, puppy love and discussions of life—washed down with chocolate sodas on warm afternoons—we had come to question almost everything we were taught at home and in school. Religion—we had argued about it so much, Catholics against agnostics against Lutherans against Christian Scientists, that we were all converted to indifferentism. Morality, which we identified with chasteness, was a lie told to our bodies. Our studies were useless or misdirected, especially our studies in English Literature: the authors we were forced to read, and Shakespeare most of all, were unpleasant to our palate; they had the taste of chlorinated water.

We were still too immature to understand the doctrine of complete despair about the modern world that would later be advanced by the followers of T. S. Eliot (before their reconciliation with the Church), but we shared in the mood that lay behind them. During the brief moments we devoted to the fate of mankind in general, we suffered from a sense of oppression. We felt that the world was rigorously controlled by scientific laws of which we had no grasp, that our lives were directed by Puritan standards that were not our own, that society in general was terribly secure, unexciting, middle class, a vast reflection of the families from which we came. Society obeyed the impersonal law of progress. Cities expanded relentlessly year by year; fortunes grew larger; more and more automobiles appeared in the streets; people were wiser and better than their ancestors—eventually, by automatic stages, we should reach an intolerable utopia of dull citizens, without crime or suffering or drama. The progression, of course, might be reversed. The period in which we were living might prove to resemble Rome under the Five Good Emperors; it might be followed by upheavals, catastrophes, a general decline. But the decay of society was psychologically equivalent to its progress: both were automatic processes that we ourselves could neither hasten nor retard. Society was something alien, which our own lives and writings could never affect: it was a sort of parlor car in which we rode, over smooth tracks, toward a destination we should never have chosen for ourselves.

Literature, our profession, was living in the shadow of its own great past. The symbols that moved us, the great themes of love and death and parting, had been used and exhausted. Where could we find new themes when everything, so it seemed, had been said already? Having devoured the world, literature was dying for lack of nourishment. Nothing was left to ourselves—nothing except to deal with marginal experiences and abnormal cases, or else to say the old things over again with a clever and apologetic twist of our own. Nothing remained except the minor note. . . . And so, having adopted it humbly, we contributed artificial little pieces to the high-school paper, in which vice triumphed over virtue, but discreetly, so as not to be censored by the faculty adviser.

We were launching or drifting into the sea of letters with no fixed destination and without a pilot. To whom could we turn for advice? The few authors we admired were separated from us either by time or else just as effectively by space and language. Among the American writers of the day there were several who had produced a good book or two good books. Except for Howells, whom we regarded as one of our enemies (if we regarded him at all), and Henry James, whom we did not read (and who lived in exile), not one of them had achieved a career. There seemed to be no writer with our own background. There was no one who spoke directly to our youth, no one for us to follow with a single heart, no one, even, against whom we could intelligently and fruitfully rebel.

Yet we read tirelessly, hour after hour; we were engaged in a desperate search for guidance. We read English authors at first, Kipling and Stevenson, then Meredith, Hardy and Gissing. In *The Private Papers of Henry Ryecroft* we found an opinion with which we agreed completely. "I have never learned to regard myself," Gissing said, "as a 'member of society.' For me there have always been two entities—myself and the world—and the normal relation between the two has been hostile."

Forgetting the hostile world, we continued our searching. We read Conrad; we read Wilde and Shaw, who were always mentioned together. From one or the other of these dramatists—or perhaps from Mencken and Nathan, then editors of *Smart Set*—we derived the sense of paradox, which became a standard for judging the writers we afterward encountered. If they were paradoxical—if they turned platitudes upside down, showed the damage wrought by virtue, made heroes of their villains—then they were "moderns"; they deserved our respect. Congreve, we learned, was a modern. Ibsen was modern also, but we were a little repelled by his symbolism and not aroused by his social message; we read him dutifully, self-consciously. Strindberg was more exciting, and we plunged into Schnitzler's early plays as if we were exploring forbidden countries in which we hoped to dwell. Reading, we imagined boys in other cities, beneath the green lamps of public libraries, scheming like ourselves to get hold of the books "not to be issued to minors," and being introduced into a special world of epigrams and *süsse Mädl*, where love affairs were taken for granted and everyone had the sense of paradox.

For us, paradox reduced itself to the simplest terms: it was the ability to say what was not expected, to fool one's audience. If, during a thunder shower, another boy looked out the classroom window and said, "It isn't raining, is it?" expecting us to answer "no," we would say "yes." By so doing, we were giving what we called a First Convolution answer.

The theory of convolutions was evolved in Pittsburgh, at Peabody High School, but it might have appeared in any city during those years before the war. It was generally explained by reference to the game of Odd or Even. You have held an even number of beans or grains of corn in your hand; you have won; therefore you take an even number again. That is the simplest argument by analogy; it is no convolution at all. But if you say to yourself, "I had an even number before and won; my opponent will expect me to have an even number again; therefore I'll take an odd number," you have entered the First Convolution. If you say, "Since I won with an even number before, my opponent will expect me to try to fool him by having an odd number this time; therefore I'll be even," you are Second Convolution. The process seems capable of indefinite extension; it can be applied, moreover, to any form of art, so long as one is less interested in what one says than in one's ability to outwit an audience. We were not conscious of having anything special to say; we wanted merely to live in ourselves and be writers.

There is, however, a practical limit to the series of convolutions. If it leads at one moment to reading Oscar Wilde because other high-school pupils have never heard of him, it leads at the next to disparaging Wilde because you admired him once and because First Convolution people still admire him. You have entered the Second Convolution: you read Schnitzler and "go beyond him" without ever understanding what he has to say. In this manner we passed through a whole series of enthusiasms—Mencken, Huneker, Somerset Maugham, Laforgue (after we learned French)—till we encountered Dostoevski, who didn't fit into our scheme, and Flaubert, whose patience overawed us.

The sense of paradox ends by having nothing left to feed upon; eventually it is self-devouring. The desire to surprise or deceive leads often to a final deception—which consists in being exactly like everybody else. This was the stage that several of us had reached by our eighteenth year. We dressed like everybody else; we talked about girls, automobiles and the World's Series. Petting was not yet fashionable: it was called "loving up" and was permitted only by unattractive girls who had to offer special inducements; but there were dances and we attended them; we rooted for the basketball team; we engaged in all the common activities (and were sorry when the time came to leave them behind). We were like others, we were normal—yet we clung to the feeling that as apprentice writers we were abnormal and secretly distinguished: we lived in the special world of art; we belonged to the freemasonry of those who had read modern authors and admired a paradox.

It was during the first years of the European war. In New York the House of Morgan was busy making loans; in Washington the President was revising his ideas of neutrality: already it was written that several million young Americans would be called from their homes, fed by the government and taught to be irresponsible heroes. In Detroit Henry Ford had begun to manufacture I don't know how many thousand or million identical motors per day or year. Greenwich Village, crowded with foreign artists, was beginning to develop new standards of living. Young women all over the country were reading Freud and attempting to lose their inhibitions. Einstein was studying in Berlin, Proust was writing in Paris, and Joyce, having lost his job as a tutor in Trieste, was in Switzerland, working sixteen hours a day on *Ulysses*. The Socialist parties of the world were supporting the war and entering cabinets of national defense, but the Russian front buckled and crumbled; Lenin from his exile was calculating the moment for a Communist revolution. All the divergent forces that would direct the history of our generation were already in action. Meanwhile, in Boston, Pittsburgh, Nashville, Chicago, we boys of seventeen and eighteen were enormously ignorant of what was going on in the world. We were reading, dancing, preparing for college-entrance examinations and, in our spare time, arguing about ourselves, ourselves and life, ourselves as artists, as lovers, the sublimation of sex and what we could possibly write about that was new.

Willa Cather
(1873–1947)

The case-history story, in which a psychiatric problem becomes the star of the piece, is a literary blight too often spread by writers who care more for the celebration of a vogue psychosis than for its victims. But "Paul's Case" is no such story; the afflicted boy, not his affliction, remains the center of interest. The story is a model, a classic portrayal of the dropout.

The special claim of literature is its authority to plumb deeply the interiors of character. In contrast to the methods used by school counselors, teachers, and circuit-riding district psychologists (methods dependent on the subject's *external* signs of speech, gesture, action, and case history), the writer's techniques of omniscient point of view, interior monologue, symbol, and imagery deliver internal evidence of the character's psyche—an intimate history that cannot be equaled by the most scrupulous of factual measurements.

Willa Cather was herself a teacher in two Pittsburgh high schools between 1901 and 1906. She had previously worked as telegraph editor and drama critic for the Pittsburgh *Daily Leader*. Her major work consists of a book of stories *The Troll Garden* (1905), and four novels: *O Pioneers!* (1913), *My Àntonia* (1918), *The Professor's House* (1925), and *Death Comes for the Archbishop* (1927).

PAUL'S CASE

It was Paul's afternoon to appear before the faculty of the Pittsburgh High School to account for his various misdemeanors. He had been suspended a week ago, and his father had called at the Principal's office and confessed his perplexity about his son. Paul entered the faculty room suave and smiling. His clothes were a trifle out-grown, and the tan velvet on the collar of his open overcoat was frayed and worn; but for all that there was something of the dandy about him, and he wore an opal pin in his neatly knotted black four-in-hand, and a red carnation in his button-hole. This latter adornment the faculty somehow felt was not properly significant of the contrite spirit befitting a boy under the ban of suspension.

Paul was tall for his age and very thin, with high-cramped shoulders and a narrow chest. His eyes were remarkable for a certain hysterical brilliancy, and he continually used them in a conscious, theatrical sort of way, peculiarly offensive in a boy. The pupils were abnormally large, as though he were addicted to belladonna, but there was a glassy glitter about them which that drug does not produce.

When questioned by the Principal as to why he was there, Paul stated, politely enough, that he wanted to come back to school. This was a lie, but Paul was quite accustomed to lying; found it, indeed, indispensable for overcoming friction. His teachers were asked to state their respective charges against him, which they did with such a rancor and aggrievedness as evinced that this was not a usual case. Disorder and impertinence were among the offences named, yet each of his instructors felt that it was scarcely possible to put into words the real cause of the trouble, which lay in a sort of hysterically defiant manner of the boy's; in the contempt which they all knew he felt for them, and which he seemingly made not the least effort to conceal. Once, when he had been making a synopsis of a paragraph at the blackboard, his English teacher had stepped to his side and attempted to guide his hand. Paul had started back with a shudder and thrust his hands violently behind him. The astonished woman could scarcely have been more hurt and embarrassed had he struck at her. The insult was so involuntary and definitely personal as to be unforgettable. In one way and another, he had made all his teachers, men and women alike, conscious of the same feeling of physical aversion. In one class he habitually sat with his hand shading his eyes; in another he always looked out of the window during the recitation; in another he made a running commentary on the lecture, with humorous intent.

His teachers felt this afternoon that his whole attitude was symbolized by his shrug and his flippantly red carnation flower, and they fell upon him without mercy, his English teacher leading the pack. He stood through it smiling, his pale lips parted over his white teeth. (His lips were continually twitching, and he had a habit of raising his eyebrows that was contemptuous and irritating to the last degree.) Older boys than Paul had broken down and shed tears under that ordeal, but his set smile did not once desert him, and his only sign of discomfort was the nervous trembling of the fingers that toyed with the buttons of his overcoat, and an occasional jerking of the other hand which held his hat. Paul was always smiling, always glancing about him, seeming to feel that people might be watching him and trying to detect something. This conscious expression, since it was as far as possible from boyish mirthfulness, was usually attributed to insolence or "smartness."

As the inquisition proceeded, one of his instructors repeated an impertinent remark of the boy's, and the Principal asked him whether he thought that a courteous speech to make to a woman. Paul shrugged his shoulders slightly and his eyebrows twitched.

"I don't know," he replied. "I didn't mean to be polite or impolite, either. I guess it's a sort of way I have of saying things regardless."

The Principal asked him whether he didn't think that a way it would be well to get rid of. Paul grinned and said he guessed so. When he was told that he could go, he bowed gracefully and went out. His bow was like a repetition of the scandalous red carnation.

His teachers were in despair, and his drawing master voiced the feeling of them all when he declared there was something about the boy which none of them understood. He added: "I don't really believe that smile of his comes altogether from insolence; there's something sort of haunted about it. The boy is not strong, for one thing. There is something wrong about the fellow."

The drawing master had come to realize that, in looking at Paul, one saw only his white teeth and the forced animation of his eyes. One warm afternoon the boy had gone to sleep at his drawing-board, and his master had noted with amazement what a white, blue-veined face it was; drawn and wrinkled like an old man's about the eyes, the lips twitching even in his sleep.

His teachers left the building dissatisfied and unhappy; humiliated to have felt so vindictive toward a mere boy, to have uttered this feeling in cutting terms, and to have set each other on, as it were, in the gruesome game of intemperate reproach. One of them remembered having seen a miserable street cat set at bay by a ring of tormentors.

As for Paul, he ran down the hill whistling the Soldiers' Chorus from *Faust*, looking wildly behind him now and then to see whether some of his teachers were not there to witness his light-heartedness. As it was now late in the afternoon and Paul was on duty that evening as usher at Carnegie Hall, he decided that he would not go home to supper.

When he reached the concert hall the doors were not yet open. It was chilly outside, and he decided to go up into the picture gallery—always deserted at this hour—where there were some of Raffelli's gay studies of Paris streets and an airy blue Venetian scene or two that always exhilarated him. He was delighted to find no one in the gallery but the old guard, who sat in the corner, a newspaper on his knee, a black patch over one eye and the other closed. Paul possessed himself of the place and walked confidently up and down, whistling under his breath. After a while he sat down before a blue Rico and lost himself. When he bethought him to look at his watch, it was after seven o'clock, and he rose with a start and ran downstairs, making a face at Augustus Cæsar, peering out from the cast-room, and an evil gesture at the Venus of Milo as he passed her on the stairway.

When Paul reached the ushers' dressing-room half a dozen boys were there already, and he began excitedly to tumble into his uniform. It was one of the few that at all approached fitting, and Paul thought it very becoming—though he knew the tight, straight coat accentuated his narrow chest, about which he was exceedingly sensitive. He was always excited when he dressed, twanging all over to the tuning of the strings and the preliminary flourishes of the horns in the music room; but tonight he seemed quite beside himself, and he teased and plagued the boys until, telling him that he was crazy, they put him down on the floor and sat on him.

Somewhat calmed by his suppression, Paul dashed out to the front of the house to seat the early comers. He was a model usher. Gracious and smiling he ran up and down the aisles. Nothing was too much trouble for him; he carried messages and brought programs as though it were his greatest pleasure in life, and all the people in his section thought him a charming boy, feeling that he remembered and admired them. As the house filled, he grew more and more vivacious and animated, and the color came to his cheeks and lips. It was very much as though this were a great reception and Paul were the host. Just as the musicians came to take their places, his English teacher arrived with checks for the seats which a prominent manufacturer had taken for the season. She betrayed some embarrassment when she handed Paul the tickets, and a *hauteur* which subsequently made her feel very foolish. Paul was startled for a moment, and had the feeling of wanting to put her out; what business had she here among all these fine people and gay colors? He looked her over and decided that she was not appropriately dressed and must be a fool to sit downstairs in such togs. The tickets had probably been sent her out of kindness, he reflected, as he put down a seat for her, and she had about as much right to sit there as he had.

When the symphony began Paul sank into one of the rear seats with a long sigh of relief, and lost himself as he had done before the Rico. It was not that symphonies, as such, meant anything in particular to Paul, but the first sigh of the instruments seemed to free some hilarious spirit within him; something that struggled there like the Genius in the bottle found by the Arab fisherman. He felt a sudden zest of life; the lights danced before his eyes and the concert hall blazed into unimaginable splendor. When the soprano soloist came on, Paul forgot even the nastiness of his teacher's being there, and gave himself up to the peculiar intoxication such personages always had for him. The soloist chanced to be a German woman, by no means in her first youth, and the mother of many children; but she wore a satin gown and a tiara, and she had that indefinable air of achievement, that world-shine upon her, which always blinded Paul to any possible defects.

After a concert was over, Paul was often irritable and wretched until he got to sleep—and tonight he was even more than usually restless. He had the feeling of not being able to let down; of its being impossible to give up this delicious excitement which was the only thing that could be called living at all. During the last number he withdrew and, after hastily changing his clothes in the dressing-room, slipped out to the side door where the singer's carriage stood. Here he began pacing rapidly up and down the walk, waiting to see her come out.

Over yonder the Schenley, in its vacant stretch, loomed big and square through the fine rain, the windows of its twelve stories glowing like those of a lighted cardboard house under a Christmas tree. All the actors and singers of any importance stayed there when they were in the city, and a number of the big manufacturers of the place lived there in the winter. Paul had often hung about the hotel, watching the people go in and out, longing to enter and leave school-masters and dull care behind him forever.

At last the singer came out, accompanied by the conductor, who helped her into her carriage and closed the door with a cordial *auf wiedersehen*—which set Paul to wondering whether she were not an old sweetheart of his. Paul followed the carriage over to the hotel, walking so rapidly as not to be far from the entrance when the singer alighted and disappeared behind the swinging glass doors which were opened by a negro in a tall hat and a long coat. In the moment that the door was ajar, it seemed to Paul that he, too, entered. He seemed to feel himself go after her up the steps, into the warm, lighted building, into an exotic, a tropical world of shiny, glistening surfaces and basking ease. He reflected upon the mysterious dishes that were brought into the dining-room, the green bottles in buckets of ice, as he had seen them in the supper party pictures of the Sunday supplement. A quick gust of wind brought the rain down with sudden vehemence, and Paul was startled to find that he was still outside in the slush of the gravel driveway; that his boots were letting in the water and his scanty overcoat was clinging wet about him; that the lights in front of the concert hall were out, and that the rain was driving in sheets between him and the orange glow of the windows above him. There it was, what he wanted—tangibly before him like the fairy world of a Christmas pantomime; as the rain beat in his face, Paul wondered whether he were destined always to shiver in the black night outside, looking up at it.

He turned and walked reluctantly toward the car tracks. The end had to come some time; his father in his night clothes at the top of the stairs, explanations that did not explain, hastily improvised fictions that were forever tripping him up, his upstairs room and its horrible yellow wallpaper, the creaking bureau with the greasy plush collar-box, and over his painted wooden bed the pictures of George Washington and John Calvin, and the framed motto, "Feed my Lambs," which had been worked in red worsted by his mother, whom Paul could not remember.

Half an hour later Paul alighted from the Negley Avenue car and went slowly down one of the side streets off the main thoroughfare. It was a highly respectable street, where all the houses were exactly alike, and where businessmen of moderate means begot and reared large families of children, all of whom went to Sabbath school and learned the shorter catechism, and were interested in arithmetic; all of whom were as exactly alike as their homes, and of a piece with the monotony in which they lived. Paul never went up Cordelia Street without a shudder of loathing. His home was next the house of the Cumberland minister. He approached it tonight with the nerveless sense of defeat, the hopeless feeling of sinking back forever into ugliness and commonness that he had always had when he came home. The moment he turned into Cordelia Street he felt the waters close above his head. After each of these orgies of living, he experienced all the physical depression which follows a debauch; the loathing of respectable beds, of common food, of a house permeated by kitchen odors; a shuddering repulsion for the flavorless, colorless mass of everyday existence; a morbid desire for cool things and soft lights and fresh flowers.

The nearer he approached the house, the more absolutely unequal Paul felt to the sight of it all; his ugly sleeping chamber; the cold bathroom with the grimy zinc tub, the cracked mirror, the dripping spigots; his father, at the top of the stairs, his hairy legs sticking out from his night-shirt, his feet thrust into carpet slippers. He was so much later than usual that there would certainly be inquiries and reproaches. Paul stopped short before the door. He felt that he could not be accosted by his father tonight; that he could not toss again on that miserable bed. He would not go in. He would tell his father that he had no car fare, and it was raining so hard he had gone home with one of the boys and stayed all night.

Meanwhile, he was wet and cold. He went around to the back of the house and tried one of the basement windows, found it open, raised it cautiously, and scrambled down the cellar wall to the floor. There he stood, holding his breath, terrified by the noise he had made; but the floor above him was silent, and there was no creak on the stairs. He found a soap-box, and carried it over to the soft ring of light that streamed from the furnace door, and sat down. He was horribly afraid of rats, so he did not try to sleep, but sat looking distrustfully at the dark, still terrified lest he might have awakened his father. In such reactions, after one of the experiences which made days and nights out of the dreary blanks of the calendar, when his senses were deadened, Paul's head was always singularly clear. Suppose his father had heard him getting in at the window and had come down and shot him for a burglar? Then, again, suppose his father had come down, pistol in hand, and he had cried out in time to save himself, and his father had been horrified to think how nearly he had killed him? Then, again, suppose a day should come when his father would remember that night, and wish there had been no warning cry to stay his hand? With this last supposition Paul entertained himself until daybreak.

The following Sunday was fine; the sodden November chill was broken by the last flash of autumnal summer. In the morning Paul had to go to church and Sabbath-school, as always. On seasonable Sunday afternoons the burghers of Cordelia Street usually sat out on their front "stoops," and talked to their neighbors on the next stoop, or called to those across the street in neighborly fashion. The men sat placidly on gay cushions placed upon the steps that led down to the sidewalk, while the women, in their Sunday "waists," sat in rockers on the cramped porches, pretending to be greatly at their ease. The children played in the streets; there were so many of them that the place resembled the recreation grounds of a kindergarten. The men on the steps—all in their shirt sleeves, their vests unbuttoned—sat with their legs well apart, their stomachs comfortably protruding, and talked of the prices of things, or told anecdotes of the sagacity of their various chiefs and over-lords. They occasionally looked over the multitude of squabbling children, listened affectionately to their high-pitched, nasal voices, smiling to see their own proclivities reproduced in their offspring, and interspersed their legends of the iron kings with remarks about their sons' progress at school, their grades in arithmetic, and the amounts they had saved in their toy banks.

On this last Sunday of November, Paul sat all the afternoon on the lowest step of his "stoop," staring into the street, while his sisters, in their rockers, were talking to the minister's daughters next door about how many shirtwaists they had made in the last week, and how many waffles some one had eaten at the last church supper. When the weather was warm, and his father was in a particularly jovial frame of mind, the girls made lemonade, which was always brought out in a red-glass pitcher, ornamented with forget-me-nots in blue enamel. This the girls thought very fine, and the neighbors joked about the suspicious colour of the pitcher.

Today Paul's father, on the top step, was talking to a young man who shifted a restless baby from knee to knee. He happened to be the young man who was daily held up to Paul as a model, and after whom it was his father's dearest hope that he would pattern. This young man was of a ruddy complexion, with a compressed, red mouth, and faded, near-sighted eyes, over which he wore thick spectacles, with gold bows that curved about his ears. He was clerk to one of the magnates of a great steel corporation, and was looked upon in Cordelia Street as a young man with a future. There was a story that, some five years ago—he was now barely twenty-six—he had been a trifle "dissipated," but in order to curb his appetites and save the loss of time and strength that a sowing of wild oats might have entailed, he had taken his chief's advice, oft reiterated to his employees, and at twenty-one had married the first woman whom he could persuade to share his fortunes. She happened to be an angular schoolmistress, much older than he, who also wore thick glasses, and who had now borne him four children, all near-sighted, like herself.

The young man was relating how his chief, now cruising in the Mediterranean, kept in touch with all the details of the business, arranging his office hours on his yacht just as though he were at home, and "knocking off work enough to keep two stenographers busy." His father told, in turn, the plan his corporation was considering, of putting in an electric railway plant at Cairo. Paul snapped his teeth; he had an awful apprehension that they might spoil it all before he got there. Yet he rather liked to hear these legends of the iron kings, that were told and retold on Sundays and holidays; these stories of palaces in Venice, yachts on the Mediterranean, and high play at Monte Carlo appealed to his fancy, and he was interested in the triumphs of cash boys who had become famous, though he had no mind for the cash-boy stage.

After supper was over, and he had helped to dry the dishes, Paul nervously asked his father whether he could go to George's to get some help in his geometry, and still more nervously asked for car fare. This latter request he had to repeat, as his father, on principle, did not like to hear requests for money, whether much or little. He asked Paul whether he could not go to some boy who lived nearer, and told him that he ought not to leave his school work until Sunday; but he gave him the dime. He was not a poor man, but he had a worthy ambition to come up in the world. His only reason for allowing Paul to usher was that he thought a boy ought to be earning a little.

Paul bounded upstairs, scrubbed the greasy odor of the dish-water from his hands with the ill-smelling soap he hated, and then shook over his fingers a few drops of violet water from the bottle he kept hidden in his drawer. He left the house with his geometry conspicuously under his arm, and the moment he got out of Cordelia Street and boarded a downtown car, he shook off the lethargy of two deadening days, and began to live again.

The leading juvenile of the permanent stock company which played at one of the downtown theatres was an acquaintance of Paul's, and the boy had been invited to drop in at the Sunday night rehearsals whenever he could. For more than a year Paul had spent every available moment loitering about Charley Edwards's dressing-room. He had won a place among Edwards's following not only because the young actor, who could not afford to employ a dresser, often found him useful, but because he recognized in Paul something akin to what churchmen term "vocation."

It was at the theatre and at Carnegie Hall that Paul really lived; the rest was but a sleep and a forgetting. This was Paul's fairy tale, and it had for him all the allurement of a secret love. The moment he inhaled the gassy, painty, dusty odor behind the scenes, he breathed like a prisoner set free, and felt within him the possibility of doing or saying splendid, brilliant things. The moment the cracked orchestra beat out the overture from *Martha*, or jerked at the serenade from *Rigoletto*, all stupid and ugly things slid from him, and his senses were deliciously, yet delicately fired.

Perhaps it was because, in Paul's world, the natural nearly always wore the guise of ugliness, that a certain element of artificiality seemed to him necessary in beauty. Perhaps it was because his experience of life elsewhere was so full of Sabbath-school picnics, petty economies, wholesome advice as to how to succeed in life, and the unescapable odors of cooking, that he found this existence so alluring, these smartly clad men and women so attractive, that he was so moved by these starry apple orchards that bloomed perennially under the limelight.

It would be difficult to put it strongly enough how convincingly the stage entrance of that theatre was for Paul the actual portal of Romance. Certainly none of the company ever suspected it, least of all Charley Edwards. It was very like the old stories that used to float about London of fabulously rich Jews, who had subterranean halls, with palms, and fountains, and soft lamps and richly apparelled women who never saw the disenchanting light of London day. So, in the midst of that smoke-palled city, enamoured of figures and grimy toil, Paul had his secret temple, his wishing-carpet, his bit of blue-and-white Mediterranean shore bathed in perpetual sunshine.

Several of Paul's teachers had a theory that his imagination had been perverted by garish fiction; but the truth was, he scarcely ever read at all. The books at home were not such as would either tempt or corrupt a youthful mind, and as for reading the novels that some of his friends urged upon him—well, he got what he wanted much more quickly from music; any sort of music, from an orchestra to a barrel organ. He needed only the spark, the indescribable thrill that made his imagination master of his senses, and he could make plots and pictures enough of his own. It was equally true that he was not stage-struck—not, at any rate, in the usual acceptation of that expression. He had no desire to become an actor, any more than he had to become a musician. He felt no necessity to do any of these things; what he wanted was to see, to be in the atmosphere, float on the wave of it, to be carried out, blue league after blue league, away from everything.

After a night behind the scenes, Paul found the school-room more than ever repulsive; the hard floors and naked walls; the prosy men who never wore frock coats, or violets in their buttonholes; the women with their dull gowns, shrill voices, and pitiful seriousness about prepositions that govern the dative. He could not bear to have the other pupils think, for a moment, that he took these people seriously; he must convey to them that he considered it all trivial, and was there only by way of a joke, anyway. He had autographed pictures of all the members of the stock company, which he showed his classmates, telling them the most incredible stories of his familiarity with these people, of his acquaintance with the soloists who came to Carnegie Hall, his suppers with them and the flowers he sent them. When these stories lost their effect, and his audience grew listless, he would bid all the boys good-bye, announcing that he was going to travel for a while, going to Naples, to California, to Egypt. Then, next Monday, he would slip back, conscious and nervously smiling; his sister was ill, and he would have to defer his voyage until spring.

Matters went steadily worse with Paul at school. In the itch to let his instructors know how heartily he despised them, and how thoroughly he was appreciated elsewhere, he mentioned once or twice that he had no time to fool with theorems, adding—with a twitch of the eyebrows and a touch of that nervous bravado which so perplexed them—that he was helping the people down at the stock company; they were old friends of his.

The upshot of the matter was that the Principal went to Paul's father, and Paul was taken out of school and put to work. The manager at Carnegie Hall was told to get another usher in his stead; the door-keeper at the theatre was warned not to admit him to the house; and Charley Edwards remorsefully promised the boy's father not to see him again.

The members of the stock company were vastly amused when some of Paul's stories reached them—especially the women. They were hard-working women, most of them supporting indolent husbands or brothers, and they laughed rather bitterly at having stirred the boy to such fervid and florid inventions. They agreed with the faculty and with his father, that Paul's was a bad case.

The east-bound train was ploughing through a January snow-storm; the dull dawn was beginning to show gray when the engine whistled a mile out of Newark. Paul started up from the seat where he had lain curled in uneasy slumber, rubbed the breath-misted window glass with his hand, and peered out. The snow was whirling in curling eddies above the white bottom lands, and the drifts lay already deep in the fields and along the fences, while here and there the long dead grass and dried weed stalks protruded black above it. Lights shone from the scattered houses, and a gang of laborers who stood beside the track waved their lanterns.

Paul had slept very little, and he felt grimy and uncomfortable. He had made the all-night journey in a day coach because he was afraid if he took a Pullman he might be seen by some Pittsburgh businessman who had noticed him in Denny & Carson's office. When the whistle woke him, he clutched quickly at his breast pocket, glancing about him with an uncertain smile. But the little, clay-bespattered Italians were still sleeping, the slatternly women across the aisle were in open-mouthed oblivion, and even the crumby, crying babies were for the nonce stilled. Paul settled back to struggle with his impatience as best he could.

When he arrived at the Jersey City Station, he hurried through his breakfast, manifestly ill at ease and keeping a sharp eye about him. After he reached the Twenty-third Street Station, he consulted a cabman, and had himself driven to a men's furnishing establishment which was just opening for the day. He spent upward of two hours there, buying with endless reconsidering and great care. His new street suit he put on in the fitting-room; the frock coat and dress clothes he had bundled into the cab with his new shirts. Then he drove to a hatter's and a shoe house. His next errand was at Tiffany's, where he selected silver-mounted brushes and a scarf-pin. He would not wait to have his silver marked, he said. Lastly, he stopped at a trunk shop on Broadway, and had his purchases packed into various travelling bags.

It was a little after one o'clock when he drove up to the Waldorf, and, after settling with the cabman, went into the office. He registered from Washington, said his mother and father had been abroad, and that he had come down to await the arrival of their steamer. He told his story plausibly and had no trouble, since he offered to pay for them in advance, in engaging his rooms: a sleep-room, sitting-room and bath.

Not once, but a hundred times Paul had planned his entry into New York. He had gone over every detail of it with Charley Edwards, and in his scrap-book at home there were pages of description about New York hotels, cut from the Sunday papers.

When he was shown to his sitting-room on the eighth floor, he saw at a glance that everything was as it should be; there was but one detail in his mental picture that the place did not realize, so he rang for the bell boy and sent him down for flowers. He moved about nervously until the boy returned, putting away his new linen and fingering it delightedly as he did so. When the flowers came, he put them hastily into water, and then tumbled into a hot bath. Presently he came out of his white bath-room, resplendent in his new silk underwear, and playing with the tassels of his red robe. The snow was whirling so fiercely outside his windows that he could scarcely see across the street; but within, the air was deliciously soft and fragrant. He put the violets and jonquils on the taboret beside the couch, and threw himself down with a long sigh, covering himself with a Roman blanket. He was thoroughly tired; he had been in such haste, he had stood up to such a strain, covered so much ground in the last twenty-four hours, that he wanted to think how it had all come about. Lulled by the sound of the wind, the warm air, and the cool fragrance of the flowers, he sank into deep, drowsy retrospection.

It had been wonderfully simple; when they had shut him out of the theatre and concert hall, when they had taken away his bone, the whole thing was virtually determined. The rest was a mere matter of opportunity. The only thing that at all surprised him was his own courage— for he realized well enough that he had always been tormented by fear, a sort of apprehensive dread that, of late years, as the meshes of the lies he had told closed about him, had been pulling the muscles of his body tighter and tighter. Until now, he could not remember a time when he had not been dreading something. Even when he was a little boy, it was always there—behind him, or before, or on either side. There had always been the shadowed corner, the dark place into which he dared not look, but from which something seemed always to be watching him—and Paul had done things that were not pretty to watch, he knew.

But now he had a curious sense of relief, as though he had at last thrown down the gauntlet to the thing in the corner.

Yet it was but a day since he had been sulking in the traces; but yesterday afternoon that he had been sent to the bank with Denny & Carson's deposit as usual—but this time he was instructed to leave the book to be balanced. There was above two thousand dollars in checks, and nearly a thousand in the bank notes which he had taken from the book and quietly transferred to his pocket. At the bank he had made out a new deposit slip. His nerves had been steady enough to permit of his returning to the office, where he had finished his work and asked for a full day's holiday tomorrow, Saturday, giving a perfectly reasonable pretext. The bank book, he knew, would not be returned before Monday or Tuesday, and his father would be out of town for the next week. From the time he slipped the bank notes into his pocket until he boarded the night train for New York, he had not known a moment's hesitation.

How astonishingly easy it had all been; here he was, the thing done; and this time there would be no awakening, no figure at the top of the stairs. He watched the snow flakes whirling by his window until he fell asleep.

When he awoke, it was four o'clock in the afternoon. He bounded up with a start; one of his precious days gone already! He spent nearly an hour in dressing, watching every stage of his toilet carefully in the mirror. Everything was quite perfect; he was exactly the kind of boy he had always wanted to be.

When he went downstairs, Paul took a carriage and drove up Fifth Avenue toward the Park. The snow had somewhat abated; carriages and tradesmen's wagons were hurrying soundlessly to and fro in the winter twilight; boys in woollen mufflers were shovelling off the doorsteps; the avenue stages made fine spots of color against the white street. Here and there on the corners were stands, with whole flower gardens blooming behind glass windows, against which the snow flakes stuck and melted; violets, roses, carnations, lilies of the valley—somehow vastly more lovely and alluring that they blossomed thus unnaturally in the snow. The Park itself was a wonderful stage winter-piece.

When he returned, the pause of the twilight had ceased, and the tune of the streets had changed. The snow was falling faster, lights streamed from the hotels that reared their many stories fearlessly up into the storm, defying the raging Atlantic winds. A long, black stream of carriages poured down the avenue, intersected here and there by other streams, tending horizontally. There were a score of cabs about the entrance of his hotel, and his driver had to wait. Boys in livery were running in and out of the awning stretched across the sidewalk, up and down the red velvet carpet laid from the door to the street. Above, about, within it all, was the rumble and roar, the hurry and toss of thousands of human beings as hot for pleasure as himself, and on every side of him towered the glaring affirmation of the omnipotence of wealth.

The boy set his teeth and drew his shoulders together in a spasm of realization; the plot of all dramas, the text of all romances, the nerve-stuff of all sensations were whirling about him like the snow flakes. He burnt like a faggot in a tempest.

When Paul came down to dinner, the music of the orchestra floated up the elevator shaft to greet him. As he stepped into the thronged corridor, he sank back into one of the chairs against the wall to get his breath. The lights, the chatter, the perfumes, the bewildering medley of color—he had, for a moment, the feeling of not being able to stand it. But only for a moment; these were his own people, he told himself. He went slowly about the corridors through the writing-rooms, smoking-rooms, reception-rooms, as though he were exploring the chambers of an enchanted palace, built and peopled for him alone.

When he reached the dining-room he sat down at a table near a window. The flowers, the white linen, the many-colored wine glasses, the gay toilettes of the women, the low popping of corks, the undulating repetitions of the *Blue Danube* from the orchestra, all flooded Paul's dream with bewildering radiance. When the roseate tinge of his champagne was added—that cold, precious bubbling stuff that creamed and foamed in his glass—Paul wondered that there were honest men in the world at all. This was what all the world was fighting for, he reflected; this was what all the struggle was about. He doubted the reality of his past. Had he ever known a place called Cordelia Street, a place where fagged-looking businessmen boarded the early car? Mere rivets in a machine they seemed to Paul,—sickening men, with combings of children's hair always hanging to their coats, and the smell of cooking in their clothes. Cordelia Street—Ah, that belonged to another time and country! Had he not always been thus, had he not sat here night after night, from as far back as he could remember, looking pensively over just such shimmering textures, and slowly twirling the stem of a glass like this one between his thumb and middle finger? He rather thought he had.

He was not in the least abashed or lonely. He had no especial desire to meet or to know any of these people; all he demanded was the right to look on and conjecture, to watch the pageant. The mere stage properties were all he contended for. Nor was he lonely later in the evening, in his loge at the Opera. He was entirely rid of his nervous misgivings, of his forced aggressiveness, of the imperative desire to show himself different from his surroundings. He felt now that his surroundings explained him. Nobody questioned his purple; he had only to wear it passively. He had only to glance down at his dress coat to reassure himself that here it would be impossible for any one to humiliate him.

He found it hard to leave his beautiful sitting-room to go to bed that night, and sat long watching the raging storm from his turret window. When he went to sleep, it was with the lights turned on in his bedroom, partly because of his old timidity, and partly so that, if he should wake in the night, there would be no wretched moment of doubt, no horrible suspicion of yellow wall-paper, or of Washington and Calvin above his bed.

On Sunday morning the city was practically snow-bound. Paul breakfasted late, and in the afternoon he fell in with a wild San Francisco boy, a freshman at Yale, who said he had run down for a "little flyer" over Sunday. The young man offered to show Paul the night side of the town, and the two boys went off together after dinner, not returning to the hotel until seven o'clock the next morning. They had started out in the confiding warmth of a champagne friendship, but their parting in the elevator was singularly cool. The freshman pulled himself together to make his train, and Paul went to bed. He awoke at two o'clock in the afternoon, very thirsty and dizzy, and rang for ice-water, coffee, and the Pittsburgh papers.

On the part of the hotel management, Paul excited no suspicion. There was this to be said for him, that he wore his spoils with dignity and in no way made himself conspicuous. His chief greediness lay in his ears and eyes, and his excesses were not offensive ones. His dearest pleasures were the gray winter twilights in his sitting-room, his quiet enjoyment of his flowers, his clothes, his wide divan, his cigarette and his sense of power. He could not remember a time when he had felt so at peace with himself. The mere release from the necessity of petty lying, lying every day and every day, restored his self-respect. He had never lied for pleasure, even at school; but to make himself noticed and admired, to assert his difference from other Cordelia Street boys; and he felt a good deal more manly, more honest, even, now that he had no need for boastful pretensions, now that he could, as his actor friends used to say, "dress the part." It was characteristic that remorse did not occur to him. His golden days went by without a shadow, and he made each as perfect as he could.

On the eighth day after his arrival in New York, he found the whole affair exploited in the Pittsburgh papers, exploited with a wealth of detail which indicated that local news of a sensational nature was at a low ebb. The firm of Denny & Carson announced that the boy's father had refunded the full amount of his theft, and that they had no intention of prosecuting. The Cumberland minister had been interviewed, and expressed his hope of yet reclaiming the motherless lad, and Paul's Sabbath-school teacher declared that she would spare no effort to that end. The rumor had reached Pittsburgh that the boy had been seen in a New York hotel, and his father had gone East to find him and bring him home.

Paul had just come in to dress for dinner; he sank into a chair, weak in the knees, and clasped his head in his hands. It was to be worse than jail, even; the tepid waters of Cordelia Street were to close over him finally and forever. The gray monotony stretched before him in hopeless, unrelieved years; Sabbath school, Young People's Meeting, the yellow-papered room, the damp dish-towels; it all rushed back upon him with sickening vividness. He had the old feeling that the orchestra had suddenly stopped, the sinking sensation that the play was over. The sweat broke out on his face, and he sprang to his feet, looked about him with his white, conscious smile, and winked at himself in the mirror. With something of the childish belief in miracles with which he had so often gone to class, all his lessons unlearned, Paul dressed and dashed whistling down the corridor to the elevator.

He had no sooner entered the dining-room and caught the measure of the music than his remembrance was lightened by his old elastic power of claiming the moment, mounting with it, and finding it all sufficient. The glare and glitter about him, the mere scenic accessories had again, and for the last time, their old potency. He would show himself that he was game, he would finish the thing splendidly. He doubted, more than ever, the existence of Cordelia Street, and for the first time he drank his wine recklessly. Was he not, after all, one of these fortunate beings? Was he not still himself, and in his own place? He drummed a nervous accompaniment to the music and looked about him, telling himself over and over that it had paid.

He reflected drowsily, to the swell of the violin and the chill sweetness of his wine, that he might have done it more wisely. He might have caught an outbound steamer and been well out of their clutches before now. But the other side of the world had seemed too far away and too uncertain then; he could not have waited for it; his need had been too sharp. If he had to choose over again, he would do the same thing tomorrow. He looked affectionately about the dining-room, now gilded with a soft mist. Ah, it had paid indeed!

Paul was awakened next morning by a painful throbbing in his head and feet. He had thrown himself across the bed without undressing, and had slept with his shoes on. His limbs and hands were lead-heavy, and his tongue and throat were parched. There came upon him one of those fateful attacks of clear-headedness that never occurred except when he was physically exhausted and his nerves hung loose. He lay still and closed his eyes and let the tide of realities wash over him.

His father was in New York; "stopping at some joint or other," he told himself. The memory of successive summers on the front stoop fell upon him like a weight of black water. He had not a hundred dollars left; and he knew now, more than ever, that money was everything, the wall that stood between all he loathed and all he wanted. The thing was winding itself up; he had thought of that on his first glorious day in New York, and had even provided a way to snap the thread. It lay on his dressing-table now; he had got it out last night when he came blindly up from dinner,—but the shiny metal hurt his eyes, and he disliked the look of it, anyway.

He rose and moved about with a painful effort, succumbing now and again to attacks of nausea. It was the old depression exaggerated; all the world had become Cordelia Street. Yet somehow he was not afraid of anything, was absolutely calm; perhaps because he had looked into the dark corner at last, and knew. It was bad enough, what he saw there; but somehow not so bad as his long fear of it had been. He saw everything clearly now. He had a feeling that he had made the best of it, that he had lived the sort of life he was meant to live, and for half an hour he sat staring at the revolver. But he told himself that was not the way, so he went downstairs and took a cab to the ferry.

When Paul arrived at Newark, he got off the train and took another cab, directing the driver to follow the Pennsylvania tracks out of the town. The snow lay heavy on the roadways and had drifted deep in the open fields. Only here and there the dead grass or dried weed stalks projected, singularly black, above it. Once well into the country, Paul dismissed the carriage and walked, floundering along the tracks, his mind a medley of irrelevant things. He seem to hold in his brain an actual picture of everything he had seen that morning. He remembered every feature of both his drivers, the toothless old woman from whom he had bought the red flowers in his coat, the agent from whom he had got his ticket, and all of his fellow-passengers on the ferry. His mind, unable to cope with vital matters near at hand, worked feverishly and deftly at sorting and grouping these images. They made for him a part of the ugliness of the world, of the ache in his head, and the bitter burning on his tongue. He stooped and put a handful of snow into his mouth as he walked, but that, too, seemed hot. When he reached a little hillside, where the tracks ran through a cut some twenty feet below him, he stopped and sat down.

The carnations in his coat were drooping with the cold, he noticed; all their red glory over. It occurred to him that all the flowers he had seen in the show windows that first night must have gone the same way, long before this. It was only one splendid breath they had, in spite of their brave mockery at the winter outside the glass. It was a losing game in the end, it seemed, this revolt against the homilies by which the world is run. Paul took one of the blossoms carefully from his coat and scooped a little hole in the snow, where he covered it up. Then he dozed a while, from his weak condition, seeming insensible to the cold.

The sound of an approaching train woke him, and he started to his feet, remembering only his resolution, and afraid lest he should be too late. He stood watching the approaching locomotive, his teeth chattering, his lips drawn away from them in a frightened smile; once or twice he glanced nervously sidewise, as though he were being watched. When the right moment came, he jumped. As he fell, the folly of his haste occurred to him with merciless clearness, the vastness of what he had left undone. There flashed through his brain, clearer than ever before, the blue of Adriatic water, the yellow of Algerian sands.

He felt something strike his chest,—his body was being thrown swiftly through the air, on and on, immeasurably far and fast, while his limbs gently relaxed. Then, because the picture-making mechanism was crushed, the disturbing visions flashed into black, and Paul dropped back into the immense design of things.

Arthur Koestler

(1905–   )

This excerpt from Arthur Koestler's autobiography *Arrow in the Blue* (1952) treats adolescent experiences that are at once conventional and grotesque. Though absolutely his own, the solemn crotchets here described may snag the memory as reminders of one's own youth.

Writing with a terseness that permits a latitude of implication, Koestler defines a ritual that isolates adults from their own adolescence: "We are not only disloyal to others, but also to our own past. The *gauche* adolescent, the foolish young man that one has been, appears so grotesque in retrospect and so detached from one's own identity that one automatically treats him with amused derision. It is a callous betrayal, yet one cannot help being a traitor to one's past."

Hungarian by birth, but an ex-soldier and correspondent in the French and British armies, Arthur Koestler is the author of *Spanish Testament* (1937) and the widely read novel *Darkness at Noon* (1941), which chronicles the ironic effects of revolution; later works include *Insight and Outlook* (1949) and *The Lotos and the Robot* (1960).

PORTRAIT OF THE AUTHOR
AT SIXTEEN

I emerged from childhood an exasperating and pathetic figure. Almost the whole of my adolescence is painful to remember. For a period of two or three years, Cyril Connolly's remark about his youth was equally true of mine: "I have always disliked myself at any given moment; the sum of these moments is my life."

I was short, slim, wore my hair parted on the side and plastered down with water and brilliantine, had a rather handsome face with unformed, infantile features and a constant smirk which looked impudent and masked by boundless timidity and insecurity.

Some twenty years later a shrewd Comintern agent said to me: "We all have inferiority complexes of various sizes, but yours isn't a complex— it's a cathedral."

The elements which shaped that structure have already been discussed or hinted at. The conviction that whatever I did was wrong, a pain to others and a disgrace to myself, had laid a permanent foundation of anxiety and guilt. The long periods of solitude, and the hectic excitement which came over me when I was allowed to see other children, transmitted their tensions to my later friendships and social contacts. In addition, there was a circumstance which for some time tortured me more than anything else: at sixteen I was the shortest boy but one in class, and that one happened to be a dwarf.

As I said before, I was slow in maturing both physically and mentally. I kept growing until around twenty-two, when I reached my present height of five feet seven. Even today I feel ill at ease if at a cocktail party I have to talk, standing, to a woman taller than I; and, as every author knows, the type of woman who rushes at you at parties to gush about your books is usually over forty-five, and over six feet tall. But what, today, is an occasional moment of mild discomfort was downright torture at sixteen. I refused to go to dancing-classes for fear that I would be forced to dance with taller partners. If friends asked me to a party, I inquired with infinite cunning about the intellectual faculties, colour of hair and eyes, and, incidentally of course, the stature of the young ladies expected to be present. The announcement that a beautiful, tall, blonde girl would be there was enough for me to plead indisposition. The examples of Napoleon, Beethoven, and other under-sized great men comforted me, but not much. Nor did they serve as a warning against the short man's traditional vanity, aggressiveness, and lust for power.

Much of this pain and distress was caused by a conversation I overheard between the parents of two of my classmates outside a bathing cabin where, unknown to them, I was changing my clothes. One said: "Isn't it terrible how quickly my boy is growing?" And the other answered: "That's no reason to worry. The terrible thing would be if he were as short as that Koestler boy." But, of course, this unpleasant experience could not have produced such a strong effect without a neurotic disposition, ready to feed on any nourishment offered by careless hands.

At seventeen I entered the university. In the *Burschenschaft* which I joined, every freshman was given a fraternity nickname. This name was conferred during an impressive ceremony; and until that solemn moment it was kept secret. The name which was sprung on me, and which I had to carry for years was "Perqueo"—taken from an old German students' song:

Es war der Zwerg Perqueo, im Heidelberger Schloss
An Gestalt kleinwinzig, am Durste riesengross.
Man schalt' ihn einen Narren; er sprach: "Ihn lieben Leut
Währt Ihr, wie ich, doch alle
Feuchtfröhlich und gescheit . . .[1]"

The end of the poem was in a way a redeeming factor.

Next to shortness, my inferiority complex fastened on my preposterously juvenile appearance. At sixteen I looked like fourteen, at twenty like sixteen, at thirty like twenty-one. Today, when appearance has caught up with age, I would no longer object to having ten years wiped off my face and my rump. Once the agonies of the past have been safely embalmed in memory they appear silly beyond belief. Yet agonies they were—such, for instance as that awkward misunderstanding with the adjutant of King Feisal of Iraq. . . .

This occurred during a visit to Bagdad in 1928. I was at that time Middle East correspondent of the Ullstein papers and had been sent out to cover one of the recurrent government crises in Iraq. On my arrival I applied for an interview with King Feisal Ibn Hussein. I was received by Tahsin Bey, the King's adjutant, in a resplendent white uniform; he had been advised of my arrival which, as befitting the representative of the biggest Continental newspaper chain, had also been announced in the local press. Tahsin Bey received me kindly; but whenever I broached the subject of politics, or the audience with His Majesty, he sidetracked the conversation and with a friendly smile inquired what young boys were taught in European schools. After the ritual number of cups of sweet and bitter coffee, and a painfully dragging conversation, he rose and concluded the talk with the question:

"And when can we now expect the visit of your papa?"

He obviously thought the representative of Ullstein's must be a middle-aged worthy who had sent his son ahead on a courtesy visit. For once, however, I proved equal to the occasion by declaring with a courteous bow:

"*Mon père, c'est moi.*"

We are not only disloyal to others, but also to our own past. The *gauche* adolescent, the foolish young man that one has been, appears so grotesque in retrospect and so detached from one's own identity that one

---

[1] There was a dwarf, Perqueo, in the castle of Heidelberg;
His stature was short, his thirst gigantic.
They called him a fool; he said: "Ye good people
If only you were like me: a tippler, serene and wise."

automatically treats him with amused derision. It is a callous betrayal, yet one cannot help being a traitor to one's past.

Worse than this betrayal is the distortion of truth which accompanies it. The agonies of youth are not funny, but distance and perspective make them appear funny, and one inadvertently falls into a patronizing, anecdotical style. I am trying to fight this impulse as I write this story, yet it is hard to recapture any sympathy for, and even less a feeling of identity with, the boy who was mortified when his classmates called him "Awtuah Koestla" because he could not roll the r's in his name; who unconsciously rose on tiptoe, like a fighting cock, when talking to taller boys; and who, at sixteen, when for the first time invited to a formal luncheon, could for an hour or more only squeeze out of himself an occasional "Yes, Madame," or "No, Madame," while growing alternately purple and pale, and being desperately aware of a condition aptly described by the French as *"suer entre les fesses."*

Timidity was the worst curse, unrelieved by the fact that it came in intermittent attacks. The timid youngster may be compared to a high-tension cable surrounded by thick layers of insulation, which protect him but also cut him off from contact with the outside world. There are several types among the timid. With some, the tension gradually relaxes as time marches on, the insulating layer becomes more flexible, shyness becomes transferred into courteous restraint—an attitude so well suited to the Anglo-Saxon temperament that it is even cultivated as a mannerism. With others, the opposite happens: the protective layer becomes a rigid, impenetrable veneer which chokes its wearer and frightens all passersby away. Then there is a third type, the one to which I belong, which may be called the "intermittent timid." In the case of the intermittent timid, phases of tongue-tiedness and cramp alternate with others of extreme garrulousness and uninhibited behaviour. Which of the two will come to the fore on a given occasion depends on circumstances beyond the subject's control. If the circumstances are such that contact is established between the live core of the cable and the environment, the current will flow freely, and the chances are that a short-circuit will occur, with a display of sparks and the blowing of fuses. Other occasions will merely produce a rubbing and grating of the environment against the insulating layer in which the timid remains encased, swathed, stifled, deaf and dumb.

Alcohol helps, but only within limits. Mostly it soaks through the insulation and makes it promiscuously conductive. If, during the initial phase, the subject is in a cramp, liquor may have the effect of intensifying the cramp until a kind of *rigor mortis* ensues. It is one of the most unpleasant social experiences.

The type of the intermittent timid should not be confused with the manic-depressive character, though the two often go together. If the manic-depressive also happens to suffer from intermittent timidity, the manic phases will facilitate the breakdown of inhibition, and *vice versa*.

Such, then, was the anatomy of the accursed shyness which I carried throughout my youth as a leper carries his bell: laughter ceases when he enters the room and the street grows empty at the sound of his footfall. My contacts with others were either nonexistent or headlong plunges into intimacy. But the latter were rare; and most of the time I felt that I was living in a portable prison of my own devising, surrounded by cold stares of bewilderment and rejection.

In this particular predicament even the Baron in the Bog's miracle-cure is of little avail. Or rather, it acts only gradually; you have to keep pulling at your hair to keep your face out of the mire until slowly, very slowly, you again find your *modus vivendi*.

The first Babo-method which I tried, the flight from timidity into cocky aggressiveness, proved a failure. It led through a series of painful beatings, both physical and moral, which were even more humiliating than the condition which they were meant to cure. The worst of these batterings lasted through my fifteenth and sixteenth years, which were spent in a small *pensionnat* for boys at Baden, near Vienna. There were about a dozen boarders in the *pensionnat*; and of these only four were over fifteen. The smaller boys lived downstairs; the four of us senior boys on the second floor. As a logical result of my character, so lovingly described above, the seniors were divided into two camps: one was known as "The Triumvirate," consisting of the other three; the other was I. This situation lasted until the end of my stay; everybody who, in his youth, has gone through the purgatory of a boarding-school can appreciate the nature of this experience.

The aggressive phase was followed by its opposite: the pose of the lonely, sensitive, starry-eyed poet, somewhere between Hamlet and Werther, doomed to early death by consumption. But this was definitely not in my line. I tried various other attitudes and poses to mask my extreme insecurity and lack of self-confidence. They were like suits bought off the rack—too tight at the waist or with sleeves inches too long. Underneath, there was no definite personality, no solid core, only fluid emotions, contradictory impulses, an amorphous bundle of tensions.

At some time during my sixteenth year I developed a new obsession; I called it the "Paradox of the Ego Spiral." The underlying problem was as old as the paradox of Achilles and the tortoise; but that did not prevent it from becoming an obsession. It went something like this:

A dog eats his supper. The dog is enjoying himself. But does the dog know that he is enjoying himself? Doubtful . . . A man reads a thriller. He is enjoying himself. He knows that he is enjoying himself. But does he know that he knows he is enjoying himself? If he is an average person, he probably doesn't . . . Now let's try it ourselves, with our superior powers of introspection. I am thinking of this problem. I know that I know that I am thinking of this problem. I know that I know that I know . . . and so on. Who, or what, is this elusive, receding "I" that is always one step removed from the process, and how can one catch up with it? As I had acquired the habit of thinking in terms of diagrams and geometrical figures, I saw the quest of that slippery, fugitive ego represented as an angular spiral; thus:

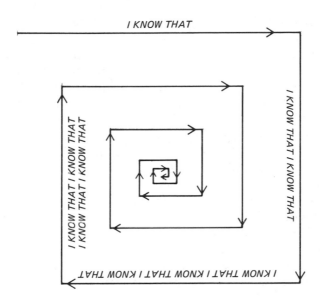

Now, it can be mathematically shown that a spiral of this kind will draw closer and closer to its centre without ever quite reaching it— just as a series of the form 1, ½, ¼, ⅛, 1/16 . . . etcetera, will generate smaller and smaller fractions, but never quite reach zero. Thus the effort to "catch the I," to achieve identity between the subject who knows and the object of its knowing, could be represented as a converging spiral which will only reach its own centre after an infinite number of involutions. Here, then, was the exact counterpoint to the arrow. The arrow went off at a tangent on its quest for the infinitely remote; the ego spiral curled inward, toward the infinitely close, which was yet as unattainable as the other.

So far so good. But what about the ego of the flatworm which could be sliced into two or more parts and regenerated into as many complete individuals? Could you cut an Ego into an "E" and a "go"? And did a two-headed calf have egos in duplicate? I found that the worm and the calf agreed quite well with my spiral. For you can't cut the centre of a spiral which is a geometrical point, into parts, but the ego spiral did not contain a centre; that spiral was not a locale, it was a function or process which could be duplicated as often as you liked. To have this point settled took a load off my chest and gave me a great feeling of satisfaction.

The more so, as convergent series have quite beautiful qualities. If you continue the series: 1, ½, ¼, ⅛, ¹⁄₁₆ . . . *ad infinitum*, and then add together all its numbers, the total sum will be exactly 2. Though we can never complete the series, we know precisely "what it is up to," as it were. Similarly, though you can never reach the core of the ego spiral, you can predict with fair precision how it will function and behave.

More than twenty-five years later, when I took up the study of psychology and neurology, I remembered my naive speculations about the arrow and the spiral, and it occurred to me that they could be regarded as archetypal symbols of two opposite trance-like states of heightened consciousness. In the "arrow state" consciousness expands towards mystic union with the All-One, while the ego is felt to dissolve in the infinite. In the opposite "spiral state" consciousness contracts, is focussed on the self, strives to establish identity between subject and object, to permeate the self with awareness of itself. The ecstasies described by most Christian mystics seem to belong to the former category, whereas certain yoga exercises, aiming at the conscious control of all functions of body and mind, seem to belong to the spiral state.

That there are two opposite types of heightened consciousness or contemplative trance, is a hypothesis which I am trying to substantiate in a work now in progress. The purpose of this digression was merely to give another example of the early original and the obsessional character of certain *leit-motifs* which keep recurring in one's development. I have always felt that *"on revient toujours"* should be altered to *"ça revient toujours."*

The lack of a clear-cut personality, of a solid centre of gravity in the flux of emotions, was in later years compensated by a neater adaptability to people and situations. Quick progress in my career as a journalist gave me a minimum of professional, though not of personal, self-confidence, and the great variety of social contacts which my job required forced me to develop a superficial technique in coping with them. For many years my relations with people, even with chance acquaintances on trains or at parties, remained emotionally as unbalanced as before, but the façade became smoother and more urbane. I became what is called a good mixer; from a hedgehog I gradually changed into a chameleon. I no longer displayed an artificial pose or mask, but a complete false personality, produced by outside conditioning and the inner need to find some *modus vivendi* with society.

Such organically grown false personalities—as distinct from consciously adopted poses—function automatically and without effort. Our society abounds in false personalities, which were developed in self-defence and later have become so ingrown that they even alter the features of the face and make it incongruent with the true personality of its owner. That may be the reason why the majority of outstanding painters, musicians, writers, and scholars, look so entirely different from what one expects. One of our most famous orchestra conductors looks like a headwaiter; our best-known painter like a wizened clown; a group-photograph of the Nobel Prize winning poets and writers would look like a meeting of chartered accountants and insurance salesmen. Perhaps Gide alone among them looked truly himself—partly because he wore a basque beret and partly because he was an exhibitionist. On the other hand, if you meet a person with a striking intellectual head and spiritually noble expression, he is sure to be either a treasury official, or an artistic dilettante and a second-rater.

There are various types of false personalities; the one to which I belong is recognizable, among other things, by the fact that he feels sure of himself when addressing a meeting or holding forth at a crowded party, but becomes the more insecure the smaller the audience, and reveals his basic timidity when alone with one other person. Genuine people are mostly the other way around.

Shyness and insecurity have remained my silent companions to this day. I have never outgrown, merely overgrown, them by a chatty, sociable, synthetic personality which I despise—as some women despise the bouncy rubber falsies which, nevertheless, they are obliged to wear to compensate for a natural defect.

Adolescence is a kind of emotional seasickness. Both are funny, but only in retrospect. The youth of sixteen that I was, with the plastered-down hair and the fatuous smirk, at once arrogant and sheepish, was emotionally seasick: greedy for pleasure, haunted by guilt, torn between feelings of inferiority and superiority, between the need for contemplative solitude and the frustrated urge for gregariousness and play; still obsessed by the arrow's flight into the Absolute, though hope of catching up with it had begun to fade; still in search of the knowing shaman, but equally worried about the possible withdrawal of the favours of Mathilda, the generous boarding-school maid. The archaic horrors of early childhood had receded but had not disappeared; they were latent, lying in wait, ready to pounce when provoked. Early intimacy with Ahor had achieved a lasting awareness of the other world, the tragic plane which existed parallel to the trivial routine of existence, even when the man-holes through which the two communicated were tightly closed and bolted under one's feet.

This latent apprehension, the awareness of guilt and impending punishment seemed to be always present, like the rhythmic beat of the surf at night along the shore. While there are voices under the open window and laughter on the pier, one is able to forget it. But when the laughter dies away and the voices are stilled, the muffled thunder swells up again, and one realizes that it has always been present; and that the waves will never stop beating their heads against the stones of the pier.

Jeannie Olive

Unlike a child, who can believe that evil is a dream or a mere inconvenience or something that happens in others, the adolescent learns of evil's ubiquity, of its resourcefulness and poise.

Who said at first to learn is like to lose? In "Society," two girls matriculate in this harsh curriculum, one as observer, the other as participant.

A native of North Carolina's Blue Ridge Mountains and a graduate of the University of North Carolina, Jeannie Olive invokes the universal theme of innocence lost, and writes of it in the dialect of Cherokee County.

SOCIETY

The weather got all mixed up that year. Indian summer idled so long on the slopes of the Blue Ridge that some of the birds never even flew south at all. Elfie and I walked to the settlement school without coats until the end of February, and the big boys of the upper grades spent their energy on the basketball court instead of having to chop wood to keep the schoolhouse warm. The rest of us, from the primer grade on up, took our lunch boxes outside at noontime and sat around the court watching practice while we ate our ham and biscuits.

"We got the best basketball team in Cherokee County," I boasted later at home. "We got Glen and Troy Grimshaw, both on the first team."

"Humph," Grandpa grunted. "So them overgrowed greazers are still hanging around the school. I thought Pope expelled them for keeps last year. I warned him."

"Mr. Pope took them back on a Bible promise to behave theirselves," I said. "They're the best players in school."

"I know about their Bible promises," Grandpa said. "They'll last just about as long as the basketball."

"Wilda, I want you to promise to have nothing to do with those big old rough boys," Ma said. "Don't you even speak to them."

"Now, Bird," Grandpa said to her, "seeing you're natured to worry about something, for God's sake worry about whether that donkey man's putting any learning in their heads. Looks to me like all the scholars' heads have turned to basketball."

The schoolmaster rode a donkey to school, and whenever Grandpa wanted to make light of him he always brought that donkey into it.

"Rufe Clemson Pope is a fine teacher," I said. "We learn a God's plenty."

"Aah," Grandpa said. "Tell me one thing you learned today. I want to know how my taxes are spent."

He pushed his chair back from the table. I was always the one through supper first, but that did me no good. I wasn't allowed to leave until excused. Ma finished second, and then we just had to sit there and wait until Grandpa finished and finally wiped the buttermilk from his whiskers and pushed his chair back.

I pretended he wasn't there and turned to Ma. "They's this new girl at school, name of Eula Bay Stiles. She wears a red hat and speaks proper. Elfie hates her."

"Eula Bay Stiles?" Ma repeated. "Any a-kin to the Stileses on Slow Creek? Down by the L and N track?"

"I don't know. Elfie said that was the ugliest hat ever she seen. She said if that hat was hern, she'd do her business in it and throw it away."

"Wilda!"

Grandpa brought his fist down on the table. "Jesus Christ, so that's how my taxes are spent! Now I asked you a simple question. You sit up straight and tell me one thing you learned today."

His whiskery face leaned over me, and I felt the smile dry on my mouth, the chair rungs dig my shoulders. I searched my head for a thing to tell and said finally, "A noun word is the name of a person, place, or thing."

"Well, then, that's better," Grandpa grudged. "Learn a little something every day. Drop by drop fills the cup."

From that time on he had a new habit. "What did you learn in school today?" It was the same old question every single night of the year. I soon figured out that if I hadn't learned anything, I'd better make up something on the way home.

Grandpa's sudden and powerful interest in the settlement school began when he was put on the school board, a mistake if ever there was one. He was enough things already. Besides Ma and me, he had all the farm hands and tenants to boss. Anybody would have thought he owned these people outright, especially the Bowlands, who lived down in the laurel slick. Tam and Minnie agreed with everything he said, though Elfie went her own way.

For another thing, Grandpa was justice of the peace. That brought him even more folks to boss. He settled all manner of local disputes before they ever got to the Greenville court. He'd never tolerated any spying on a trial, but from what little I gleaned, I vowed if I ever got in trouble I'd take it straight to the Greenville court.

Sometimes he would allow Ma and me to watch a wedding. Ma always wept, thinking, I suppose, of being a widow woman and lonesome.

"Which one of them Grimshaws do you think is the prettiest?" Elfie asked me. We had finished lunch and sat under the honey locust tree near the basketball court. Elfie was squeezing the long half-dried pods of the locust and licking out the honey wax. She had a sweet tooth that was never satisfied.

I thought of the basketball players. Troy and Glen Grimshaw pranced about the court like stallions, their shiny black heads a double span taller than the other players. They dodged, jumped, snatched the ball away, and made a ringer every time. I had to admit myself they didn't look bad.

"I mean if you was to have to choose one, which would you claim?"

"Nary one," I said. "They're both mean as stripid snakes."

"Troy's not so mean," she said, blushing.

We heard a laugh from behind the tree, and Eula Bay Stiles hopped out before us. "They, Lordee!" she said. "I just heard me a real secret."

Elfie eyed her coldly and went on twisting the locust pod.

"Elfie and Troy went for a ride, Troy fell out and Elfie cried— Lordee!"

She laughed fit to kill. I thought it was funny too, but Elfie's green eyes narrowed.

"You shet your mouth," she said, "or I'll shet it for you."

"Well for goodness," Eula Bay said in her put-on voice. "Can't you mountain children take a joke?" She turned her back on us and walked away.

That afternoon Mr. Pope got up in Society and said he'd heard some of the little girls weren't treating the new girl nice. "That's what we've got this Society for," he told us, "to learn to keep a civil tongue. We can debate our differences polite and proper instead of with fists and threats."

"*Society?* What in hell blazes is *Society?*" Grandpa blared out that night. Elfie was having supper with me. She was still feeling low and didn't raise her head.

"It's debating," I said, "and reciting poems and things. Mr. Pope makes us memorize a poem a week. He says in case we might go blind someday and not be able to read."

Grandpa wiped his whiskers. "Well, can you beat that? Did you hear that, Bird?"

Ma leaned forward with a new worry on her face. "Blind?" she repeated softly. "Go blind?"

"Why don't that jackass rider teach subjects?" Grandpa stormed. "Stick to what's in the books."

Poems are in books," Elfie said, brightening up to join the fray.

"Aaah, all right. Recite the poem."

I shut my eyes.

> "The woman was old and ragged
>   and gray
> And bent with the chill of the
>   winter's day . . ."

"Cripes!" Grandpa shouted. "That's enough of that." He turned to Elfie, who had begun to laugh. "All right, Miss Towhead, what did you learn?"

"Well, they was this old queen across the waters," she answered boldly, peering sideways at Grandpa, "and she beat up the Spanish navy and dyed her teeth blue and was a virgin."

I heard Ma suck in her breath. Grandpa said, "You're excused now." I always marveled at Elfie's nerve.

March came, and the weather man tricked us again. It changed overnight from the best to the worst. We woke up in the dark freezing cold, and Ma had to rummage around getting out more quilts fast. We ate breakfast huddled around the kitchen stove, while Grandpa raved and ranted about his sorry hired hands, who'd never finished getting in our wood supply.

Elfie and I walked to school bundled like Eskimos. The ridge path crackled under our feet, and the ruts in the Turtlepond Road were filled with spears of mush ice, like icicles turned upside down. Elfie broke off one and tasted it. "Bet we could pour sugar on the road of a cold night and make popsicles," she said.

Mr. Pope worked at the stove in the corner of the schoolroom, and the big rough boys were carrying in wood. They had sullen looks on their faces and threw their armloads of logs down so hard the windows rattled.

"Come boys, take it like sports," Mr. Pope said. "Basketball season is over, and no need to be bad-tempered about it. I've told you many a time, the only reason we have basketball in the first place is to learn to be good sports."

I saw Troy Grimshaw look at Glen and make a face. He flipped his eyelids back under the sockets and drew his mouth down like a scarecrow.

"What if Troy's face was to freeze like that?" I whispered to Elfie. "Would you say he was so pretty then?"

The primer children's benches were moved closer to the stove, and the rest of us grumbled through chattering teeth, taking turns to go up and thaw our hands. When the schoolhouse finally did get warmed up, Eula Bay Stiles complained it smelled stuffy and wanted to open a window. Mr. Pope sent her out to get a drink of water instead, but the dipper was frozen solid in the bucket and had to be brought inside.

"Now children, we're going to buckle down to work."

"*Now children*," one of the big boys mocked from the back.

Mr. Pope turned to see who it was, and behind his back a spitball hit the blackboard. At lunch he found a dead mouse in his dinner pail. Things went from bad to worse, and the worst thing happened when we were dismissed early and Mr. Pope went around back to fetch his donkey. Somebody had clipped all the hair off its tail.

That riled the teacher more than all the other things together. He called everyone back but the primer children and kept us late. "I aim to find out who did it," he warned. "Now I can put up with mischief of a sort. Pranks are pranks and boys will be boys. But one thing's sure, I'll not tolerate any molesting of my beast."

He threatened and questioned and scolded. "If any of you know who did this black deed and fail to tell, then I hold that person equally guilty and I'll mete out equal punishment."

It was almost dark when we got home. Elfie and I hurried along as fast as we could to keep warm. The hemlocks on the ridge path rose like giant ghosts in the frozen fog.

"They look like haints," Elfie said. "You ever seed a ghost-booger?"

"Reckon who done that thing at school?" I said. "Bet it was one of the Grimshaws, sure as shootin'."

"One think sure, old R. C. Pope will never know," she said. "Nobody's fool enough to tattle on a Grimshaw."

Just thinking about it, Elfie laughed the rest of the way home. "Never hoped to see me such a sight as that beast's tail," she said. "Lordee— looked like a rat's tail hung on a donkey!"

The next morning we learned that Glen Grimshaw was expelled. Mr. Pope had word of his guilt from an eyewitness. The children stared at each other's faces in wonderment. Telling was a thing rarely done at the settlement school.

"I'm satisfied it's that Eula Bay Stiles," Elfie told me. "There's your tattletail. There's the one with the slippy tongue."

"Troy don't seem to think so," I said. "I saw him talking to her before books were took up—joking and a-joshing like he was sweet on her."

"Troy's not that much of a loony," Elfie said, her face closed and brooding. "All I know is, I'd not like to be in *somebody's* shoes."

It was plain that most of the others agreed with Elfie. Anybody would have thought Eula Bay had nits in her head, the way she was shunned. Nobody would talk to her. At noon she was eating her lunch with the primer children. Only Troy Grimshaw stood by her, catching her glance whenever he could and doing his funny eyeball trick to make her laugh. It looked like Eula Bay had Troy lined up on her side, all right, and of course Mr. Pope. He bragged on her all day and allowed before all he'd never had a brighter pupil to teach. Elfie sat off in a corner, looking sick enough to die.

That afternoon in Society we had a debate. It was resolved that book sense was more useful than horse sense. Society was funny that way. All manner of things were argued, both serious and foolish. Eula Bay took the affirmative and Troy Grimshaw the negative. About four-thirty Mr. Pope sent the little fellows home, primed up the stove and let them talk on. Finally he got up and said it was over and Eula Bay won.

"You won fair and square," Troy said to her, as we gathered books and coats, "yet I'm not convinced you're right. They's knowledge stored up in folks' heads around here that's never been wrote down in books."

"Superstitions," Eula Bay said. "You all probably still believe in ghosts around here."

"Now, I'd not go so far as to say that," Troy said. "Useful things I mean, things the Cherokees knowed and passed on to the settlers. Some of it would come in mighty handy, if you was of a mind to learn."

"What, for instance?"

He picked up her books and they started for the door. Some of us followed, curious, trying to think what could be on Troy's mind.

"Why, listening with your tongue. Bet you never knowed you could learn to hear things with your tongue."

Eula Bay laughed. "Go on now. I'm not that dumb."

"Here you walk along that old L and N railroad track all the way from Slow Creek every day, and you never knowed you could listen for the train with your tongue?"

"You're crazy," she said. But she was interested, too. Anybody could tell that. When Troy started along the Slow Creek path with her, still carrying her books, she didn't object. She just kept smiling at him, never taking her eyes from his face.

"I swear to God on a stack of Bibles," Troy said. "You can ask anybody around here. These chaps all know." A few of us had been idling along behind them, burning with curiosity yet pretending not to listen. They turned around suddenly, facing us.

"Ask ary one of these chaps if you can't hear a train a-coming by touching your tongue to the railroad track."

"I got to be getting home," Abe Andrews said. "It's getting nigh on to dark."

"Me, too," another said, turning back. "See you'uns all in the mornin."

"Ma will have a dying fit if I'm late again today," I said. "Come on, Elfie."

Elfie didn't budge.

"Ask this little girl here," Troy said, "if you don't believe me. Ask her. She's got horse sense."

"Eula Bay looked Elfie up and down. "I wouldn't take anybody's word," she said. "If I wanted to know, I'd see for myself."

"Now you're talking horse sense," Troy said. "We'll all go down with you to prove it." He grabbed Eula Bay's arm and they were off down the Slow Creek trail, half running.

We stood there a moment, deciding. Elfie's face looked pinched in the dusky dark. The cold wind roared through the cove like a tunnel, flapping our coats, curling down our coat collars. My feet were beginning to feel tingly numb.

"I got to go home," I said, shivering. "Grandpa will be fit to be tied."

"Come on," Elfie said. She tugged my arm. "It won't take long. We're late anyhow. Ten minutes more won't make a speck of difference."

She began to run after them. I followed, and a few others followed me, though by the time we reached the train crossing it was too dark to see who was there and who was not. Two shadowy forms were bending down to the tracks. And then I heard Eula Bay scream.

After that all bedlam broke loose. The children were running in every direction, shouting for help, for a light, calling Mr. Pope's name. "Get some warm water," I heard somebody say. "Her tongue done stuck to the track!" All the time there was Eula Bay's ringing scream, a sound coming from deep in the throat, vibrating along the steel rail. I stood frozen in horror, numb not only in my feet but all the way up my spine.

"Just a little at a time, Eula Bay. Don't jerk." It was Mr. Pope's voice. "Pull easy. Now, try again." His flashlight pinpointed Eula Bay lying beside the track. I didn't want to look, yet was too numb to move my eyes away.

"A little more water, boys. Don't panic now, Eula Bay. Try again now."

Suddenly her head jerked upward and her body rolled over in anguish. The scream stopped but she was moaning and twisting, with her hand over her mouth. Mr. Pope picked her up quickly and wrapped her in the donkey's blanket. Then he got up bareback and held Eula Bay in front of him.

"Doc Cain first. He'll get her to the Greenville Clinic," I heard him say. And then he added, "There'll be no school tomorrow, children. Pass the word around. Instead, some of us will be making a visit to the justice of the peace. This here's a criminal act, not a schoolboy's prank."

A girl standing beside me began to sob. Mr. Pope started off toward the road, but before that he turned the beam of his flashlight slowly around us, making a complete circle.

I didn't know whether the light caught my face or not. I only know that I began to run, and someone sobbing came after me. We sped across the frozen stubble, stumbling, falling, and then were up again and running down the Turtlepond Road faster than the wind which roared at our back. It was only when I stopped on the ridge path, a pain stabbing at my side, that I realized the sobbing girl behind me was Elfie.

We leaned against a ghosty hemlock, holding tight to each other but finding no comfort.

"Never thought I'd turn out a criminal," Elfie choked. "Might as well die now as spend the rest of my life in a jailhouse."

"You couldn't know what Troy was up to," I said. "We couldn't read his mind."

"I knowed he was seeking to get even," she said, "but I never knowed he was that mean. Half the skin on her tongue . . ."

"He didn't even know she was the one that told," I interrupted quickly. I didn't want to think about Eula Bay's tongue.

"Yes, he said," Elfie confessed. "He did—he did. Happens I'm in a position to know . . ." She began sobbing again, and I understood what she meant.

"Troy was a pretty boy," she said between sobs. "You said yourself he was a pretty boy."

"Yes," I said. "I reckoned he looked right well."

Grandpa sat in front of a roaring log fire in the front room, reading a copy of *Grit*. I tried to sidle past, but he caught me.

"Aah," he said. "Late again. What excuse this time?"

"Where's Ma?" I said, moving sideways towards the stairs.

"She's out freezing her tail, tying pieces of suet meat to the juniper bushes. She thinks she's got to keep all the sparrows alive until they can get at my crops next summer."

I rushed up the stairs to my room, where I changed my dress, brushed my frizzy hair down flat, and washed the stubble scratches on my legs. All the time I kept thinking of Grandpa's talk about next summer . . .

Next summer. The words had the sound of bells ringing. But next summer was a million years away.

All through supper I sat silent, picking at my food, dreading for the moment to come. Finally Grandpa wiped the buttermilk from his whiskers and pushed his chair back.

"Well, let's hear what you learned at school today," he said.

Then I began to cry.

Part Eight

Time Future in Time Present

Time is the school in which we learn,
Time is the fire in which we burn.

Delmore Schwartz

Time Future in Time Present concludes in the spirit of Part One by stressing the interdependency of heritage, futurity, and resolute present, the bond of time that coheres in our lives and weathers the arrogance of events. Whether construed as the learning of one man or as the acquirement of a people, education is not only reliant on this interdependency but its best preserver.

Who will deny that a man's character pilots his aspirations, dickers with the unforeseen, and issues fatefully from the days he wields, hours deftly hued with the colors of his past? Axioms hide in such a question. Whether tolerated in our time as a truism, or dramatized starkly in the Fifth Century B.C. by Sophocles, the future *is* now.

If one priority of our times is that survival must become a proper study for mankind, then those who would teach are obliged to heed the *indwellingness* of futurity, not as a trite abstraction but as a felt imminence, with its threats to be mulled, its good promises helped, and its dominion advertised. Lacking these intents, any curriculum is a sham.

Though implicitly concerned with the practices and effects of teaching and learning, Part Eight does not tarry over hardware innovations or the data bank systems and teaching machines not yet vindicated. The tone of *Time Future in Time Present* is personal and revelatory, one consonant with the authority of literature rather than of politics, or the computer sciences, or philosophy.

Narratives by David Ely, Lionel Trilling, and Aldous Huxley coalesce as evidence in a foretelling. These authors are timely because they are more than seasonable; they are prescient. They honor the admonition of Albert Camus that "real generosity toward the future lies in giving all to the present."

David Ely
(1927–   )

On an obvious level "The Academy" is an indictment of authority abused. In a way characteristic of other modern institutions, the school here described cloaks its usurpations of freedom in rhetoric that is benign, that soothes while it imperils.

But the story also implies the danger of *all* indoctrinations, of their power to coerce the learner away from what he might better have been or done. In our time authoritarianism has become an open target in education: its evils are catalogued and are the first to come under suspicion. But are the tyrannies of obstinate permissiveness equally advertised? May not the lives of children be endangered as much by amorphous curricula and softheaded teaching as by common regimentation? If read in the light of these questions, "The Academy" frames one threat but warns of others.

Born in Chicago, David Ely has been a Fulbright scholar and has attended the University of North Carolina, Harvard, and Oxford. In addition to short stories, he has written film scripts and a novel, *Seconds* (1963).

THE ACADEMY

The academy lay in the center of a valley, its red-brick buildings arranged in a square. Beyond the surrounding athletic and drill fields were thick woods that rose gradually on all sides, forming a shield of privacy that made the Academy seem in fact to be, in the words of the school brochure, "a little world of its own."

Mr. Holston parked his car in the area marked for visitors. Before proceeding toward the administration building, he paused to watch several groups of uniformed cadets marching to and fro on one of the fields. There was an atmosphere of regularity and tradition that he found quite pleasing. The buildings were old and solid, their bricks weathered to a pale hue, and the stone steps worn down by generations of cadets. The concrete walkways were scrubbed clean and bordered by grass meticulously clipped and weeded. Even the trees of the forest stood in formation.

In front of the administration building was the statue of an elderly man in military dress, one hand resting benignly on the stone shoulder of a young cadet, the other arm extended in a pointing gesture. Mr. Holston supposed this might represent the Academy's founder, perhaps a retired Civil War general, but the legend inscribed on the base was so faded that he could not read it. The symbolism of the man and boy was conventional, of course—the firm but kindly teacher indicating the horizon of manhood to his youthful charge—although Mr. Holston noted that the figures were facing so that the stone commander was pointing toward the school, rather than in the direction of the outside world, which would have been more appropriate.

In the lobby of the administration building, Mr. Holston gave his name to the cadet at the reception desk, and was at once ushered down a hallway to the Director's office.

The office was as spare and neat as everything else Mr. Holston had observed about the Academy. It contained a filing cabinet, a single chair for visitors, and a desk, behind which the Director himself was in the process of rising.

The Director was a strongly built man whose white hair was closely cut in military fashion, and his handshake was vigorous. He wore the gray uniform of the school, with a single star on each shoulder to denote his rank.

"Well, Mr. Holston," he said, after the customary exchange of amenities, "I've studied your boy's transcript and test records, and I've discussed them with the Admissions Committee, and without beating around the bush, sir, we're prepared to look favorably on a formal application, if you care to make one."

"I see," said Mr. Holston, who had not expected such an immediate response. "That's very encouraging to hear." Feeling slightly ill at ease under the Director's gaze, he glanced around at the walls, which, however, were absolutely bare.

"So," continued the Director, "the only question that remains is whether you want your son to be enrolled here. I'm assuming there's no special financial problem involved, naturally."

"Oh, no. We have that all worked out." Mr. Holston hesitated, thinking that such an important matter should not be disposed of so simply. "I would like to ask about one thing," he said. "Your catalog mentioned a policy of not having any home visits the first year."

The Director nodded. "Yes. Well, we've worked out our system over a long period of time, and we've found that home visits just don't fit into the picture until the cadet is thoroughly oriented to our way of doing things. We say 'a year' merely as a general guide. Sometimes it's longer than that. Parents can visit here, of course, at specified times." The Director gazed inquiringly at Mr. Holston, who tried to think of some more questions, but could not. "Actually," the Director continued, "the cadets seem to prefer it this way, once they get started. What we're looking for, Mr. Holston, is to motivate them—motivate them to achieve success, which means success in becoming a fully oriented member of this community, and you can see how home visits might cause a little disruption in the process."

"Oh, yes," said Mr. Holston.

"Well," said the Director. "You'll want to see a little more of the Academy before making up your mind, I should imagine. Classrooms, dormitories, and so forth."

"If it isn't too much trouble."

"No trouble at all." The Director rose and escorted Mr. Holston out to the hall. "Nothing special about our classrooms," the Director remarked, stopping at one of the doors. He opened it. The instructor, a gray-haired man, roared *"Attention!"* and the entire class leaped up smartly, as the instructor did a left-face and saluted the Director. "At ease, Grimes," said the Director, returning the salute. "Proceed with instruction."

"Very good, sir."

The Director closed the door again, so that Mr. Holston had only a glimpse of the class—a roomful of gray uniformed figures, heads so closely cropped that they were almost shaven, with nothing much to distinguish one cadet from the next.

"Those were big fellows," remarked Mr. Holston, as they continued along the hallway. "I suppose they're your seniors."

"We don't go by the usual class designations, Mr. Holston. Each cadet is paced according to his needs and capacities. Our purpose is to build men, sir, and you simply can't find a formula to satisfy the requirements of every case. Now here," said the Director, pushing open a pair of swinging doors, "is our cafeteria, which is staffed by the cadets themselves. Part of our community work program."

It was the middle of the afternoon, and the cafeteria was empty, except for a few men who were mopping the floor and scrubbing the serving counters. They, too, snapped to attention when the visitors appeared, until the Director motioned for them to continue their work, as he escorted Mr. Holston on into the kitchen, where several male cooks were busy preparing food for the evening meal.

"At ease," the Director called out, for the cooks, too, had come to attention. "All modern equipment, Mr. Holston, as you can see," he said, indicating the gleaming ranges, the sinks and the neat rows of cleavers, knives, and other implements hanging on the white walls. "You will understand," he added, "that we can't run a military establishment in a sloppy fashion. We try to be thorough, sir. We have, as I say, a little world here, and it's a world that happens to be organized along military lines." He turned to an elderly cook. "Looks good, Carson."

"Thank you, sir." Carson saluted.

Mr. Holston and the Director left the kitchen by the rear door, passing into the square formed by the Academy buildings. "I suppose," said Mr. Holston, "that you find a lot of employees who like the military way. Old Army men, say."

The Director was busy returning the salute of an instructor who was marching a platoon of cadets nearby. He stood silently watching the ranks pass by. "Drill," he declared finally. "Sometimes I think its the greatest lesson of all. When a boy knows drill, Mr. Holston, then he knows something about life, don't you think?"

"Ah, yes," said Mr. Holston, a bit uncertainly. "Of course, it's a splendid training, especially when a boy goes on to have a career in the services."

"Not only there, sir, if you'll permit me. Drill has important values in civilian pursuits as well, in my opinion. And I don't mean only physical drill," the Director added, as he and his guest walked on. "We use drill techniques in classroom work, to instill habits of mental discipline and personal courtesy. We've been given hopeless cases, Mr. Holston, but we've managed in every single one, sir, to find the right answer. And the key to it has been drill, whether on the parade ground or in the classroom. Of course," he said, ushering Mr. Holston into the next building, "in some instances it takes more time than in others, and I don't mean to imply that the Academy deals primarily with so-called problem boys. Not at all. The great majority are like your own son—good, decent young fellows from fine upstanding homes." He opened a door. "This is one of our dormitories, Mr. Holston."

The room ran the length of the building. The wall was lined with beds space out to accommodate lockers, chairs and desks. The few cadets who were then studying in the room sprang from their chairs.

"Maybe you'd like to chat with one of the boys," the Director said to Mr. Holston, after he had put the cadets at ease. "Here," he said, as they approached the nearest student, who was taller than either of the men, "it's Cadet Sloan, isn't it?"

"Yes, sir."

"Well, this is Mr. Holston, Sloan, and he'll have a few words with you," said the Director, who then moved off along the row of beds, inspecting the blanket corners and testing here and there for dust.

Mr. Holston, left with Cadet Sloan, did not know quite what to say.

"Well," he began, "how do you like it here?"

"I like it very well, sir."

"That's good. Um, the food and everything . . . you find it all right?"

"Everything is very good, sir."

"Ah," said Mr. Holston, rubbing his hands together, trying to think of additional questions while Cadet Sloan gazed at him with polite attention. "Well, I suppose you're planning on some college or other, aren't you?"

"My plans aren't too definite at present, sir."

"Yes, yes. Well, I can see you're a hard worker on your books, Mr. Sloan," Mr. Holston continued, glancing first at the stack of texts on the desk and then at Cadet Sloan's face, which wore a studious look that was reinforced by little wrinkles of concentration around the eyes and mouth.

"We have plenty to do, sir, that's right."

"Your parents must be proud to have such a hard-working son."

"My parents aren't living, sir."

"Oh—I'm sorry." Mr. Holston regretted his blunder. No wonder Sloan looked drawn.

"That's all right, sir. It's been quite a while."

"Ah, yes. Well." Mr. Holston could not help being struck by the manly demeanor of Cadet Sloan. He put out his hand. "Nice to talk with you, son," he said. "And good luck."

"Thank you, sir."

The Director and his guest walked back toward the administration building. On all sides, Mr. Holston was aware of organized and purposeful activity. Several groups of cadets were marching along the paths on their way from one building to another; a soccer game was in progress on a field nearby, and on the main parade ground, a full company in dress uniform was executing a complex series of drill maneuvers.

"It's all very impressive," said Mr. Holston.

The Director smiled. "We try to keep our young men busy."

"That cadet I talked to back there," Mr. Holston added. "Sloan. He seemed to be a remarkably mature person."

"We strive to build a sense of maturity, Mr. Holston."

"Yes, yes. I can certainly tell that." Mr. Holston saw that they were approaching the stone figures of teacher and student which were turned the wrong way. He gestured toward the statues. "That's quite a piece of sculpture."

"Thank you. We're very proud of it."

Mr. Holston could not repress his curiosity. "It does seem a little— well, unconventional. I mean, the positioning. You know, facing toward the Academy instead of away from it."

The Director nodded. "Yes, most visitors notice that, Mr. Holston.

At first glance, it does seem to be a mistake, I agree." He paused beside the figures and gazed approvingly up at the stern features of the teacher. Mr. Holston thought he saw a resemblance between the Director and the statue, which, he reflected further, might be no mere fancy, for the operation of the Academy could very well be a family matter, with the leadership being passed on from one generation to the next.

"For us, you see," said the Director, continuing with his explanation, "the important thing is the Academy. This is our world, Mr. Holston. All that a boy needs is to be found right here. So that the symbolism of the figures, sir, is to represent a welcome to this little world—rather than the more conventional theme of farewell which would be indicated if the man were pointing away from the Academy."

"Of course," said Mr. Holston.

They returned to the Director's office, where an elderly man in green fatigues was polishing the desk and chairs. He stopped as they entered and stood stiffly near the wall.

"At ease, Morgan," said the Director. "That'll be all."

"Very good, sir." The elderly man saluted and hobbled out.

The Director seated himself behind the desk and briefly inspected its top for signs of dust. "Well, Mr. Holston," he said, "now you've seen something of the Academy, and I'm sure you've had an opportunity to consider a little further the question of whether it may be what you're looking for, to help your boy."

"Yes, yes. Of course." Mr. Holston nodded. "You have a fine institution here, I must say. Everything seems to be organized with . . . with real efficiency." He glanced toward the door beyond which he thought he could still hear the shuffling steps of the elderly man in fatigues. "It's a real example of what the military method can achieve," he added, feeling that perhaps he had not sufficiently expressed his admiration for all that the Director had shown him.

The Director took a folder from a drawer and placed it on the desk.

"As for my son," said Mr. Holston, "that's the important question, of course. Whether this would be the right place for him. Or rather," he amended, "whether he would be right for you. I'm sure there are many instances where boys simply don't fit in."

The Director smiled. "We don't believe in failure here, Mr. Holston. When we agree to admit a boy, sir, that means we are laying our reputation on the line." He opened the folder and took out a letter. "And without intending to boast, Mr. Holston, I think I can truthfully say that we have yet to concede defeat." He pushed the letter across the desk. Mr. Holson saw that it was an official notice of acceptance, complete except for his own signature as parent. He felt in his pocket for his fountain pen.

"In some cases, naturally," the Director continued, "we need to have more patience than in others. But patience is built into our system."

"Patience, yes," said Mr. Holston. He laid his pen beside the letter of acceptance. "Boys need patience. You're right there, of course. Some boys need a lot of that, I agree." He moved the letter slightly, so that it was squared off with the edge of the desk. "He's not a bad boy, though. Not at all," he added.

"Mr. Holston, in my experience there is no such thing as a bad boy."

"I mean, he's gotten into a couple of little scrapes—that's in the records, of course—but nothing really . . ." Mr. Holston cleared his throat.

"Boys will be boys, sir. Lack of proper motivation leads to trouble, even in the best of families. You have nothing to be ashamed of, sir."

"Oh, we're not ashamed. We just feel—my wife and I—we feel that he would be better off in the kind of atmosphere you provide here, especially during the, um, difficult years."

"That's what we're here for, Mr. Holston," said the Director.

"I mean, it's not as though we were trying to avoid our own responsibilities as parents—"

"Far from it, sir," agreed the Director.

"—but in certain situations it seems advisable to, um . . ."

"To place a boy in congenial surroundings under the proper form of supervision," said the Director, helpfully completing Mr. Holston's thought. "You're absolutely right, sir. Believe me, I deal with parents every day of the year, and I know all of the things that pass through their minds." He clasped his hands together and smiled at his visitor.

"Some people think it's a kind of rejection of the child. I mean, getting rid of him—"

"Oh, I've heard plenty of that, Mr. Holston. It's all this modern psychiatric stuff. Guilt feelings!" The Director gave a short laugh and shook his head. "I tell you, when a father and mother are prepared to undergo heavy financial sacrifice in order to see their boys receive a decent chance in life—well, if that's getting rid of him, then it's a pretty conscientious way of doing it!"

"Yes, yes," said Mr. Holston quickly. They smiled at each other. In the brief pause that followed, Mr. Holston heard the commands of the drill instructors faintly in the distance, and the muffled beat of the marching cadets. There was marching in the hallway, too, and he supposed that it was a class, moving in formation from one room to another.

"Perhaps you have some further questions," the Director remarked.

Mr. Holston picked up his pen. "Oh, not at all. No, I think you've covered everything." He tested the point of the pen against his thumb, to be sure it was working.

"This is the time for questions, Mr. Holston," the Director continued. "It's better to ask them now, I mean to say, while the Academy is fresh in your mind. Sometimes it's hard for a parent to remember later on the things he wanted to ask."

"Oh, yes, I can understand that," said Mr. Holston, studying the letter before him.

"For example, you might like to know more about our cooperative work program for the cadets. The cafeteria was an instance of that."

"It was a very fine cafeteria," said Mr. Holston. "No, I don't really have any questions about it."

"Then there's the academic program. Perhaps you feel insufficiently informed on that aspect."

"No, the catalog was quite complete. I really can't think of anything it didn't cover."

"We are great believers in the value of learning by teaching. Let me explain that. The cadets take turns, you see, in the instruction program—"

"Quite so," said Mr. Holston. "I'm sure it's a remarkably effective feature of your system."

"Oh, it is indeed. That classroom that you saw, for example—"

"Really, I have no questions," said Mr. Holston. He signed his name in the proper place, put his pen in his pocket, and pushed the letter back across the desk.

"Thank you," said the Director, placing the letter carefully in the folder. "Actually, few parents do have questions." He smiled at Mr. Holston who, however, was glancing at his watch and pushing back his chair. "They seem to sense right away whether the Academy is what they really want for their boys. Like yourself, sir, if I am not mistaken."

"Absolutely," said Mr. Holston. He stood up and touched his face with his handkerchief, for the air in the room seemed close.

The Director rose and shook his hand. "Of course, the very best guarantee of satisfaction for the parent is to see the experienced cadet and have a chance to chat with him. As you did with Sloan, I believe."

"Yes, Sloan." Mr. Holston went to the door. "I can find my way out, sir. Don't you bother."

"No bother at all, Mr. Holston," said the Director, accompanying his visitor along the hallway. "Sloan—yes, a fine cadet, Sloan. He's been with us for quite a while now. Let's see—"

"Goodbye, sir," said Mr. Holston, as they reached the front entrance.

"—it must be nearly . . ."

But Mr. Holston did not stay to hear. He went quickly down the worn stone steps, passed by the statues of the man and boy without looking up at them, and hastened to his car. On his way out, he drove by a group of cadets in sweat shirts resting by the road after a session of calisthenics. They got quickly to their feet at the command of their instructor, but Mr. Holston concentrated on his driving, and although it seemed to him that several of the cadets were bald and that others were quite gray, he gave them only a glance, and thought no more about it.

Lionel Trilling

(1905–   )

Referring to the deranged student who is a dominant character in "Of This Time, Of That Place," Lionel Trilling has written, "I did not want a pathetic story for Tertan. I thought he deserved something sterner than that. From the first, I conceived him to be an impressive figure, in some sense heroic, and he therefore made the demands on me that I come as close as I could to tragedy." In light of this intention and its result, the deeper rewards of the narrative remain for readers who weigh the sterner questions of character and event and are not content with facile judgments that explain the story away.

Though realized in a college setting, the predicament of Professor Howe, Tertan's teacher, recurs on other levels of teaching—particularly in high schools, where the fledgling behaviors of Blackburn, Casebeer, and Tertan are frequently found.

Trilling has pointed out that Tertan *is* insane: "Nothing, I fear, can reverse the diagnosis of Tertan's illness." But such a diagnosis does not reduce the story to an ironic contrast between Blackburn's immoral sanity and Tertan's noble aberration, though certainly this contrast is strong throughout. Of deeper import is the tragic loss at the center of civilized life: a man's *time*, a man's *place*—in reality vivid, chancy, palpable, and diverse—must be falsified by measurements in order to be made intelligible. Of this truth mad Tertan is the purveyor; he, more than his teacher, is contemptuously aware of the "instruments of precision." As one such instrument, Hilda and her camera freeze the immediacy of character and scene (the very transilience to which Tertan is drawn) into a Polaroid past, a forgery that can be believed. Hilda's picture-taking quite literally frames the story itself.

Considered in its broadest applications, must formal learning be merely an education in apertures, whereby reality is abridged by the machines that measure it? Or can our "instruments of precision"—our politics, our art, our science, our philosophy—engage the learner in wide prospects, in the totals of experience?

Since 1948 Lionel Trilling has been Professor of English at Columbia University. In addition to short stories and a novel entitled *The Middle of the Journey* (1947), he has written distinguished critical works: *E. M. Forster* (1943), *The Liberal Imagination* (1950), and *A Gathering of Fugitives* (1956), among others.

Of This Time, Of That Place

It was a fine September day. By noon it would be summer again, but now it was true autumn with a touch of chill in the air. As Joseph Howe stood on the porch of the house in which he lodged, ready to leave for his first class of the year, he thought with pleasure of the long indoor days that were coming. It was a moment when he could feel glad of his profession.

On the lawn the peach tree was still in fruit and young Hilda Aiken was taking a picture of it. She held the camera tight against her chest. She wanted the sun behind her, but she did not want her own long morning shadow in the foreground. She raised the camera, but that did not help, and she lowered it, but that made things worse. She twisted her body to the left, then to the right. In the end she had to step out of the direct line of the sun. At last she snapped the shutter and wound the film with intense care.

Howe, watching her from the porch, waited for her to finish and called good morning. She turned, startled, and almost sullenly lowered her glance. In the year Howe had lived at the Aikens', Hilda had accepted him as one of her family, but since his absence of the summer she had grown shy. Then suddenly she lifted her head and smiled at him, and the humorous smile confirmed his pleasure in the day. She picked up her bookbag and set off for school.

The handsome houses on the streets to the college were not yet fully awake, but they looked very friendly. Howe went by the Bradby house where he would be a guest this evening at the first dinner party of the year. When he had gone the length of the picket fence, the whitest in town, he turned back. Along the path there was a fine row of asters and he went through the gate and picked one for his buttonhole. The Bradbys would be pleased if they happened to see him invading their lawn and the knowledge of this made him even more comfortable.

He reached the campus as the hour was striking. The students were hurrying to their classes. He himself was in no hurry. He stopped at his dim cubicle of an office and lit a cigarette. The prospect of facing his class had suddenly presented itself to him and his hands were cold; the lawful seizure of power he was about to make seemed momentous. Waiting did not help. He put out his cigarette, picked up a pad of theme paper, and went to his classroom.

As he entered, the rattle of voices ceased, and the twenty-odd freshmen settled themselves and looked at him appraisingly. Their faces seemed gross, his heart sank at their massed impassivity, but he spoke briskly.

"My name is Howe," he said, and turned and wrote it on the blackboard. The carelessness of the scrawl confirmed his authority. He went on, "My office is 412 Slemp Hall, and my office-hours are Monday, Wednesday and Friday from eleven-thirty to twelve-thirty."

He wrote, "M., W., F., 11:30—12:30." He said, "I'll be very glad to see any of you at that time. Or if you can't come then, you can arrange with me for some other time."

He turned again to the blackboard and spoke over his shoulder. "The text for the course is Jarman's *Modern Plays*, revised edition. The Co-op has it in stock." He wrote the name, underlined "revised edition" and waited for it to be taken down in the new notebooks.

When the bent heads were raised again he began his speech of prospectus. "It is hard to explain—" he said, and paused as they composed themselves. "It is hard to explain what a course like this is intended to do. We are going to try to learn something about modern literature and something about prose composition."

As he spoke, his hands warmed and he was able to look directly at the class. Last year on the first day the faces had seemed just as cloddish, but as the term wore on they became gradually alive and quite likable. It did not seem possible that the same thing could happen again.

"I shall not lecture in this course," he continued. "Our work will be carried on by discussion and we will try to learn by an exchange of opinion. But you will soon recognize that my opinion is worth more than anyone else's here."

He remained grave as he said it, but two boys understood and laughed. The rest took permission from them and laughed too. All Howe's private ironies protested the vulgarity of the joke, but the laughter made him feel benign and powerful.

When the little speech was finished, Howe picked up the pad of paper he had brought. He announced that they would write an extemporaneous theme. Its subject was traditional, "Who I am and why I came to Dwight College." By now the class was more at ease and it gave a ritualistic groan of protest. Then there was a stir as fountain pens were brought out and the writing-arms of the chairs were cleared, and the paper was passed about. At last, all the heads bent to work, and the room became still.

Howe sat idly at his desk. The sun shone through the tall clumsy windows. The cool of the morning was already passing. There was a scent of autumn and of varnish and the stillness of the room was deep and oddly touching. Now and then a student's head was raised and scratched in the old, elaborate students' pantomime that calls the teacher to witness honest intellectual effort.

Suddenly a tall boy stood within the frame of the open door. "Is this," he said, and thrust a large nose into a college catalogue, "is this the meeting place of English 1A? The section instructed by Dr. Joseph Howe?"

He stood on the very sill of the door, as if refusing to enter until he was perfectly sure of all his rights. The class looked up from work, found him absurd and gave a low mocking cheer.

The teacher and the new student, with equal pointedness, ignored the disturbance. Howe nodded to the boy, who pushed his head forward and then jerked it back in a wide elaborate arc to clear his brow of a heavy lock of hair. He advanced into the room and halted before Howe, almost at attention. In a loud, clear voice he announced, "I am Tertan, Ferdinand R., reporting at the direction of Head of Department Vincent."

The heraldic formality of this statement brought forth another cheer. Howe looked at the class with a sternness he could not really feel, for there was indeed something ridiculous about this boy. Under his displeased regard the rows of heads dropped to work again. Then he touched Tertan's elbow, led him up to the desk and stood so as to shield their conversation from the class.

"We are writing an extemporaneous theme," he said. "The subject is, 'Who I am and why I came to Dwight College.'"

He stripped a few sheets from the pad and offered them to the boy. Tertan hesitated and then took the paper, but he held it only tentatively. As if with the effort of making something clear, he gulped, and a slow smile fixed itself on his face. It was at once knowing and shy.

"Professor," he said, "to be perfectly fair to my classmates"—he made a large gesture over the room—"and to you"—he inclined his head to Howe—"this would not be for me an extemporaneous subject."

Howe tried to understand. "You mean you've already thought about it—you've heard we always give the same subject? That doesn't matter."

Again the boy ducked his head and gulped. It was the gesture of one who wishes to make a difficult explanation with perfect candor. "Sir," he said, and made the distinction with great care, "the topic I did not expect, but I have given much ratiocination to the subject."

Howe smiled and said, "I don't think that's an unfair advantage. Just go ahead and write."

Tertan narrowed his eyes and glanced sidewise at Howe. His strange mouth smiled. Then in quizzical acceptance, he ducked his head, threw back the heavy, dank lock, dropped into a seat with a great loose noise and began to write rapidly.

The room fell silent again and Howe resumed his idleness. When the bell rang, the students who had groaned when the task had been set now groaned again because they had not finished. Howe took up the papers, and held the class while he made the first assignment. When he dismissed it, Tertan bore down on him, his slack mouth held ready for speech.

"Some professors," he said, "are pedants. They are Dryasdusts. However, some professors are free souls and creative spirits. Kant, Hegel and Nietzsche were all professors." With this pronouncement he paused. "It is my opinion," he continued, "that you occupy the second category."

Howe looked at the boy in surprise and said with good-natured irony, "With Kant, Hegel and Nietzsche?"

Not only Tertan's hand and head but his whole awkward body waved away the stupidity. "It is the kind and not the quantity of the kind," he said sternly.

Rebuked, Howe said as simply and seriously as he could, "It would be nice to think so." He added, "Of course I am not a professor."

This was clearly a disappointment but Tertan met it. "In the French sense," he said with composure. "Generically, a teacher."

Suddenly he bowed. It was such a bow, Howe fancied, as a stage-director might teach an actor playing a medieval student who takes leave of Abelard—stiff, solemn, with elbows close to the body and feet together. Then, quite as suddenly, he turned and left.

A queer fish, and as soon as Howe reached his office, he sifted through the batch of themes and drew out Tertan's. The boy had filled many sheets with his unformed headlong scrawl. "Whom am I?" he had begun. "Here, in a mundane, not to say commercialized academe, is asked the question which from time long immemorably out of mind has accreted doubts and thoughts in the psyche of man to pester him as a nuisance. Whether in St. Augustine (or Austin as sometimes called) or Miss Bashkirtsieff or Frederic Amiel or Empedocles, or in less lights of the intellect than these, this posed question has been ineluctable."

Howe took out his pencil. He circled "academe" and wrote "vocab." in the margin. He underlined "time long immemorably out of mind" and wrote "Diction!" But this seemed inadequate for what was wrong. He put down his pencil and read ahead to discover the principle of error in the theme. "Today as ever, in spite of gloomy prophets of the dismal science (economics) the question is uninvalidated. Out of the starry depths of heaven hurtles this spear of query demanding to be caught on the shield of the mind ere it pierces the skull and the limbs be unstrung."

Baffled but quite caught, Howe read on. "Materialism, by which is meant the philosophic concept and not the moral idea, provides no aegis against the question which lies beyond the tangible (metaphysics). Existence without alloy is the question presented. Environment and heredity relegated aside, the rags and old clothes of practical life discarded, the name and the instrumentality of livelihood do not, as the prophets of the dismal science insist on in this connection, give solution to the interrogation which not from the professor merely but veritably from the cosmos is given. I think, therefore I am (cogito etc.) but who am I? Tertan I am, but what is Tertan? Of this time, of that place, of some parentage, what does it matter?"

Existence without alloy: the phrase established itself. Howe put aside Tertan's paper and at random picked up another. "I am Arthur J. Casebeer, Jr.," he read. "My father is Arthur J. Casebeer and my grandfather was Arthur J. Casebeer before him. My mother is Nina Wimble Casebeer. Both of them are college graduates and my father is in insurance. I was born in St. Louis eighteen years ago and we still make our residence there."

Arthur J. Casebeer, who knew who he was, was less interesting than Tertan, but more coherent. Howe picked up Tertan's paper again. It was clear that none of the routine marginal comments, no "sent. str." or "punct." or "vocab." could cope with this torrential rhetoric. He read ahead, contenting himself with underscoring the errors against the time when he should have the necessary "conference" with Tertan.

It was a busy and official day of cards and sheets, arrangements and small decisions, and it gave Howe pleasure. Even when it was time to attend the first of the weekly Convocations he felt the charm of the beginning of things when intention is still innocent and uncorrupted by effort. He sat among the young instructors on the platform, and joined in their humorous complaints at having to assist at the ceremony, but actually he got a clear satisfaction from the ritual of prayer and prosy speech, and even from wearing his academic gown. And when the Convocation was over the pleasure continued as he crossed the campus, exchanging greetings with men he had not seen since the spring. They were people who did not yet, and perhaps never would, mean much to him, but in a year they had grown amiably to be part of his life. They were his fellow-townsmen.

The day had cooled again at sunset, and there was a bright chill in the September twilight. Howe carried his voluminous gown over his arm, he swung his doctoral hood by its purple neckpiece, and on his head he wore his mortarboard with its heavy gold tassel bobbing just over his eye. These were the weighty and absurd symbols of his new profession and they pleased him. At twenty-six Joseph Howe had discovered that he was neither so well off nor so bohemian as he had once thought. A small income, adequate when supplemented by a sizable cash legacy, was genteel poverty when the cash was all spent. And the literary life—the room at the Lafayette, or the small apartment without a lease, the long summers on the Cape, the long afternoons and the social evenings— began to weary him. His writing filled his mornings and should perhaps have filled his life, yet it did not. To the amusement of his friends, and with a certain sense that he was betraying his own freedom, he had used the last of his legacy for a year at Harvard. The small but respectable reputation of his two volumes of verse had proved useful—he continued at Harvard on a fellowship and when he emerged as Doctor Howe he received an excellent appointment, with prospects, at Dwight.

He had his moments of fear when all that had ever been said of the dangers of the academic life had occurred to him. But after a year in which he had tested every possibility of corruption and seduction he was ready to rest easy. His third volume of verse, most of it written in his first years of teaching, was not only ampler but, he thought, better than its predecessors.

There was a clear hour before the Bradby dinner party, and Howe looked forward to it. But he was not to enjoy it, for lying with his mail on the hall table was a copy of this quarter's issue of Life and Letters, to which his landlord subscribed. Its severe cover announced that its editor, Frederic Woolley, had this month contributed an essay called "Two Poets," and Howe, picking it up, curious to see who the two poets might be, felt his own name start out at him with cabalistic power— Joseph Howe. As he continued to turn the pages his hand trembled.

Standing in the dark hall, holding the neat little magazine, Howe knew that his literary contempt for Frederic Woolley meant nothing, for he suddenly understood how he respected Woolley in the way of the world. He knew this by the trembling of his hand. And of the little world as well as the great, for although the literary groups of New York might dismiss Woolley, his name carried high authority in the academic world. At Dwight it was even a revered name, for it had been here at the college that Frederic Woolley had made the distinguished scholarly career from which he had gone on to literary journalism. In middle life he had been induced to take the editorship of Life and Letters, a literary monthly not widely read but heavily endowed, and in its pages he had carried on the defense of what he sometimes called the older values. He was not without wit, he had great knowledge and considerable taste, and even in the full movement of the "new" literature he had won a certain respect for his refusal to accept it. In France, even in England, he would have been connected with a more robust tradition of conservatism, but America gave him an audience not much better than genteel. It was known in the college that to the subsidy of Life and Letters the Bradbys contributed a great part.

As Howe read, he saw that he was involved in nothing less than an event. When the Fifth Series of *Studies in Order and Value* came to be collected, this latest of Frederic Woolley's essays would not be merely another step in the old direction. Clearly and unmistakably, it was a turning point. All his literary life Woolley had been concerned with the relation of literature to mortality, religion, and the private and delicate pieties, and he had been unalterably opposed to all that he had called "inhuman humanitarianism." But here, suddenly, dramatically late, he had made an about-face, turning to the public life and to the humanitarian politics he had so long despised. This was the kind of incident the histories of literature make much of. Frederic Woolley was opening for himself a new career and winning a kind of new youth. He contrasted the two poets, Thomas Wormser, who was admirable, Joseph Howe, who was almost dangerous. He spoke of the "precious subjectivism" of Howe's verse. "In times like ours," he wrote, "with millions facing penury and want, one feels that the qualities of the *tour d'ivoire* are well-nigh inhuman, nearly insulting. The *tour d'ivoire* becomes the *tour d'ivresse*, and it is not self-intoxicated poets that our people need." The essay said more: "The problem is one of meaning. I am not ignorant that the creed of the esoteric poets declares that a poem does not and should not *mean* anything, that it *is* something. But poetry is what the poet makes it, and if he is a true poet he makes what his society needs. And what is needed now is the tradition in which Mr. Wormser writes, the true tradition of poetry. The Howes do no harm, but they do no good when positive good is demanded of all responsible men. Or do the Howes indeed do no harm? Perhaps Plato would have said they do, that in some ways theirs is the Phrygian music that turns men's minds from the struggle. Certainly it is true that Thomas Wormser writes in the lucid Dorian mode which sends men into battle with evil."

It was easy to understand why Woolley had chosen to praise Thomas Wormser. The long, lilting lines of *Corn Under Willows* hymned, as Woolley put it, the struggle for wheat in the Iowa fields, and expressed the real lives of real people. But why out of the dozen more notable examples he had chosen Howe's little volume as the example of "precious subjectivism" was hard to guess. In a way it was funny, this multiplication of himself into "the Howes." And yet this becoming the multiform political symbol by whose creation Frederic Woolley gave the sign of a sudden new life, this use of him as a sacrifice whose blood was necessary for the rites of rejuvenation, made him feel oddly unclean.

Nor could Howe get rid of a certain practical resentment. As a poet he had a special and respectable place in the college life. But it might be another thing to be marked as the poet of a wilful and selfish obscurity.

As he walked to the Bradbys', Howe was a little tense and defensive. It seemed to him that all the world knew of the "attack" and agreed with it. And, indeed, the Bradbys had read the essay but Professor

Bradby, a kind and pretentious man, said, "I see my old friend knocked you about a bit, my boy," and his wife Eugenia looked at Howe with her childlike blue eyes and said, "I shall *scold* Frederic for the untrue things he wrote about you. You aren't the least obscure." They beamed at him. In their genial snobbery they seemed to feel that he had distinguished himself. He was the leader of Howeism. He enjoyed the dinner party as much as he had thought he would.

And in the following days, as he was more preoccupied with his duties, the incident was forgotten. His classes had ceased to be mere groups. Student after student detached himself from the mass and required or claimed a place in Howe's awareness. Of them all it was Tertan who first and most violently signaled his separate existence. A week after classes had begun Howe saw his silhouette on the frosted glass of his office door. It was motionless for a long time, perhaps stopped by the problem of whether or not to knock before entering. Howe called, "Come in!" and Tertan entered with his shambling stride.

He stood beside the desk, silent and at attention. When Howe asked him to sit down, he responded with a gesture of head and hand, as if to say that such amenities were beside the point. Nevertheless, he did take the chair. He put his ragged, crammed briefcase between his legs. His face, which Howe now observed fully for the first time, was confusing, for it was made up of florid curves, the nose arched in the bone and voluted in the nostril, the mouth loose and soft and rather moist. Yet the face was so thin and narrow as to seem the very type of asceticism. Lashes of unusual length veiled the eyes and, indeed, it seemed as if there were a veil over the whole countenance. Before the words actually came, the face screwed itself into an attitude of preparation for them.

"You can confer with me now?" Tertan said.

"Yes, I'd be glad to. There are several things in your two themes I want to talk to you about." Howe reached for the packet of themes on his desk and sought for Tertan's. But the boy was waving them away.

"These are done perforce," he said. "Under the pressure of your requirement. They are not significant; mere duties." Again his great hand flapped vaguely to dismiss his themes. He leaned forward and gazed at his teacher.

"You are," he said, "a man of letters? You are a poet?" It was more declaration than question.

"I should like to think so," Howe said.

At first Tertan accepted the answer with a show of appreciation, as though the understatement made a secret between himself and Howe. Then he chose to misunderstand. With his shrewd and disconcerting control of expression, he presented to Howe a puzzled grimace. "What does that mean?" he said.

Howe retracted the irony. "Yes. I am a poet." It sounded strange to say.

"That," Tertan said, "is a wonder." He corrected himself with his ducking head. "I mean that is wonderful."

Suddenly, he dived at the miserable briefcase between his legs, put it on his knees, and began to fumble with the catch, all intent on the difficulty it presented. Howe noted that his suit was worn thin, his shirt almost unclean. He became aware, even, of a vague and musty odor of garments worn too long in unaired rooms. Tertan conquered the lock and began to concentrate upon a search into the interior. At last he held in his hand what he was after, a torn and crumpled copy of *Life and Letters*.

"I learned it from here," he said, holding it out.

Howe looked at him sharply, his hackles a little up. But the boy's face was not only perfectly innocent, it even shone with a conscious admiration. Apparently nothing of the import of the essay had touched him except the wonderful fact that his teacher was a "man of letters." Yet this seemed too stupid, and Howe, to test it, said, "The man who wrote that doesn't think it's wonderful."

Tertan made a moist hissing sound as he cleared his mouth of saliva. His head, oddly loose on his neck, wove a pattern of contempt in the air. "A critic," he said, "who admits *prima facie* that he does not understand." Then he said grandly, "It is the inevitable fate."

It was absurd, yet Howe was not only aware of the absurdity but of a tension suddenly and wonderfully relaxed. Now that the "attack" was on the table between himself and this strange boy, and subject to the boy's funny and absolutely certain contempt, the hidden force of his feeling was revealed to him in the very moment that it vanished. All unsuspected, there had been a film over the ·world, a transparent but discoloring haze of danger. But he had no time to stop over the brightened aspect of things. Tertan was going on. "I also am a man of letters. Putative."

"You have written a good deal?" Howe meant to be no more than polite, and he was surprised at the tenderness he heard in his words.

Solemnly the boy nodded, threw back the dank lock, and sucked in a deep, anticipatory breath. "First, a work of homiletics, which is a defense of the principles of religious optimism against the pessimism of Schopenhauer and the humanism of Nietzsche."

"Humanism? Why do you call it humanism?"

"It is my nomenclature for making a deity of man," Tertan replied negligently. "Then three fictional works, novels. And numerous essays in science, combating materialism. Is it your duty to read these if I bring them to you?"

Howe answered simply, "No, it isn't exactly my duty, but I shall be happy to read them."

Tertan stood up and remained silent. He rested his bag on the chair. With a certain compunction—for it did not seem entirely proper that, of two men of letters, one should have the right to blue-pencil the other, to grade him or to question the quality of his "sentence structure" —Howe reached for Tertan's papers. But before he could take them up, the boy suddenly made his bow-to-Abelard, the stiff inclination of the body with the hands seeming to emerge from the scholar's gown. Then he was gone.

But after his departure something was still left of him. The timbre of his curious sentences, the downright finality of so quaint a phrase as "It is the inevitable fate" still rang in the air. Howe gave the warmth of his feeling to the new visitor who stood at the door announcing himself with a genteel clearing of the throat.

"Doctor Howe, I believe?" the student said. A large hand advanced into the room and grasped Howe's hand. "Blackburn, sir, Theodore Blackburn, vice-president of the Student Council. A great pleasure, sir."

Out of a pair of ruddy cheeks a pair of small eyes twinkled good-naturedly. The large face, the large body were not so much fat as beefy and suggested something "typical"—monk, politician, or innkeeper.

Blackburn took the seat beside Howe's desk. "I may have seemed to introduce myself in my public capacity, sir," he said. "But it is really as an individual that I came to see you. That is to say, as one of your students to be."

He spoke with an English intonation and he went on, "I was once an English major, sir."

For a moment Howe was startled, for the roast-beef look of the boy and the manner of his speech gave a second's credibility to one sense of his statement. Then the collegiate meaning of the phrase asserted itself, but some perversity made Howe say what was not really in good taste even with so forward a student, "Indeed? What regiment?"

Blackburn stared and then gave a little pouf-pouf of laughter. He waved the misapprehension away. "*Very* good, sir. It certainly is an ambiguous term." He chuckled in appreciation of Howe's joke, then cleared his throat to put it aside. "I look forward to taking your course in the romantic poets, sir," he said earnestly. "To me the romantic poets are the very crown of English literature."

Howe made a dry sound, and the boy, catching some meaning in it, said, "Little as I know them, of course. But even Shakespeare who is so dear to us of the Anglo-Saxon tradition is in a sense but the preparation for Shelley, Keats and Byron. And Wadsworth."

Almost sorry for him, Howe dropped his eyes. With some embarrassment, for the boy was not actually his student, he said softly "Wordsworth."

"Sir?"

"Wordsworth, not Wadsworth. You said Wadsworth."

"Did I, sir?" Gravely he shook his head to rebuke himself for the error. Wordsworth, of course—slip of the tongue." Then, quite in command again, he went on. "I have a favor to ask of you, Doctor Howe. You see, I began my college course as an English major,"—he smiled—"as I said."

"Yes?"

"But after my first year I shifted. I shifted to the social sciences. Sociology and government—I find them stimulating and very *real.*" He paused, out of respect for reality. "But now I find that perhaps I have neglected the other side."

"The other side?" Howe said.

"Imagination, fancy, culture. A well-rounded man." He trailed off as if there were perfect understanding between them. "And so, sir, I have decided to end my senior year with your course in the romantic poets."

His voice was filled with an indulgence which Howe ignored as he said flatly and gravely, "But that course isn't given until the spring term."

"Yes, sir, and that is where the favor comes in. Would you let me take your romantic prose course? I can't take it for credit, sir, my program is full, but just for background it seems to me that I ought to take it. I do hope," he concluded in a manly way, "that you will consent."

"Well, it's no great favor, Mr. Blackburn. You can come if you wish, though there's not much point in it if you don't do the reading."

The bell rang for the hour and Howe got up.

"May I begin with this class, sir?" Blackburn's smile was candid and boyish.

Howe nodded carelessly and together, silently, they walked to the classroom down the hall. When they reached the door Howe stood back to let his student enter, but Blackburn moved adroitly behind him and grasped him by the arm to urge him over the threshold. They entered together with Blackburn's hand firmly on Howe's biceps, the student inducting the teacher into his own room. Howe felt a surge of temper rise in him and almost violently he disengaged his arm and walked to the desk, while Blackburn found a seat in the front row and smiled at him.

II

The question was, At whose door must the tragedy be laid?

All night the snow had fallen heavily and only now was abating in sparse little flurries. The windows were valanced high with white. It was very quiet; something of the quiet of the world had reached the class, and Howe found that everyone was glad to talk or listen. In the room there was a comfortable sense of pleasure in being human.

Casebeer believed that the blame for the tragedy rested with heredity. Picking up the book he read, "The sins of the fathers are visited on their children." This opinion was received with general favor. Nevertheless,

Johnson ventured to say that the fault was all Pastor Manders' because the Pastor had made Mrs. Alving go back to her husband and was always hiding the truth. To this Hibbard objected with logic enough, "Well then, it was really all her husband's fault. He *did* all the bad things." De Witt, his face bright with an impatient idea, said that the fault was all society's. "By society I don't mean upper-crust society," he said. He looked around a little defiantly, taking in any members of the class who might be members of upper-crust society. "Not in that sense. I mean the social unit."

Howe nodded and said, "Yes, of course."

"If the society of the time had progressed far enough in science," De Witt went on, "then there would be no problem for Mr. Ibsen to write about. Captain Alving plays around a little, gives way to perfectly natural biological urges, and he gets a social disease, a venereal disease. If the disease is cured, no problem. Invent salvarsan and the disease is cured. The problem of heredity disappears and li'l Oswald just doesn't get paresis. No paresis, no problem—no problem, no play."

This was carrying the ark into battle, and the class looked at De Witt with respectful curiosity. It was his usual way and on the whole they were sympathetic with his struggle to prove to Howe that science was better than literature. Still, there was something in his reckless manner that alienated them a little.

"Or take birth-control, for instance," De Witt went on. "If Mrs. Alving had some knowledge of contraception, she wouldn't have had to have li'l Oswald at all. No li'l Oswald, no play."

The class was suddenly quieter. In the back row Stettenhover swung his great football shoulders in a righteous sulking gesture, first to the right, then to the left. He puckered his mouth ostentatiously. Intellect was always ending up by talking dirty.

Tertan's hand went up, and Howe said, "Mr. Tertan." The boy shambled to his feet and began his long characteristic gulp. Howe made a motion with his fingers, as small as possible, and Tertan ducked his head and smiled in apology. He sat down. The class laughed. With more than half the term gone, Tertan had not been able to remember that one did not rise to speak. He seemed unable to carry on the life of the intellect without this mark of respect for it. To Howe the boy's habit of rising seemed to accord with the formal shabbiness of his dress. He never wore the casual sweaters and jackets of his classmates. Into the free and comfortable air of the college classroom he brought the stuffy sordid strictness of some crowded, metropolitan high school.

"Speaking from one sense," Tertan began slowly, "there is no blame ascribable. From the sense of determinism, who can say where the blame lies? The preordained is the preordained and it cannot be said without rebellion against the universe, a palpable absurdity."

In the back row Stettenhover slumped suddenly in his seat, his heels held out before him, making a loud, dry, disgusted sound. His body sank until his neck rested on the back of his chair. He folded his hands across his belly and looked significantly out of the window, exasperated not only with Tertan, but with Howe, with the class, with the whole system designed to encourage this kind of thing. There was a certain insolence in the movement and Howe flushed. As Tertan continued to speak, Howe stalked casually toward the window and placed himself in the line of Stettenhover's vision. He stared at the great fellow, who pretended not to see him. There was so much power in the big body, so much contempt in the Greek-athlete face under the crisp Greek-athlete curls, that Howe felt almost physical fear. But at last Stettenhover admitted him to focus and under his disapproving gaze sat up with slow indifference. His eyebrows raised high in resignation, he began to examine his hands. Howe relaxed and turned his attention back to Tertan.

"Flux of existence," Tertan was saying, "produces all things, so that judgment wavers. Beyond the phenomena, what? But phenomena are adumbrated and to them we are limited."

Howe saw it for a moment as perhaps it existed in the boy's mind— the world of shadows which are cast by a great light upon a hidden reality as in the old myth of the Cave. But the little brush with Stettenhover had tired him, and he said irritably, "But come to the point, Mr. Tertan."

He said it so sharply that some of his class looked at him curiously. For three months he had gently carried Tertan through his verbosities, to the vaguely respectful surprise of the other students, who seemed to conceive that there existed between this strange classmate and their teacher some special understanding from which they were content to be excluded. Tertan looked at him mildly, and at once came brilliantly to the point. "This is the summation of the play," he said and took up his book and read, "Your poor father never found any outlet for the over-mastering joy of life that was in him. And I brought no holiday into his home, either. Everything seemed to turn upon duty and I am afraid I made your poor father's home unbearable to him, Oswald. Spoken by Mrs. Alving."

Yes that was surely the "summation" of the play and Tertan had hit it, as he hit, deviously and eventually, the literary point of almost everything. But now, as always, he was wrapping it away from sight. "For most mortals," he said, "there are only joys of biological urgings, gross and crass, such as the sensuous Captain Alving. For certain few there are the transmutations beyond these to a contemplation of the utter-whole."

Oh, the boy was mad. And suddenly the word, used in hyperbole, intended almost for the expression of exasperated admiration, became literal. Now that the word was used, it became simply apparent to Howe that Tertan was mad.

It was a monstrous word and stood like a bestial thing in the room. Yet it so completely comprehended everything that had puzzled Howe, it so arranged and explained what for three months had been perplexing him that almost at once its horror became domesticated. With this word Howe was able to understand why he had never been able to communicate to Tertan the value of a single criticism or correction of his wild, verbose themes. Their conferences had been frequent and long but had done nothing to reduce to order the splendid confusion of the boy's ideas. Yet, impossible though its expression was, Tertan's incandescent mind could always strike for a moment into some dark corner of thought.

And now it was suddenly apparent that it was not a faulty rhetoric that Howe had to contend with. With his new knowledge he looked at Tertan's face and wondered how he could have so long deceived himself. Tertan was still talking, and the class had lapsed into a kind of patient unconsciousness, a coma of respect for words which, for all that most of them knew, might be profound. Almost with a suffusion of shame, Howe believed that in some dim way the class had long ago had some intimation of Tertan's madness. He reached out as decisively as he could to seize the thread of Tertan's discourse before it should be entangled further.

"Mr. Tertan says that the blame must be put upon whoever kills the joy of living in another. We have been assuming that Captain Alving was a wholly bad man, but what if we assume that he became bad only because Mrs. Alving, when they were first married, acted toward him in the prudish way she says she did?"

It was a ticklish idea to advance to freshmen and perhaps not profitable. Not all of them were following.

"That would put the blame on Mrs. Alving herself, whom most of you admire. And she herself seems to think so." He glanced at his watch. The hour was nearly over. "What do you think, Mr. De Witt?"

De Witt rose to the idea; he wanted to know if society couldn't be blamed for educating Mrs. Alving's temperament in the wrong way. Casebeer was puzzled, Stettenhover continued to look at his hands until the bell rang.

Tertan, his brows louring in thought, was making as always for a private word. Howe gathered his books and papers to leave quickly. At this moment of his discovery and with the knowledge still raw, he could not engage himself with Tertan. Tertan sucked in his breath to prepare for speech and Howe made ready for the pain and confusion. But at that moment Casebeer detached himself from the group with which he had been conferring and which he seemed to represent. His constituency remained at a tactful distance. The mission involved the time of an assigned essay. Casebeer's presentation of the plea—it was based on the freshmen's heavy duties at the fraternities during Carnival Week—cut across Tertan's preparations for speech. "And so some of us fellows thought," Casebeer concluded with heavy solemnity, "that we could do a better job, give our minds to it more, if we had more time."

Tertan regarded Casebeer with mingled curiosity and revulsion. Howe not only said that he would postpone the assignment but went on to talk about the Carnival, and even drew the waiting constituency into the conversation. He was conscious of Tertan's stern and astonished stare, then of his sudden departure.

Now that the fact was clear, Howe knew that he must act on it. His course was simple enough. He must lay the case before the Dean. Yet he hesitated. His feeling for Tertan must now, certainly, be in some way invalidated. Yet could he, because of a word, hurry to assign to official and reasonable solicitude what had been, until this moment, so various and warm? He could at least delay and, by moving slowly, lend a poor grace to the necessary, ugly act of making his report.

It was with some notion of keeping the matter in his own hands that he went to the Dean's office to look up Tertan's records. In the outer office the Dean's secretary greeted him brightly, and at his request brought him the manila folder with the small identifying photograph pasted in the corner. She laughed. "He was looking for the birdie in the wrong place," she said.

Howe leaned over her shoulder to look at the picture. It was as bad as all the Dean's-office photographs were, but it differed from all that Howe had ever seen. Tertan, instead of looking into the camera, as no doubt he had been bidden, had, at the moment of exposure, turned his eyes upward. His mouth, as though conscious of the trick played on the photographer, had the sly superior look that Howe knew.

The secretary was fascinated by the picture. "What a funny boy," she said. "He looks like Tartuffe!"

And so he did, with the absurd piety of the eyes and the conscious slyness of the mouth and the whole face bloated by the bad lens.

"Is he *like* that?" the secretary said.

"Like Tartuffe? No."

From the photograph there was little enough comfort to be had. The records themselves gave no clue to madness, though they suggested sadness enough. Howe read of a father, Stanislaus Tertan, born in Budapest and trained in engineering in Berlin, once employed by the Hercules Chemical Corporation—this was one of the factories that dominated the sound end of the town—but now without employment. He read of a mother Erminie (Youngfellow) Tertan, born in Manchester, educated at a Normal School at Leeds, now housewife by profession. The family lived on Greenbriar Street which Howe knew as a row of once elegant homes near what was now the factory district. The old mansion had long ago been divided into small and primitive apartments. Of Ferdinand himself there was little to learn. He lived with his parents, had attended a Detroit high school and had transferred to the local school in his last year. His rating for intelligence, as expressed in numbers, was high, his scholastic record was remarkable, he held a college scholarship for his tuition.

Howe laid the folder on the secretary's desk. "Did you find what you wanted to know?" she asked.

The phrases from Tertan's momentous first theme came back to him. "Tertan I am, but what is Tertan? Of this time, of that place, of some parentage, what does it matter?"

"No, I didn't find it," he said.

Now that he had consulted the sad, half-meaningless record he knew all the more firmly that he must not give the matter out of his own hands. He must not release Tertan to authority. Not that he anticipated from the Dean anything but the greatest kindness for Tertan. The Dean would have the experience and skill which he himself could not have. One way or another the Dean could answer the question, "What is Tertan?" Yet this was precisely what he feared. He alone could keep alive—not forever but for a somehow important time—the question, "What is Tertan?" He alone could keep it still a question. Some sure instinct told him that he must not surrender the question to a clean official desk in a clear official light to be dealt with, settled and closed.

He heard himself saying, "Is the Dean busy at the moment? I'd like to see him."

His request came thus unbidden, even forbidden, and it was one of the surprising and startling incidents of his life. Later when he reviewed the events, so disconnected in themselves, or so merely odd, of the story that unfolded for him that year, it was over this moment, on its face the least notable, that he paused longest. It was frequently to be with fear and never without a certainty of its meaning in his own knowledge of himself that he would recall this simple, routine request, and the feeling of shame and freedom it gave him as he sent everything down the official chute. In the end, of course, no matter what he did to "protect" Tertan, he would have had to make the same request and lay the matter on the Dean's clean desk. But it would always be a landmark of his life that, at the very moment when he was rejecting the official way, he had been, without will or intention, so gladly drawn to it.

After the storm's last delicate flurry, the sun had come out. Reflected by the new snow, it filled the office with a golden light which was almost musical in the way it made all the commonplace objects of efficiency shine with a sudden sad and noble significance. And the light, now that he noticed it, made the utterance of his perverse and unwanted request even more momentous.

The secretary consulted the engagement pad. "He'll be free any minute. Don't you want to wait in the parlor?"

She threw open the door of the large and pleasant room in which the Dean held his Committee meetings, and in which his visitors waited. It was designed with a homely elegance on the masculine side of the eighteenth-century manner. There was a small coal fire in the grate and the handsome mahogany table was strewn with books and magazines. The large windows gave on the snowy lawn, and there was such a fine width of window that the white casements and walls seemed at this moment but a continuation of the snow, the snow but an extension of casement and walls. The outdoors seemed taken in and made safe, the indoors seemed luxuriously freshened and expanded.

Howe sat down by the fire and lighted a cigarette. The room had its intended effect upon him. He felt comfortable and relaxed, yet nicely organized, some young diplomatic agent of the eighteenth century, the newly fledged Swift carrying out Sir William Temple's business. The rawness of Tertan's case quite vanished. He crossed his legs and reached for a magazine.

It was that famous issue of *Life and Letters* that his idle hand had found and his blood raced as he sifted through it, and the shape of his own name, Joseph Howe, sprang out at him, still cabalistic in its power. He tossed the magazine back on the table as the door of the Dean's office opened and the Dean ushered out Theodore Blackburn.

"Ah, Joseph!" the Dean said.

Blackburn said, "Good morning, Doctor." Howe winced at the title and caught the flicker of amusement over the Dean's face. The Dean stood with his hand high on the door-jamb and Blackburn, still in the doorway, remained standing almost under the long arm.

Howe nodded briefly to Blackburn, snubbing his eager deference. "Can you give me a few minutes?" he said to the Dean.

"All the time you want. Come in." Before the two men could enter the office, Blackburn claimed their attention with a long full "er." As they turned to him, Blackburn said, "Can *you* give *me* a few minutes, Doctor Howe?" His eyes sparkled at the little audacity he had committed, the slightly impudent play with hierarchy. Of the three of them Blackburn kept himself the lowest, but he reminded Howe of his subaltern relation to the Dean.

"I mean, of course," Blackburn went on easily, "when you've finished with the Dean."

"I'll be in my office shortly," Howe said, turned his back on the ready "Thank you, sir," and followed the Dean into the inner room.

"Energetic boy," said the Dean. "A bit beyond himself but very energetic. Sit down."

The Dean lighted a cigarette, leaned back in his chair, sat easy and silent for a moment, giving Howe no signal to go ahead with business.

He was a young Dean, not much beyond forty, a tall handsome man with sad, ambitious eyes. He had been a Rhodes scholar. His friends looked for great things from him, and it was generally said that he had notions of education which he was not yet ready to try to put into practice.

His relaxed silence was meant as a compliment to Howe. He smiled and said, "What's the business, Joseph?"

"Do you know Tertan—Ferdinand Tertan, a freshman?"

The Dean's cigarette was in his mouth and his hands were clasped behind his head. He did not seem to search his memory for the name. He said, "What about him?"

Clearly the Dean knew something, and he was waiting for Howe to tell him more. Howe moved only tentatively. Now that he was doing what he had resolved not to do, he felt more guilty at having been so long deceived by Tertan and more need to be loyal to his error.

He's a strange fellow," he ventured. He said stubbornly, "In a strange way he's very brilliant." He concluded, "But very strange."

The springs of the Dean's swivel chair creaked as he came out of his sprawl and leaned forward to Howe. "Do you mean he's so strange that it's something you could give a name to?"

Howe looked at him stupidly. "What do you mean?" he said.

"What's his trouble?" the Dean said more neutrally.

"He's very brilliant, in a way. I looked him up and he has a top intelligence rating. But somehow, and it's hard to explain just how, what he says is always on the edge of sense and doesn't quite make it."

The Dean looked at him and Howe flushed up. The Dean had surely read Woolley on the subject of "the Howes" and the *tour d'ivresse*. Was that quick glance ironical?

The Dean picked up some papers from his desk, and Howe could see that they were in Tertan's impatient scrawl. Perhaps the little gleam in the Dean's glance had come only from putting facts together.

"He sent me this yesterday," the Dean said. "After an interview I had with him. I haven't been able to do more than glance at it. When you said what you did, I realized there was something wrong."

Twisting his mouth, the Dean looked over the letter. "You seem to be involved," he said without looking up. "By the way, what did you give him at mid-term?"

Flushing, setting his shoulders, Howe said firmly, "I gave him A-minus."

The Dean chuckled. "Might be a good idea if some of our nicer boys went crazy—just a little." He said, "Well," to conclude the matter and handed the papers to Howe. "See if this is the same thing you've been finding. Then we can go into the matter again."

Before the fire in the parlor, in the chair that Howe had been occupying, sat Blackburn. He sprang to his feet as Howe entered.

"I said my office, Mr. Blackburn." Howe's voice was sharp. Then he was almost sorry for the rebuke, so clearly and naively did Blackburn seem to relish his stay in the parlor, close to authority.

"I'm in a bit of a hurry, sir," he said, "and I did want to be sure to speak to you, sir."

He was really absurd, yet fifteen years from now he would have grown up to himself, to the assurance and mature beefiness. In banks, in consular offices, in brokerage firms, on the bench, more seriously affable, a little sterner, he would make use of his ability to be administered by his job. It was almost reassuring. Now he was exercising his too-great skill on Howe. "I owe you an apology, sir," he said.

Howe knew that he did, but he showed surprise.

"I mean, Doctor, after your having been so kind about letting me attend your class, I stopped coming." He smiled in deprecation. "Extracurricular activities take up so much of my time. I'm afraid I undertook more than I could perform."

Howe had noticed the absence and had been a little irritated by it after Blackburn's elaborate plea. It was an absence that might be interpreted as a comment on the teacher. But there was only one way for him to answer. "You've no need to apologize," he said. "It's wholly your affair."

Blackburn beamed. "I'm so glad you feel that way about it, sir. I was worried you might think I had stayed away because I was influenced by—" he stopped and lowered his eyes.

Astonished, Howe said, "Influenced by what?"

"Well, by—" Blackburn hesitated and for answer pointed to the table on which lay the copy of *Life and Letters*. Without looking at it, he knew where to direct his hand. "By the unfavorable publicity, sir." He hurried on. "And that brings me to another point, sir. I am vice president of Quill and Scroll, sir, the student literary society, and I wonder if you would address us. You could read your own poetry, sir, and defend your own point of view. It would be very interesting."

It was truly amazing. Howe looked long and cruelly into Blackburn's face, trying to catch the secret of the mind that could have conceived this way of manipulating him, this way so daring and inept—but not entirely inept—with its malice so without malignity. The fact did not yield its secret. Howe smiled broadly and said, "Of course I don't think you were influenced by the unfavorable publicity."

"I'm still going to take—regularly, your credit—your romantic poets course next term," Blackburn said.

"Don't worry, my dear fellow, don't worry about it."

Howe started to leave and Blackburn stopped him with, "But about Quill, sir?"

"Suppose we wait until next term? I'll be less busy then."

And Blackburn said, "Very good, sir, and thank you."

In his office the little encounter seemed less funny to Howe, was even in some indeterminate way disturbing. He made an effort to put it from his mind by turning to what was sure to disturb him more, the Tertan letter read in the new interpretation. He found what he had always found, the same florid leaps beyond fact and meaning, the same headlong certainty. But as his eye passed over the familiar scrawl it caught his own name, and for the second time that hour he felt the race of his blood.

"The Paraclete," Tertan had written to the Dean, "from a Greek word meaning to stand in place of, but going beyond the primitive idea to mean traditionally the helper, the one who comforts and assists, cannot without fundamental loss be jettisoned. Even if taken no longer in the supernatural sense, the concept remains deeply in the human consciousness inevitably. Humanitarianism is no reply, for not every man stands in the place of every other man for this other comrade's comfort. But certain are chosen out of the human race to be the consoler of some other. Of these, for example, is Joseph Barker Howe, Ph.D. Of intellects not the first yet of true intellect and lambent instructions, given to that which is intuitive and irrational, not to what is logical in the strict word, what is judged by him is of the heart and not the head. Here is one chosen, in that he chooses himself to stand in the place of another for comfort and consolation. To him more than another I give my gratitude, with all respect to our Dean who reads this, a noble man, but merely dedicated, not consecrated. But not in the aspect of the Paraclete only is Dr. Joseph Barker Howe established, for he must be the Paraclete to another aspect of himself, that which is driven and persecuted by the lack of understanding in the world at large, so that he in himself embodies the full history of man's tribulations and, overflowing upon others, notably the present writer, is the ultimate end."

This was love. There was no escape from it. Try as Howe might to remember that Terton was mad and all his emotions invalidated, he could not destroy the effect upon him of his student's stern, affectionate regard. He had betrayed not only a power of mind but a power of love. And, however firmly he held before his attention the fact of Tertan's madness, he could do nothing to banish the physical sensation of gratitude he felt. He had never thought of himself as "driven and persecuted" and he did not now. But still he could not make meaningless his sensation of gratitude. The pitiable Tertan sternly pitied him, and comfort came from Tertan's never-to-be-comforted mind.

III

In an academic community, even an efficient one, official matters move slowly. The term drew to a close with no action in the case of Tertan, and Joseph Howe had to confront a curious problem. How should he grade his strange student, Tertan?

Tertan's final examination had been no different from all his other writing, and what did one "give" such a student? De Witt must have his A, that was clear. Johnson would get a B. With Casebeer it was a question of a B-minus or a C-plus, and Stettenhover, who had been crammed by the team tutor to fill half a blue-book with his thin feminine scrawl, would have his C-minus which he would accept with mingled indifference and resentment. But with Tertan it was not so easy.

The boy was still in the college process and his name could not be omitted from the grade sheet. Yet what should a mind under suspicion of madness be graded? Until the medical verdict was given, it was for Howe to continue as Tertan's teacher and to keep his judgment pedagogical. Impossible to give him an F: he had not failed. B was for Johnson's stolid mediocrity. He could not be put on the edge of passing with Stettenhover, for he exactly did not pass. In energy and richness of intellect he was perhaps even De Witt's superior, and Howe toyed grimly with the notion of giving him an A, but that would lower the value of the A De Witt had won with his beautiful and clear, if still arrogant, mind. There was a notation which the Registrar recognized— Inc., for Incomplete, and in the horrible comedy of the situation, Howe considered that. But really only a mark of M for Mad would serve.

In his perplexity, Howe sought the Dean, but the Dean was out of town. In the end, he decided to maintain the A-minus he had given Tertan at mid-term. After all, there had been no falling away from that quality. He entered it on the grade sheet with something like bravado.

Academic time moves quickly. A college year is not really a year, lacking as it does three months. And it is endlessly divided into units which, at their beginning, appear larger than they are—terms, half-terms, months, weeks. And the ultimate unit, the hour, is not really an hour, lacking as it does ten minutes. And so the new term advanced rapidly, and one day the fields about the town were all brown, cleared of even the few thin patches of snow which had lingered so long.

Howe, as he lectured on the romantic poets, became conscious of Blackburn emanating wrath. Blackburn did it well, did it with enormous dignity. He did not stir in his seat, he kept his eyes fixed on Howe in perfect attention, but he abstained from using his notebook, there was no mistaking what he proposed to himself as an attitude. His elbow on the writing-wing of the chair, his chin on the curled fingers of his hand, he was the embodiment of intellectual indignation. He was thinking his own thoughts, would give no public offense, yet would claim his due, was not to be intimidated. Howe knew that he would present himself at the end of the hour.

Blackburn entered the office without invitation. He did not smile; there was no cajolery about him. Without invitation he sat down beside Howe's desk. He did not speak until he had taken the blue-book from his pocket. He said, "What does this mean, sir?"

It was a sound and conservative student tactic. Said in the usual way it meant, "How could you have so misunderstood me?" or "What does this mean for my future in the course?" But there were none of the humbler tones in Blackburn's way of saying it.

Howe made the established reply, "I think that's for you to tell me."

Blackburn continued icy. "I'm sure I can't, sir."

There was a silence between them. Both dropped their eyes to the blue-book on the desk. On its cover Howe had penciled: "F. This is very poor work."

Howe picked up the blue-book. There was always the possibility of injustice. The teacher may be bored by the mass of papers and not wholly attentive. A phrase, even the student's handwriting, may irritate him unreasonably. "Well," said Howe, "Let's go through it."

He opened the first page. "Now here: you write, In *The Ancient Mariner*, Coleridge lives in and transports us to a honey-sweet world where all is rich and strange, a world of charm to which we can escape from the humdrum existence of our daily lives, the world of romance. Here, in this warm and honey-sweet land of charming dreams we can relax and enjoy ourselves."

Howe lowered the paper and waited with a neutral look for Blackburn to speak. Blackburn returned the look boldly, did not speak, sat stolid and lofty. At last Howe said, speaking gently, "Did you mean that, or were you just at a loss for something to say?"

"You imply that I was just bluffing?" The quotation marks hung palpable in the air about the word.

"I'd like to know. I'd prefer believing that you were bluffing to believing that you really thought this."

Blackburn's eyebrows went up. From the height of a great and firm-based idea he looked at his teacher. He clasped the crags for a moment and then pounced, craftily, suavely. "Do you mean, Doctor Howe, that there aren't two opinions possible?"

It was superbly done in its air of putting all of Howe's intellectual life into the balance. Howe remained patient and simple. "Yes, many opinions are possible, but not this one. Whatever anyone believes of *The Ancient Mariner*, no one can in reason believe that it represents a—a honey-sweet world in which we can relax."

"But that is what I *feel*, sir."

This was well-done, too. Howe said, "Look, Mr. Blackburn. Do you really relax with hunger and thirst, the heat and the sea-serpents, the dead men with staring eyes, Life in Death and the skeletons? Come now, Mr. Blackburn."

Blackburn made no answer, and Howe pressed forward. "Now, you say of Wordsworth, 'Of peasant stock himself, he turned from the effete life of the salons and found in the peasant the hope of a flaming revolution which would sweep away all the old ideas. This is the subject of his best poems.'"

Beaming at his teacher with youthful eagerness, Blackburn said, "Yes, sir, a rebel, a bringer of light to suffering mankind. I see him as a kind of Prothemeus."

"A kind of what?"

"Prothemeus, sir."

"Think, Mr. Blackburn. We were talking about him only today and I mentioned his name a dozen times. You don't mean Prothemeus. You mean—" Howe waited, but there was no response.

"You mean Prometheus."

Blackburn gave no assent, and Howe took the reins. "You've done a bad job here, Mr. Blackburn, about as bad as could be done." He saw Blackburn stiffen and his genial face harden again. "It shows either a lack of preparation or a complete lack of understanding." He saw Blackburn's face begin to go to pieces and he stopped.

"Oh, sir," Blackburn burst out, "I've never had a mark like this before, never anything below a B, never. A thing like this has never happened to me before."

It must be true, it was a statement too easily verified. Could it be that other instructors accepted such flaunting nonsense? Howe wanted to end the interview. "I'll set it down to lack of preparation," he said. "I know you're busy. That's not an excuse, but it's an explanation. Now, suppose you really prepare, and then take another quiz in two weeks. We'll forget this one and count the other."

Blackburn squirmed with pleasure and gratitude. "Thank you, sir. You're really very kind, very kind."

Howe rose to conclude the visit. "All right, then—in two weeks."

It was that day that the Dean imparted to Howe the conclusion of the case of Tertan. It was simple and a little anti-climactic. A physician had been called in, and had said the word, given the name.

"A classic case, he called it," the Dean said. "Not a doubt in the world," he said. His eyes were full of miserable pity, and he clutched at a word. "A classic case, a classic case." To his aid and to Howe's there came the Parthenon and the form of the Greek drama, the Aristotelian logic, Racine and the Well-Tempered Clavichord, the blueness of the Aegean and its clear sky. Classic—that is to say, without a doubt, perfect in its way, a veritable model, and, as the Dean had been told, sure to take a perfectly predictable and inevitable course to a foreknown conclusion.

It was not only pity that stood in the Dean's eyes. For a moment there was fear too. "Terrible," he said, "it is simply terrible."

Then he went on briskly. "Naturally, we've told the boy nothing. And, naturally, we won't. His tuition's paid by his scholarship, and we'll continue him on the rolls until the end of the year. That will be kindest. After that the matter will be out of our control. We'll see, of course, that he gets into the proper hands. I'm told there will be no change, he'll go on like this, be as good as this, for four to six months. And so we'll just go along as usual."

So Tertan continued to sit in Section 5 of English 1A, to his classmates still a figure of curiously dignified fun, symbol to most of them of the respectable but absurd intellectual life. But to his teacher he was now very different. He had not changed—he was still the greyhound casting for the scent of ideas, and Howe could see that he was still the same Tertan, but he could not feel it. What he felt as he looked at the boy sitting in his accustomed place was the hard blank of a fact. The fact itself was formidable and depressing. But what Howe was chiefly aware of was that he had permitted the metamorphosis of Tertan from person to fact.

As much as possible he avoided seeing Tertan's upraised hand and eager eye. But the fact did not know of its mere factuality, it continued its existence as if it were Tertan, hand up and eye questioning, and one day it appeared in Howe's office with a document.

"Even the spirit who lives egregiously, above the herd, must have its relations with the fellowman," Tertan declared. He laid the document on Howe's desk. It was headed "Quill and Scroll Society of Dwight College. Application for Membership."

"In most ways these are crass minds," Tertan said, touching the paper. "Yet as a whole, bound together in their common love of letters, they ∠ranscend their intellectual lacks since it is not a paradox that the whole is greater than the sum of its parts."

"When are the elections?" Howe asked.

"They take place tomorrow."

"I certainly hope you will be successful."

"Thank you. Would you wish to implement that hope?" A rather dirty finger pointed to the bottom of the sheet. "A faculty recommender is necessary," Tertan said stiffly, and waited.

"And you wish me to recommend you?"

"It would be an honor."

"You may use my name."

Tertan's finger pointed again. "It must be a written sponsorship, signed by the sponsor." There was a large blank space on the form under the heading, "Opinion of Faculty Sponsor."

This was almost another thing and Howe hesitated. Yet there was nothing else to do and he took out his fountain pen. He wrote, "Mr. Ferdinand Tertan is marked by his intense devotion to letters and by his exceptional love of all things of the mind." To this he signed his name, which looked bold and assertive on the white page. It disturbed him, the strange affirming power of a name. With a business-like air, Tertan whipped up the paper, folding it with decision, and put it into his pocket. He bowed and took his departure, leaving Howe with the sense of having done something oddly momentous.

And so much now seemed odd and momentous to Howe that should not have seemed so. It was odd and momentous, he felt, when he sat with Blackburn's second quiz before him, and wrote in an excessively firm hand the grade of C-minus. The paper was a clear, an indisputable failure. He was carefully and consciously committing a cowardice. Blackburn had told the truth when he had pleaded his past record. Howe had consulted it in the Dean's office. It showed no grade lower than a B-minus. A canvass of some of Blackburn's previous instructors had brought vague attestations to the adequate powers of a student imperfectly remembered, and sometimes surprise that his abilities could be questioned at all.

As he wrote the grade, Howe told himself that his cowardice sprang from an unwillingness to have more dealings with a student he disliked. He knew it was simpler than that. He knew he feared Blackburn: that was the absurd truth. And cowardice did not solve the matter after all. Blackburn, flushed with a first success, attacked at once. The minimal passing grade had not assuaged his feelings and he sat at Howe's desk and again the blue-book lay between them. Blackburn said nothing. With an enormous impudence, he was waiting for Howe to speak and explain himself.

At last Howe said sharply and rudely, "Well?" His throat was tense and the blood was hammering in his head. His mouth was tight with anger at himself for his disturbance.

Blackburn's glance was almost baleful. "This is impossible, sir."

"But there it is," Howe answered.

"Sir?" Blackburn had not caught the meaning but his tone was still haughty.

Impatiently Howe said, "There it is, plain as day. Are you here to complain again?"

"Indeed I am, sir." There was surprise in Blackburn's voice that Howe should ask the question.

"I shouldn't complain if I were you. You did a thoroughly bad job on your first quiz. This one is a little, only a very little, better." This was not true. If anything, it was worse.

"That might be a matter of opinion, sir."

"It is a matter of opinion. Of my opinion."

"Another opinion might be different, sir."

"You really believe that?" Howe said.

"Yes." The omission of the "sir" was monumental.

"Whose, for example?"

"The Dean's, for example." Then the fleshy jaw came forward a little. "Or a certain literary critic's, for example."

It was colossal and almost too much for Blackburn himself to handle.

The solidity of his face almost crumpled under it. But he withstood his own audacity and went on. "And the Dean's opinion might be guided by the knowledge that the person who gave me this mark is the man whom a famous critic, the most eminent judge of literature in this country, called a drunken man. The Dean might think twice about whether such a man is fit to teach Dwight students."

Howe said in quiet admonition, "Blackburn, you're mad," meaning no more than to check the boy's extravagance.

But Blackburn paid no heed. He had another shot in the locker. "And the Dean might be guided by the information, of which I have evidence, documentary evidence,"—he slapped his breast pocket twice— "that this same person personally recommended to the college literary society, the oldest in the country, that he personally recommended a student who is crazy, who threw the meeting into an uproar—a psychiatric case. The Dean might take that into account."

Howe was never to learn the details of that "uproar." He had always to content himself with the dim but passionate picture which at that moment sprang into his mind, of Tertan standing on some abstract height and madly denouncing the multitude of Quill and Scroll who howled him down.

He sat quiet a moment and looked at Blackburn. The ferocity had entirely gone from the student's face. He sat regarding his teacher almost benevolently. He had played a good card and now, scarcely at all unfriendly, he was waiting to see the effect. Howe took up the blue-book and negligently sifted through it. He read a page, closed the book, struck out the C-minus and wrote an F.

"Now you may take the paper to the Dean," he said. "You may tell him that after reconsidering it, I lowered the grade."

The gasp was audible. "Oh, sir!" Blackburn cried. "Please!" His face was agonized. "It means my graduation, my livelihood, my future. Don't do this to me."

"It's done already."

Blackburn stood up, "I spoke rashly, sir, hastily. I had no intention, no real intention, of seeing the Dean. It rests with you—entirely, entirely. I *hope* you will restore the first mark."

"Take the matter to the Dean or not, just as you choose. The grade is what you deserve and it stands."

Blackburn's head dropped. "And will I be failed at mid-term, sir?"

"Of course."

From deep out of Blackburn's great chest rose a cry of anguish. "Oh, sir, if you want me to go down on my knees to you, I will, I will."

Howe looked at him in amazement.

"I will, I will. On my knees, sir. This mustn't, mustn't happen."

He spoke so literally, meaning so very truly that his knees and exactly

his knees were involved and seeming to think that he was offering something of tangible value to his teacher, that Howe, whose head had become
icy clear in the nonsensical drama, thought, "The boy is mad," and began
to speculate fantastically whether something in himself attracted or
developed aberration. He could see himself standing absurdly before the
Dean and saying, "I've found another. This time it's the Vice-president
of the Council, the manager of the debating team and secretary of Quill
and Scroll."

One more such discovery, he thought, and he himself would be
discovered! And there, suddenly, Blackburn was on his knees with a
thump, his huge thighs straining his trousers, his hand outstretched in a
great gesture of supplication.

With a cry, Howe shoved back his swivel chair and it rolled away
on its casters half across the little room. Blackburn knelt for a moment
to nothing at all, then got to his feet.

Howe rose abruptly. He said, "Blackburn, you will stop acting like
an idiot. Dust your knees off, take your paper and get out. You've
behaved like a fool and a malicious person. You have half a term to do
a decent job. Keep your silly mouth shut and try to do it. Now get out."

Blackburn's head was low. He raised it and there was a pious light
in his eyes. "Will you shake hands, sir?" he said. He thrust out his hand.

"I will not," Howe said.

Head and hand sank together. Blackburn picked up his blue-book
and walked to the door. He turned and said, "Thank you, sir." His back,
as he departed, was heavy with tragedy and stateliness.

IV

After years of bad luck with the weather, the College had a perfect day
for Commencement. It was wonderfully bright, the air so transparent,
the wind so brisk that no one could resist talking about it.

As Howe set out for the campus he heard Hilda calling from the
back yard. She called, "Professor, professor," and came running to him.

Howe said, "What's this 'professor' business."

"Mother told me," Hilda said. "You've been promoted. And I want
to take your picture."

"Next year," said Howe. "I won't be a professor until next year. And
you know better than to call anybody professor."

"It was just in fun," Hilda said. She seemed disappointed.

"But you can take my picture if you want. I won't look much different
next year." Still, it was frightening. It might mean that he was to stay
in this town all his life.

Hilda brightened. "Can I take it in this?" she said, and touched the
gown he carried over his arm.

Howe laughed. "Yes, you can take it in this."

"I'll get my things and meet you in front of Otis," Hilda said. "I have the background all picked out."

On the campus the Commencement crowd was already large. It stood about in eager, nervous little family groups. As he crossed, Howe was greeted by a student, capped and gowned, glad of the chance to make an event for his parents by introducing one of his teachers. It was while Howe stood there chatting that he saw Tertan.

He had never seen anyone quite so alone, as though a circle had been woven about him to separate him from the gay crowd on the campus. Not that Tertan was not gay, he was the gayest of all. Three weeks had passed since Howe had last seen him, the weeks of examination, the lazy week before Commencement, and this was now a different Tertan. On his head he wore a panama hat, broad-brimmed and fine, of the shape associated with South American planters. He wore a suit of raw silk, luxurious, but yellowed with age and much too tight, and he sported a whangee cane. He walked sedately, the hat tilted at a devastating angle, the stick coming up and down in time to his measured tread. He had, Howe guessed, outfitted himself to greet the day in the clothes of that ruined father whose existence was on record in the Dean's office. Gravely and arrogantly he surveyed the scene—in it, his whole bearing seemed to say, but not of it. With his haughty step, with his flashing eye, Tertan was coming nearer. Howe did not wish to be seen. He shifted his position slightly. When he looked again, Tertan was not in sight.

The chapel clock struck the quarter hour. Howe detached himself from his chat and hurried to Otis Hall at the far end of the campus. Hilda had not yet come. He went up into the high portico and, using the glass of the door for a mirror, put on his gown, adjusted the hood on his shoulders and set the mortarboard on his head. When he came down the steps, Hilda had arrived.

Nothing could have told him more forcibly that a year had passed than the development of Hilda's photographic possessions from the box camera of the previous fall. By a strap about her neck was hung a leather case, so thick and strong, so carefully stitched and so molded to its contents that it could only hold a costly camera. The appearance was deceptive, Howe knew, for he had been present at the Aikens' pre-Christmas conference about its purchase. It was only a fairly good domestic camera. Still, it looked very impressive. Hilda carried another leather case from which she drew a collapsible tripod. Decisively she extended each of its gleaming legs and set it up on the path. She removed the camera from its case and fixed it to the tripod. In its compact efficiency the camera almost had a life of its own, but Hilda treated it with easy familiarity, looked into its eye, glanced casually at its gauges. Then from a pocket she took still another leather case and drew from it a small instrument through which she looked first at Howe, who began to feel inanimate and lost, and then at the sky. She made some adjustment on the instrument, then some adjustment on the camera. She swept the scene with her eye, found a spot and pointed the camera in its direction. She walked to the spot, stood on it and beckoned to Howe. With each new leather case, with each new instrument, and with each new adjustment she had grown in ease and now she said, "Joe, will you stand here?"

Obediently Howe stood where he was bidden. She had yet another instrument. She took out a tape-measure on a mechanical spool. Kneeling down before Howe, she put the little metal ring of the tape under the tip of his shoe. At her request, Howe pressed it with his toe. When she had measured her distance, she nodded to Howe who released the tape. At a touch, it sprang back into the spool. "You have to be careful if you're going to get what you want," Hilda said. "I don't believe in all this snap-snap-snapping," she remarked loftily. Howe nodded in agreement, although he was beginning to think Hilda's care excessive.

Now at last the moment had come. Hilda squinted into the camera, moved the tripod slightly. She stood to the side, holding the plunger of the shutter-cable. "Ready," she said. "Will you relax, Joseph, please?" Howe realized that he was standing frozen. Hilda stood poised and precise as a setter, one hand holding the little cable, the other extended with curled dainty fingers like a dancer's, as if expressing to her subject the precarious delicacy of the moment. She pressed the plunger and there was the click. At once she stirred to action, got behind the camera, turned a new exposure. "Thank you," she said. "Would you stand under that tree and let me do a character study with light and shade?"

The childish absurdity of the remark restored Howe's ease. He went to the little tree. The pattern the leaves made on his gown was what Hilda was after. He had just taken a satisfactory position when he heard in the unmistakable voice, "Ah, Doctor! Having your picture taken?"

Howe gave up the pose and turned to Blackburn who stood on the walk, his hands behind his back, a little too large for his bachelor's gown. Annoyed that Blackburn should see him posing for a character study in light and shade, Howe said irritably, "Yes, having my picture taken."

Blackburn beamed at Hilda. "And the little photographer?" he said. Hilda fixed her eyes on the ground and stood closer to her brilliant and aggressive camera. Blackburn, teetering on his heels, his hands behind his back, wholly prelatical and benignly patient, was not abashed at the silence. At last Howe said, "If you'll excuse us, Mr. Blackburn, we'll go on with the picture."

"Go right ahead, sir. I'm running along." But he only came closer. "Doctor Howe," he said fervently, "I want to tell you how glad I am that I was able to satisfy your standards at last."

Howe was surprised at the hard, insulting brightness of his own voice, and even Hilda looked up curiously as he said, "Nothing you have ever done has satisfied me, and nothing you could ever do would satisfy me, Blackburn."

With a glance at Hilda, Blackburn made a gesture as if to hush Howe—as though all his former bold malice had taken for granted a kind of understanding between himself and his teacher, a secret which must not be betrayed to a third person. "I only meant, sir," he said, "that I was able to pass your course after all."

Howe said, "You didn't pass my course. I passed you out of my course. I passed you without even reading your paper. I wanted to be sure the college would be rid of you. And when all the grades were in and I did read your paper, I saw I was right not to have read it first."

Blackburn presented a stricken face. "It was very bad, sir?"

But Howe had turned away. The paper had been fantastic. The paper had been, if he wished to see it so, mad. It was at this moment that the Dean came up behind Howe and caught his arm. "Hello, Joseph," he said. "We'd better be getting along, it's almost late."

He was not a familiar man, but when he saw Blackburn, who approached to greet him, he took Blackburn's arm, too. "Hello, Theodore," he said. Leaning forward on Howe's arm and on Blackburn's, he said, "Hello, Hilda dear." Hilda replied quietly, "Hello, Uncle George."

Still clinging to their arms, still linking Howe and Blackburn, the Dean said, "Another year gone, Joe, and we've turned out another crop. After you've been here a few years, you'll find it reasonably upsetting— you wonder how there can be so many graduating classes while you stay the same. But of course you don't stay the same." Then he said, "Well," sharply, to dismiss the thought. He pulled Blackburn's arm and swung him around to Howe. "Have you heard about Teddy Blackburn?" he asked. "He has a job already, before graduation—the first man of his class to be placed." Expectant of congratulations, Blackburn beamed at Howe. Howe remained silent.

"Isn't that good?" the Dean said. Still Howe did not answer and the Dean, puzzled and put out, turned to Hilda. "That's a very fine-looking camera, Hilda." She touched it with affectionate pride.

"Instruments of precision," said a voice. "Instruments of precision." Of the three with joined arms, Howe was the nearest to Tertan, whose gaze took in all the scene except the smile and the nod which Howe gave him. The boy leaned on his cane. The broad-brimmed hat, canting jauntily over his eye, confused the image of his face that Howe had established, suppressed the rigid lines of the ascetic and brought out the baroque curves. It made an effect of perverse majesty.

"Instruments of precision," said Tertan for the last time, addressing no one, making a casual comment to the universe. And it occurred to

Howe that Tertan might not be referring to Hilda's equipment. The sense of the thrice-woven circle of the boy's loneliness smote him fiercely. Tertan stood in majestic jauntiness, superior to all the scene, but his isolation made Howe ache with a pity of which Tertan was more the cause than the object, so general and indiscriminate was it.

Whether in his sorrow he made some unintended movement toward Tertan which the Dean checked, or whether the suddenly tightened grip on his arm was the Dean's own sorrow and fear, he did not know. Tertan watched them in the incurious way people watch a photograph being taken, and suddenly the thought that, to the boy, it must seem that the three were posing for a picture together made Howe detach himself almost rudely from the Dean's grasp.

"I promised Hilda another picture," he announced—needlessly, for Tertan was no longer there, he had vanished in the last sudden flux of visitors who, now that the band had struck up, were rushing nervously to find seats.

"You'd better hurry," the Dean said. "I'll go along, it's getting late for me." He departed and Blackburn walked stately by his side.

Howe again took his position under the little tree which cast its shadow over his face and gown. "Just hurry, Hilda, won't you?" he said. Hilda held the cable at arm's length, her other arm crooked and her fingers crisped. She rose on her toes and said "Ready," and pressed the release. "Thank you," she said gravely and began to dismantle her camera as he hurried off to join the procession.

Aldous Huxley

(1894–1963)

Educated at Eton and Oxford, Aldous Huxley was the son of Julia Arnold (Matthew Arnold's niece) and the grandson of the eminent biologist Thomas Henry Huxley (1825–1895). In 1946, fifteen years after the first appearance of his *Brave New World*, in a foreword written for the American edition of the novel, Aldous Huxley said, ". . . *Brave New World* is a book about the future and, whatever its artistic or philosophical qualities, a book about the future can interest us only if its prophecies look as though they might conceivably come true. From our present vantage point, fifteen years further down the inclined plane of modern history, how plausible do its prognostications seem?" If posed today, this question would draw the response "plausible in the extreme," for current popularizations of biological knowledge like Gordon Rattray Taylor's *The Biological Time Bomb* read awesomely like paraphrases of the forty-year-old novel.

Brave New World, from which the following excerpt is taken, is the story of a technological utopia where suffering has been outlawed and a god named Ford is worshipped. The citizen's environmental conditioning and genetic composition are predetermined by the World State. The traditional values of Western man are considered savage.

In regard to American education, a severe question haunts the following scenes: Which of the pedagogic theories and practices now in fashion would seem to foreshadow the results depicted in *Brave New World*?

Other fiction by Aldous Huxley includes *Crome Yellow* (1921), *Point Counter Point* (1928), and *The Devils of Loudon* (1952). His principal non-fiction works are *Grey Eminence* (1941), *The Art of Seeing* (1942), and *Themes and Variations* (1950).

THE STATE
CONDITIONING CENTER

I

A squat grey building of only thirty-four stories. Over the main entrance the words, CENTRAL LONDON HATCHERY AND CONDITIONING CENTRE, and, in a shield, the World State's motto, COMMUNITY, IDENTITY, STABILITY.

The enormous room on the ground floor faced towards the north. Cold for all the summer beyond the panes, for all the tropical heat of the room itself, a harsh thin light glared through the windows, hungrily seeking some draped lay figure, some pallid shape of academic goose-flesh, but finding only the glass and nickel and bleakly shining porcelain of a laboratory. Wintriness responded to wintriness. The overalls of the workers were white, their hands gloved with a pale corpse-coloured rubber. The light was frozen, dead, a ghost. Only from the yellow barrels of the microscopes did it borrow a certain rich and living substance, lying along the polished tubes like butter, streak after luscious streak in long recession down the work tables.

"And this," said the Director opening the door, "is the Fertilizing Room."

Bent over their instruments, three hundred Fertilizers were plunged, as the Director of Hatcheries and Conditioning entered the room, in the scarcely breathing silence, the absent-minded, soliloquizing hum or whistle, of absorbed concentration. A troop of newly arrived students, very young, pink and callow, followed nervously, rather abjectly, at the Director's heels. Each of them carried a notebook, in which, whenever the great man spoke, he desperately scribbled. Straight from the horse's mouth. It was a rare privilege. The D. H. C. for Central London always made a point of personally conducting his new students round the various departments.

"Just to give you a general idea," he would explain to them. For of course some sort of general idea they must have, if they were to do their work intelligently—though as little of one, if they were to be good and happy members of society, as possible. For particulars, as every one knows, make for virtue and happiness; generalities are intellectually necessary evils. Not philosophers but fret-sawyers and stamp collectors compose the backbone of society.

427

"To-morrow," he would add, smiling at them with a slightly menacing geniality, "you'll be settling down to serious work. You won't have time for generalities. Meanwhile . . ."

Meanwhile, it was a privilege. Straight from the horse's mouth into the notebook. The boys scribbled like mad.

Tall and rather thin but upright, the Director advanced into the room. He had a long chin and big rather prominent teeth, just covered, when he was not talking, by his full, floridly curved lips. Old, young? Thirty? Fifty? Fifty-five? It was hard to say. And anyhow the question didn't arise; in this year of stability, A. F. 632, it didn't occur to you to ask it.

"I shall begin at the beginning," said the D. H. C. and the more zealous students recorded his intention in their notebooks: *Begin at the beginning.* "These," he waved his hand, "are the incubators." And opening an insulated door he showed them racks upon racks of numbered test-tubes. "The week's supply of ova. Kept," he explained, "at blood heat; whereas the male gametes," and here he opened another door, "they have to be kept at thirty-five instead of thirty-seven. Full blood heat sterilizes." Rams wrapped in theremogene beget no lambs.

Still leaning against the incubators he gave them, while the pencils scurried illegibly across the pages, a brief description of the modern fertilizing process; spoke first, of course, of its surgical introduction— "the operation undergone voluntarily for the good of Society, not to mention the fact that it carries a bonus amounting to six months' salary"; continued with some account of the technique for preserving the excised ovary alive and actively developing; passed on to a consideration of optimum temperature, salinity, viscosity; referred to the liquor in which the detached and ripened eggs were kept; and, leading his charges to the work tables, actually showed them how this liquor was drawn off from the test-tubes; how it was let out drop by drop onto the specially warmed slides of the microscopes; how the eggs which it contained were inspected for abnormalities, counted and transferred to a porous receptacle; how (and he now took them to watch the operation) this receptacle was immersed in a warm bouillon containing free-swimming spermatozoa—at a minimum concentration of one hundred thousand per cubic centimetre, he insisted; and how, after ten minutes, the container was lifted out of the liquor and its contents re-examined; how, if any of the eggs remained unfertilized, it was again immersed, and, if necessary, yet again; how the fertilized ova went back to the incubators; where the Alphas and Betas remained until definitely bottled; while the Gammas, Deltas and Epsilons were brought out again, after only thirty-six hours, to undergo Bokanovsky's Process.

"Bokanovsky's Process," repeated the Director, and the students underlined the words in their little notebooks.

One egg, one embryo, one adult—normality. But a bokanovskified egg will bud, will proliferate, will divide. From eight to ninety-six buds, and every bud will grow into a perfectly formed embryo, and every embryo into a full-sized adult. Making ninety-six human beings grow where only one grew before. Progress.

"Essentially," the D.H.C. concluded, "bokanovskification consists of a series of arrests of development. We check the normal growth and, paradoxically enough, the egg responds by budding."

Responds by budding. The pencils were busy.

He pointed. On a very slowly moving band a rack-full of test-tubes was entering a large metal box, another rack-full was emerging. Machinery faintly purred. It took eight minutes for the tubes to go through, he told them. Eight minutes of hard X-rays being about as much as an egg can stand. A few died; of the rest, the least susceptible divided into two; most put out four buds; some eight; all were returned to the incubators, where the buds began to develop; then, after two days, were suddenly chilled, chilled and checked. Two, four, eight, the buds in their turn budded; and having budded were dosed almost to death with alcohol; consequently burgeoned again and having budded—bud out of bud out of bud—were thereafter—further arrest being generally fatal—left to develop in peace. By which time the original egg was in a fair way to becoming anything from eight to ninety-six embryos—a prodigious improvement, you will agree, on nature. Identical twins—but not in piddling twos and threes as in the old viviparous days, when an egg would sometimes accidentally divide; actually by dozens, by scores at a time.

"Scores," the Director repeated and flung out his arms, as though he were distributing largesse. "Scores."

But one of the students was fool enough to ask where the advantage lay.

"My good boy!" The Director wheeled sharply round on him. "Can't you see? Can't you *see?*" He raised a hand; his expression was solemn. "Bokanovsky's Process is one of the major instruments of social stability!"

Major instruments of social stability.

Standard men and women; in uniform batches. The whole of a small factory staffed with the products of a single bokanovskified egg.

"Ninety-six identical twins working ninety-six identical machines!" The voice was almost tremulous with enthusiasm. "You really know where you are. For the first time in history." He quoted the planetary motto. "Community, Identity, Stability." Grand words. "If we could bokanovskify indefinitely the whole problem would be solved."

Solved by standard Gammas, unvarying Deltas, uniform Epsilons. Millions of identical twins. The principle of mass production at last applied to biology.

"But, alas," the Director shook his head, "we *can't* bokanovskify indefinitely."

Ninety-six seemed to be the limit; seventy-two a good average. From the same ovary and with gametes of the same male to manufacture as many batches of identical twins as possible—that was the best (sadly a second best) that they could do. And even that was difficult.

"For in nature it takes thirty years for two hundred eggs to reach maturity. But our business is to stabilize the population at this moment, here and now. Dribbling out twins over a quarter of a century—what would be the use of that?"

Obviously, no use at all. But Podsnap's Technique had immensely accelerated the process of ripening. They could make sure of at least a hundred and fifty mature eggs within two years. Fertilize and bokanovskify—in other words, multiply by seventy-two—and you get an average of nearly eleven thousand brothers and sisters in a hundred and fifty batches of identical twins, all within two years of the same age.

"And in exceptional cases we can make one ovary yield us over fifteen thousand adult individuals."

Beckoning to a fair-haired, ruddy young man who happened to be passing at the moment. "Mr. Foster," he called. The ruddy young man approached. "Can you tell us the record for a single ovary, Mr. Foster?"

"Sixteen thousand and twelve in this Centre," Mr. Foster replied without hesitation. He spoke very quickly, had a vivacious blue eye, and took an evident pleasure in quoting figures. "Sixteen thousand and twelve; in one hundred and eighty-nine batches of identicals. But of course they've done much better," he rattled on, "in some of the tropical Centres. Singapore has often produced over sixteen thousand five hundred; and Mombasa has actually touched the seventeen thousand mark. But then they have unfair advantages. You should see the way a negro ovary responds to pituitary! It's quite astonishing, when you're used to working with European material. Still," he added, with a laugh (but the light of combat was in his eyes and the lift of his chin was challenging), "still, we mean to beat them if we can. I'm working on a wonderful Delta-Minus ovary at this moment. Only just eighteen months old. Over twelve thousand seven hundred children already, either decanted or in embryo. And still going strong. We'll beat them yet."

"That's the spirit I like!" cried the Director, and clapped Mr. Foster on the shoulder. "Come along with us, and give these boys the benefit of your expert knowledge."

Mr. Foster smiled modestly. "With pleasure." They went.

In the Bottling Room all was harmonious bustle and ordered activity. Flaps of fresh sow's peritoneum ready cut to the proper size came shooting up in little lifts from the Organ Store in the sub-basement. Whizz and then, click! the lift-hatches flew open; the bottle-liner had only to reach out a hand, take the flap, insert, smooth-down, and before the lined bottle had had time to travel out of reach along the endless band, whizz, click! another flap of peritoneum had shot up from the depths, ready to be slipped into yet another bottle, the next of that slow interminable procession on the band.

Next to the Liners stood the Matriculators. The procession advanced; one by one the eggs were transferred from their test-tubes to the larger containers; deftly the peritoneal lining was slit, the morula dropped into place, the saline solution poured in . . . and already the bottle had passed, and it was the turn of the labellers. Heredity, date of fertilization, membership of Bokanovsky Group—details were transferred from test-tube to bottle. No longer anonymous, but named, identified, the procession marched slowly on; on through an opening in the wall, slowly on into the Social Predestination Room.

"Eighty-eight cubic metres of card-index," said Mr. Foster with relish, as they entered.

"Containing *all* the relevant information," added the Director.

"Brought up to date every morning."

"And co-ordinated every afternoon."

"On the basis of which they make their calculations."

"So many individuals, of such and such quality," said Mr. Foster.

"Distributed in such and such quantities."

"The optimum Decanting Rate at any given moment."

"Unforeseen wastages promptly made good."

"Promptly," repeated Mr. Foster. "If you knew the amount of overtime I had to put in after the last Japanese earthquake!" He laughed goodhumouredly and shook his head.

"The Predestinators send in their figures to the Fertilizers."

"Who give them the embryos they ask for."

"And the bottles come in here to be predestined in detail."

"After which they are sent down to the Embryo Store."

"Where we now proceed ourselves."

And opening a door Mr. Foster led the way down a staircase into the basement.

The temperature was still tropical. They descended into a thickening twilight. Two doors and a passage with a double turn insured the cellar against any possible infiltration of the day.

"Embryos are like photograph film," said Mr. Foster waggishly, as he pushed open the second door. "They can only stand red light."

And in effect the sultry darkness into which the students now followed him was visible and crimson, like the darkness of closed eyes on a summer's afternoon. The bulging flanks of row on receding row and tier above tier of bottles glinted with innumerable rubies, and among the rubies moved the dim red spectres of men and women with purple eyes and all the symptoms of lupus. The hum and rattle of machinery faintly stirred the air.

"Give them a few figures, Mr. Foster," said the Director, who was tired of talking.

Mr. Foster was only too happy to give them a few figures.

Two hundred and twenty metres long, two hundred wide, ten high. He pointed upwards. Like chickens drinking, the students lifted their eyes towards the distant ceiling.

Three tiers of racks: ground floor level, first gallery, second gallery.

The spidery steel-work of gallery above gallery faded away in all directions into the dark. Near them three red ghosts were busily unloading demijohns from a moving staircase.

The escalator from the Social Predestination Room.

Each bottle could be placed on one of fifteen racks, each rack, though you couldn't see it, was a conveyor traveling at the rate of thirty-three and a third centimetres an hour. Two hundred and sixty-seven days at eight metres a day. Two thousand one hundred and thirty-six metres in all. One circuit of the cellar at ground level, one on the first gallery, half on the second, and on the two hundred and sixty-seventh morning, daylight in the Decanting Room. Independent existence—so called.

"But in the interval," Mr. Foster concluded, "we've managed to do a lot of them. Oh, a very great deal." His laugh was knowing and triumphant.

"That's the spirit I like," said the Director once more. "Let's walk around. You tell them everything, Mr. Foster."

Mr. Foster duly told them.

Told them of the growing embryo on its bed of peritoneum. Made them taste the rich blood surrogate on which it fed. Explained why it had to be stimulated with placentin and thyroxin. Told them of the *corpus luteum* extract. Showed them the jets through which at every twelfth metre from zero to 2040 it was automatically injected. Spoke of those gradually increasing doses of pituitary administered during the final ninety-six metres of their course. Described the artificial maternal circulation installed in every bottle at Metre 112; showed them the reservoir of blood-surrogate, the centrifugal pump that kept the liquid moving over the placenta and drove it through the synthetic lung and waste product filter. Referred to the embryo's troublesome tendency to anæmia, to the massive doses of hog's stomach extract and foetal foal's liver with which, in consequence, it had to be supplied.

Showed them the simple mechanism by means of which, during the last two metres out of every eight, all the embryos were simultaneously shaken into familiarity with movement. Hinted at the gravity of the so-called "trauma of decanting," and enumerated the precautions taken to minimize, by a suitable training of the bottled embryo, that dangerous shock. Told them of the test for sex carried out in the neighborhood of Metre 200. Explained the system of labelling—a T for the males, a circle for the females and for those who were destined to become freemartins a question mark, black on a white ground.

"For of course," said Mr. Foster, "in the vast majority of cases, fertility is merely a nuisance. One fertile ovary in twelve hundred—that would really be quite sufficient for our purposes. But we want to have a good choice. And of course one must always have an enormous margin of safety. So we allow as many as thirty per cent of the female embryos to develop normally. The others get a dose of male sex-hormone every twenty-four metres for the rest of the course. Result: they're decanted as freemartins—structurally quite normal (except," he had to admit, "that they *do* have the slightest tendency to grow beards), but sterile. Guaranteed sterile. Which brings us at last," continued Mr. Foster, "out of the realm of mere slavish imitation of nature into the much more interesting world of human invention."

He rubbed his hands. For of course, they didn't content themselves with merely hatching out embryos: any cow could do that.

"We also predestine and condition. We decant our babies as socialized human beings, as Alphas or Epsilons, as future sewage workers or future . . ." He was going to say "future World controllers," but correcting himself, said "future Directors of Hatcheries," instead.

The D.H.C. acknowledged the compliment with a smile.

They were passing Metre 320 on Rack 11. A young Beta-Minus mechanic was busy with screw-driver and spanner on the blood-surrogate pump of a passing bottle. The hum of the electric motor deepened by fractions of a tone as he turned the nuts. Down, down . . . A final twist, a glance at the revolution counter, and he was done. He moved two paces down the line and began the same process on the next pump.

"Reducing the number of revolutions per minute," Mr. Foster explained. "The surrogate goes round slower; therefore passes through the lung at longer intervals; therefore gives the embryo less oxygen. Nothing like oxygen-shortage for keeping an embryo below par." Again he rubbed his hands.

"But why do you want to keep the embryo below par?" asked an ingenuous student.

"Ass!" said the Director, breaking a long silence. "Hasn't it occurred to you that an Epsilon embryo must have an Epsilon environment as well as an Epsilon heredity?"

It evidently hadn't occurred to him. He was covered with confusion.

"The lower the caste," said Mr. Foster, "the shorter the oxygen." The first organ affected was the brain. After that the skeleton. At seventy per cent of normal oxygen you got dwarfs. At less than seventy eyeless monsters.

"Who are no use at all," concluded Mr. Foster.

Whereas (his voice became confidential and eager), if they could discover a technique for shortening the period of maturation what a triumph, what a benefaction to Society!

"Consider the horse."

They considered it.

Mature at six; the elephant at ten. While at thirteen a man is not yet sexually mature; and is only full-grown at twenty. Hence, of course, that fruit of delayed development, the human intelligence.

"But in Epsilons," said Mr. Foster very justly, "we don't need human intelligence."

Didn't need and didn't get it. But though the Epsilon mind was mature at ten, the Epsilon body was not fit to work till eighteen. Long years of superfluous and wasted immaturity. If the physical development could be speeded up till it was as quick, say, as a cow's, what an enormous saving to the Community!

"Enormous!" murmured the students. Mr. Foster's enthusiasm was infectious.

He became rather technical; spoke of the abnormal endocrine coordination which made men grow so slowly; postulated a germinal mutation to account for it. Could the effects of this germinal mutation be undone? Could the individual Epsilon embryo be made a revert, by a suitable technique, to the normality of dogs and cows? That was the problem. And it was all but solved.

Pilkington, at Mombasa, had produced individuals who were sexually mature at four and full-grown at six and a half. A scientific triumph. But socially useless. Six-year-old men and women were too stupid to do even Epsilon work. And the process was an all-or-nothing one; either you failed to modify at all, or else you modified the whole way. They were still trying to find the ideal compromise between adults of twenty and adults of six. So far without success. Mr. Foster sighed and shook his head.

Their wanderings through the crimson twilight had brought them to the neighborhood of Metre 170 on Rack 9. From this point onwards Rack 9 was enclosed and the bottle performed the remainder of their journey in a kind of tunnel, interrupted here and there by openings two or three metres wide.

"Heat conditioning," said Mr. Foster.

Hot tunnels alternated with cool tunnels. Coolness was wedded to discomfort in the form of hard X-rays. By the time they were decanted the embryos had a horror of cold. They were predestined to emigrate to the tropics, to be miners and acetate silk spinners and steel workers. Later on their minds would be made to endorse the judgment of their bodies. "We condition them to thrive on heat," concluded Mr. Foster. "Our colleagues upstairs will teach them to love it."

"And that," put in the Director sententiously, "that is the secret of happiness and virtue—liking what you've *got* to do. All conditioning aims at that: making people like their unescapable social destiny."

In a gap between two tunnels, a nurse was delicately probing with a long fine syringe into the gelatinous contents of a passing bottle. The students and their guides stood watching her for a few moments in silence.

"Well, Lenina," said Mr. Foster, when at last she withdrew the syringe and straightened herself up.

The girl turned with a start. One could see that, for all the lupus and the purple eyes, she was uncommonly pretty.

"Henry!" Her smile flashed redly at him—a row of coral teeth.

"Charming, charming," murmured the Director and, giving her two or three little pats, received in exchange a rather deferential smile for himself.

"What are you giving them?" asked Mr. Foster, making his tone very professional.

"Oh, the usual typhoid and sleeping sickness."

"Tropical workers start being inoculated at Metre 150," Mr. Foster explained to the students. "The embryos still have gills. We immunize the fish against the future man's diseases." Then, turning back to Lenina, "Ten to five on the roof this afternoon," he said, "as usual."

"Charming," said the Director once more, and, with a final pat, moved away after the others.

On Rack 10 rows of next generation's chemical workers were being trained in the toleration of lead, caustic soda, tar, chlorine. The first of a batch of two hundred and fifty embryonic rocket-plane engineers was just passing the eleven hundred metre mark on Rack 3. A special mechanism kept their containers in constant rotation. "To improve their sense of balance," Mr. Foster explained. "Doing repairs on the outside of a rocket in mid-air is a ticklish job. We slacken off the circulation when they're right way up, so that they're half starved, and double the flow of surrogate when they're upside down. They learn to associate topsy-turvydom with well-being; in fact, they're only truly happy when they're standing on their heads.

"And now," Mr. Foster went on, "I'd like to show you some very interesting conditioning for Alpha Plus Intellectuals. We have a big batch of them on Rack 5. First Gallery level," he called to two boys who had started to go down to the ground floor.

"They're round about Metre 900," he explained. "You can't really do any useful intellectual conditioning till the foetuses have lost their tails. Follow me."

But the Director had looked at his watch. "Ten to three," he said. "No time for the intellectual embryos, I'm afraid. We must go up to the Nurseries before the children have finished their afternoon sleep."

Mr. Foster was disappointed. "At least one glance at the Decanting Room," he pleaded.

"Very well then." The Director smiled indulgently. "Just one glance."

II

Mr. Foster was left in the Decanting Room. The D.H.C. and his students stepped into the nearest lift and were carried up to the fifth floor.

INFANT NURSERIES. NEO-PAVLOVIAN CONDITIONING ROOMS, announced the notice board.

The Director opened a door. They were in a large bare room, very bright and sunny; for the whole of the southern wall was a single window. Half a dozen nurses, trousered and jacketed in the regulation white viscose-linen uniform, their hair aseptically hidden under white caps, were engaged in setting out bowls of roses in a long row across the floor. Big bowls, packed tight with blossom. Thousands of petals, ripe-blown and silkily smooth, like the cheeks of innumerable little cherubs, but of cherubs, in that bright light, not exclusively pink and Aryan, but also luminously Chinese, also Mexican, also apoplectic with too much blowing of celestial trumpets, also pale as death, pale with the post-humous whiteness of marble.

The nurses stiffened to attention as the D.H.C. came in.

"Set out the books," he said curtly.

In silence the nurses obeyed his command. Between the rose bowls the books were duly set out—a row of nursery quartos opened invitingly each at some gaily coloured image of beast or fish or bird.

"Now bring in the children."

They hurried out of the room and returned in a minute or two, each pushing a kind of tall dumb-waiter laden, on all its four wire-netted shelves, with eight-month-old babies, all exactly alike (a Bokanovsky Group, it was evident) and all (since their caste was Delta) dressed in khaki.

"Put them down on the floor."

The infants were unloaded.

"Now turn them so that they can see the flowers and books."

Turned, the babies at once fell silent, then began to crawl towards those clusters of sleek colours, those shapes so gay and brilliant on the white pages. As they approached, the sun came out of a momentary eclipse behind a cloud. The roses flamed up as though with a sudden passion from within; a new and profound significance seemed to suffuse the shining pages of the books. From the ranks of the crawling babies came little squeals of excitement, gurgles and twitterings of pleasure.

The Director rubbed his hands. "Excellent!" he said. "It might almost have been done on purpose."

The swiftest crawlers were already at their goal. Small hands reached out uncertainly, touched, grasped, unpetaling the transfigured roses, crumpling the illuminated pages of the books. The Director waited until all were happily busy. Then, "Watch carefully," he said. And, lifting his hand, he gave the signal.

The Head Nurse, who was standing by a switchboard at the other end of the room, pressed down a little lever.

There was a violent explosion. Shriller and ever shriller, a siren shrieked. Alarm bells maddeningly sounded.

The children started, screamed; their faces were distorted with terror.

"And now," the Director shouted (for the noise was deafening), "now we proceed to rub in the lesson with a mild electric shock."

He waved his hand again, and the Head Nurse pressed a second lever. The screaming of the babies suddenly changed its tone. There was something desperate, almost insane, about the sharp spasmodic yelps to which they now gave utterance. Their little bodies twitched and stiffened; their limbs moved jerkily as if to the tug of unseen wires.

"We can electrify that whole strip of floor," bawled the Director in explanation. "But that's enough," he signalled to the nurse.

The explosions ceased, the bells stopped ringing, the shriek of the siren died down from tone to tone into silence. The stiffly twitching bodies relaxed, and what had become the sob and yelp of infant maniacs broadened out once more into a normal howl of ordinary terror.

"Offer them the flowers and the books again."

The nurses obeyed; but at the approach of the roses, at the mere sight of those gaily-coloured images of pussy and cock-a-doodle-doo and baa-baa black sheep, the infants shrank away in horror; the volume of their howling suddenly increased.

"Observe," said the Director triumphantly, "observe."

Books and loud noises, flowers and electric shocks—already in the infant mind these couples were compromisingly linked; and after two hundred repetitions of the same or a similar lesson would be wedded indissolubly. What man has joined, nature is powerless to put asunder.

"They'll grow up with what the psychologists used to call an 'instinctive' hatred of books and flowers. Reflexes unalterably conditioned. They'll be safe from books and botany all their lives." The Director turned to his nurses. "Take them away again."

Still yelling, the khaki babies were loaded on to their dumb-waiters and wheeled out, leaving behind them the smell of soul milk and a most welcome silence.

One of the students held up his hand; and though he could see quite well why you couldn't have lower-caste people wasting the Community's time over books, and that there was always the risk of their reading something which might undesirably decondition one of their reflexes, yet . . . well, he couldn't understand about the flowers. Why go to the trouble of making it psychologically impossible for Deltas to like flowers?

Patiently the D.H.C. explained. If the children were made to scream at the sight of a rose, that was on grounds of high economic policy. Not so very long ago (a century or thereabouts), Gammas, Deltas, even Epsilons, had been conditioned to like flowers—flowers in particular and wild nature in general. The idea was to make them want to be going out into the country at every available opportunity, and so compel them to consume transport.

"And didn't they consume transport?" asked the student.

"Quite a lot," the D.H.C. replied. "But nothing else."

Primroses and landscapes, he pointed out, have one grave defect: they are gratuitous. A love of nature keeps no factories busy. It was decided to abolish the love of nature, at any rate among the lower classes; to abolish the love of nature, but *not* the tendency to consume transport. For of course it was essential that they should keep on going to the country, even though they hated it. The problem was to find an economically sounder reason for consuming transport than a mere affection for primroses and landscapes. It was duly found.

"We condition the masses to hate the country," concluded the Director. "But simultaneously we condition them to love all country sports. At the same time, we see to it that all country sports shall entail the use of elaborate apparatus. So that they consume manufactured articles as well as transport. Hence those electric shocks."

"I see," said the student, and was silent, lost in admiration.

There was a silence; then, clearing his throat, "Once upon a time," the Director began, "while our Ford was still on earth, there was a little boy called Reuben Rabinovitch. Reuben was the child of Polish-speaking parents." The Director interrupted himself. "You know what Polish is, I suppose?"

"A dead language."

"Like French and German," added another student, officiously showing off his learning.

"And 'parent'?" questioned the D.H.C.

There was an uneasy silence. Several of the boys blushed. They had not yet learned to draw the significant but often very fine distinction between smut and pure science. One, at last, had the courage to raise a hand.

"Human beings used to be . . ." he hesitated; the blood rushed to his cheeks. "Well, they used to be viviparous."

"Quite right." The Director nodded approvingly.

"And when the babies were decanted . . ."

" 'Born,' " came the correction.

"Well, then they were the parents—I mean, not the babies, of course; the other ones." The poor boy was overwhelmed with confusion.

"In brief," the Director summed up, "the parents were the father and the mother." The smut that was really science fell with a crash into the boys' eye-avoiding silence. "Mother," he repeated loudly rubbing in the science; and, leaning back in his chair, "These," he said gravely, "are unpleasant facts; I know it. But then most historical facts *are* unpleasant."

He returned to Little Reuben—to Little Reuben, in whose room, one evening, by an oversight, his father and mother (crash, crash!) happened to leave the radio turned on.

("For you must remember that in those days of gross viviparous reproduction, children were always brought up by their parents and not in State Conditioning Centres.")

While the child was asleep, a broadcast programme from London suddenly started to come through; and the next morning, to the astonishment of his crash and crash (the more daring of the boys ventured to grin at one another), Little Reuben woke up repeating word for word a long lecture by that curious old writer ("one of the very few whose works have been permitted to come down to us"), George Bernard Shaw, who was speaking, according to a well-authenticated tradition, about his own genius. To Little Reuben's wink and snigger, this lecture was, of course, perfectly incomprehensible and, imagining that their child had suddenly gone mad, they sent for a doctor. He, fortunately, understood English, recognized the discourse as that which Shaw had broadcasted the previous evening, realized the significance of what had happened, and sent a letter to the medical press about it.

"The principle of sleep-teaching, or hypnopædia, had been discovered." The D.H.C. made an impressive pause.

The principle had been discovered; but many, many years were to elapse before that principle was usefully applied.

"The case of Little Reuben occurred only twenty-three years after Our Ford's first T-Model was put on the market." (Here the Director made a sign of the T on his stomach and all the students reverently followed suit.) "And yet . . ."

Furiously the students scribbled. *"Hypnopædia, first used officially in A.F. 214. Why not before? Two reasons. (a) . . ."*

"These early experimenters," the D.H.C. was saying, "were on the wrong track. They thought that hypnopædia could be made an instrument of intellectual education . . ."

(A small boy asleep on his right side, the right arm stuck out, the right hand hanging limp over the edge of the bed. Through a round grating in the side of a box a voice speaks softly.

"The Nile is the longest river in Africa and the second in length of all the rivers of the globe. Although falling short of the length of the

Mississippi-Missouri, the Nile is at the head of all rivers as regards the length of its basin, which extends through 35 degrees of latitude . . ."

At breakfast the next morning, "Tommy," some one says, "do you know which is the longest river in Africa?" A shaking of the head. "But don't you remember something that begins: The Nile is the . . ."

"The - Nile - is - the - longest - river - in - Africa - and - the - second - in - length - of - all - the - rivers - of - the - globe . . ." The words come rushing out. "Although - falling - short - of . . ."

"Well now, which is the longest river in Africa?"

The eyes are blank. "I don't know."

"But the Nile, Tommy."

"The - Nile - is - the - longest - river - in - Africa - and - second . . ."

"Then which river is the longest, Tommy?"

Tommy burst into tears. "I don't know," he howls.)

That howl, the Director made it plain, discouraged the earliest investigators. The experiments were abandoned. No further attempt was made to teach children the length of the Nile in their sleep. Quite rightly. You can't learn a science unless you know what it's all about.

"Whereas, if they'd only started on *moral* education," said the Director, leading the way towards the door. The students followed him, desperately scribbling as they walked and all the way up in the lift. "Moral education, which ought never, in any circumstances, to be rational."

"Silence, silence," whispered a loud speaker as they stepped out at the fourteenth floor, and "Silence, silence," the trumpet mouths indefatigably repeated at intervals down every corridor. The students and even the Director himself rose automatically to the tips of their toes. They were Alphas, of course; but even Alphas have been well conditioned. "Silence, silence." All the air of the fourteenth floor was sibilant with the categorical imperative.

Fifty yards of tiptoeing brought them to a door which the Director cautiously opened. They stepped over the threshold into the twilight of a shuttered dormitory. Eighty cots stood in a row against the wall. There was a sound of light regular breathing and a continuous murmur, as of very faint voices remotely whispering.

A nurse rose as they entered and came to attention before the Director.

"What's the lesson this afternoon?" he asked.

"We had Elementary Sex for the first forty minutes," she answered. "But now it's switched over to Elementary Class Consciousness."

The Director walked slowly down the long line of cots. Rosy and relaxed with sleep, eighty little boys and girls lay softly breathing. There was a whisper under every pillow. The D.H.C. halted and, bending over one of the little beds, listened attentively.

"Elementary Class Consciousness, did you say? Let's have it repeated a little louder by the trumpet."

At the end of the room a loud speaker projected from the wall. The Director walked up to it and pressed a switch.

". . . all wear green," said a soft but very distinct voice, beginning in the middle of a sentence, "and Delta Children wear khaki. Oh no, I don't want to play with Delta children. And Epsilons are still worse. They're too stupid to be able to read or write. Besides they wear black, which is such a beastly colour. I'm *so* glad I'm a Beta."

There was a pause; then the voice began again.

"Alpha children wear grey. They work much harder than we do, because they're so frightfully clever. I'm really awfully glad I'm a Beta, because I don't work so hard. And then we are much better than the Gammas and Deltas. Gammas are stupid. They all wear green, and Delta children wear khaki. Oh no, I *don't* want to play with Delta children. And Epsilons are still worse. They're too stupid to be able . . ."

The Director pushed back the switch. The voice was silent. Only its thin ghost continued to mutter from beneath the eighty pillows.

"They'll have that repeated forty or fifty times more before they wake; then again on Thursday, and again on Saturday. A hundred and twenty times three times a week for thirty months. After which they go on to a more advanced lesson."

Roses and electric shocks, the khaki of Deltas and a whiff of asafœtida—wedded indissolubly before the child can speak. But wordless conditioning is crude and wholesale; cannot bring home the finer distinctions, cannot inculcate the more complex courses of behaviour. For that there must be words, but words without reason. In brief, hypnopædia.

"The greatest moralizing and socializing force of all time."

The students took it down in their little books. Straight from the horse's mouth.

Once more the Director touched the switch.

". . . so frightfully clever," the soft, insinuating, indefatigable voice was saying, "I'm really awfully glad I'm a Beta because . . ."

Not so much like drops of water, though water, it is true, can wear holes in the hardest granite; rather, drops of liquid sealing-wax, drops that adhere, incrust, incorporate themselves with what they fall on, till finally the rock is all one scarlet blob.

"Till at last the child's mind *is* these suggestions, and the sum of the suggestions *is* the child's mind. And not the child's mind only. The adult's mind too—all his life long. The mind that judges and desires and decides—made up of these suggestions. But all these suggestions are *our* suggestions!" The Director almost shouted in his triumph. "Sugges-

tions from the State." He banged the nearest table. "It therefore follows . . ."

A noise made him turn round.

"Oh, Ford!" he said in another tone, "I've gone and woken the
children."

III

Outside, in the garden, it was playtime. Naked in the warm June sunshine, six or seven hundred little boys and girls were running with shrill
yells over the lawns, or playing ball games, or squatting silently in twos
and threes among the flowering shrubs. The roses were in bloom, two
nightingales soliloquized in the boskage, a cuckoo was just going out of
tune among the lime trees. The air was drowsy with the murmur of bees
and helicopters.

The Director and his students stood for a short time watching a
game of Centrifugal Bumble-puppy. Twenty children were grouped in
a circle round a chrome steel tower. A ball thrown up so as to land on
the platform at the top of the tower rolled down into the interior, fell
on a rapidly revolving disk, was hurled through one or other of the
numerous apertures pierced in the cylindrical casing, and had to be
caught.

"Strange," mused the Director, as they turned away, "strange to
think that even in Our Ford's day most games were played without more
apparatus than a ball or two and a few sticks and perhaps a bit of
netting. Imagine the folly of allowing people to play elaborate games
which do nothing whatever to increase consumption. It's madness. Now-
adays the Controllers won't approve of any new game unless it can be
shown that it requires at least as much apparatus as the most complicated
of existing games." He interrupted himself.

"That's a charming little group," he said, pointing.

In a little grassy bay between tall clumps of Mediterranean heather,
two children, a little boy of about seven and a little girl who might have
been a year older, were playing, very gravely and with all the focussed
attention of scientists intent on a labour of discovery, a rudimentary
sexual game.

"Charming, charming!" the D.H.C. repeated sentimentally.

"Charming," the boys politely agreed. But their smile was rather
patronizing. They had put aside similar childish amusements too recently
to be able to watch them now without a touch of contempt. Charming?
but it was just a pair of kids fooling about; that was all. Just kids.

"I always think," the Director was continuing in the same rather
maudlin tone, when he was interrupted by a loud boo-hooing.

From a neighbouring shrubbery emerged a nurse, leading by the hand a small boy, who howled as he went. An anxious-looking little girl trotted at her heels.

"What's the matter?" asked the Director.

The nurse shrugged her shoulders. "Nothing much," she answered. "It's just that this little boy seems rather reluctant to join in the ordinary erotic play. I'd noticed it once or twice before. And now again to-day. He started yelling just now . . ."

"Honestly," put in the anxious-looking little girl, "I didn't mean to hurt him or anything. Honestly."

"Of course you didn't, dear," said the nurse reassuringly. "And so," she went on, turning back to the Director, "I'm taking him in to see the Assistant Superintendent of Psychology. Just to see if anything's at all abnormal."

"Quite right," said the Director. "Take him in. You stay here, little girl," he added, as the nurse moved away with her still howling charge. "What's your name?"

"Polly Trotsky."

"And a very good name too," said the Director. "Run away now and see if you can find some other little boy to play with."

The child scampered off into the bushes and was lost to sight.

"Exquisite little creature!" said the Director, looking after her. Then, turning to his students, "What I'm going to tell you now," he said, "may sound incredible. But then, when you're not accustomed to history, most facts about the past *do* sound incredible."

He let out the amazing truth. For a very long period before the time of Our Ford, and even for some generations afterwards, erotic play between children had been regarded as abnormal (there was a roar of laughter); and not only abnormal, actually immoral (no!): and had therefore been rigorously suppressed.

A look of astonished incredulity appeared on the faces of his listeners. Poor little kids not allowed to amuse themselves? They could not believe it.

"Even adolescents," the D.H.C. was saying, "even adolescents like yourselves . . ."

"Not possible!"

"Barring a little surreptitious auto-erotism and homosexuality—absolutely nothing."

"*Nothing?*"

"In most cases, till they were over twenty years old."

"Twenty years old?" echoed the students in a chorus of loud disbelief.

"Twenty," the Director repeated. "I told you that you'd find it incredible."

"But what happened?" they asked. "What were the results?"

"The results were terrible." A deep resonant voice broke startlingly into the dialogue.

They looked around. On the fringe of the little group stood a stranger—a man of middle height, black-haired, with a hooked nose, full red lips, eyes very piercing and dark. "Terrible," he repeated.

The D.H.C. had at that moment sat down on one of the steel and rubber benches conveniently scattered through the gardens; but at the sight of the stranger, he sprang to his feet and darted forward, his hand outstretched, smiling with all his teeth, effusive.

"Controller! What an unexpected pleasure! Boys, what are you thinking of? This is the Controller; this is his fordship, Mustapha Mond."

In the four thousand rooms of the Centre the four thousand electric clocks simultaneously struck four. Discarnate voices called from the trumpet mouths.

"Main Day-shift off duty. Second Day-shift take over. Main Day-shift off . . ."

In the lift, on their way up to the changing rooms, Henry Foster and the Assistant Director of Predestination rather pointedly turned their backs on Bernard Marx from the Psychology Bureau: averted themselves from that unsavoury reputation.

The faint hum and rattle of machinery still stirred the crimson air in the Embryo Store. Shifts might come and go, one lupus-coloured face give place to another; majestically and for ever the conveyors crept forward with their load of future men and women. . . .

Suggestions for Further Reading

This bibliography is selective rather than comprehensive. Its aim is to assist the reader who desires other stories, novels, and personal narratives than those provided or previously suggested in *The Literature of Learning*. The following lists might well be preceded by a catalogue of the great books of Western and Eastern culture. For who will deny that the catholic literature of learning is discovered in the works of Tolstoy, Shakespeare, Lao Tzu, Melville, Cervantes, Dante, Dostoevsky, Goethe, Chaucer, Homer, Sophocles, Molière, Buddha, Joyce, and Faulkner, among others? Because lists of these authors and their works are available everywhere and easily secured by inquiring readers, the following bibliography is given over to literature that is predominantly contemporary and understandably absent from traditional listings.

The bibliography is divided into sections determined by the literary genres represented. These sections are then subdivided according to the *levels* of learning (elementary, secondary, and collegiate) surveyed in the readings. A category labeled *General* is reserved for sources within each genre that do not have specific or extended school settings but whose themes are germane.

Novels

Whereas novels devoted to college life are perhaps too numerous, worthwhile novels of high school and junior high experience are comparatively rare. And novels imbued with the milieu of the elementary school are virtually nonexistent.

I. General

Jean-Jacques Rousseau, *Émile*, 1762
Henry James, *Roderick Hudson*, 1876
        The Portrait of a Lady, 1881

Mark Twain, *Huckleberry Finn*, 1885
Thomas Mann, *Buddenbrooks*, 1901
Joseph Conrad, *Youth*, 1902
Jack London, *Martin Eden*, 1909
Theodore Dreiser, *The "Genius"*, 1915
James Joyce, *Portrait of the Artist as a Young Man*, 1916
André Gide, *The Immoralist*, 1921
Thomas Wolfe, *Look Homeward, Angel*, 1929
        Of Time and the River, 1935
        The Web and the Rock, 1939
James T. Farrell, *Young Lonigan*, 1932
        The Young Manhood of Studs Lonigan, 1934
        Judgment Day, 1935
Richard Wright, *Black Boy*, 1937
William Faulkner, *The Bear*, 1942
James Michener, *The Fires of Spring*, 1949
Ralph Ellison, *Invisible Man*, 1952
Saul Bellow, *The Adventures of Augie March*, 1953
Hermann Hesse, *The Journey to the East*, 1956
James Agee, *A Death in the Family*, 1957
Claude Brown, *Manchild in the Promised Land*, 1965

II. Junior and Senior High School

Leo Rosten, *The Education of Hyman Kaplan*, 1937
J. D. Salinger, *The Catcher in the Rye*, 1951
William Goldman, *Temple of Gold*, 1957
E. R. Braithwaite, *To Sir, With Love*, 1959
John Knowles, *A Separate Peace*, 1959
John Updike, *The Centaur*, 1963
Jeremy Larner, *Drive, he said*, 1964

III. College

F. Scott Fitzgerald, *This Side of Paradise*, 1920
Robert Nathan, *Peter Kindred*, 1920
        Mister Whittle and the Morning Star, 1947
Stephen Vincent Benét, *The Beginning of Wisdom*, 1921
Willa Cather, *The Professor's House*, 1925
Sinclair Lewis, *Arrowsmith*, 1925
Carl Van Doren, *The Ninth Wave*, 1926
Bernard DeVoto, *We Accept with Pleasure*, 1934
John Erskine, *Bachelor—of Arts*, 1934
Vardis Fisher, *Passions Spin the Plot*, 1934
        We Are Betrayed, 1935
        Orphans in Gethsemane, 1960
George Santayana, *The Last Puritan*, 1936

George Stewart, *Doctor's Oral*, 1939
Wallace Stegner, *Fire and Ice*, 1941
James T. Farrell, *My Days of Anger*, 1943
Robert Penn Warren, *At Heaven's Gate*, 1943
Albert Guérard, *The Hunted*, 1944
William Maxwell, *The Folded Leaf*, 1945
Calder Willingham, *End as a Man*, 1947
Shirley Jackson, *Hangsaman*, 1951
Robie Macauley, *The Disguises of Love*, 1952
Mary McCarthy, *The Groves of Academe*, 1952
Randall Jarrell, *Pictures from an Institution*, 1954
May Sarton, *Faithful Are the Wounds*, 1955
    The Small Room, 1962
Vladimir Nabokov, *Pnin*, 1957
    Pale Fire, 1962
Howard Nemerov, *The Homecoming Game*, 1957
Stringfellow Barr, *Purely Academic*, 1958
George P. Elliott, *Parktilden Village*, 1958
Mark Harris, *Wake Up, Stupid*, 1959
William Van O'Conner, *Campus on the River*, 1959
Bernard Malamud, *A New Life*, 1961
J. D. Salinger, *Franny and Zooey*, 1961
Philip Roth, *Letting Go*, 1962
Louis Simpson, *Riverside Drive*, 1962
Ken Kolb, *Getting Straight*, 1967
Erich Segal, *Love Story*, 1970

Short Stories

I. General

Henry James, "The Pupil"
Franz Kafka, "Report to the Academy"
Bernard Malamud, "A Summer's Reading"
Calvin Trillin, "Lester Drentluss Turns Black with Desire"

II. Elementary

John Henrik Clarke, "The Boy Who Painted Christ Black"
James Gould Cozzens, "The Animals' Fair"
Alphonse Daudet, "The Last Class"
Shirley Jackson, "After You, My Dear Alphonse"
    "Charles"
Frank O'Connor, "The Idealist"
William Saroyan, "First Day of School"
    "Death of Children"
Mary Elizabeth Vroman, "See How They Run"
Jessamyn West, "The Singing Lesson"

III. Junior and Senior High School

James Gould Cozzens, "Someday You'll Be Sorry"
F. Scott Fitzgerald, "The Freshest Boy"
Martha Foley, "One with Shakespeare"
William Harlan Hale, "Mr. Minnow in Trouble"
Langston Hughes, "One Friday Morning"
John Langdon, "The Blue Serge Suit"
Victoria Lincoln, "The Glass Wall"
John O'Hara, "Do You Like It Here?"
John Updike, "In Football Season"
                "A Sense of Shelter"
                "Tomorrow, and Tomorrow, and So Forth"

IV. College

Sinclair Lewis, "Young Man Axelbrod"
Robie Macauley, "The Chevigny Man"
Samuel Sandmel, "The Colleagues of Mr. Chips"
Mark Schorer, "In Uniform"
                "To the Wind"
Roger Shattuck, "Workout on the River"
Irwin Shaw, "The Eighty-yard Run"

Personal Narratives

This section is composed of sources that are full-length volumes. For books containing autobiographical *essays*, the reader should consult the subsequent category devoted to anthologies.

I. General

Jean-Jacques Rousseau, *The Confessions*, 1783
André Gide, *The Journals* (in four volumes) 1889–1949
Lincoln Steffens, *The Autobiography of Lincoln Steffens*, 1931
Vincent Sheean, *Personal History*, 1935
Esther Cloudman Dunn, *Pursuit of Understanding*, 1945
Stephen Leacock, *The Boy I Left Behind Me*, 1946
John Erskine, *My Life as a Teacher*, 1948
James Baldwin, *Nobody Knows My Name*, 1961

II. Elementary

Florence McGehee, *Please Excuse Johnny*, 1952
Sean O'Casey, *I Knock at the Door*, 1956
Herbert Kohl, *Thirty-six Children*, 1968
Sunny Decker, *An Empty Spoon*, 1969

III. Junior and Senior High School

Joan Dunn, *Retreat from Learning*, 1955
Constance Melaro, *Bitter Harvest*, 1965
Mary Frances Green and Orletta Ryan, *The Schoolchildren*, 1966
Deborah James, *The Taming: A Teacher Speaks*, 1969
Charles G. Rousculp, *Chalk Dust on My Shoulder*, 1969

IV. College

Bliss Perry, *And Gladly Teach*, 1935
Christian Gauss, *The Papers of Christian Gauss*, 1957

Anthologies

The market, as always, is now gluttered with interchangeable anthologies. Most of these books, when not platitudinous, are merely earnest and helplessly abstract. However, the works cited below, though surely unequal in content and editorial inspiration, do have a common aim—to evoke experience as well as to analyze it. In keeping with the focus of this bibliography, worthy collections solely given over to *expository* writings are not cited, for these titles are handily included in customary lists.

> *Great Teachers*, edited by Houston Peterson. New Brunswick, N.J.: Rutgers University Press, 1946.
> A compendium of tributes to Alexander Agassiz, Christian Gauss, Mark Hopkins, and other memorable teachers. Written by notable pupils, these selections are almost exclusively devoted to college teaching.
> *Issues in Education: An Anthology of Controversy*, edited with notes and commentaries by Bernard Johnston. Boston, Mass.: Houghton Mifflin Company, 1964.
> Arranged thematically around current issues are selections by such figures as Plato, Milton, Comenius, Rousseau, Herbert Spencer, Emerson, and T. H. Huxley, and contemporary figures such as John Dewey, Robert Hutchins, Sidney Hook, Alfred North Whitehead, James Agee, Russell Kirk, Bertrand Russell, and John Ciardi.
> *The Teacher*, edited by Morris Ernst. Englewood Cliffs, N.J.: Prentice-Hall, Inc., 1968.
> Stressing the idiosyncratic traits of successful teaching, this volume brings together light reminiscences ranging from the informal to the flimsy.
> *Teacher's Treasure Chest*, edited by Leo Duell. Englewood Cliffs, N.J.: Prentice-Hall, Inc., 1956.
> A collection replete with ladies' magazine sentiment and my-favorite-teacher salutes. A very uneven anthology containing a few first-rate poems and recollections.

Three Thousand Years of Educational Wisdom, edited with commentaries by Robert Ulich. Cambridge, Mass.: Harvard University Press, 1954.

A superb anthology of unexpendable readings from ancient times to the early twentieth century. Eastern as well as Western sources are included; lucid and scholarly editorial notes prevail throughout.

Unseen Harvests, edited by Emory S. Basford and Claude M. Fuess. New York: Crowell-Collier and Macmillan, Inc., 1947.

A collection of fictional and expository writings ranging from the trivial to the substantial, with a clear emphasis on the latter. Informal in arrangement and intent, there are readings here for varied temperaments and persuasions. A book primarily edited for browsing.

Index of Authors